More Bestselling For Dummies Titles by Eric Tyson

Investing For Dummies®

A *Wall Street Journal* bestseller, this book walks you through how to build wealth in stocks, real estate, an d small business as well as other investments.

Mutual Funds For Dummies®

This best-selling guide is now updated to include current fund and portfolio recommendations. Using the practical tips and techniques, you'll design a mutual fund investment plan suited to your income, lifestyle, and risk preferences.

Taxes For Dummies®

The complete, best-selling reference for completing your tax return and making tax-wise financial decisions year-round. Tyson coauthors this book with tax experts David Silverman and Margaret Munro.

Home Buying For Dummies®

America's #1 real estate book includes coverage of online resources in addition to sound financial advice from Eric Tyson and frontline real estate insights from industry veteran Ray Brown. Also available from America's best-selling real estate team of Tyson and Brown — *House Selling For Dummies* and *Mortgages For Dummies*.

Real Estate Investing For Dummies®

Real estate is a proven wealth-building investment, but many people don't know how to go about making and managing rental property investments. Real estate and property management expert Robert Griswold and Eric Tyson cover the gamut of property investment options, strategies, and techniques.

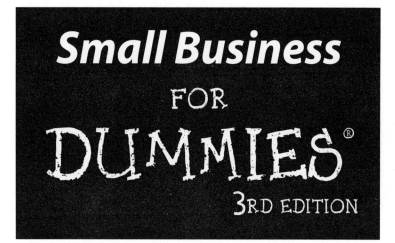

Small Business
FOR
DUMMIES®
3RD EDITION

by Eric Tyson and Jim Schell

WILEY

Wiley Publishing, Inc.

Small Business For Dummies®, 3rd Edition

Published by
Wiley Publishing, Inc.
111 River St.
Hoboken, NJ 07030-5774
www.wiley.com

WILEY

About the Authors

Eric Tyson, MBA: A personal financial writer, lecturer, and former financial counselor, for the past two-plus decades Eric has been his own boss. He works with and teaches people from a myriad of income levels and backgrounds, so he knows the small business ownership concerns and questions of real folks just like you.

After toiling away for too many years as a management consultant to behemoth financial-service firms, Eric decided to take his knowledge of the industry and commit himself to making personal financial management accessible to everyone. Despite being handicapped by a joint BS in Economics and Biology from Yale and an MBA from Stanford, Eric remains a master at "keeping it simple."

An accomplished freelance personal-finance writer, Eric is the author or co-author of numerous other *For Dummies* national bestsellers on personal finance, taxes, investing, and home buying, and is a syndicated columnist. His *Personal Finance For Dummies* won the Benjamin Franklin Award for Best Business Book.

Eric's work has been critically acclaimed in hundreds of publications and programs, including *Newsweek, The Los Angeles Times, The Chicago Tribune, Kiplinger's Personal Finance Magazine, The Wall Street Journal, Bottom Line Personal,* as well as NBC's *Today* show, ABC, CNBC, PBS's *Nightly Business Report,* CNN, FOX-TV, CBS national radio, Bloomberg Business Radio, and Business Radio Network.

Jim Schell: Contrary to what some people may think, Jim has not always been a grizzled veteran of the small-business wars. Raised in Des Moines, Iowa, and earning a BA in Economics at the University of Colorado, Jim served in the U.S. Air Force in Klamath Falls, Oregon. Jim's entrepreneurial genes eventually surfaced when he and three Minneapolis friends started The Kings Court, at the time the nation's first racquetball club. Two years later, Jim bought General Sports, Inc. After another two years, he started National Screenprint, and, finally, he partnered with an ex-employee in Fitness and Weight Training Corp. Each of the start-ups was bootstrapped, and each was privately held. For several years, Jim involved himself in the management of all four businesses at the same time. His third business, National Screenprint, ultimately grew to $25 million in sales and 200 employees.

Relocating to San Diego, Jim began a long-simmering writing career, authoring four books (*The Brass Tacks Entrepreneur, Small Business Management Guide, The Small Business Answer Book,* and *Understanding Your Financial Statements*) and numerous columns for business and trade magazines.

Citing culture shock, Jim and his wife, Mary — a sales trainer and longtime business partner — relocated to Bend, Oregon, where he continued his writing career. He also kicked off his fifth start-up, Opportunity Knocks (OK), a business that uses volunteers to organize, administrate, and facilitate the formation of small-business owners into teams that will serve as a member's board of advisors. Jim has three grown sons — Jim, Todd, and Mike — and five grandchildren.

Dedication

To my wife, Judy; to my family, especially my parents, Charles and Paulina; to my friends; and to my counseling clients and students of my courses, for teaching me how to teach them about managing their finances.

— Eric Tyson

This book is dedicated to The Rocky Road, and to all those friends, employees, and customers who have traversed it with me. Most of all, it is dedicated to my wife, Mary, without whom The Rocky Road would have been The Dead End.

— Jim Schell

Authors' Acknowledgments

Many people contribute to the birth of a book, and this book is no exception. First, Eric would like to express his deep debt of gratitude to James Collins, who inspired him when he was a young and impressionable business school student. Jim encouraged Eric to try to improve some small part of the business world by being an entrepreneur and focusing solely on what customers needed rather than on what made the quickest buck.

The technical reviewer for this book, Barbara Findlay Schenck, helped improve our book, and we are thankful for that.

Thanks to all the good people in the media and other fields who have taken the time to critique and praise our previous writing so that others may know that it exists and is worth reading. And to those who may not open the book because of its bright yellow color and low-brow title, "You can't judge a book by its cover!" Now that we've got your attention, flip through the pages and find out why readers everywhere know and trust books *For Dummies*.

And a final and heartfelt thanks to all the people on the front lines and behind the scenes who helped to make this book and Eric's others a success. A big round of applause, please, for Alissa Schwipps as project editor and Josh Dials and Kelly Ewing as copy editors. Their attention to detail and ability to ask good questions helped make this book the best that it could be. Thanks also to the Composition, Graphics, Proofreading, and Indexing staffs for their great efforts in producing this book.

P.S. Thanks to you, dear reader, for buying this book.

Publisher's Acknowledgments

We're proud of this book; please send us your comments through our Dummies online registration form located at www.dummies.com/register/.

Some of the people who helped bring this book to market include the following:

Acquisitions, Editorial, and Media Development

Senior Project Editor: Alissa Schwipps

(Previous Edition: Marcia L. Johnson)

Acquisitions Editor: Mike Baker

Copy Editors: Josh Dials, Kelly Ewing

(Previous Edition: Elizabeth Kuball)

Editorial Program Coordinator: Erin Calligan Mooney

Technical Editor: Barbara Findlay Schenck

Senior Editorial Manager: Jennifer Ehrlich

Editorial Assistants: Joe Niesen, Leeann Harney, David Lutton

Cartoons: Rich Tennant (www.the5thwave.com)

Composition Services

Project Coordinator: Patrick Redmond

Layout and Graphics: Stacie Brooks, Reuben W. Davis, Alissa D. Ellet, Joyce Haughey, Melissa K. Jester

Proofreaders: Laura Bowman, David Faust, John Greenough

Indexer: Potomac Indexing, LLC

Publishing and Editorial for Consumer Dummies

Diane Graves Steele, Vice President and Publisher, Consumer Dummies

Joyce Pepple, Acquisitions Director, Consumer Dummies

Kristin A. Cocks, Product Development Director, Consumer Dummies

Michael Spring, Vice President and Publisher, Travel

Kelly Regan, Editorial Director, Travel

Publishing for Technology Dummies

Andy Cummings, Vice President and Publisher, Dummies Technology/General User

Composition Services

Gerry Fahey, Vice President of Production Services

Debbie Stailey, Director of Composition Services

Contents at a Glance

Table of Contents

Part II: Buying an Existing Business *105*

Chapter 6: Exploring Buying a Business 107

Chapter 7: Finding the Right Business to Buy 119

Introduction

· ·

Small business is many things to those of us who have participated in it or have dreamed about participating in it. Without a doubt, this concept of "being your own boss" is an alluring one.

Not everyone can be a boss, however — at least not a good or successful one. If you're currently someone's employee (not a boss), fantasizing about owning a business of your own is perfectly natural on those days when you're fed up with your current boss or job. Your fantasy is made even more attractive by the rags-to-riches stories you hear about entrepreneurs who've turned their visions into millions or even billions of dollars.

But in the midst of your dreams, know that small-business ownership has some not-so-appealing aspects as well. Most often, many years of hard work and tons of tough choices are required before the risks you take are turned into rewards. And, most difficult of all, the entrepreneurial career can be lonely at the top. Of course, the thrill of being the ultimate decision-maker may be exactly what attracts you to small business in the first place, but you should realize that this attraction has its downsides, the most prominent of which is that it breeds trial and error, and trial and error begets mistakes. Mistakes are the most expensive (and most dangerous) way for the small-business owner to learn.

But wait, before you plod back to your day job, we have some good news for you: The mistakes that you're likely to make have already been made by those who have gone before you — including us. If you can somehow avoid the trial and error that leads to them (which is what we're here to help you do), your chances for success will multiply many times over.

Despite the previously mentioned downsides, it's impossible to describe the sense of accomplishment you'll get from starting and running your own successful business. Like so many before you, you'll know the thrill of creation, you'll feel the pride of watching that creation grow, and you'll realize that your work and your vision have filled an identifiable void for your customers, for your employees, and, of course, for you and your family.

If you visit the small-business section of a larger bookstore, you'll find plenty of books on the topic of small business. The problem we see, however, is that most of them aren't worthy of your time or dollars. *Forbes* magazine once said of the marketplace for small-business books, "Warning: Most how-to books on entrepreneurship aren't worth a dime." The marketplace apparently agrees — the vast majority of small-business books disappear from the bookstore shelves within their first year or two. We're proud to say that this updated and revised third edition launches the 10th year of this book's history! We're grateful for reviewers' kind words, such as the praise from Hattie Bryant, creator of the PBS series *SmallBusinessSchool,* who said of our book, "No one should try to start a business without this book."

Michael Gerber, author of *The E-Myth* series of business books (HarperBusiness), makes the point that "the one common denominator in every successful entrepreneur is an insatiable appetite to learn." If Michael is right, and we believe that he is, you've passed the first test of the successful entrepreneur: By purchasing this book, you've displayed a desire to learn. Keep it up — you're on the right track.

Small business isn't rocket science. You don't need to be a genius to start and run a successful small business. What you do need is help, which is exactly why we wrote this book. We're pleased that you chose us as your guides into the stimulating world of small business.

About This Book

You'll find within the following pages the backgrounds and philosophies that serve as a guide to the advice we provide — advice from the field that makes our small-business book stand out from the rest.

We're small-business experienced, and we share the benefits of that experience with you. Between us, we have six decades of experience in starting and running seven successful small businesses. In addition, we've worked with thousands of small-business owners. Jim has led numerous small-business peer networking groups and has provided volunteer counseling services to small-business owners. Eric conducted financial counseling for small-business owners, taught financial-management courses, and is a former management consultant.

Throughout this book, we share the experience we've gained, in the hopes that you'll use our advice to purge the trial and error from your inventory of management tools. We also share an ample collection of straight-from-the-horse's-mouth anecdotes in the following pages, each one based on a true story.

We take an objective view of small-business ownership. Although we firmly believe in the creative power of small business, we're not here to be its pitchmen.

Sadly, too many small-business books are written by folks with an agenda: a franchise to sell, a multilevel marketing scheme to promote, or a high-priced seminar to foist on the reader. Free of conflicts of interest, we're here to pass on the truth and let you decide. If you're the type of person who wants to get into this competitive career field, we'd like you to enter the race informed as well as inspired.

We take a holistic approach. Because small business can at times be both demanding and intoxicating, running your own shop can threaten to consume your life. Although everyone knows that life is more than just business, striking a balance and staying in control can represent a colossal challenge. With that in mind, we take particular care to present the realities of running a small business within the larger (and more important) framework of maintaining a happy personal and financial life.

We're committed to updating this book so that you have the best and latest information and advice at your fingertips. Tax laws change, benefits change, technology changes, and so do many other facets of the small-business world. That's why we've remained on top of these changes and revised this book.

Conventions Used in This Book

Every book has its own conventions, and this one is no different. To make the most of the information we provide, keep your eye out for these conventions:

- ✔ *Italics* highlight new terms that we define.
- ✔ **Boldfaced** text indicates the keywords in explanatory bulleted lists and action steps in how-to numbered lists.
- ✔ `Monofont` sets Web addresses apart.

In addition, you can safely skip text highlighted with the Technical Stuff icon or formatted in gray-shaded sidebars without missing anything you need to know. This text provides plenty of helpful information, but the information isn't crucial to your understanding of the topic at hand.

Foolish Assumptions

Many small-business books assume that their readers are ready to make the leap into small business and are cognizant of the risks and pitfalls. We don't make that assumption here, and neither should you. That's why we include sections designed to help you decide whether small business is really for you. We spell out the terms of starting your own business, break down the tasks, and point out the dangers. We don't think that you're incapable of making the decision yourself; we just know that time is your most precious resource, and we think we can help you save it. Too many years of your life will be lost if you make the wrong choice.

Much of this book also is targeted to running and managing your existing small business intelligently. Even if you have a great idea, operating a small business is much harder than it appears, so we show you the best ways to manage and grow your enterprise.

How to Use This Book

We've organized this book to satisfy different reading and personal styles. Some of you may read it from cover to cover, while others will refer to it to answer a specific question or address an immediate concern. For this reason, each chapter of the book is designed to stand on its own. We're flexible — read it as a project or use it as a reference guide.

Much like every small-business owner, this book must wear a number of hats. It can serve as your resource in many ways.

For making big decisions

Your first small-business decision may be to admit that you're not ready for this career — at least not yet. If you're straddling the fence, Chapter 1 is intended to help you dismount onto one side or the other. We help you make the right choice by presenting you with a test that helps you determine whether this career works for you.

Make no mistake about it, no matter how creatively you and your lawyer may attempt to structure your deal, this business of small business involves risk. Therefore, before exposing yourself to such risk, we suggest that you get your personal finances in order. Enter Chapter 2, which covers personal money management.

As a road map

The road in the early stages of a small business has so many detours and forks that you're bound to lose sight of the road itself. Chapters 3, 4, and 5 provide you with the map you need to reach your destination. In these chapters, we overturn all the stones of a typical small business start-up, from writing a gangbuster business plan to creating the right legal framework to locating the financing that suits your needs.

Wait. You say you're considering buying an existing business as opposed to starting one from scratch? That's fine, too, but you should ask some finely tuned questions prior to making that decision. "What are the advantages of buying an existing business over starting a new one? What kind of business should I buy? How should I determine the price I can pay? What are the tax implications? What are the first things I should do after the sale is completed?" You find the answers to these questions (and many more) in Chapters 6 through 9.

As a problem solver and a frame of reference

You'll soon discover that small-business ownership is really one never-ending exercise in problem solving. Chapters 10 through 19 are designed to help solve small business's most compelling problems. Here's a partial list of those problems:

- **Sales creation:** No sales, no income, no business survival. Period.

- **Marketing:** Although such small-business functions as sales, accounting, and operations are primarily black-and-white issues, not so with marketing. Marketing is gray, fuzzy, and hard to define (go ahead, try defining the word *marketing* right now in one easy sentence), one of those aspects of doing business that doesn't come naturally to most people.

- **Employees:** Deciding when and whom to hire is a vital but difficult decision. Then, even when you've hired the right employees for the right jobs, you're faced with the never-ending task of motivating and retaining them — and sometimes replacing them.

- **Operational issues:** Operations is that long list of day-to-day responsibilities, beginning with how you spend your day from the time you walk in the office or store in the morning until the time you go home at night. These issues include everything from collecting accounts receivable to understanding financial statements to taking good care of your customers. And don't forget the foremost operational issue: managing the lifeblood of your business — cash.

- **Long-range planning:** Small-business owners recognize that long-range planning is important, but unfortunately they're too busy dealing with day-to-day business minutiae to get around to it. They say they'll do planning tomorrow, but alas, tomorrow never comes.

- **Accounting and bookkeeping issues:** Double-entry accounting systems? Cash flow projections? Current ratios and quick ratios and inventory turns? You're probably saying, "Give me a break. What does all this have to do with my chocolate-chip cookie business?" You'll see!

- **Technology issues:** Today, new telecommunications and information-gathering tools are appearing faster than politicians promising to cut taxes and improve government services. Keeping up is sometimes challenging, but you must do it.

- **Locating new financing or revising existing financing:** Capital is the food that feeds every small business. If you lack money, you may not be able to get your business headed in the desired direction. No capital equals no fuel to make your business go.

- **Everything else:** This category includes, but isn't limited to, such issues as product development, pricing, budgeting, business expansion, government regulations, customer service, ownership issues, and lifestyle issues.

As a mentor

It ought to be a rule: Every small-business owner should have his or her own mentor. Sadly, too few do. Meanwhile, the small-business owner's *Fortune* 500 cousins long ago learned the mentorship lesson, resulting in the fact that every new management employee today has a mentor lurking in the wings nearby. Those mentors typically are business veterans — people who've learned business's lessons the hard way. Mentors guide and teach, and that's exactly what certain chapters in this book are intended to do.

Chapters 20 through 22 act as the mentor you need to assist you in building your business. These chapters share a collection of suggestions, advice, and tips on subjects designed to make the difference between maintaining a stagnant or mediocre business and growing a healthy one. Included in these chapters are tips on such topics as how to effectively utilize technology, how to improve your personal management skills, and where to find the best tools with which to grow your business.

Icons Used in This Book

To help you find the information you need to assist you on your entrepreneurial path, we've placed icons throughout the text to highlight important points.

This symbol indicates time-tested tips to make your small-business journey more profitable and easier. Often straight from the heart of experience, we'll clue you in on what works for us as we navigate the oft-troubled waters of small-business life.

We present tales from our own experiences to save you some trial and error. Enjoy the company of your fellow entrepreneurs and benefit from the lessons they've learned.

The path of small-business ownership can be fraught with peril. Some deals may be too good to be true, and some people may have their own interests at heart, not yours. This icon points out the dangers and helps steer you clear.

This icon points out stuff too good (and too important) to forget.

This icon asks you to do some thinking and checking before you take the plunge. You have a lot of important choices to make when running a small business, so don't rush in.

If you like to sweat the dull stuff, this icon points out the inner workings of the business world that you're likely to ignore as you get down to the real work.

Where to Go from Here

It's up to you where you go from here, but if you're just beginning to think about small business, we recommend that you read straight through, cover to cover, to maximize your small-business intelligence. But the A-to-Z approach isn't necessary. If you feel pretty confident in your knowledge of certain areas, pick the ones that you're most interested in learning about by skimming the Table of Contents or by relying on the well-crafted Index at the back of the book.

Part I
Becoming an Entrepreneur

The 5th Wave   By Rich Tennant

"It's quite a business plan, Ms. Strunt. It's the first
one I've read whose mission statement says,
'...keeps me out of trouble'."

In this part . . .

Do you have the right stuff to start and run your own business? In Part I you can test your entrepreneurial aptitude, ensure that your personal finances can withstand the strain, and then start making your dream a reality with a well-designed business plan and a survey of financial and ownership options.

Chapter 1

Is Small Business for You?

In This Chapter

▶ Understanding the role of small business

▶ Knowing the skills small-business owners need

▶ Determining whether you have what it takes to run a successful small business

▶ Being aware of the reasons to own (and not to own) a small business

▶ Identifying alternatives to starting a business

An old friend of ours, who has been a small-business owner for more years than most of us have been alive, says, "Small business is a place where you can take your dog to the office whenever you choose." That's a good way of looking at it, but we offer several other viewpoints as well.

We also give you a set of 20 questions to ask yourself about your skills, talents, and capabilities. If you're honest with yourself — don't worry, there are no right or wrong answers — this test will give you the information you need to determine whether running a small business is the right move for you. And if you find that running a small business isn't for you, we provide several alternatives, which may give you exactly what you're looking for.

Owning and running a small business can be rewarding — personally and financially — but only if you have what it takes to succeed. This chapter gives you all the know-how you need to be sure that you're making the right decision.

Of course, you probably won't make the decision about whether to go into the small-business world based upon your desire to spend more time with your pet! Lots of important issues — from your financial situation, to your desire to create a needed product or provide a needed service, to your ability to be a jack-of-all-trades — will influence your decision to become an entrepreneur. This chapter helps you understand the realities of starting and running a small business and how and why it may or may not work for you.

12

Defining What Is a Business

The lingo of the business world — cash flow, profit and loss statements, accounts receivable, debt-to-equity ratio, and so on — makes small-business ownership appear far more complicated than it really is. Don't be fooled. You're probably more acquainted with the basic concepts of doing business than you think. If you've ever participated in a bake sale, been paid for a musical performance, or operated a baby-sitting, painting, or lawn-mowing service, you've been involved in a small business.

Being a small-business owner doesn't mean that you have to work 70 hours a week, get to make a six-figure income, or have a breakthrough product or service that earns you national recognition. We know many successful small-business owners who work at their craft 40 hours a week or less and some who work part-time at their business while on someone else's payroll. The vast majority of small-business owners we know provide products or services quite similar to what's already in the marketplace and make reasonable but not extraordinary sums of money — and are perfectly happy doing so!

Small (and large) business basics

It's a hot summer afternoon, and you're sweating it out under the shade of an elm tree in your front yard. "Boy, it's hot," you say to yourself, sighing. "I could sure go for a glass of lemonade." And that's when you seize upon your business idea. With no lemonade stand in sight, you figure that you've found an untapped market of thirsty customers.

You start by asking some of your neighbors if they would buy lemonade from you, and you quickly discover that the quality, service, and location of your proposed business may attract a fair number of customers. You've just conducted your first market research.

After you determine that your community has a need for your business, you also need to determine the location of your business. Although you could set up in front of your house, you decide that your street doesn't get enough traffic. To maximize sales, you decide to set up your stand on the corner down the road. Luckily, Mrs. Ormsby gives you permission to set up in front of her house, provided that she gets a free glass of lemonade. You've just negotiated your first lease, and you've just had your first experience at bartering.

With a tiny bit of creativity and ego, you determine the name of your business: The World's Best Lemonade Stand. Several transactions with parents and the grocery store later, and you have your lemonade stand (the store), your cash box, a table, a pitcher (your furniture and fixtures), and the lemonade (your inventory). The World's Best Lemonade Stand is now ready for business!

From the moment you first realized that you weren't the only one who might be interested in buying some lemonade, you faced the same business challenges and issues that all small-business owners face. As a matter of fact, the business challenges and issues your lemonade stand faces are the same that Microsoft and every other *Fortune* 500 company faces. The basics of doing business are the same, no matter what size the business is:

- **Sales:** Microsoft sells software applications; you sell lemonade. A sale is a sale no matter what the product or service or how large or small the ticket price.

- **Cost of goods:** Microsoft buys packaging materials and advertising space for its software from its vendors and suppliers; you buy lemons and sugar and paper cups for your lemonade from the grocery store.

- **Expenses:** Microsoft has employee wages and pension plans (or employee benefits; see Chapter 16); you have sign-making costs and bubble-gum expenditures to keep your employees happy (also a form of employee benefits).

- **Profit:** Profit is what's left over after Microsoft subtracts the cost of its goods and expenses from its sales; the same is true for your lemonade stand.

The formula for Business 101

To take these Business 101 concepts (sales, cost of goods, expenses, and profit) one step further, not only are the terms described in the preceding section the same for any and every business, but many associated financial basics are the same, too. Here's what we mean:

- **Accounts payable:** Microsoft owes money to its vendors who provide it with packaging materials and advertising space; you owe money to your parents who provide you with lemons.

- **Accounts receivable:** Microsoft has money due from its dealers, who stock the company's software applications on their shelves. You have money due to you from Mrs. Huxtable, who wandered by thirsty but without her purse.

- **Cash flow:** Microsoft has money coming in and going out through various transactions with customers, dealers, and vendors (sometimes cash flows positively, sometimes negatively), and so do you. (See Chapter 13 for much, much more on this important, but sometimes murky, concept.)

- **Assets:** Microsoft has its office buildings and technical equipment; you have your lemonade stand and cash box.

- **Liabilities:** Microsoft owes people (vendors) money; so do you (your parents).

- **Net worth:** Net worth is what's left over after Microsoft subtracts what it owes (its *liabilities*) from what it owns (its *assets*). Ditto for your small-business enterprise.

Small business by the numbers

The Small Business Administration defines *small business* as any business with fewer than 500 employees. Co-author Jim's fourth small business had 200 employees, and in our minds anyway, that wasn't small. With 200 employees, you have, say 400 dependents, maybe 1,000 customers, and 100 or so of the business's vendors all depending on you, trusting in you, and waiting for the mail to deliver their next check. That certainly isn't small by our standards — not if you measure size in terms of responsibility anyway.

For those to whom numbers are important, however, our definition of *small business* is any business with 100 employees or less, a category that includes more than 98 percent of all U.S. businesses.

The latest year's U.S. government figures tell us that there are 26.8 million small businesses. Of those, nearly 18 million have no employees. Meanwhile, each year in excess of 600,000 new businesses open their doors. This kind of growth is an indicator of the appeal of owning a small business. (Or maybe it's an indicator of the lack of appeal of working for someone else.)

Not only do small businesses create opportunities for their owners, but they also create jobs. Small firms create about three-quarters of the new jobs in the United States, employing about 57 million Americans in the process. In addition, small businesses give everyone a chance to participate; women own approximately 40 percent of the small businesses (and the number of women-owned businesses is growing at twice the rate of the other categories), Hispanics 7 percent, African Americans 5 percent, and Asians 5 percent.

What all this says is that small business is not really small — it is large, diverse, and growing. Not only is it not small when speaking in terms of the sheer numbers of small businesses and their employees, it's also not small when talking about the tenacity and knowledge required to start and run a small business, which is where the remainder of this book comes in. You provide the tenacity part of the equation; we provide the knowledge.

This comparison between The World's Best Lemonade Stand and Microsoft could go much deeper and longer. Although the basics of the two businesses are the same, the differences are primarily due to size. In business, *size* is a synonym for *complexity*.

So, you may be thinking, if business is so simple, why isn't everyone doing it — and succeeding at it? The reason is that even though the basics of business are simple, the details are not. Consider the various ways in which you grant your customers credit, collect the resulting accounts receivable, and, unfortunately, sometimes write them off when you're not paid. Consider the simple concept of sales: How do you pay the people who make those sales, where and how do you deploy them, and how do you organize, supervise, and motivate them? And how do you compile and make sense of your financial figures? How much should you pay your vendors for their products? And when you need money, should you consider taking in shareholders or should you borrow from the bank? And, lest we forget, how should you deal with the Internal Revenue

Service (IRS) and Occupational Safety and Health Administration (OSHA) and your state's workers' compensation department? These are but a few of the complex details that muddy the waters of business.

Small business: Role model for big business

Jack Welch, while CEO of General Electric, once said in a speech to his division managers, "Think small. What General Electric is trying relentlessly to do is to get that small-company soul . . . and small-company speed . . . inside our big-company body."

Think small? What's happening here? Why would the CEO of a gigantic company like GE want his employees to be thinking small? Because Jack Welch knew that small can be beautiful and because success and survival in the business arena always favors the agile over the cumbersome, the small over the big. Thanks to this "small is beautiful" trend — and thanks to increasing technological advances — you no longer have to be big to appear big; everyone can compete in most of today's marketplaces.

Different people and businesses, similar issues

Okay, so we've defined the term *small business* and identified the people who create and run one, but what about your particular small business? After all, in your eyes anyway, the business you have in mind or the one you're already running is different than anyone else's. Different products, different services, different legal entity, and the list goes on.

The term *small business* covers a wide range of product and service offerings. A ten-person law practice is a small business. A doctor's office is a small business. Architects, surveyors, and dentists are also in the business of owning and operating small businesses.

How about a Subway franchisee? You guessed it. Small business. Ditto with freelance writers (hence, we, your humble authors, are both small-business owners), consultants, and the dry cleaner on the corner of State and Main. Each one is a small business.

A business is also a small business regardless of its entity. You say that you're a part owner in a limited liability partnership? Then you're involved in a small business. Sole proprietorships, C Corporations, nonprofits, and limited liability corporations — all are small businesses, as long as they have fewer than 100 employees. (We define these various business entities in Chapter 5.)

Think about it. All these businesses have several common denominators. They all need:

✔ Marketing to make their products or services known

✔ Sales to get their products or services in the hands of the customer

✔ Varying degrees of administration and financial accounting to satisfy a number of internal informational needs, as well as the needs of the IRS

Beyond the similarities in this list, each business is significantly different from another. Some need employees, some don't; some require vast investments in real estate, equipment, and elaborate information systems; some can get by with a desk, computer, and phone. Some may need to borrow money to get the business up and running; many others get by with what's in the owner's savings account.

Our definition of a small-business owner

A *small-business owner* (or entrepreneur), by our definition anyway, is anyone who owns a business that has 100 or fewer employees, period. Everyone who hangs out a shingle qualifies for the title no matter whether the business is private, public, barely surviving, or soaring off the charts.

You're a small-business owner if you've been in the saddle one day, one week, or one decade. You're a small-business owner whether you're male or female and have a college degree or not. You're a small-business owner if you work out of your home or on a fishing boat somewhere off the coast of Alaska.

Everyone has his or her own definition of the small-business owner. We find these three of particular interest; pick one or pick them all:

✔ **Webster's Dictionary:** A person who organizes and manages a business undertaking, assuming the risk for sake of profit.

✔ **Peter Drucker:** Someone who gets something new done. (The late Peter Drucker is the Father of Modern Management. His books have virtually defined contemporary U.S. management theory. Drucker primarily wrote for large companies.)

✔ **Us:** A person who is motivated by independence, creativity, and growth, rather than by the security of an employer's paycheck.

All people have their own collection of unique characteristics that determine who they are, what makes them happy, and where they belong in this world. On those not-as-frequent-as-they-should-be occasions when our characteristics align snugly with the kind of work we are doing, we know how Cinderella felt when her foot slipped effortlessly into the glass slipper offered by the Prince.

In all fairness, we must warn those of you who are considering our vocation that owning your own business can be addictive. We love it usually, hate it occasionally, and need it always, and we wouldn't trade professions with anybody — except for maybe Tiger Woods.

Do You Have the Right Stuff?

Unfortunately, to truly discover whether you have the right stuff to run your own small business, you need to take a little test. Tests don't always have to be a pain in the posterior, and they can be relatively painless when you don't have to study for them, there are no right or wrong answers, and you're the only one who needs to know the outcome. So be prepared to take a painless but potentially revealing test: The Small-Business Owner's Aptitude Test.

Some words of caution here: This test is not scientific in its basis. However, we think it's potentially useful because it's based on our combined six decades of experience working *as* entrepreneurs, as well as *alongside* them. This test is meant to provide a guideline and not to cast in concrete your choice to start or buy a business. The results will be most meaningful when it comes time to make your decision if you are in the highest- or the lowest-scoring groups. For those of you who fall somewhere in the middle, we recommend some serious soul searching, consultation with friends and other small-business owners, and a large grain of salt.

Instructions

Score each of the following 20 questions with a number from 1 (the entrepreneurially unfriendly response) to 5 (the entrepreneurially friendly response). You determine your appropriate numerical score by assessing the relative difference between the two options and by how fervently you feel about the answer.

For example, one question asks, "Do you daydream about business opportunities while commuting to work, flying on an airplane, or waiting in the doctor's office?" Give yourself a 5 if you find yourself doing this a lot, a 1 if you never do this, and a 2, 3, or 4, depending upon the degree of work-related daydreaming you do. (A business, especially one that you own yourself, can be downright fun and all-consuming. For most successful entrepreneurs, their minds are rarely far away from their businesses, often thinking of new products, new marketing plans, and new ways to find customers.)

To make the test even more meaningful, have someone who doesn't have a vested interest in or strong opinions about your decision — such as a good friend or co-worker — also independently take the test, with you as the subject. We seldom have unbiased opinions of ourselves, and having an unrelated third party take the test on your behalf gives a more accurate view.

Then compare the two scores — the score you arrived at when you took the test compared to the score your friend or peer compiled for you. Our guess is that your true entrepreneurial aptitude, at least according to our experience, will lie somewhere between the two scores.

The questions

After reading each question, simply circle your numerical response or write it down on a separate sheet of paper.

1. **In the games that you play, do you play harder when you fall behind, or do you have a tendency to fold your cards and cut your losses? (5 if you play harder, 1 if you wilt under pressure)**

   5   4   3   2   1

2. **When you go to a sports event or concert, do you try to figure out the promoter's or the owner's gross revenues? (5 if you often do, 1 if you never do)**

   5   4   3   2   1

3. **When things take a serious turn for the worse, is your first impulse to look for someone to blame, or is it to look for alternatives and solutions? (5 if you look for alternatives and solutions, 1 if you complain)**

   5   4   3   2   1

4. **Using your friends and/or co-workers as a barometer, how would you rate your energy level? (5 if it is high, 1 if it is low)**

   5   4   3   2   1

5. **Do you daydream about business opportunities while commuting to work, flying on an airplane, waiting in the doctor's office, or other quiet times? (5 if you often do, 1 if you never do)**

   5   4   3   2   1

6. **Look back on the significant changes you've made in your life — schools, jobs, relocations, relationships. Have you fretted and worried about those changes and not acted, or have you looked forward to them with excitement and been able to make those tough decisions after doing some research? (5 if you looked forward to the decisions and tackled them after doing your homework, 1 if you've been overwhelmed with worry about them and paralyzed from action for too long)**

   5   4   3   2   1

7. **Is your first consideration of any opportunity always the upside or is it always the downside? (5 if you always see the upside and recognize the risks, 1 if you dwell on the downside to the exclusion of considering the benefits)**

   5   4   3   2   1

8. Are you happiest when you are busy or when you have nothing to do? (5 if you are always happiest when busy, 1 if you are always happiest when you have nothing to do)

   5   4   3   2   1

9. As an older child or young adult, did you often have a job or a scheme or an idea to make money? (5 if always, 1 if never)

   5   4   3   2   1

10. Did you work part-time or summer jobs as a youth, or did you not work/primarily recreate/enjoy a total break over the summer? (5 if you often worked, 1 if you never did)

    5   4   3   2   1

11. Did your parents own a small business? (5 if they worked many years owning small businesses, 1 if they never did)

    5   4   3   2   1

12. Have you worked for a small business for more than one year? (5 if you have, 1 if you haven't)

    5   4   3   2   1

13. Do you like being in charge, in control, and at the center of attention? (5 if you really crave those things, 1 if you detest those things)

    5   4   3   2   1

14. How comfortable are you with borrowing money to finance an investment, such as buying a home? (5 if owing money is not a problem, 1 if it's a huge problem)

    5   4   3   2   1

15. How creative are you? (5 if extremely creative, 1 if not creative at all)

    5   4   3   2   1

16. Do you have to balance your checkbook to the penny or is "close" good enough? (5 if "close" is good enough, 1 if to the penny)

    5   4   3   2   1

17. When you fail at a project or task, does it scar you forever or does it inspire you to do it better the next time? (5 if it inspires you for the next time, 1 if it scars you forever)

    5   4   3   2   1

18. When you truly believe in something, whether it's an idea, a product, or a service, are you able to sell it? (5 if almost always, 1 if never)

    5   4   3   2   1

19. **In your current social and business environment, are you most often a follower or a leader? (5 if almost always a leader, 1 if always a follower)**

    5   4   3   2   1

20. **How good are you at achieving/keeping your New Year's resolutions? (5 if you almost always achieve/keep them, 1 if you never do)**

    5   4   3   2   1

Scoring the test

Now total your score. Here's how to assess your totals:

> **80 to 100:** Go for it. If you read this book and continue to show a willingness to be a sponge, you should succeed!
>
> **60 to 79:** You probably have what it takes to successfully run your own business, but take some time to look back over the questions you scored the lowest on and see whether you can discern any trends.
>
> **40 to 59:** Too close to call. Review the questions on which you scored poorly and don't scrimp on learning more to tilt the scales in your favor.
>
> **0 to 39:** We could be wrong, but you're probably better off working as an employee or pursuing one of the other alternatives to starting your own business.

Analyzing your results

The truth about a subjective test such as this one is that it can serve as a helpful indicator, but it isn't always right. Too many other factors go into the passing, or failing, of tests. And so it is with our Small-Business Owner's Aptitude Test. It can be a helpful indicator, but it won't provide you with the definitive answer. We issue this disclaimer because the Small-Business Owner's Aptitude Test is, in effect, a measure of the way you have acted in the past and not necessarily how you will perform in the future.

Your future as a small-business owner will hold many surprises. (By the time you finish this book, you'll be prepared for many of them.) The skills and traits that you need to cope with those surprises will ultimately determine whether your choice to start or buy a small business is the right one. What exactly are those skills?

> ✔ **Numbers skills:** These skills include those related to borrowing money, accounting for it, and reporting on the financial performance of your company. (See Chapters 5, 10, and 13 for more information.)

- ✔ **Sales skills:** The small-business owner is always selling someone — be it his customers, employees, or vendors.

- ✔ **Marketing skills:** Everyone has to market her product or service — no one is exempt. (See Chapter 11 for details on marketing.)

- ✔ **Leadership skills:** The small-business owner is the Grand Poobah of his venture. Grand Poobahs are only as good as the manner in which the business's employees are led. (See Chapter 15 for more information.)

Does this mean that if you don't have these skills, you should remain on the receiving end of a paycheck? Thankfully, it does not.

Many successful entrepreneurs who have come before you made it without being able to personally perform all the skills necessary to run a business. But what we're saying is that, over the course of your career, you'll have to either develop these skills or involve someone in the business who already has them (a partner, a key employee, or a hired advisor or consultant, for example).

Skills aside, successful entrepreneurs either have or adopt several required traits:

- ✔ **Confidence:** Small-business owners have to be able to coexist with risk and possibly debt. Capitalism offers its participants no guarantees; thus, the small business and consequently its owner are usually at risk and sometimes in debt. And yet, its owner still has to sleep at night.

- ✔ **Intuition:** Call it intuition or call it gut instinct, the small-business owner has to call things right more often than wrong, or he will be calling it quits.

- ✔ **Optimism:** Rarely pessimistic, successful small-business owners see good fortune, not misfortune; upsides, not downsides; and opportunities, not problems. The small-business owner can always hire a devil's advocate (that's what lawyers and accountants are for), but the enthusiasm and optimism necessary to drive the vision must come from the entrepreneur.

- ✔ **Drive:** Successful small-business owners are driven to create a product, service a customer, and build a successful business. Like the craving for chocolate, this drive doesn't go away.

- ✔ **Passion:** An entrepreneur's passion is infectious. Your employees, your vendors, and your customers — everyone you come in contact with — can feel your passion and feed off it.

Does this mean that if you don't have these five traits, you should remain on the receiving end of a paycheck? Well, let us answer by saying that we recognize that being a good employee today also requires some of these traits, so owning a business is not your only option. However, if you don't have most of these traits in healthy supply, you're probably going to be better off as an employee instead of a small-business owner.

Identifying the Pros and Cons of Owning a Small Business

Assuming that you've determined that you do have what it takes to own a small business, allow us to help you take the next step and dive in.

Even if you passed the test and qualify as a prospective small-business owner, this decision you're about to make is not a simple, clear-cut one. After all, you can find as many compelling reasons why you should not own a business as you can find reasons why you should. In the following section, we present many of these reasons.

These two lists, incidentally, are in no particular order. Everyone is different. The reasons Bill Gates may have decided to start Microsoft may be vastly different from the reasons John Dough decided to buy his own pizza business. You won't find right or wrong reasons to start or buy a business; you'll only find right or wrong criteria that go into forming those reasons.

The reasons to own

We can think of many reasons to give your boss the heave-ho. In this section, though, we stick with the best reasons why people choose to own a business:

- **The satisfaction of creation:** Have you ever experienced the pride of building a chair, preparing a gourmet meal, or repairing a vacuum cleaner? Or how about providing a needed counseling service that helps people solve their vexing financial problems? The small-business owner is treated to the thrill of creation on a daily basis, not to mention the satisfaction of solving a customer's problem.

- **Establishment of their own culture:** No more standing around the water cooler complaining about "the way things are around here." After you've started your own business, the way things are around here is a direct function of the way you intend them to be.

- **Financial upside:** Consider Charles Schwab, Oprah Winfrey, and Steve Jobs. It's no surprise that these one-time small-business owners are among the nation's wealthiest individuals. (A recent SBA study concluded definitively that although small-business ownership is risky, small-business owners had a significantly higher probability of being classified as high income and high wealth.)

- **Self-sufficiency:** For many people, working for someone else has proven to be a less-than-gratifying experience. As a result of such unfulfilling experiences, some people have discovered that if they want to provide for themselves and their families, they'd better create the opportunity themselves. It's either that or be willing to occasionally spend a long wait in the unemployment line.

✔ **Flexibility:** Perhaps you prefer to work in the evenings because that's when your spouse works or you want to spend more time with the kids during the day. Or you may prefer taking frequent three-day-weekend jaunts rather than a few full-week vacations every year. As a small-business owner, despite the long hours you work, you should have more control over keeping a schedule that works best for you. After all, you're the boss, and you can usually tailor your schedule to meet your personal needs, as well as those of your customers.

✔ **Special perks:** As you discover in Chapter 17, small-business owners have several advantages over many employees. For example, small-business owners can sock away more than $45,000 per year free of federal and state income taxes into their retirement accounts. And yes, similar to those corporate execs who wine and dine their clients and then write off the expenses, small-business owners also have the option of writing off such costs as long as they adhere to IRS rules. Chapter 18 explains what makes these rules tick and how they can work for you.

Minimizing start-up risk with part-time ventures

Some people believe that starting your own business is the riskiest of all small-business options. However, if you're starting a business that specifically uses your skills and expertise, the risk may not be nearly as great as you think. Besides, risk is relative: Those who are employed by someone else are taking a risk, too — a risk that their employer will continue to offer them the opportunity to remain employed.

One way to minimize the risk of starting a full-time business is to work into a part-time one. Suppose for a moment that you're a computer troubleshooter at a large company and making $50,000 per year. You're considering establishing your own computer consulting service and would be happy making a comparable amount of money. If you find through your research that others performing the services you intend to provide are charging $50 per hour, you'll need to actually spend about 20 hours a week consulting (assuming that you work 50 weeks per year). Because you can run your consulting business from your home (which can generate small tax breaks) and you can do it without purchasing costly new equipment, your expenses should be minimal. (**Note:** We've ignored your employer's benefits here, which, of course, have value, too.)

Rather than leaving your day job and diving into your new business without the safety of a regular paycheck, you have the option of starting to moonlight as a consultant. Over the course of a year or two, if you can average ten hours a week of consulting, you're halfway to your goal. Then, after you leave your job and can focus all your energies on your business, getting to 20 hours per week of billable work won't be such a stretch.

Many businesses, by virtue of leveraging their owner's existing skills and expertise, can be started with low start-up costs. You can begin building the framework of your company using *sweat equity* (the time and energy you invest in your business, as opposed to the capital) in the early, part-time years. As long as you know your competition and can offer your customers a valued service at a reasonable cost, the principal risk with your part-time business is that you won't do a good job marketing what you have to offer. When you can figure out how to market your skills, that's the time to make the break.

The reasons not to own

In light of the resounding potential benefits, why would any reasonable soul elect to continue receiving a paycheck? Why wouldn't everyone want to own a business? Let us count the nays:

- **Responsibility:** As a small-business owner, not only does your family depend on your business success, so do your partners, your employees and their families, your customers, and sometimes your vendors. As much as we love our small businesses, every now and then even the most enthusiastic of us wax nostalgic for the good old days when we would punch our time card and leisurely walk out the door — really, truly, done for the day. If you're the type of person who sometimes takes on more responsibility than you can handle and works too many hours, beware that another drawback of running your own business is that you may be prone to becoming a workaholic.

- **Competition:** Although some people thrive on competition, that same competition comes back to haunt you by threatening your security. You soon find out that a host of hungry competitors is pursuing your customers and threatening your livelihood, whether by cutting prices or offering a more complete package of unique services. Sure, competition is what makes capitalism go 'round, but you should remember that in order to have a competition, someone's going to win and someone's going to lose.

- **Change:** Products and services come, and products and services go. Nothing is sacred in the business of doing business, and the pace of change today is significantly faster than it was a generation ago — and it shows no signs of slowing down. If you don't enjoy change and the commotion it causes, then perhaps the stability that a larger, more bureaucratic organization provides is best for you.

- **Chance:** Interest rates, the economy, theft, fire, natural disasters, sickness, pestilence — the list goes on. Any of these random events can send your business reeling.

- **Red tape:** Taxes, health-care reform, bureaucracy, tariffs, duties, treaties, OSHA, FDA, NAFTA, glurg, glurg, glurg.

- **Business failure:** And finally, as if this list of a small-business's enemies isn't long enough, the owner faces the specter of the ultimate downside: business failure in the form of bankruptcy. This is the stage where the owner stands back and watches the creditors swoop in like vultures to devour his remaining business assets.

Now contrast the small-business owner's failure to the *Fortune* 500 employee who fails, collecting a tidy severance check as he packs up his calculator and waves good-bye on his way to register for unemployment compensation. No life's savings lost for this person, no second mortgages hanging over his or her home, no asterisks on the credit report. In our opinion, no other failure in the business world is as painful as that facing the small-business owner. More than any other reason, this extreme cost of failure is the primary reason that owning a small business isn't for everyone.

Exploring Alternatives to Starting a Business

More than a few small-business owners and entrepreneurial cheerleaders would have you believe that every employee would be happy and financially better off running his own small business. The reality is, of course, that the grass is not always greener on the other side of the fence. Small business isn't the only game in town; in some cases, it isn't even the best option available for you.

If, after taking the Small-Business Owner's Aptitude Test earlier in this chapter, you feel that you don't fit the profile of the typical entrepreneur, don't despair. Some folks are happier working for a company, be it either for-profit or nonprofit. Here are several options for you to consider, in lieu of becoming an entrepreneur:

- **Become a better employee.** Companies of all sizes need good employees, and good companies are willing to go to a lot of trouble and expense to hire, retain, and pay them. (If you're not presently working for one of those good companies, you have plenty to choose from. Get your resume updated!) Keep improving your work ethic. Your willingness to put in the extra hours when needed and your accompanying willingness to accept more responsibility will bring a smile to the faces of employers. Keep learning. You don't need a PhD, a master's degree, or even an undergraduate college degree to succeed in business because of the amount of knowledge that you can pick up on your own through mentors, experience, and plenty of reading.

If you haven't completed your college or graduate degree and the industry you're in places particular value in those who have, investing the time and money it takes to finish your degree can pay big dividends. (More than a few of today's enlightened businesses will finance all or at least a part of that education for you. Just ask.) Talk to others who have taken a similar mid-career educational path and see what they have to say.

✔ **Be an entrepreneur inside a larger company.** If you can find or create an entrepreneurial enterprise inside (or alongside) a larger company, in addition to significant managerial and operational responsibility, in many cases you can also negotiate sharing in the financial success that you help to create. Entrepreneurial opportunities can come from within businesses of all sizes, shapes, and forms. One large company — 3M, a *Fortune* 500 company — has long taken pride in a corporate culture that allows its employees to take an idea and build it into a separate company within 3M. Post-it Notes, those handy, sticky notes found everywhere in the offices of the world, is an example of a business started within a business by 3M employees.

Developing a business within a business can be a win-win situation for everyone. The employees involved can be compensated for the results of their newfound business, companies like 3M add another terrific and profitable product to their empire, and a new business venture may be spun off to make more products and hire more employees, keeping the local economy humming.

✔ **Move from a large company to a small company.** Although we're not aware of any statistics measuring the movement of employees from large businesses to small businesses (or vice versa), we would guess the scale tilts significantly in favor of employees moving from large businesses to small businesses for several reasons: Employees get well-rounded experience working with small companies; small-business employees have opportunities for more responsibility; and employee decisions and actions have much more impact on a small business, and that impact is more visible than in a large business.

✔ **Buy an existing business.** In the likely event that you don't have a specific idea for a business you want to start, but you have exhibited business-management skills, consider buying an established business. Although buying someone else's business can, in some cases, be riskier than starting your own, at least you know exactly what you're getting into right from the start. The good news, however, is that you often don't have to waste time and energy creating an infrastructure — it's already in place, which allows you, the buyer, to dive right into the business, without having to waste time on the peripherals.

Buying an existing business often requires that you shell out more money at the outset, in the form of a down payment to buy the business. Thus, if you don't have the ability to run the business and it performs poorly, you have a lot more to lose financially.

✔ **Invest in someone else's business.** If you find that managing the day-to-day headaches of a small business is not for you, perhaps a viable alternative would be to consider investing in someone else's small business — assuming that you have the ability to identify potentially successful businesses. In our experience, however, few people have the knowledge to be investors in other people's small businesses. (For more information on this subject, see Chapter 5.)

Chapter 2

Laying Your Personal Financial Foundation

*W*hether you dream about owning your own business or you're currently living the reality of the good and the bad that comes from being your own boss, you know that money is important. Just as your car won't run without gasoline, you can't sustain a roof over your head and provide food, clothing, and the rest of life's necessities if you can't pay for them.

Likewise, you can't continue buying what you want and need for your business without money. Of course, today's easy access to consumer credit — witness the never-ending stream of credit-card solicitations cramming your mailbox and some retailers' E-Z layaway terms — can allow you to live beyond your means for quite a while.

But if you continue spending more money than you take in and adding to your debt pile, you can easily and quickly end up with more debt and interest on that debt than you can handle. Your next stop may be bankruptcy, a fate this chapter would like to help you avoid.

Getting Your Financial Ducks in Order

Having your personal finances in order is one of the most under-recognized keys to achieving success in your small business. Just one significant money oversight or mistake can derail your entrepreneurial dreams or venture. The following sections present several good reasons why your chances for success as a small-business owner are higher if your personal finances are in top shape.

Cutting the umbilical cord

One of the primary reasons why many aspiring entrepreneurs continue to work for someone else is the financial and accompanying psychological obstacles they face in leaving the security of a regular paycheck. The pressure and uncertainty of living paycheck to paycheck to meet monthly obligations serves as a huge wet blanket for most budding entrepreneurs' enthusiasm — and it doesn't do much to boost their resolve to leave behind the comfort of their paychecks and benefits.

Unless you prepare yourself fiscally and emotionally to leave your day job, you may never discover that you have untapped potential to run your own business. Money and mind issues cause many aspiring entrepreneurs to remain indentured servants to their employers and can cause those who do break their bondage to soon return to the relative comfort of being employees.

If you decide to start your own business, you'll quickly discover what every successful entrepreneur before you has discovered: You have a finite amount of time and energy. If your mind is preoccupied with personal financial problems, and resolving those problems requires too much of your thought and effort, something has to give. That something is likely to be either your family or your business — or, perhaps both.

In the early years of your start-up business, you'll almost surely experience a reduction in your take-home income. You must accept this scenario as fact, plan accordingly, stick with those plans, and make them work.

Improving your business survival odds

If you're successful in leaving your job and getting your business venture off the ground, you'll need to manage your money well to ensure continued success. Money is a precious resource that, when squandered, is gone forever.

Of course, if you're wealthy to begin with, you can go on for quite some time before a lack of money forces you to give up your venture. But most of us who start small businesses aren't Rockefellers or Gettys to begin with — after all, one of the attractions of achieving small-business success is building your own nest egg. Getting your financial house in order before you start your business can buy you critical time to make a success of your start-up.

Maintaining harmony on the home front

The financial and emotional stress that small business puts on many entrepreneurs not only affects them directly but also impacts family members — especially spouses and children — even more. Young children can pick up on the stress and feel the hurt of neglect from parents who forget their role as parents in their quest for success. Spouses can grow resentful of all the money and time their workaholic partners put into the fledgling business.

After years of hard work in the business and neglect of their partners and friends, successful and unsuccessful small-business owners alike can end up with a set of divorce papers and fewer friends. (Of course, workaholic employees and company executives can end up in the same lonely boat, too.) Business success, if it comes as the result of ignoring your personal life, can be a lonely and unfulfilling reward.

Before you commit to launching your small business, consider this short but highly important list of things to accomplish on the home front:

- ✔ **Set aside time to talk about concerns.** Schedule time with your spouse and other family members to discuss their concerns and needs related to your starting a small business. Be sure to ask the following:

  - How do they feel about the financial burden?

  - What do they think about leaving the corporate security?

  - What concerns do they have about your working late hours?

  - Do they see working from home (assuming that you're starting a home business) as a good thing or a bad thing?

  - What role, if any, would they like to play in the new business?

  Especially important is to come to an understanding as to what personal assets (savings, home equity, and so on) you all agree can be used in the business. If you haven't discussed and assessed your personal financial situation, now's the time to do so.

  Allow your family members to speak their minds and get their concerns out on the table. Although it's easy to say and much harder to do, be sure that you don't get defensive or make them feel that they can't be heard. Your first job is to listen and really *hear* what they have to say.

- ✔ **Seek outside assistance for impasses.** Running your own business is demanding and stressful. You don't need the added pressure of problems on the home front. If your initial discussions with family members reveal problems that aren't easily resolved, the time to get help is before your business is up and running. After your spouse has filed for divorce or your kids are messed up on drugs, the damage too often is done. Marriage/ family counseling with an experienced counselor can be an invaluable preventive investment. Finding a mentor or another entrepreneur who has built a business of his or her own can give you the additional insight of experience. You may also try reading some quality self-help/family-relationship books.

Creating Your Money To-Do List

We hope you agree that getting your personal finances in order before you set up shop makes a lot of sense. But you have so much to do and so little time! Where to begin and what to do? This section provides a short list of the important financial tasks you need to undertake.

Assess your financial position and goals

Where do you stand in terms of retirement planning? How much do you want to have saved to pay for your children's educational costs? What kind of a home do you want to buy?

These and other important questions can help shape your personal financial plans. Sound financial planning isn't accomplished by faithfully balancing your checkbook or investing in stocks based upon a friend's tip. Rather, smart financial management is about taking a hard look at where you are, figuring out where you want to go, and making sure that you're prepared for occasional adverse conditions along the way — a process, incidentally, that is not unlike what you'll be doing when you run your own business.

Measuring your net worth

First, give yourself a financial physical. Start with measuring your *net worth,* which is the difference between your financial assets and financial liabilities.

Begin by totaling up your financial assets (all your various bank accounts, stocks, mutual funds, and so on) and subtracting from that the sum total of all your liabilities (credit-card debt, auto loans, student loans, and so on). *Note:* Because most people don't view their home as a retirement asset, we've left your home's value and mortgage out of your net worth calculations. (Personal property [furniture, cars, and so on] doesn't count as a financial asset.) However, you may include this amount if you want, especially if you're willing to tap your home's equity to accomplish goals such as retiring.

Now, don't jump to conclusions based on the size of the resulting number. If you're young and still breaking into your working years, your net worth is bound to be relatively low — perhaps even negative. Relax. Sure, you have work to do, but you have plenty of time ahead of you.

Ideally, as you approach the age of 40, your net worth should be greater than a year's worth of gross income; if your net worth equals more than a few years of income, you're well on the road toward meeting larger financial goals, such as retirement.

Of course, the key to increasing your net worth is making sure that more money is coming in than is going out. To achieve typical goals such as retirement, you should be saving about 10 percent of your gross (pretax) income. If you have big dreams or you're behind in the game, you may need to save 15 percent or more.

If you know that you're saving enough, or if you know it won't be *that* hard to start saving enough, then don't bother tracking your spending. On the other hand, if you have no idea how you'll start saving that much, you're going to need to determine where you're spending your money.

Telling good debt from bad

Next, categorize your liabilities as either good debt or bad debt:

- ✔ **Good debt** refers to money borrowed for a long-term investment that appreciates over time, such as a home, an education, or a small business.

- ✔ **Bad debt** is money borrowed for a consumer purchase, such as a car, an Italian silk suit, or a vacation to Cancun.

Why is bad debt bad? Because it's costly to carry, and if you carry too much, it's like a financial cancer. If the outstanding balances of all your credit cards and auto loans divided by your annual gross income is exceeding 25 percent of your income, you've entered a danger zone, where interest payments can start to snowball out of control.

Don't even consider starting a small business until you've paid off all your consumer debt.

Not only are the interest rates on consumer debt relatively high, but also the things you buy with consumer debt lose their value over time. A financially healthy amount of bad debt — like a healthy amount of cigarette smoking — is none.

Reducing debt

If you have outstanding consumer debt, pay it off sooner rather than later. If you must tap into savings to pay down your consumer debts, then do it. Many people resist digging into savings, feeling as if they're losing hard-earned money. Remember that the growth of your money is determined by your net worth — the difference between your assets and liabilities. Paying off an outstanding credit-card balance with an interest rate of 14 percent is like finding an investment with a guaranteed return of 14 percent — tax free. (**Note:** We recognize that small-business owners sometimes finance their small business via credit cards, and in some cases, because this would be investment debt and investment debt is "good debt," we feel this situation may be acceptable. We discuss business financing options in Chapter 5.)

If you don't have any available savings with which to pay off your high-interest-rate debts, you'll have to climb out of debt one month at a time. The fact that you're in hock and without savings is a sign that you've been living beyond your means. Devote 10 to 15 percent of your income toward paying down your consumer loans. If you have no idea where you'll get this money, detail your spending by expense category, such as rent, eating out, clothing, and so on, as we discuss in the preceding section. You'll probably find that your spending doesn't reflect what's important to you, and you'll see fat to trim. (This process is similar to budgeting and expense management in business, and not being able to manage your personal expenses may be a wake-up call for your business proposal.)

While paying down your debt, you should always look for ways to lower your interest rate. Apply for low-interest-rate cards to which you can transfer balances from your highest-interest-rate cards. Haggling with your current credit-card company for a lower interest rate sometimes works. Also, think about borrowing against the equity in your home, against your employer-sponsored retirement account, or from family — all options that should lower your interest rate significantly.

 If you're having a hard time kicking the credit-card habit, get out your scissors and cut up your cards. The convenience of purchasing with plastic can still be had with a Visa or MasterCard debit card, which is linked directly to your checking account so that you can't spend beyond your means. Merchants who take Visa or MasterCard credit cards also accept these companies' debit cards.

Buying insurance

Another action you should take before you address your longer-term financial goals is making sure that you're properly covered by insurance. Without proper insurance coverage, an illness or an accident could quickly turn into a devastating financial storm.

Buy long-term disability insurance if you lack it. This most overlooked form of insurance protects against a disability curtailing your greatest income-generating asset: your ability to earn money. If anyone depends on your employment income, buy term life insurance, which, in the event of your death, leaves money to those financially dependent upon you. Make sure that your health insurance policy is a comprehensive one. Ideally, your lifetime benefits should be unlimited; if the policy has a maximum, it should be at least a few million dollars. (We provide more details on these important coverages later in this chapter in the section "Assessing and Replacing Benefits.")

Also check your auto and home policies' liability coverage, which protects you in the event of a lawsuit; you should have at least enough to cover twice your assets.

And for all your insurance policies, take the highest deductible you can afford. Of course, if you have a claim, you'll have to pay more of the initial expense out of your own pocket, but you'll save significantly on premiums. Buy insurance to cover the potentially catastrophic losses, not the small stuff.

Planning for the long term

In co-author Eric's experience as a financial counselor, he has seen many examples prove that earning a high income does not guarantee a high rate of savings. The best savers he knows tend to be goal oriented — earmarking savings for specific purposes.

If you know that you're an undisciplined saver, you may consider adopting the technique of designating certain savings or investment accounts toward specific goals. After all, if you're feeling tempted to buy a luxury car, it's a lot harder to take money out of an account earmarked for Timmy's college education than from a general account called "savings."

Perhaps because it's the furthest away of our long-term goals, retirement is the most difficult to get in focus. Retirement is also much tougher to plan for than most goals because of all the difficult-to-make assumptions — inflation, life expectancy, Social Security benefits, taxes, rate of return, and so on — that go into the calculations.

Use a good retirement planning workbook or program. Check out T. Rowe Price (www.troweprice.com; 800-638-5660) or Vanguard.com's Web site. These retirement planners help to transform a fuzzy dream into a concrete action plan, forcing you to get specific about retirement issues you may not have thought about and opening your eyes to the power of compounding interest and the importance of saving now.

Goal-specific saving is challenging for most people given competing goals. Even a respectable 10 to 15 percent of your income may not be enough to accomplish such goals as saving for retirement, accumulating a down payment for a home, saving for children's college expenses, and tucking away some money for starting a small business.

So you must make some tough choices and prioritize your goals. Only you know what's important to you, which means that you're the most qualified person to make these decisions. But we want to stress the importance of contributing to retirement accounts, whether you use a 401(k), SEP-IRA, Keogh, or IRA. Not only do retirement accounts shelter your investment earnings from taxation, but these accounts are also generally tax deductible.

With the money you're socking away, be sure you invest wisely. Doing so is not as difficult as most financial advisors and investment publications make it out to be. (Of course, they want to make it sound complicated in order to gain your confidence, your business, and fees.)

What's your reward for whipping your finances into shape and staying the course? Although it's true that money can't buy happiness, managing your personal finances efficiently can open up your future life options, such as switching into a lower-paying but more fulfilling career, starting your own business, or perhaps working part-time at a home-based business when you have kids so that you can be an involved parent. Work at achieving financial success and then be sure to make the most of it.

Shrink your spending

Do all you can to reduce your expenses and lifestyle to a level that fits with the entrepreneurial life that you want to lead. Now is the time to make your budget lean and entrepreneurially friendly.

Determine what you spend each month on rent, mortgage, groceries, eating out, insurance, and so on. Your checkbook register, your credit-card statement, and your memory of cash purchases should help you piece together what you spend on various things in a typical month. The best way to track your expenses is to pay either by credit card or debit card. Cash doesn't provide you a paper trail to reconcile your expenses at the end of the month.

Beyond the bare essentials of food, shelter, health care, and clothing, most of what you spend money on is discretionary — in other words, luxuries. Even the dollars you spend on the so-called necessities, such as food and shelter, are usually only part necessity, with the balance being luxury.

If you refuse to question your current spending, or if you view all your current spending as necessary, you'll probably have no option but to continue your career as an employee. You'll never be able to pursue your dream! Over-spending won't make you happy; you'll be miserable over the years if your excess spending makes you feel chained to a job you don't like. Life is too short to spend most of it working at a full-time job that doesn't make you happy.

Build up your cash reserves

Shrinking your spending is a means to an end — that end being the ability to save what you don't spend for a rainy day. In the embryonic years of your business, you're going to see too many rainy days — you may even experience years predominated by rain.

Your wherewithal to stick with an entrepreneurial endeavor will depend in part on your war chest of cash. At a minimum, you should have three to six months of living expenses invested in an accessible account, such as a money market fund with low operating expenses. If you have consumer debt, after you finish paying off your debt, your top financial priority should be building this fund. The bigger the war chest, the better; if you can accumulate a year's worth of living expenses, great.

Stabilize income with part-time work

One way to pursue your entrepreneurial dreams, and not starve while doing so, is to continue working part-time in a regular job at the same time you're working part-time in your own business. If you have a job that allows you to work part-time, seize the opportunity. Some employers will even allow you to maintain your benefits.

When co-author Eric was planning to start his financial counseling business, he was able to cut back his full-time job to half-time for four months, using his time away from his regular job to start his financial counseling business. In the first year of co-author Jim's initial entrepreneurial venture, he also continued his full-time job for a wood-products business.

In addition to the monetary security you get from a regular job, splitting your time allows you to adjust gradually to a completely new way of making a living. Some people have a difficult time adjusting if they quit their job cold turkey and start working full-time as an entrepreneur.

One option is to completely leave your current job but line up work that will provide a decent income for at least some of your weekly work hours. Consulting for your former employer is a time-tested first "entrepreneurial" option with low risk — just one of many reasons why you should endeavor to leave your current job without burning bridges in the process.

Another option to working part-time is to depend on your spouse's income while you work on beefing up your own. Obviously, this option involves sacrifice from the love of your life, so be sure to talk things through with your partner to minimize misunderstandings and resentments. Perhaps someday you'll be in a position to return the favor — that's what Eric did. His wife, Judy, was working in education when Eric started an entrepreneurial venture after business school. They lived a Spartan lifestyle on her income. Several years later, when Eric's business was on solid footing, Judy left her job to start her own business.

Assessing and Replacing Benefits

For some aspiring entrepreneurs, the thought of losing their employee benefits is even scarier than cutting off their paychecks. Insurance coverages in particular — especially health insurance — seem daunting to replicate outside of the friendly confines of a corporation or nonprofit institution.

Some people are so intimidated by the thought of giving up their benefits that they jettison their dreams of becoming small-business owners. One father said to co-author Eric, "I can't go into business for myself because health insurance is too costly." That's unfortunate: Neither health insurance nor any other benefit need stand in the way of your small-business dreams.

You may be surprised at how quickly and inexpensively you can replicate your employer's benefits in your own business. And, as you can see in this section and in even more detail in Chapter 16, as a small-business owner, you may have access to some valuable benefits that your employer doesn't or can't offer you. So if you're dreaming of starting your own business, don't view your employer's benefits package as a ball and chain tying you to your current job.

Retirement savings plans and pensions

If your employer offers retirement savings programs, such as a 401(k) plan or a pension plan, don't despair about not having these benefits in the future if you should start your own business. Of course, what you've already earned and accumulated *(vested)* as an employee is yours.

Some of the best benefits of self-employment are the available retirement savings plans — SEP-IRAs (Simplified Employee Pension Individual Retirement Accounts) and Keoghs. SEP-IRAs and Keoghs allow sheltering of far more money than most corporate retirement plans do. With SEP-IRA and Keogh plans, you can plow away up to 20 percent of your net income on a tax-deductible basis.

Retirement plans are a terrific way for you, as a business owner, and your employees to tax-shelter a healthy portion of earnings. Especially if you don't have employees, making regular contributions to one of these plans is usually a no-brainer. If you do have employees, the decision is a bit more complicated but still often a great idea. Small businesses with a number of employees should always consider 401(k) plans. We explain all these plans in Chapter 16.

Health insurance

If you're in good health and you've decided to start your own business, start investigating what will happen to your coverage when you leave your job. The first option to explore is whether your existing coverage through your employer's group plan can be converted into individual coverage. If it can, great; just don't act on this option until you've explored other health plans on your own, which may offer similar benefits at lower cost. Also get proposals for individual coverage from major health plans in your area. Be sure to select a high deductible, if available, to keep costs down.

Thanks to the Health Insurance Portability and Accountability Act, you may be able to secure an individual health-insurance policy even if you have existing health problems. Employers with 20 or more employees are required by law to provide (at your expense) health insurance for 18 months (under government regulations called *COBRA*) after you terminate employment. If you've previously had group health-insurance coverage for at least 18 consecutive months, you've used up your COBRA coverage from your last employer, and you apply within two months of the ending of that coverage, you're guaranteed to have access to an individual health-insurance policy regardless of your medical condition.

Thanks to tax law changes in recent years, health savings accounts (HSAs) have become far more attractive and increasingly available. Like the best retirement accounts, HSAs offer an upfront tax deduction on contributions as well as tax-free compounding of investment earnings over time. HSAs also offer tax-free withdrawals so long as the money is used for eligible expenses. So, unlike any retirement account, HSAs are so-called triple-tax-free accounts. For all the details on these terrific tax-saving vehicles for small business owners and their employees, please see Chapter 16.

Disability insurance

Well in advance of leaving your job, be sure that you secure long-term disability insurance. Long-term disability insurance protects your income in the event of a disability. If you're like most people, your greatest financial asset is your ability to earn employment income. If you suffer a disability and are unable to work, how will you and your family manage financially? Most people, of course, couldn't manage their current lifestyle if their employment income disappeared.

Don't wait until you leave your job to shop for disability coverage. After you quit your job and no longer have steady employment income, you won't be able to qualify for a long-term disability policy. Most insurers will then want to see at least six months of self-employment income before they're willing to write a policy for you. The risk then is, if you become disabled during this time, you're completely without insurance.

Several proven sources for securing long-term disability insurance include the following:

- ✔ **Professional associations:** Thanks to the purchasing power of the group, associations that you may be a member of — or could become a member of — often offer less costly disability coverage than what you could buy on your own.

- ✔ **Insurance agents:** Also consider shopping for an individual disability policy through agents who specialize in such coverage.

Life insurance

If you have life-insurance coverage through your employer, odds are you can replicate it on your own. If you have dependents (children, a spouse, or others) who rely on your income, you need life insurance.

The amount of life insurance you carry should be determined by how much annual income you're trying to protect and over how many years. For example, to replace your income over the next decade, multiply your annual after-tax income by 8.5. Thus, if you're annually making $30,000 after taxes, you should buy about $250,000 of life insurance. You only need to replace your after-tax income because the death benefits on a life-insurance policy are free of income tax.

Term life insurance, which is pure life insurance protection, offers the best way to buy needed coverage at the lowest cost.

Other policies, such as universal, whole, and variable life, which are collectively referred to as *cash-value policies,* combine life-insurance coverage with an investment account. For an equivalent amount of coverage, a cash-value policy typically costs about eight times what a term policy costs. Furthermore, in the early years of a cash-value policy, the bulk of that cost difference builds little in the way of cash value and instead goes mostly to pay insurance agent commissions and administrative costs.

In the long run, you would do best to separate your life insurance from your investments. Buy term insurance and invest your savings through your employer's retirement savings plan. Contributions to 401(k) plans and the like typically offer an upfront tax deduction at the federal and state levels. Money put into a cash-value life-insurance plan offers no such deduction.

The good news is that if you need life insurance, you can probably purchase an individual life-insurance policy at a lower cost than you could purchase such coverage through your employer.

Insurance agency quotation services send you a handful of relatively user-friendly proposals from the highest-rated, lowest-cost companies available. Like other agencies, the services receive a commission if you buy a policy from them, which you're under no obligation to do. They'll ask you for your date of birth, whether you smoke, and how much coverage you'd like. Reputable firms in this line of work include SelectQuote (800-343-1985; www.selectquote.com) and Term4Sale (www.term4sale.com).

Dental, vision, and other insurance

You may have other insurance programs besides the traditional health, life, and disability. Some employers offer insurance plans for dental and vision care, and occasionally some other unusual benefits, such as prepaid legal plans.

As an aspiring or new entrepreneur, you can't afford to waste money. Insurance programs that cover small potential out-of-pocket losses aren't worth purchasing. Don't waste your money buying such policies. Remember that insurance companies are in business to make money. On average, insurers pay out no more than about 60 cents in claims per dollar paid to them in policyholder premiums. The other 40-plus percent goes to administration and profits.

Social Security taxes

Another "benefit" of working for an employer is that the employer pays for half (7.65 percent of your income) of your Social Security and Medicare taxes. Don't despair of the extra cost of having to pay both halves of this tax when operating your own business. Although you do have to pay the entire tax (15.3 percent of your income) when you're self-employed, the IRS allows you to take half of this amount as a tax deduction on your Form 1040. The value of your deduction depends on your marginal tax rate; if you are in, say, the 28-percent federal income tax bracket, then the actual cost of your self-employment tax is 5.51 percent $[7.65 - (7.65 \times 0.28)]$. Thus, the tax isn't as painful as you think. (State tax deductions decrease the effective costs of self-employment taxes even further.)

When pricing your products or services, you can build the cost of this tax, as well as other benefits you'll pay for out of your own pocket, into your calculations. (After all, this is what your current employer does.) We explain pricing strategies in Chapter 11.

Time off

All work and no play make Mary and John dull and probably overstressed entrepreneurs. When you work for a company, we trust that it provides you with certain holidays and at least a couple of weeks of vacation each year. You may never have considered that your paycheck covers the cost of these normal workdays when you're allowed time off.

Again, when you price your products and services, you should factor in that between holidays and two to three weeks of annual vacation, you'll probably not be working about 5 weeks out of the 52 weeks in a year. Although some new entrepreneurs don't take much vacation time or many holidays off, we certainly don't want you to plan for that — you'll burn yourself out and not be much fun to be around!

Managing Your Personal Finances Post-Launch

It continues to amaze us: We see savvy small-business owners who are successful when it comes to managing their companies. However, when you glance at their personal finances, they may look like personal financial misfits — underinsured, overextended on credit, undiversified in investments, behind on retirement planning, and so on.

Dismissing this trait as a mere foible, in much the same way that you may chuckle at a genius with a messy desk, is easy to do. Such sloppiness with personal financial management is an unfortunate tendency, however, because it downplays the seriousness of the problem: Poorly managed personal finances can destroy a business, no matter how successful and well run it is. Also, we've noticed that poor personal financial management often leads to more of the same on a business level. Old habits are not easily changed.

This chapter focuses on getting your finances in order before you start your business. However, keeping your personal finances on track (living within your means, planning how much you need to save for various goals, selecting sound investments, and maintaining catastrophic and cost-effective insurance coverage) post-launch is vital to your financial future as well as to the viability of your business. If you don't know how to do these things well, we have a recommendation for you: Pick up a copy of the latest edition of Eric's book, *Personal Finance For Dummies* (Wiley).

As a small-business owner, you also need to be especially careful to stay on top of your required tax payments for both yourself and your employees. (We cover small-business tax issues in Chapter 18.) You also need to protect your personal finances from business-related lawsuits — an important topic we cover in Chapters 5 and 17.

Chapter 3

Finding Your Niche

. . . .

. . . .

*A*lthough your business niche and the idea behind your business are important, neither the niche nor the idea makes the primary difference when it comes to the survival of your business. Rather, the primary difference will be made by *you!* The niche and the idea are only a small part of the puzzle. In this chapter, we give you more puzzle pieces to play with, including the cornerstone piece (that's you again), and we explain why you need to put them together to assure your business's success.

Why You Don't Need a New Idea

Most small-business owners dive into their niches because they love the product or service they provide. The annals of small business are filled with the tales of founders who cared so deeply about their product or service that they subsequently decided to make it their life's work so that they could enjoy getting up in the morning again.

Examples abound of businesses that have grown and prospered as a result of an entrepreneur's passion for a particular activity:

- ✔ Jim Gentes was a passionate biker who had ideas about bike helmets that led him to found Giro.
- ✔ L.L. Bean developed a line of outdoor gear that he couldn't find elsewhere.
- ✔ John Bogle founded the Vanguard Group of mutual funds in order to deliver low-cost funds that served investors' best interests.

Of course, many small-business owners (the vast majority, in fact) don't break new ground. Plenty of tax preparers, dry cleaners, and restaurant owners happily make themselves a comfortable living doing what many others before them have already done.

Unfortunately, having a groundbreaking idea or extensive product knowledge and enthusiasm has little real influence on your long-term business success. Even if you make the best chocolate chip cookies this side of Mrs. Fields, your business could still crash and burn. Maybe you don't sell enough cookies, or you have a hard time accounting for the ones you do sell, or you sell ocean tankers filled with cookies but your prices are too low to make a profit or your customers won't pay their bills.

Having a good product and knowing the product well are only the beginning of building a successful business; you must also perform a long list of sometimes arduous day-to-day chores in order to be a successful small-business owner. Those chores may be to

- Find good customers and convince them to buy (see Chapter 12).

- Deal with difficult, hard-to-please customers.

- Provide cost-effective customer service that retains customer loyalty.

- Understand financial statements, including balance sheets, profit and loss statements, and cash flow statements (see Chapter 13).

- Grant credit and know how, and to whom, to grant it.

- Collect *receivables* (the money you're owed).

- Juggle and prioritize the payment of *payables* (the money you owe to others).

- Understand the mystifying concept of cash flow and then manage it.

- Compute inventory turn, days-in-receivables, current ratios, and return on sales (we cover all these items in Chapter 13).

- Use such management tools as organization charts, job descriptions, and performance reviews (see Chapter 15).

- Purchase the right computer and software and then learn how to use it.

- Collect and disburse sales tax, income tax, and FICA, and perform all those other services the government requires of small businesses (we explain government requirements in Chapter 17).

- Protect yourself from lawsuits — both from your employees and your customers — including sexual harassment suits and product liability suits.

- Avoid (and deal with when you can't) such headaches as OSHA (Occupational Safety and Health Administration), workers' compensation, and unemployment problems.

- Deal with drug- and alcohol-related problems, pacify smokers and non-smokers, and recognize and deal with the malingerers, the embezzlers, and the shoplifters.

> ✔ Know how, and when, to use small claims court.
>
> ✔ Know how to hire, fire, train, motivate, and hold employees accountable; control expenses; manage crises; balance cultures; deal with bankers; budget; forecast — the list goes on and on.

Of course, not all businesses have to deal with all the items in the preceding list. If your business doesn't have inventory, for example, you won't have to deal with the myriad issues relating to that.

Our point here is that the niche or idea won't ultimately make or break your business; the day-to-day running of the business itself is what ultimately determines success — or failure.

Stated another way, you show us a crackerjack business person, and we'll show you someone who can get rich in the cookie business whether or not he or she has the foggiest idea about how to bake the darned things.

Inventing Something New

Benjamin Franklin, Thomas Edison, Wilbur & Orville Wright — the annals of American history are filled with numerous people who created something new that changed an industry and even our way of life. Most people know the "famous" inventors, but many unknown folks invent something that becomes a business success.

Co-author Jim had a marine biologist friend who invented a device to count and sort fish eggs. The inventor added on a small manufacturing facility to the back of his garage and sold or leased his device to fish and conservation departments all over the world. For ten years he, his wife, and his oldest son manufactured fish egg sorters and built a strong business with real value, before selling it to a younger buyer interested in growing the business.

In this section, we highlight some helpful places to turn to (and harmful ones to run from) if you aspire to be an inventor.

Say yes to useful invention resources

In 1999, the American Inventor's Protection Act was passed by Congress and signed into law to better protect American entrepreneurs who create something that could be patented or otherwise protected, including new products, services, or processes.

One reason the Act was passed in 1999 was to protect would-be inventors from hyped invention promotion firms, which take your money and provide you little (if anything) in return (see the next section for more).

Fortunately, a number of truly helpful resources exist, including those in the following list, which are among the best and most interesting for would-be inventors:

- ✔ *American Inventor* **TV show on ABC:** Each season, a panel of judges screens hundreds of inventions and inventors in major cities around the country in the search for winners. In recent seasons, the grand prize winner got $1,000,000 in prize money and resources to promote his invention while semifinalists got smaller amounts. Winning can pay off; the first year's winner designed an infant car seat and entered into a partnership with Evenflo. For information on auditioning, go to www. americaninventor.tv.

- ✔ **Nolo Press books on patents and inventions:** Nolo Press (www.nolo. com), publisher of hundreds of legal books and software programs since 1971, has numerous helpful books on patents and inventions.

- ✔ **Peer networking groups:** Most larger communities have peer networking groups of inventors. Check with your local Chamber of Commerce or local economic development department.

- ✔ **United Inventors Association (UIA):** This nonprofit was founded by Roberta Toole in 1990. Its Web site (www.uiausa.org) is a treasure trove of resources for inventors worldwide. Membership is required to access most of their resources and costs $97.

- ✔ **U.S. Patent and Trademark Office:** For a government operation, the USPTO Web site (www.uspto.gov) has a lot to offer would-be inventors. Click Inventor Support and then Inventor Resources to find an array of listings. The complaints section is a public forum for consumer complaints against invention promotion firms.

Run away from invention promotion firms

Hundreds of invention promotion firms annually siphon hundreds of millions of dollars from naive wannabe entrepreneurs. Government regulators are slowly and belatedly taking some action. The following is excerpted from an excellent summary by the Federal Trade Commission (FTC) on invention promotion firms.

". . . many inventors pay thousands of dollars to firms that promise to evaluate, develop, patent, and market inventions. Unfortunately, many of these firms do little or nothing for their fee.

The Federal Trade Commission (FTC) has found that many invention promotion firms claim — falsely — that they can turn almost any idea into cash. But, the agency says, smart inventors can learn to spot the sweet-sounding promises of a fraudulent promotion firm. Here's how to follow up if you hear the following lines:

We think your idea has great market potential. *Few ideas — however good — become commercially successful. If a company fails to disclose that investing in your idea is a high-risk venture, and that most ideas never make any money, beware.*

Our company has licensed a lot of invention ideas successfully. *If a company tells you it has a good track record, ask for a list of its successful clients. Confirm that these clients have had commercial success. If the company refuses to give you a list of their successful clients, it probably means they don't have any.*

You need to hurry and patent your idea before someone else does. *Be wary of high-pressure sales tactics. Although some patents are valuable, simply patenting your idea does NOT mean you will ever make any money from it.*

Congratulations! We've done a patent search on your idea, and we have some great news. There's nothing like it out there. *Many invention promotion firms claim to perform patent searches on ideas. Patent searches by fraudulent invention promotion firms usually are incomplete, conducted in the wrong category, or unaccompanied by a legal opinion on the results of the search from a patent attorney. Because unscrupulous firms promote virtually any idea or invention without regard to its patentability, they may market an idea for which someone already has a valid, unexpired patent. In that case, you may be the subject of a patent infringement lawsuit — even if the promotional efforts on your invention are successful.*

Our research department, engineers, and patent attorneys have evaluated your idea. We definitely want to move forward. *This is a standard sales pitch. Many questionable firms do not perform any evaluation at all. In fact, many don't have the "professional" staff they claim.*

Our company has evaluated your idea, and now wants to prepare a more in-depth research report. It'll be several hundred dollars. *If the company's initial evaluation is 'positive,' ask why the company isn't willing to cover the cost of researching your idea further.*

Our company makes most of its money from the royalties it gets from licensing its clients' ideas. Of course, we need some money from you before we get started. *If a firm tells you this, but asks you to pay a large fee — upfront or to agree to make credit payments — ask why they're not willing to help you on a contingency basis. Unscrupulous firms make almost all their money from advance fees.*

The American Inventors Protection Act of 1999 gives you certain rights when dealing with invention promoters. Before an invention promoter can enter into a contract with you, it must disclose the following information about its business practices during the past five years:

- *How many inventions it has evaluated*
- *How many of those inventions got positive or negative evaluations*
- *Its total number of customers*
- *How many of those customers received a net profit from the promoter's services*
- *How many of those customers have licensed their inventions due to the promoter's services*

This information can help you determine how selective the promoter has been in deciding which inventions it promotes and the degree of success he has enjoyed. Invention promoters also must give you the names and addresses of all invention promotion companies they have been affiliated with over the past 10 years. Use this information to determine whether the company you're considering doing business with has been subject to complaints or legal action. Call the U.S. Patent and Trademark Office (USPTO) at 1-866-767-3848, and the Better Business Bureau, the consumer protection agency, and the Attorney General in your state or city, and in the state or city where the company is headquartered.

If a promoter causes you financial injury by failing to make the required disclosures, by making any false or fraudulent statements or representations, or by omitting any fact, you have the right to sue the promoter and recover the amount of your injury plus costs and attorneys' fees."

Choosing Your Business

Before we begin helping you decide the venture that would be best for you, you need to understand the four major business categories: retailing, service, manufacturing, and wholesaling.

Consider your category

The following lists some important characteristics you need to know about the four major industry groups:

✔ **Retailing:** Retailing is the general category that most people are familiar with, because the typical American deals with at least one retailer every day. Because you're familiar with the retail business, the learning curve is usually much easier in retailing than in the other three categories (although this benefit is true as well for your retailing competitors). Also, because most retail businesses deal primarily with cash or near-cash equivalents (credit cards), funding requirements for accounts receivable are relatively low compared with some of the other business categories, which means, in turn, that the capital requirements for entry can be relatively low, depending upon how much inventory is required. (See Chapter 5 to determine your initial cash needs.)

E-commerce (retailing over the Internet) is changing the parameters of the retailing category. The barrier to entry in retail-oriented entrepreneurial endeavors is becoming smaller as some successful retailing entrepreneurs choose Web pages over storefronts. However, success online isn't as easy or as lucrative as some would have you believe.

✔ **Service:** The service industry is the fastest growing of the four categories, in part due to the low cost of entry (that is, you need no significant inventory outlays and minimal equipment). Additionally, if you're among the increasing number of service providers who choose to work out of their homes, occupancy expenses are relatively low and tax advantages are a potential perk.

✔ **Manufacturing:** Save up your hard-earned cash if you're thinking of becoming a manufacturer; this category is a veritable cash-guzzling machine. Inventory, accounts receivable, equipment, physical plant, employees — you name the cash-draining asset, and most manufacturers have gotta have it.

Although manufacturing is typically the most expensive of the four categories in terms of capital requirements, it offers great potential for rewards. Look at the high-tech industry for examples of wealth being created (not just for the founders but for key employees as well) in short periods of time; companies such as Microsoft, Intel, and Compaq were start-up manufacturers not that long ago.

✔ **Wholesaling:** The middleman in capitalism's distribution channel, *wholesalers* act as intermediaries between manufacturers and the retailers or the consumers. The wholesaler's role is to buy large quantities of products at discounted prices from manufacturers, break them down into smaller quantities, and sell them at a markup over the wholesale price to retailers or consumers. Like manufacturers, wholesalers require significant cash outlays for inventory, receivables, the physical plant, and employees; thus, the start-up capital requirements for wholesalers are correspondingly high.

> ## "How hard can it be to run a card shop?"
>
> Our hero (we'll call him Aaron) decides that it's time to make a lifestyle change. He and his family relocate to Bend, Oregon, where, he figures, the world rotates at half the speed it does in the San Francisco Bay Area.
>
> Aaron, a marketing consultant for a high-powered firm, decides to become a Hallmark franchisee, so he and his wife purchase an existing store in a Bend mall. Because Aaron had been consulting with Hallmark for several years on how to resolve its marketing issues, he figures he knows the industry inside and out.
>
> "Hey," he tells his friends in a statement he will regret for years, "how hard can it be to run a card shop?"
>
> Aaron will find out *exactly* how hard it can be to run a card shop. Suddenly, instead of having to know everything there is to know about *Fortune* 500–style marketing, he has to know a smattering of everything there is to know about accounting and bookkeeping procedures; hiring, training, motivating, and firing employees; payroll; government regulations; cash flow; budgeting; inventory; dealing with bankers, lawyers, and accountants; and. . . . Well, you get the point.
>
> "When I was consulting and would work with Hallmark management in problems relating to its franchisees," he says today, "my marketing firm's management and I would go nuts. We'd say things like 'Those little guys just don't get it,' and we'd want to tear out our hair in frustration."
>
> "Well, I'm one of those 'little guys' today, and it's me who's tearing out what's left of my hair in frustration. We small-business owners see the world through a different set of sunglasses than the corporate consultants."
>
> Would Aaron do it all over again?
>
> "Well, yes. The change in scenery has been worth it. But I can tell you this much," he says, returning an out-of-place Charlie Brown birthday card to its rightful slot. "There are two kinds of businesses in this world. The first is where you have to be a jack of only one trade. The second is where you have to be a jack of all trades, and you are the person who is responsible for ensuring that everything else is taken care of. I went from the first to the second, and now I know that the two aren't even in the same universe."

Take advantage of "accidental opportunities"

Many small-business owners are "accidental" entrepreneurs — that is, they simply stumble on a business to start or to buy. Maybe a favorite retail store suddenly comes up for sale, or a friend informs them of a can't-miss opportunity, or a customer of the business that person is working for now invites him or her to do some freelance consulting — an invitation that turns into a business opportunity. In these cases, the lucky entrepreneur doesn't set out to own a business. Instead, he or she stumbles on the right opportunity. As with so many other directions people take in life, the time and the place just happen to be right.

When considering your "accidental opportunity," if you don't enjoy what you do, your chances for success will decrease. Make sure that your accidental opportunity is in a niche that you like.

Inventory your skills, interests, and job history

Most people aren't lucky or fortunate enough to stumble upon the right business. And the kinds of people who discover the right business are often those who are willing to go to a lot of trouble to find the right opportunities.

In this section, we help you actively seek the right business to buy or start. We assist you in matching your skills, interests, and job history with the right situation. We help you select the niche that works best for you, given who you are, what you like to do, and what you're capable of doing.

To properly make this selection, you need to do some introspection. The following questions are designed to help you take a look at your business acumen. (You can get a piece of paper and treat these questions like a quiz if you want to.) The answers to these questions give you the inventory you need to help select possible businesses for you.

When in doubt as to an answer, ask a good friend or your spouse for advice. Oftentimes, they know you best.

1. **What top three business skills have you displayed over your business career?**

   Examples include such categories as sales, accounting, marketing, administration, writing, communications, quantitative analysis, hiring, training, employee motivation, product development, customer service, focus, delegation, accountability, attention to detail, and so on.

2. **In which of the business skills are you the weakest?**

3. **Over your working history (include part-time and full-time jobs), what three jobs have you enjoyed the most and why?**

   After listing the three, consider (and list) the reasons why you liked those particular jobs.

4. **During your working history, what three jobs have you enjoyed the least and why?**

   Similar to Question #3, consider and then list the reasons why you disliked those particular jobs.

5. **What are your top-three overall personal skills?**

   Examples include leadership, communication, intelligence, creativity, vision, cheerleading, invention and/or innovation, listening, problem solving, counseling, and so on.

6. **If this were a perfect world and you could select the industry in which you'd like to spend the rest of your life, what would be your top-three choices?**

   Examples include sports, music, movies, art, finance, education, telecommunications, electronics, computers, medicine, architecture, agriculture, transportation, insurance, real estate, financial services, food and beverage services, apparel design and manufacture, furniture and home products, outdoor products, printing, photography, chemistry, plastics, and so on.

7. **Many people turn a hobby or special interest (such as photography, golf, coin collecting) into a business. What three favorite hobbies or special interests of yours might be conducive to creating a business?**

8. **Given what you know about the retailing, service, manufacturing, and wholesale career choices, rank these four in order of desirability.**

Don't expect to answer these questions and determine that — eureka! — you should immediately open a retail clothing store, or start a financial consulting business, or import rare ostrich eggs. Instead, these questions are an attempt to help you inventory your skills, interests, and job history. Then, as a result of that inventory, we hope to stimulate the thought processes that will assist you in developing a list of businesses that may work for you.

If, for example, your strengths (and interests) are in sales, you may want to consider a business where sales is the primary function of the business (manufacturer's representative, for instance). If you indicate that you have weaknesses in such areas as attention to detail, delegation, and administration, you may want to consider operating a business solo as opposed to one requiring employees. If you determine that over your job history, you didn't like those jobs where you dealt directly with customers, the retail business would probably not work for you.

These questions are intended to help you take an introspective look at yourself and lead you to where you would logically fit in the broad spectrum of business opportunities available. That's why we say you'll find no quick answers here, but rather an opportunity to jump-start the narrowing-down process. Come back to these questions several times over a period of weeks — few people arrive at a solution the first time through.

Narrow your choices

Drumroll, please! In this section, we continue the process of assisting you in selecting the right business for you (if, that is, you haven't already selected it).

When considering a business opportunity, you need to answer the following questions in order to assure yourself that the business you're considering is the right one for you:

✔ **Is it a business that suits your personality?**

- Consider a retail business if you like dealing with people, don't mind keeping regular hours, and can handle being tied to one spot for long periods of time. The converse, of course, also applies. If you don't like dealing with people, keeping regular hours, or being tied to one spot for long periods of time, don't consider the retail business.

- Consider the service business if you like dealing with people, solving problems, and working in spurts and flurries.

- Consider a wholesaling business if you're a detail-oriented person, if you enjoy supervising employees, and if you don't mind risking the significant amount of capital that carrying and distributing inventory requires.

- Consider the manufacturing business if you're a quality-conscious and detail-oriented person who enjoys searching for solutions to such engineering-oriented issues as process and flow and quality control. You should also enjoy supervising employees.

Within each of the four major categories, you can get more specific and narrow your choices down to specific industries. For example:

- If you like working with numbers, consider the financial services or accounting/tax-preparation business.

- If you don't mind working unusual hours, consider the restaurant or entertainment business.

- If you don't mind spending long periods of time sitting at a desk, consider a banking, telephone sales, or consulting business.

✔ **Is it a business or product in which you have experience?** Experience is the world's best teacher. If you don't have it, your competitors who do have it are bound to have a sizable competitive edge over you. Sixty percent of successful business owners have gravitated to products or services in industries with which they were previously familiar.

✔ **Is it a business you can afford?** A service business is usually the least expensive of the four business categories, followed by retailing, wholesaling, and, finally, manufacturing. For more information on how to compute the cash requirements of your business, see Chapter 5. (Yes, you should take into consideration the amount of money you can borrow, or find investors for, when considering this question.)

✔ **Is it a business with too much risk?** Can you live with the risk inherent in this business? Generally, the bigger the capital requirement, the larger the risk. Are you sure you're prepared to live with the risk of starting a manufacturing company? If not, consider becoming a service provider instead — it's more suited to the average pocketbook. (If you have an idea for a new widget but don't have the resources to manufacture it, you can always outsource the manufacturing of it, and then you can sell, service, and maintain it yourself.)

✔ **Is it a business in which you have a competitive advantage?** Can you make, service, or sell your product better? If not, you need to ask yourself what will motivate your customers to work with you. (If your answer is price, you're in trouble already, unless you've figured out a clear and high-quality way to create and deliver a product or service cheaper and better than the industry leaders.)

✔ **Is it a business in which you can become a specialist?** There's power in being a specialist; there's danger in being a generalist. Today's movers and shakers have learned from past experience; focus on doing those things you can do better than anyone else. (Consider all those takeovers of a few years ago, with steel companies buying insurance companies and filmmakers buying bookstores. Many of those odd companions are companions no more. Many were spun off to other businesses more knowledgeable about that industry and better able to provide a quality product at a competitive price.)

Go in search of fast growth

Every year *Inc.* magazine publishes its list of "The 500 Fastest Growing Companies in America." This list includes tomorrow's potential goliaths of the business world. Such companies as Microsoft, Timberland, Oracle, and Cablevision have graced and then graduated from the list since its inception.

We've gone through the most recent list and categorized these fast-growing companies by industry. So, if you're looking for the fast track, this list of fastest-growing small-business niches in the United States may prove helpful to you:

Industry	*Number of Inc. 500 Companies*
IT Services	56
Human Resources	50
Advertising & Marketing	48
Software	39
Government Services	38
Health	35
Financial Services	35
Retail	27
Telecommunications	26
Construction	21
Business Services	20
Real Estate	14
Energy	14

Timing your start-up

When is the best time to start your new business? Should you begin your new enterprise when the economy is strong or when the economy is in a recession? Does the economy even matter? What economic forces should drive your decision?

Forget the economy, folks. We won't come right out and say that the economy doesn't matter, because depending upon your niche, it can. But by and large, the economy doesn't matter. When the economy is booming, it could be the best time to start a business, because people are in a strong buying mode. But there are downsides to starting a business in booming economies. For example, unemployment is usually low (which means good employees are hard to find).

Economic recessions can also cut both ways. The bad news about recessions is that consumers are wary buyers in recessions, and wary buyers mean low margins, and low margins usually mean low profits. But the good news is that they serve as sort-out time (that is, they sort out the weak businesses from the strong ones and allow the strong ones to survive and grow). As the weak businesses disappear, they leave in their place an opportunity for newer, stronger competitors to surface.

The bottom line: The best time to start a business is when the timing is right for you and for your niche. If you're prepared in terms of finances and experience (see Chapters 1 and 2), if the niche is right and available (as discussed throughout this chapter), and if you're passionate about what you do, the time is right. If you and the niche aren't prepared, the time is wrong. No economic indicators can tell you this. Your gut is the best economic indicator we know.

From the *Inc.* 500 fast-growth companies list, it's also worth noting the niches enjoying the fastest growth. They include Environmental Services, Food & Beverage, Media, Health, and Telecommunications.

A number of past *Inc.* 500 fastest-growing companies are no longer in business. Risk and growth are common bedfellows, and one entrepreneur's riches may lead to another entrepreneur's rags. Thankfully for most of us, other, less glamorous industries offer plenty of room for success. Because the industry you choose can greatly affect your success, consider the following industry-specific questions:

- ✔ **Do you believe in the industry you plan to do business in?** Industries such as the tobacco industry or the firearms industry or the debt-collection industry are not for everyone. Be sure to select an industry that will allow you to sleep at night and feel good about what you're doing.

- ✔ **Is it an industry that isn't overcrowded or dominated by a few well-marketed companies?** You say you're thinking about a coffee house or a bagel shop? Good luck. You'd better know something or be prepared to offer a different product or service than Starbucks, Bruegger's, or Noah's Bagels. Every industry has a saturation point; you want to make sure that your chosen industry isn't one of them. (You can usually determine the saturation point by observing how successful the existing businesses are. Such success can usually be measured by observation — the condition of the business's premises, the quality and professionalism of the employees, and the prices charged; for example, is there room in the prices to make a profit?)

✔ **Is this business in an industry that is moving at a pace that you could be comfortable with?** Some industries move faster than others — the biotech industry moves faster than the gift-shop industry. Make sure that you have a comfort level with the pace of your chosen industry. Some industries will leave you breathless (and money-less) if you can't keep up with the pace. The gift-shop industry will leave you bleary eyed and passionless if you thrive on the rush you get from constant activity and change.

✔ **Is it a business, and an industry, that you can get passionate about?** Can you love the product and the customers? Passion helps sell — it sells products to customers and it sells vision to employees.

Take advantage of government resources

Everyone likes to poke fun at our government (hey, what are governments for anyway?). But now and then, when we least expect it, our government surprises us and does something right. The small-business arena is one of those areas where the government has made giant strides when it comes to doing something right. We cite the following examples:

✔ **The Small Business Administration (SBA):** The SBA offers a wide variety of educational materials and seminars for both current and aspiring small-business owners. They also provide financial assistance through loans and loan-guarantee programs. In recent years, these programs have become significantly more user-friendly, and today the SBA is an excellent resource for the capital-seeking small-business owner who has trouble finding funding through the conventional private-sector sources. For more information on SBA loans, see Chapter 5; for more information on how the SBA can be of assistance locally, call your nearest field office.

✔ **Service Corps of Retired Executives (SCORE):** Federally funded, SCORE consists of more than 10,000 volunteers in hundreds of cities across the United States who provide free counseling and advice to prospective or existing small businesses.

SCORE, an excellent concept to be sure, can be a tad on the hit-or-miss side, however, due to the fact that the majority of SCORE's volunteers are ex-large-company employees. Thus, not all of them have known what it's like to have been there as their own small business takes off. If you happen to be assigned to the right volunteer, however, SCORE can be the best deal in town — occasionally even providing you with a much-needed mentor. SCORE is definitely a service worth trying, especially given its cost to you, which is absolutely nothing — it's free! Visit its Web site at www.score.org (or call 800-634-0245 for the SCORE office nearest you) to pose online questions to counselors or to contact the office nearest you.

✔ **Small Business Development Centers (SBDCs):** There are 700 SBDCs in the United States, most of which are located on college and university campuses. The SBDC program is sponsored by the SBA in partnership with state and local governments, the educational community, and the private sector. Its mission is to provide business counseling, training, and various other educational resources to help both start-ups and existing small businesses.

Unlike SCORE, SBDC services are provided on a fee basis, and SBDC employees (they are not volunteers) are usually educators. Most have not owned a small business of their own. As a result, similar to SCORE, the services they offer can be hit or miss. Call 703-271-8700 for the SBDC center nearest you or visit its Web site at www.sba.gov/sbdc.

✔ **The SBA Answer Desk:** A free service of the SBA, you can call 800-827-5722 to speak with a living, breathing SBA employee who will provide you with a thorough list of governmental resources and referrals, along with a smattering of advice. Questions can be specific or general; ultimately, you'll be referred to a Web site, a SCORE or SBDC chapter, or an SBA publication.

✔ **State Department of Commerce and/or Economic Development Departments:** Most state Departments of Commerce or Economic Development Departments have small-business assistance centers, most of which are replicated on the Web. These centers contain information on licensing and permit regulations and provide information packets on starting and running a business. Check your state government pages, use an Internet search engine, or call your state's Department of Commerce or Economic Development Department. (Some states include commerce under the office of the secretary of state.)

Recognizing Your Number One Asset — You

Turn back the clock to the middle of the 20th century. Imagine you're a small-town banker somewhere in the state of Arkansas. In the course of a day's business, you look up from your desk to see a man in his 30s stride into your office and plop down a proposal. It seems this fellow intends to buy a soft ice cream machine to put on the sidewalk outside of his Ben Franklin dime store, and he wants you to help him finance it.

"Oh, brother," you think to yourself. "This guy must be one pickle short of a barrel. If he can't scrape up $1,800 from the profits on his little dime store, what makes him think I should finance this new venture? $1,800 is a lot of ice cream cones."

Then you pause in the midst of your thoughts and take a deeper look into the man's eyes as he passionately describes his vision for peddling ice cream cones on the sidewalk. And lo and behold, you see a fire burning inside as he explains his ideas for selling ice cream and attracting customers to shop in his store while they enjoy the ice cream cone. And the more the man talks, the more you come to understand that this fellow is driven by a dream, a dream that goes far beyond peddling ice cream. After listening for longer than you had intended, you make an uncharacteristic decision to cough up the dough — not because of the uniqueness of the entrepreneur's idea but because of the uniqueness of the entrepreneur himself. Despite the humdrum notion of selling ice cream on the sidewalk, you fork over the check. Then you sit back and watch as two years later he pays off the five-year note and goes on to eventually create Wal-Mart, the mightiest retailer in the land.

Yes, you, the banker, made your decision based on the man, Sam Walton, and not his ice cream machine. It was only natural that the success of his business would follow.

Avowedly, most of us are not Sam Walton. We don't have his sense of detail, his drive, his leadership abilities, or his vision for his niche. But the world has plenty of room for folks who don't build Wal-Marts. Visit any community in the United States, and even the smallest will have a number of Sam Waltons, those small-business owners who made their furniture store the best in the three-county area, those small-business owners who build the best fly rods in the great Northwest, and those small-business owners who sell more ice cream cones than anyone north of Boston. You don't have to be the largest retailer in the world to be a smashing success. Plenty of mini Sam Waltons are hanging around.

And so it will be with the rest of us who follow in those footsteps — we alone will either make or break our company. Sure, the niche will be important, but we will select it. And certainly our employees will be important, but we will choose the people we hire (and the people we fire). And, of course, our products (or services) will be important, but we will have the final word in defining them. Everything that happens within our business will have our own personal stamp on it. Nothing will be outside of our grasp.

Today's venture capitalists have for many years understood the same lesson that Sam Walton's banker learned in the course of that long-ago meeting. The small-business owner is the Number One determinant of his or her company's success or failure.

Chapter 4

Crafting Your Plans

. . . .

In This Chapter

▶ Drafting a mission statement

▶ Recognizing the importance of business plans

▶ Creating a business plan

▶ Updating your plan

. . . .

*A*fter you've made the commitment to start your own business, you need to embark on your first meaningful hands-on task: developing and writing your business plan. But before you get started, you need to write a mission statement to set the stage for the plan. Over the life of your business, you'll use that mission statement in many ways, from creating a vision for your business's future (that is, the big-picture overview) to developing a year-to-year strategy to setting annual goals for you and your employees.

Your Mission: Impossible If You Fail to Define It

A good mission statement is a written, easy-to-remember sentence, a short list of bullet points, or a paragraph illustrating your business's goals and purpose in life. Or, as Jim believes, it is what makes your company special. Mission statements come in many sizes, shapes, and forms, but they all have one common purpose: to guide you and your employees in making the critical decisions that affect the direction of your company. Additionally, your mission statement should identify your company to outsiders — your customers, your vendors, the media, and others.

To give you an idea of how well-developed mission statements identify the businesses behind them, we invite you to match the following companies with their mission statements (well, if these aren't official mission statements, we think they ought to be):

Company	Mission Statement
1. Disney	A. "To give unlimited opportunity to women."
2. Boeing	B. "To solve unsolved problems innovatively."
3. 3M	C. "To make people away from home feel that they're among friends and really wanted."
4. Mary Kay	D. "To make people happy."
5. Marriott	E. "To push the leading edge of aviation, taking on huge challenges and doing what others cannot do."

Our guess? You didn't have much trouble coming up with the following matches:

- ✔ **Disney:** "To make people happy." (This one clearly meets the requirement of easy to remember.)

- ✔ **Boeing:** "To push the leading edge of aviation, taking on huge challenges and doing what others cannot do." (A tad fluffy perhaps, but certainly challenging.)

- ✔ **3M:** "To solve unsolved problems innovatively." (No restrictions to the range of niches here. No wonder its products range from fishing line to sealing tape to Post-it Notes to Thinsulate Insulation.)

- ✔ **Mary Kay:** "To give unlimited opportunity to women." (And Mary Kay has done exactly that — for women and for men. Countless new businesses over the years have emulated their networking approach to sales.)

- ✔ **Marriott:** "To make people away from home feel that they're among friends and really wanted." (This mission statement says what the company is trying to do; at the same time, it provides guidelines to its employees on how to deal with customers.)

In the following pages, we help you write your mission statement.

Writing your mission statement

What about your business? How should your mission statement read?

- ✔ If you were to own a bookstore, would your mission statement state "to sell books" or "to increase the educational and enjoyment levels of customers"?

- ✔ If you were to own a contracting business, would your mission statement read "to build houses" or "to provide affordable building solutions for customers"?

✔ If you were writing a how-to book for small-business owners, would your mission statement read "to write a 400-page business book" or "to provide readers with solutions to their business problems and suggestions for taking advantage of their business opportunities"?

Notice the common inference in all these mission statements to the key word *solutions.*

Every successful company these days is in the business of providing solutions to customers' needs, desires, or problems. Thus, the question you should answer when creating your mission statement is, "What solution do I provide, and what must I do to make sure that the solution I provide is consistently delivered?"

Also, be sure to give yourself plenty of room to grow (within your niche) when developing your business's mission statement. When a bookstore owner defines the business as "education and enjoyment," the owner leaves open the option to sell DVDs, rather than just books. The contractor has the option to build garages, barns, and outbuildings, in addition to homes. The writer retains the option to develop DVDs, not to mention to serve as a consultant or hold seminars.

One more point: Mission statements aren't forever. Mission statements, like people and environments, can change. Your business may morph into something entirely different as time passes. That's certainly acceptable, as long as you recognize the change and make sure that your mission statement keeps pace with the direction of your business.

Keeping your mission in people's minds

After your company is up and running, be sure to display your mission statement in the following places:

✔ On the walls and bulletin boards in the most visible places in your business, as a constant reminder to you, your employees, and your customers.

✔ In the executive summary section of your business plan (see the next section). Investors and other important outsiders are often busy and appreciate reading the highlights of your plan first and then selectively delving into the details as they feel necessary.

✔ On the first page of your employee manual, if your business is large enough to warrant one. (We discuss such manuals in Chapter 15.) This prominent placement demonstrates to employees what should be their Number One concern when they come to work each day.

✔ On every document your company generates, including but not limited to stationery, faxes, newsletters, and e-mails. Okay, this may seem to be overkill, but it helps everyone to internalize the company's purpose.

The power of a mission statement

Co-author Jim facilitated a "Strategic Meeting" for the Central Oregon Regional Housing Authority (CORHA), a Redmond, Oregon–based organization that offers affordable housing to the citizens within its designated geographical boundaries. The agenda of the Strategic Meeting included a review of CORHA's existing mission statement, which, at the time, read "to provide affordable housing opportunities to Central Oregon residents."

Following an hour of discussion with the key staff and board members who were in attendance, the group ultimately crafted and agreed upon a new mission statement. That new, shorter mission statement read "to foster dignity through affordable housing."

Suddenly, instead of CORHA being an organization that was in the business of "providing affordable housing," the organization was now in the business of "fostering dignity." Affordable housing was simply the tool by which that dignity would be fostered. You can imagine the impact such a change in mission had on CORHA's employees — and the manner in which they treated customers.

Such is the power of a well-worded, well-thought-out mission statement. This mission statement made this organization "special," and at the same time it defined the manner in which it treats its customers — a huge dividend for such a small investment.

Your Business Plan: Don't Start Up without It

You say you don't need a plan?

Sure, and neither did Wrong Way Corrigan, Alice in Wonderland, or Dr. Livingstone (who presumed to know where he was going as he disappeared into the African bush), as well as tens of thousands of other folks who got lost along their way. If you prepare a well-defined plan, and if you update your plan as you proceed, point A will lead to point B, rather than to point Q or to no point at all. And so it is with your business.

If ensuring that you're traveling in the right direction isn't enough reason to prepare a plan, talk to some of the people in the business of loaning or investing money (see Chapter 5). These folks won't even think about doling out their cash unless you present a quality business plan. And it had better be a humdinger of a plan, at that.

A business plan serves two distinct purposes: to serve as your business's road map and to attract loans or investments. The first reason points out why you should have a plan even if you don't intend to solicit outside funding.

Using your business plan as a road map

Bankers, venture capitalists, and other folks who see a lot of business proposals have discovered that viable ideas are a dime a dozen — the idea itself won't make or break a business; the person behind the idea and the idea's execution holds the key to business success. (Or, as someone once said, "Anyone who can take a shower can have a good idea. What matters is what happens *after* you towel off.") So how do you show the business plan reader what kind of person is behind the idea? And where does the execution of that idea begin?

Execution begins in the business plan. Sure, the content of the business plan begins its steady march to obsolescence the same day the ink is dry — things happen fast in small business. However, although the business plan itself is of obvious importance, of even more importance is the process you go through when you're writing your plan and the knowledge you gain from that process. A well-thought-out business-plan-writing process asks the right questions, forcing you to research and think through the solutions at the outset, anticipating and minimizing the chance of major problems, instead of having to crisis-manage them all later.

An example of this foresight is the "Risk" section of the business plan. Most entrepreneurs do not envision the risks inherent in starting a business, as optimism and a half-full glass rule the day. Having to write the Risk section, however, forces you to not only itemize the risks but, where possible, explain how you intend to manage them.

If you value time, money, and pleasantness of experience, you wouldn't take a trip to a new destination without first consulting a map, would you? Why should running your business be any different?

Finding financing with business plans

Lenders and professional investors read a business plan as much to find out about the preparer as to understand the business. They look for thoroughness, professionalism, and attention to detail in the plan, in addition to the presentation of a credible scenario for running a successful business. After all, thoroughness, professionalism, and attention to detail are the same traits they want to see in the person responsible for managing the money they invest in or lend to the business. What better early indication of these characteristics than the business plan?

The sophisticated investor has learned from experience — horses don't win races; jockeys do. The jockey is you, the business owner, and the business plan is the first official indication of the kind of race your horse is going to run.

Business plans take a lot of time and focus to prepare well and are not to be confused with an afternoon jaunt at the beach. Similar to successfully locating the right financing and finding the right mentor, developing a successful business plan separates the potential doers from the dreamers.

By and large, only the truly committed take the trouble to prepare a business plan. You find some exceptions, of course; some potential small-business owners have enough of their act together to carry a good business plan in their head. And, yes, some of those business owners have gone on to achieve great success. But you'd have a hard time convincing us that these same business owners couldn't have accomplished even greater success and avoided some early mistakes if they had taken the time to record and refine their ideas in a tangible business plan. The depth of this early commitment to writing a business plan directly correlates to your chance for success. And a well-thought-out business plan demonstrates the depth of commitment necessary to end up at the helm of a successful small business.

Writing Your Business Plan

How detailed should you make your plan? A simple, more short-term-focused plan (ten pages or so) is adequate if, say, you're a home-office business and the plan is for your benefit alone. However, if you intend to expand your business, hire employees, and even open multiple locations, then your plan should cover the long-term issues more extensively and, thus, be lengthier (say, 20 to 50 pages). Finally, no matter what size or direction you contemplate for your business, if you intend to use the plan as a tool to look for outside investors, an even more complete business plan is necessary.

All business plans don't need to contain all the parts described in the following sections. For business plans going to outsiders such as bankers from whom you are seeking money or some other commitment, you should cover all the following bases. If your business plan is solely for your own use, at a minimum you should cover the marketing and financial management sections.

Whichever length you decide upon, your plan can always be added to and/or upgraded. Later on, after you've completed the plan and your business takes off, you will have plenty of opportunities to rewrite and update your plan.

Here are several additional pointers on the actual writing of the plan:

- ✔ **Always double-space.** Double-spacing allows for easier reading and provides room for making hand-written notes or comments.
- ✔ **Begin each part (Description of the Business, Management Summary, Marketing Plan, and so on) on a new page.** Within each section, the text can be continuous, but be sure to make significant space breaks between each section.

✔ **Feel free to change the wording or add titles to our recommended sections.** No two businesses are exactly the same.

Note: Although you should maintain the order of the parts, you can always vary the order of the sections within those parts.

✔ **Prepare and present the business plan so that it's tailored to the end user.** If you're giving it to a professional, such as a banker, because you're seeking funding, make the plan look professional. It should be professionally bound.

In the following sections, we give you a suggested format for your business plan. Whether you use this particular format or adapt one of your own, your business plan should address the issues listed.

Part 1: Business description

This part is intended to provide the reader with an overview of the business. After reviewing this part, the reader should understand exactly what business you're in, its legal entity, and how your business intends to differentiate itself from its competitors. Don't take this challenge lightly; the reader's decision to peruse the plan in more depth will be guided by his initial reaction to this description.

A. Mission statement

Write as described earlier in this chapter (see "Your Mission: Impossible If You Fail to Define It").

B. Summary of the business

This category answers the basic question, "What business am I in?" You should precede this summary with a one-sentence definition of exactly what the business will do or does, the same to-the-point definition you'll ultimately use to explain your business to everyone from bankers to customers to cocktail party acquaintances.

If you can't define the business in one sentence, something is probably wrong with your vision and focus of what your business should be.

The concept of your business doesn't have to be unique or extraordinary. Electricians, tax preparers, and computer consultants will always be in demand. More businesses succeed through being managed efficiently and wisely than by providing a new and unique product or service.

If you want your business to really be different, you can put a new twist on a concept that has been around for a while. Suppose that you're a veterinarian, but you recognize that more than a few people in your area are too busy to bring their pets to your office for treatment. Thus, you may create a new business — say, Vet on Wheels. (After all, Domino's decided it could vastly expand its customer base by delivering pizzas instead of waiting for customers to walk in the door.) You also have the option to run your veterinarian business the traditional way (that is, by offering quality services at a competitive price to walk-in customers). Plenty of room in the pet-care industry exists for both.

C. Legal description

Is your business a sole proprietorship, partnership, C Corporation, S Corporation, or limited liability corporation? (See complete details on these options in Chapter 5.)

D. Competitive edge

Answer the following questions to clearly communicate how you intend to differentiate your company from your competitors:

- ✓ **Who are your competitors, and what (in your opinion) is currently their competitive edge?** Here you want to identify your competitors' strengths so that you can, in the early stages of your business anyway, avoid directly competing against them.

- ✓ **What are your competitors' weaknesses?** By identifying their weaknesses, you open the opportunity to hit 'em where they're the most vulnerable.

- ✓ **What will distinguish your products or services from those of your competitors?** This distinction doesn't have to be something new and unique. Simply doing something better usually suffices. If you're operating a lawn-care business, for customers who use your services throughout the grass-cutting season, you could trim their bushes at no charge as a customer loyalty bonus.

- ✓ **Service, quality, or price — which of the three do you intend to emphasize?** Remember, you can't be all things to all people. Where do you intend to position your product in the marketplace? Do you intend to be the top service and quality provider within your niche, or do you plan to concentrate on the low end of the niche by focusing mainly on price? (You can find a number of positions in every marketplace, so there should be plenty of room for you if you do what you do better than those you compete against.)

It is extremely difficult, if not impossible, for most small businesses to be the "low-cost" player in a niche. In most cases, the small business should focus on service and quality and leave the low pricing to someone else.

TRUE STORY

What business do you really want to be in?

The fifth small business that co-author Jim started, called Opportunity Knocks (OK), organizes small-business owners into teams and facilitates monthly board-of-advisor meetings for its members. OK members (12 to a team) use those monthly meetings to solve their problems, get feedback on their ideas, and receive support from their peers.

At the first meeting of one of Jim's OK home-office teams, a woman (we'll call her Kate) presented her critical issue. She designed, manufactured, and sold custom, hand-painted kitchen and bathroom tile, but she was spending most of her time performing the manufacturing functions (hand-painting the tiles) with little time left over to design new products and gain new customers.

"Kate," one member of her team inquired, "did you go into business to become a tile painter?"

"No," Kate replied. "I started the business because I wanted to be a tile designer and sell my designs across the country."

"Then you should be designing, selling, and marketing your tile, not painting them," another team member suggested. "Outsource the manufacturing and do the design, sales, and marketing yourself."

You could see a light go on inside Kate's head. Right there in front of her newly formed "board of advisors," she made the decision to make a major change in the focus of her business. Now, she spends her days designing, marketing, and selling her products, while an outside vendor handles the production.

Don't wait for someone else to ask, "What business do you really want to be in?" Ask yourself the question and then answer it in your business plan.

Part 2: Management

The management section is the most important of all business plan categories in those cases where you intend to use the business plan as a vehicle to raise money. Intelligent investors recognize that the success or failure of a business hinges on the quality of the management team. Hence, this management section is one of the first places investors look when they pick up your plan. If they aren't impressed with the management team, potential investors won't go any further.

Begin your management section with biographies of the principal members of your business: the president, vice president, sales and marketing managers, board members, and so on. Be accurate in outlining their backgrounds and remember that the prudent investor checks references. You should, incidentally, pay the most attention to the section pertaining to the person making the most difference to the business — you!

Be sure to include in the descriptive biographical paragraphs such information as

- ✔ Education
- ✔ Prior positions
- ✔ Noteworthy achievements

You're selling your management team to the reader; don't leave out the important elements.

If you use the business plan only as a road map and not as an inducement for investment, the management summary is less important. Putting the qualifications and employment histories of the major players on paper, however, may help you better think through whether the players fit well together and make a synergetic and complementary team.

Part 3: Marketing plan

The marketing plan portion of your business plan provides the reader with an overview of the industry in which your business competes, a description of your business's potential customers, and how you intend to sell, distribute, and promote your product or service.

This part of the plan is often the most difficult — and the most important — for companies to complete. Many competing products and services will fall within your niche. The difficulty, of course, will be in differentiating and highlighting yours to prospective customers and then convincing them to make the purchase. The marketing portion of the plan will make or break your success in this aspect of the business.

A. The industry at large

In this section of the plan, provide an overview of the industry (within the geographical area you expect your business to cover) by answering the following questions:

- ✔ How competitive is the industry?
- ✔ What are the growth opportunities?
- ✔ Who are the industry leaders?
- ✔ Where are the niches in addition to yours?

You can usually obtain the answers to these questions by reviewing Web sites, talking to customers, and speaking with people at your industry's trade associations. Another reliable source would be those who are already in specified niches within the industry, such as wholesalers or manufacturers' reps.

INVESTIGATE

Research model companies

If your business provides products or services similar to those offered by others, identify one, two, or three of your successful competitors that seem most similar to what you'd like your company to be like. Which of these companies do you want to emulate? In what areas can you improve or differentiate your offerings to create a unique niche and to attract customers to your business over competing alternatives?

Even if you have an innovative and unique concept, identify those companies in related, and even dissimilar, fields to find those you want to mimic. Never underestimate the value of mimicry; many successful entrepreneurs are inveterate copycats.

For the model companies you examine, answer the following questions:

✔ Why did they choose their location?

✔ How do they promote their services and products?

✔ What types of customers do they attract?

✔ What are their revenues, expenses, and profitability?

✔ How have they grown and expanded over time?

✔ What are their plans for the future?

How can you determine all this? Ask the model company's customers or become a customer yourself (before you open your own doors, of course). Or, if the model company is a publicly held company, buy a few shares of their stock or obtain their filed financial statements and documents. Or better yet, talk to the vendors that are common to your two businesses. Most vendors, in an attempt to be a "friend" to their customers, will spill more beans than they should about their customers.

B. Potential customers

If your business sells to consumers rather than to other businesses, consider gender, age, income, geographic location, marital status, number of children, education, housing situation (rent or own), and the reasons they may want your product or service. Which of these demographics represent your desired customers?

Create a profile of how your target market behaves as customers. Consider what motivates them to buy and how they buy, including

✔ Whether they rely on recommendations from others

✔ Their product usage-rate tendencies

✔ Their purchase occasions

✔ Whether they buy online, on credit, or on impulse

You'll need this target customer profile information later on, when it comes time to select the right media advertising vehicle to use.

On the other hand, if you sell to businesses, you must understand similar demographic issues that relate to them. What types of businesses will buy your product and services? Who within those businesses will be the ultimate decision-makers, and how can you reach them? What problems of the ultimate decision-makers will you solve with your products or services?

C. The benefits of your product or service

Too many businesses know exactly how to describe the "features" of their products or services, but don't know how to point out the "benefits." Today's consumers, particularly the more sophisticated ones, are more interested in hearing about the benefits of your gizmo than they are about its features.

You're manufacturing a new computer? Don't tell me about its dimensions and its horsepower; tell me about what it will do for me that the others won't. You're selling a promotional product? Don't tell me about where it's manufactured or how much it weighs; tell me about how it can benefit the growth of my business.

D. Geography

Identify your primary geographic focus — that is, where do you expect your customers to come from? Will your customer focus be within local markets? Statewide? National? International? Clearly, your advertising and other promotions will be quite different if you're marketing overseas as opposed to simply your hometown.

E. Distribution

How do you plan to get your products or services to the marketplace? Describe your role in the industry and your distribution plan. Are you a manufacturer? Service provider? Wholesaler? Retailer? Will you utilize a direct sales force? Manufacturers' reps? Catalogs? Telemarketing? Direct mail? An e-commerce Web site? Explain how you intend to create and organize your distribution system. (See Chapter 11 for the information you'll need in order to answer these questions.)

F. Advertising

You need to identify how you can best reach your potential customers. Will it be via newspaper, radio, television, magazines, direct mail, Internet, or telemarketing? Which are most economically feasible within your budget? Which mediums do your desired customers most heavily utilize? What internal programs or external agencies can you use? (See Chapter 11 for more about advertising.)

G. Public relations

Public relations is the art of keeping your name before the public in a positive way other than through paid advertising. Public relations involves such activities as employee, community, industry, and government relations; customer and prospective customer relations; and — the best-known aspect of public relations — publicity.

Publicity resources are usually free; the trick is to get the attention of the writer or reporter who can do you the most good when your competitors and, indeed, just about everyone else in the business world, are trying to do the same thing. A good public relations plan can help you build a positive image in the minds of those in your target audience and guide your efforts as you seek to generate publicity that can expand awareness of your product or service.

This section of your business plan should answer the following questions:

- ✔ What public relations techniques will you use?
- ✔ What is your business's publicity hook, and why will it interest editors, reporters, and those in the audience?
- ✔ How will you build relationships with those in your target market, as well as with select editorial contacts?
- ✔ How can you tap into your network of friends and business associates in order to build a positive image of your business and to gain editorial introductions?

For example, in the restaurant business, one of the best public relations hits is a favorable review in the local newspaper. You can find, within your community and in other media outlets, many similar and effective public relations resources. Consider participating in career day at a local school, sponsoring a runner in a charity marathon, or designating a portion of a road or highway to be maintained by your business. And don't forget the simple press release, alerting the media and community to worthwhile achievements of your company and its people. (See Chapter 11 for more about public relations.)

H. Pricing

In this section, explain your short-term and long-term pricing. Include information on costs and profit expectations, along with a thorough review of your competitors' pricing and your perceived position within the industry. Do you intend to be the low-cost provider? The high-end producer? How do you intend to position your product?

When pricing your products, always consider the current competitive climate first. Research the pricing of similar services or products in the marketplace, and then price your product accordingly. Don't make the mistake early on of pricing your products based upon some predetermined profit margin that you or your accountant would like to achieve. Price instead on what your competitive research (primarily talking to customers) determines the market will bear.

And don't be afraid to sell your services or products at healthy margins when the opportunity presents itself. Rest assured, it won't last forever. (For more on pricing, see Chapter 11.)

1. Sales terms and credit policies

A sale is never complete until you deposit the proceeds safely in your business account. With this in mind, you need to spell out the terms of the sale and the conditions governing the granting of credit and the acceptance of payment before you make your first sale. For more on the subject of sales, see Chapter 11.

Part 4: Operations

This part outlines the nuts and bolts of the operational issues of your company. The scope of your operations or management plan covers a wide range of functions, from dealing with employees to purchasing from vendors to maintaining your company's accounting records.

A. Employees

Many small businesses are one-person operations. So much the better if you fall into this category — you'll suffer none of the headaches of hiring, motivating, training, and firing employees. You'll only have to worry about you, which, if you're anything like your humble authors, should be no small project in itself.

However, for those of you who plan to have employees, you'll need to answer the following questions in this section of the business plan:

✔ How will you assemble your team — by leasing your employees or by hiring them outright?

✔ Where will you find the employees you intend to hire yourself?

✔ What benefits will you offer?

✔ What motivational incentives will you use?

✔ Will you assemble an employee manual?

✔ Will you offer a retirement plan?

✔ Will there be down-the-road opportunities for ownership for key employees?

✔ How will you train your employees?

See Chapters 15 and 16 for a discussion of these employee issues.

B. Compensation

Too many small businesses hire their first employees without first devising an overall compensation plan. Such an oversight inevitably leads to a lack of uniformity in compensation. When employees perceive that you're not compensating them fairly relative to other employees and that you haven't communicated an objective reason for this discrepancy, a line may begin to form outside your office.

For purposes of the business plan, you need to objectively define the basics of your compensation plan for hourly, salaried, and commissioned employees. You need to include bonus plans and perks. (For more on compensation plans, see Chapter 16.)

C. Vendors and outside resources

What vendors and outside resources do you intend to use? How do you plan to kick off your relationship with key vendors? Vendor accessibility is an important issue in many industries. Frequently, the best vendors don't make their line of products available to every customer, especially the new kid on the block with no history, no prior connections in the industry, and an anemic balance sheet. You'll need to have the answers to their qualifying questions before you make your first call. Completion of this section will provide you with the material you'll need to respond to their queries.

D. Accounting and/or bookkeeping

Answer the following questions when describing who will take care of your accounting and bookkeeping duties:

- ✔ Will you hire an experienced bookkeeper? CPA? Controller? Chief financial officer (see Chapter 10)?
- ✔ Do you intend to computerize your accounting system?
- ✔ What accounting software package will you use?
- ✔ Do you plan to outsource your bookkeeping or accounting? What outside resource will you use?

For those businesses that intend to use the business plan as a tool to invite a loan or an investment, this section is particularly important. The smart lender or investor wants to be sure that the financial responsibilities of running the business are in good hands. This is especially true when the entrepreneur isn't particularly strong on the financial side of business.

Part 5: Risks

You, as well as potential lenders and investors in your business, will care and should care about the potential risks in your business. The better you understand them, the better able you'll be to anticipate them, minimize them, and keep your business in business.

Risk: You have to see it to beat it

You must first recognize risk before you can face it. Mary, an experienced small-business veteran, was asked to serve on the board of a local nonprofit agency that was having serious financial problems. Its recently fired executive director had, over a period of years, spent hundreds of thousands of the agency's dollars on personal cars, vacations, and even a second home. The agency faced serious financial problems; not only had it lost money to the crooked director, but due to the resulting adverse publicity, many of the nonprofit's sources for donations began drying up.

Before agreeing to accept the position, Mary asked the board chairperson for a current business plan (that is, a plan on how the nonprofit expected to turn around its financial problems). To the nonprofit's credit, it had prepared one.

Following an interview with the executive director and the chairman, she turned down the board position.

"The business plan read like an ad-agency marketing brochure," she later explained. "All it talked about was the wonderful opportunity for the agency to make a difference, the terrific future of the nonprofit's cause, and the need for such a charity in the local community. It was as if their cash-flow problems, their public image, and their publicity problems didn't exist."

"My interview with the executive director and the board chairman was more of the same," Mary continued. "A good break here, a random event there, and everything was bound to come up roses. Try as I did to change the subject and discuss the immediate risks that faced the agency and their need to confront them, neither the director nor the chairperson would face up to the risks that currently faced the agency. Failure was right around the corner, yet they refused to acknowledge it, much less do anything about it."

"You know," Mary laughed, "one of the things I love about small-business owners is their unbridled optimism. Their glasses are always half-full; there is nothing they can't do, given a little time and a lot of hard work. That's the good news! The bad news is that there has to be the voice of the devil's advocate somewhere in the back of a successful business owner's head that recognizes and helps formulate sensible actions to minimize that risk."

"The experiences of this nonprofit are a perfect example," Mary concluded. "If you refuse to recognize the risk in the beginning, you're eventually going to be blindsided by it."

When asked what she looked for in the nonprofit's turnaround plan, she replied, "A good turnaround plan is not that different from a good business plan. I would look first to the people issue — that is, what is the nonprofit going to do to replace the departing executive director, and how do they intend to motivate and upgrade their current staff? After that, I would want to know what they intend to do to solve their image problems."

Risks are inherent in every business, and yours will be no exception. Identify those risks. Be candid and thorough in describing your risks. Investors and lenders know there are risks in every business, and they will be looking for honesty and awareness here, not ambivalence or avoidance. They know how to recognize the difference.

Part 6: Financial management plan

Your good idea is likely to turn into your worst nightmare if you don't examine or fail to be realistic about the financial aspect of your business. If you're one of those creative types or a mover and a shaker who hates to work with numbers, you may decide to blow off the financial part of the business plan. Doing so, we're sorry to tell you, could cost you, at the minimum, the dollars that you need to grow your business; at the maximum, it could cost you the very existence of the business itself. Along with marketing, financial management is the most-often neglected part of every small-business venture. Don't let it be yours!

Before you launch your business, you should first do the research you need to come up with the financial figures we describe here. We not only suggest that you do these projections, but also that you make this process mandatory — especially if you need to seek outside financing.

You should do your projections on a spreadsheet using a program such as Microsoft Excel. If you don't know how to use a spreadsheet, we suggest you either find out how (from computer training companies in your community or good books on the topic) or have someone do it for you. And if you don't understand the difference between a profit and loss statement and a balance sheet, turn to Chapter 13. Spreadsheets and financial statements are tools that every successful small-business owner must eventually understand. You can find out how to use them now or later — but we strongly suggest that sooner is better.

When compiling your business plan, you need to consider the three types of financial statements covered in the following sections.

A. Pro forma profit and loss statement

A *pro forma profit and loss statement* is a projected income and expense plan, and it summarizes your estimated revenue and expenses over a specified period of time. The accuracy of your profit and loss pro forma depends on the quality of the assumptions you make. If you make good assumptions going in, then you can expect meaningful results. An important part of the value of preparing a pro forma profit and loss statement is that it forces you to think through the questions that you need to answer to arrive at the assumptions you make.

Estimating your expenses for your pro forma will be relatively easy. The most difficult assumptions you'll have to make will be your sales and other income (revenues) and your gross margin (gross profit.) Many small-business owners will generate two or even three separate pro formas — for example, a best-case scenario, a middle-case scenario, and a worst-case scenario.

You should prepare your profit-and-loss projections for the first three years of your business (unless you're seeking venture capital funding, in which case five years may be required). Anything longer requires too many far-out, hard-to-make assumptions. Compute the first year's pro forma on a month-to-month basis, and the second and third years' on a quarterly basis.

If you don't know how to read financial documents, much less prepare them, we suggest that you pick up a copy of the latest edition of co-author Eric's best-selling book *Investing For Dummies* (Wiley) and/or take a good class in how to read financial statements at a local college. Also, you can take advantage of computerized business plan software packages, most of which include financial projection templates.

B. Balance sheet

The *balance sheet* measures your business's resources (assets) and obligations (liabilities) at a particular time. This balance sheet concept is important to understand and, incidentally, is just as relevant to your personal financial situation as it is to your business one. As a matter of fact, if you apply for a loan at a financial institution, you'll almost certainly have to submit a personal balance sheet. (If you aren't currently keeping one for your family's assets, you should be.)

Although we recommend balance-sheet projections for every business, they're especially relevant for those businesses that have significant noncash assets tied up in such categories as inventory and accounts receivable.

As with the profit and loss statement, you should prepare a projected balance sheet for the first three years of business; project the first year on a monthly basis, and the second and third years on a quarterly basis.

C. Cash-flow projections

Cash flow is the amount of cash that moves through your business in the form of receipts (representing an increase in cash) and expenses and capital expenditures (representing a decrease in cash). Cash flow is the practical side of the accounting equation, representing the cash required to keep your business operating on a day-to-day basis.

Don't confuse cash flow with profitability, which measures the results of the entire operation of the business (of which cash is only one important part) over a given period of time. Profitability provides the benchmarks for measuring the effectiveness of your operations, but cash flow pays the bills.

As a prospective business owner, you should project your business's cash needs before going into business so that you know how much money you need to raise. As with profit-and-loss and balance-sheet projections, you should project cash flow needs for the first three years of the business. For more information on cash flow, see Chapter 13.

Before doing your financial projections, consider the following:

- ✔ Ask your tax advisor (if you're working with one) to show you examples of similar financial projections from other business plans to use as a guideline.

- ✔ Don't bother projecting more than three years out; the assumptions you must use will be too vague. (Exception: Some outside investors may require five-year projections.)

- ✔ Thoroughly identify the assumptions you make. The garbage-in, garbage-out theory is alive and well when applied to projecting financial results. The conclusions you reach will be no better than the quality of your assumptions. You should prominently itemize these assumptions as well, in order to allow the reader to know exactly what they are and how they were made.

- ✔ In the likely event that you don't know how to produce the pro forma profit and loss statement, balance sheet, and cash-flow projections, you can

  - Hire a tax advisor.

  - Hire a business-plan consultant.

  - Purchase a business-plan-software package.

  - Learn to use spreadsheet software and do the projections yourself.

Keeping Your Plan Current

Guarantees are dangerous in small business, but we can make two without hesitation:

- ✔ The immediate progress of your business will deviate from your original plan.

- ✔ Your business will change dramatically over what you've envisioned. And that's just the first year!

Deviation and change are constants in this sometimes roller-coaster endeavor, but deviation and change are why many small-business owners select this career in the first place.

To make the necessary adjustments in response to this deviation and change, you must keep your business plan current. Take a day away from the office and the phone every 6 to 12 months and dissect the important portions of your business plan — particularly those involving staffing, marketing, distribution, and product development — and answer the following questions:

- ✔ Has the business developed according to plan within each of these areas (staffing, marketing, distribution, and product development)? If not, why?

- ✔ In areas where the business hasn't developed according to plan, do you want to get back on track? What adjustments will you make in each area to get back on track?

- ✔ Given the passage of time, where do you want your business to be a year from now, and how and what changes should you make to support that new direction?

Then work at making your changes to the plan, remembering that, if those changes have a financial impact on your business (and most important changes will), you must also apply the changes to the pro forma profit and loss statement and to your balance sheet and cash-flow projections.

A significant change in bottom-line income will obviously impact key balance sheet numbers, which in turn will affect such key measures as the debt-to-equity ratio and the current ratio. (See Chapter 13 for an explanation of these terms.) Extreme variations in these ratios influence your credit lines, your relationships with lenders and vendors, and your long-range plans for capital expenditures and new hires.

Creating a business plan is a one-time experience, but keeping it up to date is an ongoing task — which is, when you think about it, not unlike the relationship between starting a business and actually running and maintaining one.

Chapter 5

Financing, Ownership, and Organizational Decisions

. . . .

In This Chapter

▶ Figuring the amount of money you'll need to launch your business

▶ Assessing how, and where, to finance your business

▶ Deciding about partners and/or shareholders

▶ Selecting the legal entity that works best for you

. . . .

*W*e hope you're discovering where you want to go with your small business as you read this book. Assuming that you've decided to commit to the journey, it's time to begin making some important decisions about how you're going to reach your goals. In this chapter, we help you estimate how much cash you need to get started, where you can expect to obtain that money, whether you'll be traveling alone or with others, and what kind of vehicle can get you there.

Determining Your Start-Up Cash Needs

You must understand that your business's initial cash requirements will include not only one-time start-up costs, but also working capital and a reserve. Here's a further description of each of these requirements:

✔ **One-time start-up costs:** Start-up costs include such one-time expenses as legal fees, licenses and permits, deposits, furniture and fixtures, inventory, leasehold improvements (remodels or additions to the store or office space you rent or lease), signage, and everything you need to initially open for business. Consult another business's profit and loss statement (P & L), or a pro forma P & L sample on a business plan template, for a listing of the typical day-to-day ongoing expenses you're going to incur (see Chapter 13).

✔ **Working capital:** *Working capital* is the cash you'll need to remain open for business. This includes such ongoing, everyday expenditures as replacement inventory and raw materials, accounts receivable, hiring of employees, and the general day-to-day operation of your business until such time as you become consistently profitable and can fund operations out of internally generated cash flow. Don't forget to include debt payments — both interest and principal — when arriving at this figure. (Although principal payments aren't an expense, they reduce available capital.)

✔ **Reserve:** The *reserve* is an amount consisting of enough capital to overcome forecasting mistakes and/or make up for variances from your budget. If you end up having neither forecasting mistakes nor budget variances, we suggest you give the *Guinness Book of World Records* a call!

So where's all this money going to come from? You have two basic methods with which to finance your start-up:

✔ **Bootstrapping:** The internal generation of initial financing, using primarily your own personal resources, and sometimes complemented by various forms of equity investments or loans from family, friends, and relatives.

✔ **Outsourcing:** The external generation of financing for both start-up expenses and ongoing business needs, using outside resources such as banks, angels, and venture capitalists (which we cover later in this chapter).

Bootstrapping is a much more likely source of funds than outsourcing for most start-ups. Besides, providers of outsourced funds also aren't likely to give you the money you need unless they see that you've done your bootstrapping first. (For more on bootstrapping, see the section "Using Your Own Money: Bootstrapping" later in this chapter.)

Whether you bootstrap the financing of your business or whether you finance it using money from outsiders, you should first estimate your cash needs. If you plan to go the bootstrapping route, estimate your cash needs to minimize the chances of running out of money, a situation which can lead to the failure of your business and the loss of all the invested capital. If you plan to outsource your capital, estimate your cash needs to ensure potential lenders that you have solid projections for your future cash needs.

If you do end up obtaining outside capital, nothing shouts inexperience like having to go back to your source at a later date and asking for more money. Looking for a surefire way to raise a red flag in front of your banker or investor? Tell him or her you made a mistake in forecasting, and you need more capital than you had originally asked for. Whether you'll get your capital the second time around is up for grabs, but one thing is certain: You'll get increased scrutiny. Bankers and investors don't like oversights and mistakes, especially when it comes to issues dealing with their money.

So, what's the obvious solution? Just as remodeling work on a home almost always takes longer and costs more than expected, many entrepreneurs find that their start-up costs more than they originally expected. That's why you should allow yourself sufficient time to investigate, reflect upon, and estimate the costs associated with starting your chosen business.

If you've completed your profit and loss statement, balance sheet, and cash-flow projections, the following exercise should be simple. If you haven't, this exercise will be a headache, so do yourself a favor and go to Chapters 4 and 13 now!

This worksheet is designed to help you estimate your business's capital requirements:

Estimated Capital Requirement Worksheet

1. Add all one-time, pre-opening costs, such as legal fees; licenses and permits; deposits; furniture and fixtures; inventory; leasehold improvements; logo, stationery, and signage; insurance; and so on (your "one-time start-up costs").   ———————

2. Add your projected early-month consecutive losses from your profit and loss statement. Be sure to include debt payments, both interest and principal (the first part of your "working capital").   ———————

3. Add the anticipated purchase of assets from your balance sheet for the first year: equipment, inventory, furniture and fixtures (the second part of your "working capital").   ———————

4. Add lines 1, 2, and 3.   ———————

5. Multiply the number you arrived at in Step 4 by 0.25 to get your reserve. (**_Note:_** The percentage required by this reserve figure will vary depending on the experience of the person or persons starting and running the business. The more experienced you are, the less the reserve will have to be; the less experienced you are, the higher it will have to be. A reserve of 25 percent represents our best guess as an average.)   ———————

6. Add the amount in Step 4 to the amount in Step 5 to get your total capital requirements.   ———————

This total capital requirements figure represents the amount of capital your business will require from all sources before start-up. After you determine how much capital you need, the even harder work begins — finding it.

Using Your Own Money: Bootstrapping

If your small-business start-up is like most others, you probably won't utilize outside capital. Bootstrapping will have to do.

Inc. magazine now annually publishes the *Inc.* 5000, a listing of fast-growing private companies in the United States. A recent survey of the *Inc.* 5000 showed the sources of original financing from those *Inc.* 5000 companies (see Table 5-1).

Table 5-1	Where Financing Money May Come From
Resource Tapped	*Percentage of CEOs Who Tapped Resources*
Self-financed	82%
Loans from friends, family, or business associates	22%
Bank loans	18%
Lines of credit	18%
Venture capital	8%
SBA or other government funds	4%

Note: The total exceeds 100 percent because some CEOs tapped more than one resource.

Bootstrapping sources emerge as the clear-cut winner in the start-up financing competition, even for this exclusive list of fast-track, rapid-growth companies. If you think about it, it makes sense that bootstrapping is so pervasive and works so well. First, what better way to instill discipline and make things work efficiently than to have a limited supply of funds? Second, because you care deeply about risking your own money or that of family or friends, you have a powerful incentive to work hard and smart at making your business succeed.

So take heart if you think that you need vast sums of cash to start a small business or if you have been turned down (perhaps more than once) by outside sources of funding. As you can see in Table 5-1, the entrepreneurial traits of hard work, perseverance, and, yes, good old-fashioned scrounging can help you locate the money that you need to start your business.

Profiling bootstrappers

Bootstrappers come in all sizes, shapes, and forms. Some prefer to conduct their growing businesses alone, some jump from start-up to start-up, and some make the transition from small business to large business.

Here are profiles of several typical bootstrappers:

- ✔ **Eric:** Before co-author Eric set out to start his financial counseling business, he kept his expenses low enough to save about half of his employment earnings each year over several years, which provided a nice nest egg to finance his business start-up. While living in Boston and still single, Eric shared apartments with anywhere from two to four roommates to keep his rental expenses low. As he made the transition into his entrepreneurial endeavor, Eric worked half-time for four months so that his salaried income didn't completely disappear.

- ✔ **Jim:** Co-author Jim's fourth business (all four were bootstrapped) was started to provide a needed service to his sporting goods business. He purchased a screen-printing company from its owner for $10,000, moved the business out of the owner's basement, and funded its growth from the revenues of the sporting goods business until the screen-printing company was profitable and could stand on its own. Eighteen years later, he sold the business when its revenues reached $25 million.

- ✔ **Ted Waitt:** Ted quit college to take a job selling PCs, and then, as so many bootstrappers do, quit that job to start his own company. Using a portion of his grandmother's nest egg as collateral, he borrowed $10,000 to start a business in his father's South Dakota barn. That business would later become Gateway 2000, one of the nation's leading computer manufacturers with billions in revenue.

These examples point out the typical pattern of bootstrapping. The founder and/or family and friends provide the start-up capital. Profits from the business, money from outside resources (banks, shareholders, and so on), or a combination of both funds future growth.

Tapping into bootstrapping sources

Bootstrapping, as the examples in the preceding section point out, begins at home. If you're like us and the majority of entrepreneurs, here's how you can go about locating the funds you need to finance your start-up:

1. **Take stock of your personal assets and liabilities.**

   As we discuss in Chapter 2, you should get your personal finances in order and determine where you stand in terms of common important goals such as retirement planning. Only then can you begin to determine what portion of your assets you'll feel comfortable using in your business.

2. **Assuming that your parents and family are financially able to help, gingerly approach them.**

The family resource is appropriately known as *relationship investing* or *relationship lending*. Although relationship investing is a widely used resource for raising money, it is also the most potentially dangerous. Telling the bank you can't meet repayment obligations is one thing; telling a close relative that you've lost his money is quite another. The good news is that you'll work that much harder to succeed when family or friends are involved; the bad news is that the investment could damage existing relationships. Proceed with great care and be clear with family and friends as to the risks, including the risk that they could lose their entire investment if your business gets into trouble!

3. **Ask friends, especially those friends who can bring expertise to the table along with their money.**

Be aware, however, that the risks involved when borrowing money from friends are similar to the risks when borrowing from family. The downsides can be just as painful.

4. **If Steps 1, 2, and 3 still aren't enough, start looking for a, gulp, partner (or partners).**

We talk more about the role of partners in the section "Exploring Ownership Options" later in this chapter. Suffice it to say that partners are a roll of the dice — make a good roll, and your business will prosper beyond what it could with you alone; make a bad roll, and your problems could be multiplied.

5. **When all else fails, look to the outside resources, even though they're historically unlikely to fund start-ups.**

Look for angels first before heading for the banks, the Small Business Administration, and Small Business Investment Companies (we explain these all later in this chapter). If your idea or concept is compelling enough, and if *you* are compelling enough, you may even consider approaching venture capitalists.

After you've tapped out your own resources, but before you begin probing family and friends, you should remember to tape the Golden Rule of Bootstrapping to the middle of your forehead and then take a long look in the mirror. In the event that you haven't come across it yet, the Golden Rule of Bootstrapping states the following:

Do not do unto others until you've done unto yourself.

Or, stated in words that apply specifically to your search for capital:

If you aren't willing to risk your own money, why should anyone else risk theirs, especially family and friends?

The purpose of the Golden Rule of Bootstrapping is to make sure that you, the bootstrapper, don't even *think* about asking your family, friends, and relatives for money before you've contributed yourself. The first question family and friends inevitably will ask is, "How much of your own money are you investing?"

These are some of the most common places to find bootstrapping capital:

- ✔ **Savings, investments, and salable assets:** This is always the first place to look. Theoretically, all you're doing here is simply transferring your assets from one investment (your savings account) to another (your new business). Okay, so you're increasing your risk by a quantum leap, but you're also increasing your opportunity for reward.

- ✔ **The family and friends network:** Be sure to make your relationship loans as official as possible — always create a promissory note complete with a fixed interest rate (at least 1 percent over prime to avoid IRS scrutiny) and include cast-in-stone payback terms. Consult a lawyer when larger loans (in excess of $10,000) are required.

- ✔ **Life insurance:** If you own life insurance policies with a cash value, you probably shouldn't, because term life insurance is a far better deal (see Chapter 2). Consider cashing in such policies and putting that money to far better use — your business. Remember, however, that you may owe some income tax on accumulated interest (in excess of the premiums you paid) from your life insurance policy.

  Ask yourself whether you really need life insurance at all. If you have no financial dependents, you won't need it to replace your income if you pass away. If you do need life insurance, however, secure good term life coverage before you cancel or cash in your current policy. Otherwise, your dependents will be in trouble if you pass away after you've canceled your current policy but before you've secured new coverage.

- ✔ **Credit cards:** Credit cards provide expensive money, perhaps, but easy money as well. No personal guarantees here, no bankers looking over your shoulder; just sign your name and get on with the business at hand. In the increasingly competitive credit-card market, interest rates on some cards are around 10 percent, so be sure to shop around rather than simply accumulating a balance on whatever platinum-hued card currently happens to be in your wallet or pitched through an ad. And, when you carry a balance from month to month, always make your credit-card payments on time unless you enjoy paying even higher interest rates — in many cases upwards of 20 percent.

✔ **Home equity:** Proceed with extreme care when borrowing against home equity. A misstep could cost you the roof over your family's head. Don't even consider this option until you've thoroughly reviewed your overall personal financial situation (see Chapter 2).

Outsourcing for Your Capital Needs

As you can see by referring to Table 5-1 earlier in the chapter, outsourcing institutions — banks, the Small Business Administration (SBA), Small Business Investment Companies (SBICs), angel investors, and venture capitalists — are *not* primary resources for start-up capital. This is because most of these outsourcers are looking for either significant collateral and operating history (banks and the SBA) or a business in an industry with uncommon opportunities for return on investment (venture capitalists). Meanwhile, angels are the most versatile of the outsourcing resources, but they're also the most difficult to find. We talk about each of these resources in this section.

Outsourcers, with the possible exception of SBICs, have a well-deserved role in the financing world; that role just doesn't happen to be at the start-up stage. After your business has matured and has a track record, the outsourcers may become a part of the financing game for your business.

The first thing to discover when considering which outsourcer to use is whether they're loaning you money (banks, SBA, and others) or investing their money (venture capitalists, some angels, and the like). Or, stated another way, will they be creditors or will they be part owners?

Outsourcing resources fall into two general categories: banks and, er, nonbanks.

Banking on banks

Contrary to the popular opinion that bankers enjoy turning down prospective borrowers, bankers are in business to lend money. Every time bankers sit down in front of a prospective borrower, they hope that what they're about to see is a deal that will work. After all, *no loans* means no investment income for the bank, and no investment income means no marble columns — and without marble columns, what would hold up their gold-inlaid ceilings? Make no mistake about it, banks are in business to lend money and make profits, which banks do by playing the spread — charging you more to use their money than they're paying somebody else (namely, depositors) to get it.

Most banks don't make start-up loans to small-business owners unless an owner's collateral is such that it will cover 100 percent of the loan. Examples of such collateral include real estate (including home equity) and stocks and bonds.

A bank's primary role in the small-business lending arena is funding growth — for example, financing the expansion of a small business that has a track record. Most banks can offer a wide variety of creative loan packages designed to finance the existing small business. These loans include the following financing possibilities:

- ✔ **Asset-based financing** is a general term describing the situation whereby a lender accepts as collateral the assets of a company in exchange for a loan. Most asset-based loans are collateralized against either *accounts receivable* (money owed by customers for products or services sold but not yet paid for), inventory, or equipment. Accounts receivable is the favorite of the three because it can be converted into cash more quickly (theoretically within 30 days, if these are terms you are offering). Banks advance funds only on a percentage of receivables or inventory, the typical percentages being 75 percent of receivables and 50 percent, or less, of inventory.

  For example, using these percentages, if your business has $30,000 in receivables due from customers and $50,000 in inventory, the bank may loan you 75 percent of $30,000 (which equals $22,500) and 50 percent of $50,000 (which equals $25,000). The total of the two ($47,500) would then be available for you to use as working capital. These percentages vary based on the industry and the quality of the receivables and the inventory.

- ✔ A **line of credit** involves the bank's setting aside designated funds for the business to draw against the ebb and flow of cash as needs dictate. As line-of-credit funds are used, the credit line is reduced; conversely, when payments are made, the line is replenished.

  An advantage of line-of-credit financing is that no interest is accrued unless the funds are actually used. Ironically, the best time to arrange for your business's line of credit is when your business is doing well and you need the money the least. Why? Because that's when getting approval from the banker for the line of credit will be easiest, and you'll qualify for the best loan terms.

  Don't make the mistake of overlooking a line of credit just because you don't presently need money. (Remember, a "line" doesn't cost anything if you don't draw against it.) Establish your credit line when things are going well. Sooner or later, if you're like most small businesses, you'll need the cash.

✔ A **letter of credit** is a guarantee from the bank that a specific obligation of the business will be honored. Letters of credit are most often used to buy products sight unseen from overseas vendors. The bank generates its income in these situations by charging fees for making the guarantee.

✔ **Floor planning** is another form of asset-based lending in which the borrower's inventory is used as collateral for the loan. Car dealerships often use floor planning as their primary financing tool.

Getting money from nonbanks

Banks don't have a lock on the small-business lending market. Investment brokerage firms and major business conglomerates are important players in the small-business lending market, too.

Most nonbank lenders find their niche by specializing in a specific category of loan, such as leasing or asset-based financing. Leasing companies (where you can lease your business's equipment or furniture and fixtures), for example, are the most common nonbank financing resource, with 25 percent of small businesses availing themselves of some sort of leasing financing. *Leasing,* in case you've never done it, is basically a rental — you pay a monthly fee for the use of an item, and at the end of the lease term you return the item to the company that leased it to you.

A compilation of nonbank resources follows in this section.

The Small Business Administration (SBA)

An SBA loan is a loan made by a local lender (bank or nonbank) that is, in turn, guaranteed by a federal agency called the Small Business Administration (SBA). The SBA provides its backup guarantee as an inducement for banks to make loans that otherwise may be too risky from a banker's perspective. Only in rare cases does the SBA actually provide the money itself.

SBA loans usually provide longer repayment terms and lower down-payment requirements than conventional bank loans. They're available to most for-profit small businesses that don't exceed the SBA's parameters on size (which can vary depending on the industry). SBA loans can be used for a number of reasons, including (in infrequent cases) start-up monies if you have sufficient collateral in long-term, tangible assets, such as real estate, machinery, and equipment.

Getting an SBA loan isn't a sure thing; to the contrary, the agency is extremely selective about whom it approves. Take a look at the primary criteria the SBA looks for when considering guaranteeing a loan:

✔ The owner must have invested at least 30 percent of the required capital and be willing to guarantee the balance of the loan.

✔ The owner must be active in the management of the business.

✔ All principals must have a clean credit history.

✔ The business must project adequate cash flow to pay off the loan, and the debt/net-worth ratio must fall within the SBA's approved guidelines.

SBA loans have a reputation for being cumbersome and subject to enormous red tape. This reputation had been deserved in years past, but technology has made inroads everywhere, even in the government. The SBA's LowDoc Program (short for "low documentation"), for loans under $100,000, promises to process loan requests in less than 48 hours and requires you to fill out only a one-page application form. Other documentation you can be expected to furnish when applying for an SBA loan in excess of $100,000 includes a personal financial statement, three years of tax returns, and three years of financial projections.

To find a local bank or nonbank institution that works with the SBA, look in the Yellow Pages for SBA Approved Lending Sources (ALS) or call the SBA at 800-827-5722. If you're on the Internet, see www.sba.gov for more information about SBA loans that may work for you.

Small Business Investment Companies

Small Business Investment Companies (SBICs) are privately owned, quasi-venture capital firms organized under the auspices of the SBA. SBICs either lend money to, or invest money in, small businesses primarily within their local area. Categorized as *Federal Licensees* (meaning the federal government has given the SBIC its stamp of approval), SBICs either fund start-ups or provide operating funds with which to expand existing businesses. Through their relationship with the SBA, they're also able to offer particularly favorable terms and conditions to *disadvantaged businesses* (businesses owned by women and minorities).

Hundreds of SBICs operate around the country. To find out more about them, call the SBA at 800-827-5722, check out the SBA's Web site (www.sba.gov), or contact a nearby Small Business Development Center (discussed in Chapter 3).

Certified Development Companies

Another program of the SBA, the Certified Development Company (CDC) program (also known as the 504 Loan Program), provides long-term (10- and 20-year), fixed-rate loans for small businesses. This program focuses on financing fixed assets, such as real estate (land and buildings). CDCs work with a local lender; typical financing may include 50 percent from the local lender, 40 percent from the CDC, and 10 percent down from the small business being helped. The asset being purchased acts as the collateral.

Several hundred CDCs exist nationwide. For the CDC nearest you, call the SBA at 800-827-5722 or visit the SBA's Web site (www.sba.gov) and inquire about the 504 Loan Program.

Your state's Economic Development Department

Many states have an Economic Development Department (sometimes a stand-alone governmental agency, possibly housed within the state's Department of Commerce) that offers a variety of loan programs to statewide businesses. The programs offered are usually modeled after SBA loans but can often offer better terms and conditions than the SBA, especially for those businesses that employ many employees. Such state departments will also generally offer *microloan* programs designed to assist small-business start-ups. Call or visit your state's Web site for further information.

Angels: Investors with heart

Angels are individuals — usually ex-entrepreneurs who are experienced enough to understand and live with the financial risks they take — with money available to lend or invest. The angels' motives may vary: Most seek to increase their net worth, some want to help aspiring entrepreneurs, and some simply crave being a part of the action.

Angels come in many forms: Some fly in flocks (that is, belong to angel organizations or investment groups), some work solo, some look for a piece of the company's ownership (equity), and others prefer lending (debt). Almost all angels demand personal involvement in your business, however, and in many cases, the know-how an angel can bring to the table is worth more than the capital itself.

Angels are like the highway patrol — the time that you need them the most is the time they're the most difficult to find. Movements are afoot, however, to make the identity of angels more accessible. According to the Yellow Pages Publishers Association, "angels" will soon be a Yellow Pages heading in most telephone books (along with "psychic life readings" and "body piercing").

One angel's investing criteria

Angels do their investment thing for a number of reasons, ranging from greed to boredom to altruism. The best angels we know, however, are those who invest not because they're looking to make money, but because they enjoy the thrill of the start-up and working with aspiring entrepreneurs. One such fellow is Norm Brodsky, who also writes a column for *Inc.* magazine.

Brodsky, who views himself as much as a mentor as he does an angel, lists four basic rules for the angel investor:

Rule #1: Invest in people who want your help, not your money. Brodsky is looking for people who will listen. If they aren't ready to listen and are unwilling to take an old pro's advice, Brodsky sees no compelling reason to get involved.

The lesson for you: Angels are usually ex-entrepreneurs with deeply ingrained ideas on how to create and build a business. Be willing to use their ideas and suggestions, or you'll probably lose the angel. The flip side, of course, is to be sure that an angel's view of the world and your business mission match. No investment is worth compromising your principles and vision.

Rule #2: When possible, go it alone. Independence is, and always will be, one of the entrepreneur's primary traits, in Brodsky's mind anyway. Entrepreneurs need to have things done their way, not someone else's way.

The lesson for you: One angel is preferable to a team of angels. In general, Brodsky believes that the "too-many-cooks-spoil-the-broth" principle is at work here. In some situations, however, more than one angel may be preferable — for example, when one angel doesn't have enough cash to meet the business's growth needs or where one angel may add flavors to the broth that the other angel doesn't.

Rule #3: Take a majority stake (become a partner) until your investment has been paid. Preservation of capital is of the utmost importance to sophisticated angels. They know that if they don't preserve it, they won't have it to invest again.

The lesson for you: Expect your angel to be demanding on the issue of ownership; he wants a voice in the direction of the business. He or she needs to have control, at least until it is obvious that the business is going to be successful and that the investment goals will be achieved.

In the end, of course, if you don't have enough money to go it alone and it may be the angel who makes the difference in whether your business gets off the ground, he or she will have great influence over the ultimate terms. We suggest, however, that you not give up the controlling equity in your company (51 percent) unless doing so is absolutely, positively your last course of action in obtaining financing. The amount of equity to be ceded is always negotiable — try to hold out for at least 51 percent for yourself.

Rule #4: Retain the right to force a payout (payback including interest) of the loan or investment. A business's profitability doesn't necessarily foretell a payout, unless it's specified in the agreement. Although the profitability of the business is important to the angel, the payout of the loan or investment is even more important. Success without a return isn't success; it's only grounds for disagreement.

The lesson for you: Expect your angel to demand in writing a payout that would come from future earnings, even though you'd prefer to spend or invest the cash elsewhere.

Meanwhile, the SBA spawned Active Capital (`activecapital.org`), and you'll discover a mix-and-match format designed to bring together aspiring small-business start-ups and "accredited small-business investors." The "accredited small-business investor" must have a net worth in excess of $1 million or individual annual income in excess of $200,000 (or $300,000 joint income).

If you want to find an angel in your own backyard, your state or city may have an angel-matching program. Ask local bankers, accountants, financial advisors, or lawyers for their input on how to find a local angel-matching program; call your local Chamber of Commerce; or contact your state's Department of Commerce.

Venture capital

Venture capital firms and organizations offer cash in exchange for equity in start-up companies, so they are, in effect, an organized version of angel investing. As opposed to more conservative sources of capital, which look closely at a business's past performance and its collateral before handing out cash, venture capital firms focus primarily on future prospects when looking at a business plan. Thus, venture capital is useful for a few sophisticated businesses in higher-risk, higher-reward industries. Venture capital firms look for the possibility of hefty annual returns (30 percent or more) on their investments in order to offset the losses that are sure to occur within their high-risk portfolios.

Few small-business start-ups are in a position to take advantage of venture capital financing. The typical venture capital firm funds only 2 percent of the deals it sees, and that 2 percent has to meet a wide range of investment criteria, such as highly attractive niches, sophisticated management, and potential for high return — criteria that the typical small-business start-up can't begin to meet. Don't be disappointed at not qualifying for venture capital funding. As this chapter details, many other, more appropriate financing resources exist for small businesses.

Minority funding resources

The resources for low-income and minority funding (which in many cases is defined to include women-owned businesses) are many. Look to the following for starters:

- The National Bankers Association (NBA) in Washington, D.C., represents minority-owned banks that target loans to minority-owned businesses. For the nearest member bank in your area, call the NBA at 202-588-5432 or visit its Web site at `www.nationalbankers.org`.

- Most states have an agency that provides one-stop assistance on financial services for small businesses. Check the library or the phone book for such an agency in your state and then ask about state-operated minority funding resources.

✔ On the federal level, the Small Business Administration can help direct callers to local organizations that can, in turn, help locate low-income and minority funding opportunities. Call the SBA at 800-827-5722 for the resource nearest you or surf its Web site at www.sba.gov.

✔ The U.S. Commerce Department's Minority Business Development Agency funds Business Development Centers nationwide whose function is, in part, to help minority-owned start-up businesses. Call 888-324-1551 for more information or visit its Web site at www.mbda.gov.

Exploring Ownership Options

In theory, all businesses have three ownership options:

✔ Privately held, with the founder being the only shareholder

✔ Privately held, sharing ownership with partners or other shareholders

✔ Publicly held, meaning that shares in your company are available to the general public via the stock market

In reality, of course, most businesses only have the first two of these options — going it alone or having partners or minority shareholders. Few businesses have the management, resources, and appeal needed to go public, either at the start-up stage or in the course of the business's growth.

There is no right or wrong answer as to which of the three options you should use, but there is a right or wrong way to determine which works best for you. At the heart of making that decision is . . . you guessed it . . . you! You are the primary ingredient that will determine which of the three options will work best for your business. Your criteria to use in making this decision will include the kind of person you are, the way you communicate, the way you delegate, and the manner in which you work with people.

The kind of business you intend to start also can be a factor. If, for example, you intend to start a high-tech manufacturing business, you may find that the key employees you want will demand some ownership (such as stock options; see Chapter 16) as part of their compensation packages. On the other hand, if you intend to go into the consulting business, sole ownership is the likely ticket for you.

The following sections offer a brief discussion of the pros and cons of each of the three ownership options.

The role of business incubators

A *business incubator* is, quite simply, a building that is divided into units of space, which are then leased to early-stage small businesses. The result is a collection of offices and small warehouses filled with businesses (most likely in the light manufacturing, service, or technology sectors) that have one thing in common: They're businesses in the early stages of development. Each of the businesses has problems and needs that are similar, and each is in need of a variety of help, ranging from technical assistance to shared business opportunities to a simple pat on the back. Attesting to the benefits that incubators offer is the fact that today almost 1,000 incubators are operating in North America, up from only 15 in 1980.

Business incubators aren't intended to provide permanent homes to their client businesses but rather to provide them with a temporary nurturing environment, until such time as the business is financially healthy. Upon reaching more predictable profitability, the incubated business can then be expected to "graduate" and move on to a typical office or warehouse building.

The advantages of working in a business incubator environment are many; here are but a few of the most important ones:

- **Financing:** Most incubators offer some kind of access to capital. We should mention here that incubator companies are carefully screened; thus, a business that has been accepted into an incubator offers somewhat of a stamp of approval on the business in the eyes of potential lenders and investors. Also,

angels tend to hover around business incubators, so acceptance into one is usually a surefire way to get in touch with the local angel community.

- **Shared opportunities:** Sales leads, new business opportunities, strategic alliances — all are part of an incubator's offerings.

- **Shared business services:** A number of important business services can be found inside an incubator, including but not limited to telephone answering, bookkeeping services, access to fax and copy machines, and a wide variety of services and equipment that would otherwise require outlays by the start-up business.

- **Affordable rents and flexible real estate:** Rental costs are often a bit below market, and the sizes of the offices and warehouses vary widely, thereby affording clients more flexibility.

- **Networking with peers:** Imagine a collection of small-business owners, people like you, in every workspace in your building. Being a small-business owner doesn't have to be lonely.

We recommend that you consider a business incubator right from the get-go, unless yours is a business that depends on a geographic location that the incubator can't provide. To find the small-business incubator nearest you, call the National Business Incubation Association at 740-593-4331 or visit its Web site at www.nbia.org.

You as the sole owner

Sole ownership is always the least conflictive and most popular of the three options for starting a company, assuming that you have access to the necessary funds to launch your business, industry knowledge, and energy to make a go of the business by yourself. Sure, the leverage and financial benefits that partners and shareholders bring to the table can be worth their weight in potential opportunities, but decision-making in shared ownership situations requires consensus, and consensus can take a lot of time. Besides, consensus doesn't always represent your own personal best interests, and when your name is on the dotted line, your personal best interests should be at or near the top of the reasons for making decisions.

Being the only owner has the following advantages:

- ✔ **It's generally easier, quicker, and less expensive.** No lawyers are required to write partnership agreements and assist in determining answers to all the questions that partnership agreements require.

- ✔ **The profits belong solely to you.**

- ✔ **You have no need for consensus.** Your way is the only way.

- ✔ **You don't waste time catering to the often-aggravating demands of shareholders, minority or otherwise.** There's no possibility of shareholder lawsuits.

Being the only owner also has the following disadvantages:

- ✔ **You have no one to share the risk with.**

- ✔ **Your limited skills will have to make do until you can hire someone with complementary skills.**

- ✔ **Single ownership can be lonely.** Many times, you'll wish you had someone with whom to share the problems and stress. You may be able to do this with trusted, senior employees. Of course, if you have good friends and/or a strong marriage partner, these people can be a source of much-needed support.

Still confused as to whether you want to go it alone or share ownership? Answer the following questions to help with the decision:

- ✔ **Do you believe that you need a partner?** Do you absolutely, positively need a partner? To provide cash? Knowledge? If you do, that settles the issue; if you don't, continue with the following questions.

    The preceding reasons are the correct ones for needing a partner. Incorrect reasons include picking a partner because he or she is your friend or picking a partner because you're afraid of running a business by yourself.

✔ **Are you capable of working with partners or shareholders?** Will you have a problem sharing the decisions and the profits as well as the risks?

✔ **Does your business fit the multiple ownership profile?** In other words, does this business have room for two partners, and is it a business that has the growth potential to support two partners? Will a partner have an important role in the organization? Would his or her complementary skills enhance the business's chance for success?

✔ **What are the legal requirements of multiple ownership?** Can you live within these legal parameters? (Read the remainder of this chapter and then consult with an attorney if you still have questions.)

✔ **What do you have in common with other business owners who have opted for multiple ownership? Where do you see conflicts?** Ask your banker, accountant, or attorney for the names of other business owners who have opted for multiple ownership. Interview those owners. Get their feedback on the list of pluses and minuses.

✔ **What's the likelihood of finding a partner with complementary skills and a personality compatible with yours?** This ability depends on how wired into the business community you are and the line of work you're going into. If you have a lot of business contacts and know exactly what you want, finding a partner may be easy. More typically, it isn't.

After you answer these questions, you should have enough information to make the decision. Make a list of pros and cons. Will your business have a better chance of success with just you at the helm, or are other skills immediately needed? Take your time.

If you opt for multiple ownership, you'll live with the decision for a long, long time. If you elect sole ownership at the start, however, you can always seek partners later if you feel that you need them for the business success that you desire.

Sharing ownership with partners or minority shareholders

As discussed in the preceding section, partners make sense when they can bring needed capital to the business along with complementary management skills. Unfortunately, partners also present the opportunity for turmoil, and, especially in the early stages of a business's growth, turmoil takes time, burns energy, and costs money — all of which most small-business founders lack.

If you're one of those rare individuals who is fortunate enough to have found the right partner, go for it; work out a deal. We've seen this proven many times over: A partnership in the right hands will outperform a sole proprietorship in the right hands, any day.

Having *minority shareholders* (any and all shareholders who collectively own less than 50 percent) can also make sense, especially after the business is out of the blocks and has accumulated value. The most common methods of putting stock in the hands of employees include stock-option plans, bonuses, and Employee Stock Ownership Plans (ESOPs). See Chapter 16 for more details.

Here's a warning based on our personal experience: Minority shareholders can be a pain; they have legal rights that often run counter to the wishes of the majority. Because majority shareholders are ceded the right to make the final decisions, courts have determined that minority shareholders must have an avenue of appeal. Thus, minority shareholders, particularly in our litigious society, sometimes look to the courts whenever they feel their rights of ownership are being violated. Unfortunately, shareholder suits are a sign of the times.

As a result of this potentially tenuous relationship, you should always — we repeat, *always!* — involve an attorney when inviting minority shareholders to the party, and you should always include a buy-sell agreement in the deal. In the event that the relationship doesn't turn out to be what all parties expected, buy-sell agreements establish procedures for issuing, valuing, and selling shares of the company, including how to determine the value of shares when one or more of the owners wants to cash out.

Occasionally, especially where venture capital financing is involved, the founder of the business may find himself or herself working for majority shareholders. Fortunately, this situation rarely occurs because the typical small-business founder has already proven that taking orders from others is not exactly one of his or her inherent strengths. We've found that, on the infrequent occasions when this situation does occur, more often than not the founder of the company is the first one to get the boot when the going gets tough, as the chief financiers step in to protect their investment. That's why we strongly recommend that you find a way to retain majority control.

Going public: Cashing in

No question about it, the lure of liquidity and the possibility of interest-free capital can be overpowering to the small-business owner, especially after years of personally guaranteeing debt, scraping for money, and living on a reduced (or no) salary. Many small-business owners at one time or another fantasize about going public, yet few businesses ever make it. Several reasons exist for this, the first and foremost of which is that the stock markets are selective; they function for businesses that have outstanding track records and that meet particular hurdles. (Although we realize that this last statement may be a bit hard to swallow if you've personally lost money investing in newly issued stock that went belly up, it still, generally, holds true.)

Here's what it takes to get your stock listed on one of the major U.S. stock exchanges:

- ✔ **National Association of Securities Dealers Automated Quotation system (NASDAQ):** NASDAQ has companies ranging from small emerging firms to large firms such as Microsoft. Listing requirements include either a market value of at least $8 million and pretax income from continuing operations of at least $1 million or a market value of at least $18 million, 400 or more shareholders, and an operating history of at least two years. Tens of thousands of other companies are in the over-the-counter market, but these companies are so low priced and/or infrequently traded that they aren't listed on NASDAQ.

  In case you care — and it's okay if you don't — NASDAQ is an electronic network that allows brokers to trade "over the counter" from their offices all over the country.

- ✔ **American Stock Exchange (AMEX):** AMEX is the second-largest stock exchange in the United States and lists typically mid-size firms. Listing requirements include a pretax annual income of at least $750,000 or a market value of at least $15 million.

- ✔ **New York Stock Exchange (NYSE):** The NYSE is the largest stock exchange in the world in terms of total volume and value of shares traded. It lists more than 2,000 companies, which tend to be among the oldest, largest, and best-known American corporations. To be listed on the NYSE, among other criteria, a company must annually earn at least $2.5 million before taxes and must have a market value of at least $100 million.

In truth, going public has downsides that are easily overlooked. Although the capital raised may be interest free, it is by no means hassle-free. You'll find that the army of outside shareholders that comes with going public, in concert with the Securities and Exchange Commission (SEC), requires an avalanche of public filings. Yes, the public business is liquid, but at what cost to management's time? You'll also pay hefty fees to investment bankers to issue stock and to the stock exchange to initiate your listing and to maintain it over time. And, in public companies, every shareholder, customer, media person, and competitor can peer into your financial records and ask you those questions that you may not have the time or the desire to answer, and they may discover things that you really don't want them to know.

Going public only works for a sophisticated chosen few, so don't waste a lot of time fantasizing about being the CEO of a public company. Given the entrepreneurial characteristics of the vast majority of people who typically decide to start businesses, public companies and small-business owners are like a size-9 shoe on a size-12 foot.

Deciding Whether to Incorporate

Before we discuss the variety of legal entities available to you, we must first pass on one piece of overriding advice. Today's high cost of legal consultations notwithstanding, making the entity decision is one of those half dozen or so times when consulting a good lawyer usually makes sense. (See Chapter 21 for information on quality legal software.)

The entity options we describe in the upcoming sections are only intended to serve as guidelines. Although the entity decision you make won't necessarily be forever (your legal framework can and may change as your business changes), the choice you make now is bound to have significant short-term financial and legal implications — implications that will far exceed the cost of any upfront legal fees.

On a related issue, a good attorney may, at the time you're making the entity decision, ask you what your exit strategy is for your business. If you reply that your exit strategy may be to eventually sell the business, it will affect the options he will recommend to you. Too often, we've seen business owners who suddenly decide they want to sell their businesses be told by their tax advisors or attorneys that, as a result of bad entity decisions early on, they'll be taxed twice at the time of the sale. (*Note:* If your business is currently a C Corporation, make sure that this entity really, truly fits your needs. We'll bet there are better options.)

The first decision that you must make, in the process of determining which legal entity to adopt, is to incorporate or not to incorporate. After you have made that choice, if your decision is to incorporate, your choices are then to become a C Corporation, a Subchapter S Corporation, or a limited liability corporation (LLC).

If you prefer to do most of the incorporating work yourself without involving an attorney, refer to the book *Incorporating Your Business For Dummies,* by The Company Corporation (Wiley). You can also visit the Web site www.corporate.com for more information and assistance on the subject. In the following sections, we discuss the factors involved in your decision to incorporate or remain unincorporated, as well as your options within each category. Be sure to research all aspects of this issue, because a host of tax, liability, and administrative issues should be considered before you decide.

Unincorporated options

The preponderance of small-business entities are unincorporated for any number of valid reasons (such as the cost and complexity of the incorporating process; we talk about that process in the section "Incorporated business entities" later in this chapter). If you decide to remain unincorporated, your business will automatically become either a sole proprietorship or, if you have a partner or partners, a partnership.

Sole proprietorship

If you're a typical small-business owner, especially one of the home-office variety (see Chapter 20), your first consideration should always be the sole proprietorship, which is generally the simplest and least costly way to structure a business. Simply open your door, hang out your shingle, and zap, zap, you're a sole proprietorship. Little muss, little fuss, and little paperwork.

So why doesn't everyone become a sole proprietorship if it's so simple? The primary reason is the personal liability issue. The sole proprietor is personally liable for the business and puts his or her nonbusiness assets at risk. If you've selected an industry in which the chances for liability are high (consulting, for example), you should at least consider the option of incorporating.

Most people decide to open their businesses by using their own names as the principal owners. If you decide to use a fictitious name or a trade name, however, you'll need to file a Certificate of Conducting Business Under an Assumed Name with your state or local town/city/county clerk. You can obtain the forms from good self-help law books; the filing fee is minimal. For most small-business start-ups, using your own name is the best, and simplest, choice.

Other important characteristics of the sole proprietorship include the following:

- Ownership must be limited to a single owner or a married couple.
- Taxable income is subject to both income and self-employment tax (see Chapter 18).
- Business losses may offset income from other personal sources subject to certain limitations.
- Some states allow protection of personal assets from business risks by owning them jointly with a spouse or by transferring them to a spouse or children. (Check with an attorney or your state's attorney general's office.)
- Insurance is available to cover some of the risks of a sole proprietorship. (Check with associations that are appropriate for your profession; also check with local insurance agents who specialize in working with small-business owners.)

✔ Legal termination of the business is easy for the sole proprietorship, especially compared to all the legal ramifications required when terminating something like a C Corporation. When putting an end to a sole proprietorship, simply close the doors and (assuming that you have no outstanding creditors) walk away.

Partnerships

Similar to a sole proprietorship, a *general partnership* (also known as a *standard partnership*) can also be initiated by simply opening the doors. In a partnership, all partners are personally liable for their obligations to the partnership.

A partnership may include two or more partners and is similar to the sole proprietorship — little paperwork is required in the formation stage. The individual partners are taxed on their percentage of the partnership income; therefore, the partnership itself, similar to the sole proprietorship, doesn't pay taxes.

The downside of a partnership is that the partners can be held personally liable. Because of this liability issue, partnerships can be particularly sticky relationships unless the partners are capable of resolving disagreements amicably.

In addition to the general partnership, you can create a business entity known as a *limited partnership* — a combination of at least one general partner and one or more limited partners. The limited partners are liable only to the extent of the cash and/or property they've contributed to the partnership; the general partners are liable for everything else. The general partners are the managing partners; the limited partners are passive investors only.

Although not legally required for a partnership to conduct its business, we strongly recommend that you (working with an attorney) prepare a partnership agreement when you make the decision to involve a partner or partners. We recommend its preparation in order to outline what happens should various and inevitable problems or issues arise, such as one partner wanting out of the business or the need for the infusion of new capital in unequal contributions by the partners.

In the absence of a partnership agreement, the division of ownership, profits, and liabilities among partners will be legally assumed to be equal, regardless of whether some partners have contributed more assets or time than others to the business.

A good partnership agreement should include the following specifics:

✔ **The duration of the partnership:** Generally, a partnership agreement's duration is "in perpetuity." You may have reasons why one partner or another may specify that the agreement will lapse, such as when a business reaches a certain size or when profits are available to repay one partner's initial investment.

✓ **The time or money each partner will contribute:** The time and money contributed will rarely be the same throughout the duration of a partnership. When an unplanned difference between the two exists (for example, one partner works longer hours than the other, or one partner contributes new money to the company while the other does not), a good partnership agreement spells out a way to equate the disparity.

✓ **The methods for making business decisions:** Generally speaking, someone has to have the final word in the likely event the partners have disagreements.

✓ **The sharing of profits and losses:** Normally, profit sharing (as well as loss sharing) will be in concert with the percentage of ownership. However, you may have occasions when one partner will receive more than the other. These occasions, which should be spelled out in the partnership agreement, may include new responsibilities, new investments, or new workloads.

✓ **The determination of when to distribute profits:** Partners' wishes on this issue aren't always consistent; one partner may want to take money out of the partnership, while the other may want to leave the money in to help the company grow.

✓ **The dissolution or restructuring of the partnership in the event of death or disability of a partner:** Sooner or later, death and/or disability is going to happen, and when it does, you must have a way to determine the valuation of the partnership for estate or cash-out purposes and for redefining the ongoing business.

Incorporated business entities

A *corporation* is considered a legal entity of its own; thus, its owners (shareholders or stockholders) aren't personally liable for the business's liabilities, losses, and risks. Shareholders can come and go, but, unlike a sole proprietorship or a partnership, the business will continue to exist in spite of any change in the corporation's ownership.

Generally speaking, the decision to incorporate is usually made either as a result of the business's growth and the issues that accompany that growth or when the personal tax considerations of one or more of the owners warrant incorporation. The desired benefits of making the incorporation decision usually include the following:

TRUE STORY

Husband-and-wife partnerships: A union not always made in heaven

Daryl and Helen's business started out the way many husband-and-wife partnerships do, evolving from the skills of the husband. Daryl was an Earthmover extraordinaire and had been driving those monstrous yellow machines you see rumbling around highway construction projects since he graduated from high school. He could turn a rolling hill into a parking lot quicker than you could utter the word excavate. After ten years of moving dirt for someone else, Daryl decided it was time to start moving it for himself, whereupon he started Whitney and Sons Excavations. Who better to take care of the bookkeeping and office chores than his wife Helen?

The company grew in the early years, both in revenues and in profits. At the beginning, Daryl was an enthusiastic hands-on manager, directing every job himself. Several years passed, and the company had 20 employees and bank borrowings to finance hundreds of thousands of dollars in heavy equipment. Daryl's workdays were long and emotionally draining. Instead of driving the Earthmovers, he was "baby-sitting" other people who drove them. Meanwhile, Daryl and Helen's personal problems had escalated — they were learning the lesson so many husband-and-wife partnerships have learned over the years: Although the husband may be a talented craftsman, this doesn't necessarily mean he can manage a group of employees (including his wife).

The company's bottom line turned to red, employee unrest multiplied, and cash disappeared. Helen's job became harder and harder. She was the one who had to manage the bank loans and vendor payables, and she was the one who had to scrounge to find the cash to make the payrolls. She hated her job — not the bookkeeping part, but the cash-managing part — keeping unhappy bankers and vendors and employees at bay as she juggled the company's waning assets. Daryl and Helen's communications, never great even at the beginning of their partnership, worsened, and they soon had to seek marriage counseling.

Finally, Daryl and Helen could take it no more. They swallowed their pride and declared bankruptcy. Helen took a job as an accountant for Brown County while Daryl, you guessed it, hired on as a Cat driver for a large company in a neighboring county. The marriage sputtered for another year or so before both Daryl and Helen decided too much damage had been done. Sadly, that partnership ended, too.

The moral of this story? No matter what the legal entity, a husband-and-wife business is a partnership, in the true sense of the word. Just because you can manufacture a widget together, don't assume that you can manage a company. Partnerships are risky arrangements. The good ones prosper; the bad ones can ruin friendships and marriages. If a husband and wife don't communicate well *before* they go into business, they shouldn't expect to begin communicating well *after* they go into business together.

Yes, many wonderful companies have evolved thanks to fruitful and binding partnerships between spouses. Sadly, however, too many more have failed. Tread carefully as you ponder the decision to enter into another partnership.

- ✔ **Shielding the company's principals from personal liability.** Consider whether the type of business you're getting into or are already in has high potential for lawsuits.

- ✔ **Providing an opportunity to raise capital by selling stock.**

- ✔ **Enabling the business owners to more quickly and easily transfer ownership from one shareholder to another.**

- ✔ **Allowing for the adoption of a variety of employee benefits (such as the corporation's ability to fully tax-deduct employee health and disability insurance premiums paid) not available to other types of unincorporated entities.** See Chapter 16 for a discussion of benefits.

Every corporation should execute a buy-sell agreement, which always involves the assistance of an attorney competent in this area. Among other things, the buy-sell agreement dictates how a person's shares of stock will be handled if that person retires from the business, becomes disabled, or dies. This exit-strategy issue is one of the most overlooked potential problems among entrepreneurs.

Given the benefits of incorporating, you may assume that you'll find significant disadvantages to incorporating; otherwise, everyone would do it. Correct-amundo! The primary disadvantages of incorporating are the following:

- ✔ **The cost and hassle of the incorporation procedure and complying with the public agencies (federal and state) that oversee corporations.** The act of incorporation can be expensive, especially from the perspective of a budding entrepreneur with limited cash and few or no customers. The cost depends on the state in which you incorporate. Costs can range from about $100 to approximately $1,000 for incorporation fees, and the corporation must pay an annual tax that varies by state. These costs don't include attorney's fees or any other fees that may crop up.

  Filings can take from a few days to several weeks, again depending on the state and who's handling the process within that state. In some states, filings can take up to two months because the secretary of state and county officials must review them.

- ✔ **The hassle and potential liability from shareholder lawsuits involved in dealing with shareholders.**

- ✔ **The "double taxation" that occurs in a C Corporation when dividends are paid.** When corporations earn profits, those profits are taxed at the corporate level. If some of those profits are then paid in dividends to company shareholders, company shareholders also must pay income tax on the dividends, hence the term *double taxation*.

If you decide to incorporate, you have three kinds of corporations to consider: the C Corporation, the Subchapter S Corporation, and the limited liability corporation. We discuss each in the sections that follow.

C Corporations

Most big businesses and some small corporations elect C, or regular corporation status, primarily because of their need for the liability protection that C Corporations offer. Because of their size and the public nature of their business, these large corporations don't qualify for either Subchapter S or limited liability company status.

C Corporations are taxed as an entity separate from any of the individuals comprising it, and all the profits of the business are taxed at the corporate level. And, if some of those profits are paid in dividends to the corporation's shareholders, the shareholders are obligated to pay ordinary income tax on those dividends. The result of this is the so-called double-taxation status of corporations.

As with the other types of corporations, C Corporations are expensive and time-consuming to create. The process includes the owners of the business (the shareholders and stockholders) agreeing on the following:

- The name of the business
- The number of shares of stock the company can sell, the class of stock, and its value
- The number of shares the owners will buy
- The amount of money (or other assets) the owners will contribute to buy shares of stock
- The directors and officers who will manage the corporation

Subchapter S Corporations

Named after the Internal Revenue Code section that allows it, Subchapter S is the corporation of the "little folks" — smaller companies that need the liability protection afforded but don't have the issue of multiple shareholders to worry about. Subchapter S status is reserved for businesses with no more than 75 shareholders. Both new and existing businesses may elect to adopt Subchapter S status.

When would you consider an S Corporation? As with a C Corporation, an S Corporation provides the liability protection, but unlike a C Corporation, it avoids the double-taxation status by allowing the income of the corporation to pass through to its owners/shareholders. The major difference between an S Corporation and a C Corporation (or an LLC) is that the S Corporation income is subject to only one tax — the personal income tax.

S Corporation status is the usual choice of small-business owners who make the decision to incorporate for liability purposes. This is especially true for start-up businesses because early-stage losses can be offset against your personal income.

Before deciding to create a Subchapter S Corporation, you should consider the profitability expectations of the business. In the start-up years, if you're like most small businesses, you can expect your business to lose money. In this case, opting for Subchapter S status is advisable, because you can offset your business losses against your personal income. In later years, as your business becomes profitable, paying taxes at the corporate rate rather than the personal rate may become more advantageous, so you'd be wise to switch to C Corporation status.

The election of Subchapter S status has many other varied ramifications. We strongly recommend that an attorney or qualified tax advisor help you to make this decision.

Limited liability corporations: A hybrid invention

The limited liability corporation (LLC) is the newer kid on the corporate block. The IRS officially awarded the LLC favorable tax status in 1988; since then, all 50 states and the District of Columbia allow this unique entity. An LLC is a hybrid entity. It combines the benefits of a corporation with those of a partnership:

✔ Like a corporation, investors in an LLC don't face personal liability for the debts or obligations of the LLC.

✔ Like a partnership, the LLC is afforded favorable tax treatment because the income and losses of the business flow through to the individual investors, who are called *members,* and are reported only once on each investor's personal income tax return.

Another advantage of an LLC is its flexibility. Unlike an S Corporation, an LLC can be structured to allocate the profits of the business differently among the various members, while at the same time preserving the flow-through tax treatment. An LLC has the added advantage over a partnership of providing the members with limited liability. The relationship of the members in an LLC is controlled by an operating agreement, a document not unlike a partnership agreement. The operating agreement can be quite complex.

LLCs are relatively new, so we recommend that you consult an attorney with significant experience in establishing LLCs for small businesses like yours to help you decide whether an LLC can work for your business and to help draft the operating agreement. Be sure to find an attorney who really understands the ins and outs of LLCs. Ask for attorney referrals from other business owners who've incorporated.

Part II
Buying an Existing Business

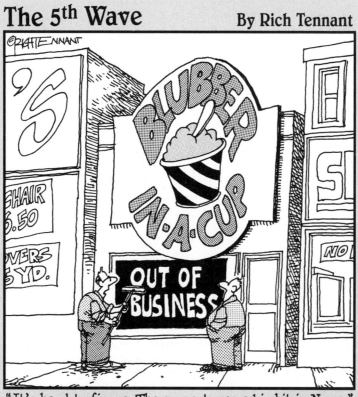

The 5th Wave   By Rich Tennant

"It's hard to figure. The concept was a big hit in Nome."

In this part . . .

Some small-business owners are better suited to buying an existing small business than to starting one from scratch. This part explores the advantages and disadvantages of buying an existing business and helps you determine what kind of business to buy and what you should pay for it. In this part, we also cover the tax implications and potential employee issues involved with buying an existing business, and we provide you with a process for moving forward.

Chapter 6

Exploring Buying a Business

. . . .

In This Chapter

▶ Understanding good reasons to buy a small business

▶ Identifying who's likely to fail when going the purchase route

▶ Measuring your likelihood of success

. . . .

After a business has been created, it can have a life of its own. The umbilical cord to its creator can be cut, and the business can pass through the hands of various owners. In some cases, a great small business can outlive its original owners — assuming, of course, that subsequent owners have the necessary entrepreneurial and management skills.

In this chapter, we tell you the reasons why you should buy a business; we also steer you clear when your personality and resources don't make purchasing a good match.

Understanding Why to Buy a Business

Every year, hundreds of thousands of small businesses change hands. Why? For the same reasons that many people purchase an already-built home instead of building from scratch. Because building a home or a business takes a lot of time and work, with lots of potential for problems.

We don't mean for you to take this building analogy too far. After all, you can start most small businesses without drawing on your carpentry skills. However, as with buying an existing home, you may find that the advantages of buying someone else's business outweigh the advantages of building one yourself.

Dissatisfaction: A catalyst for change

As sometimes happens in life, those who end up buying a business often end up doing so as a result of some outside force or circumstance that propels them in that direction.

Consider the case of David, a veterinarian who worked for an owner who agreed to offer David 10 percent of the practice after David had worked there for a number of years. Over time, however, the owner engaged in various legal maneuverings that allowed him to wiggle out of the offer. David became dejected and upset; he'd been a loyal and highly competent employee over the years. His customers enjoyed working with him and requested his services when scheduling future appointments. David couldn't understand how the owner could treat him so poorly despite his years of excellent service to the business. David couldn't see and understand that the owner was greedy and unethical because David was neither.

The silver lining to this story was that this horrible experience was the catalyst David needed to go into business for himself. Instead of building a practice from scratch, however, David bought an existing practice — and he's glad that he did. David hit the ground running with the established practice, yet through his energies and talents, he made the practice bigger and better. Today, David is a contented small-business owner and a multimillionaire to boot.

As if this issue of saving time and energy in the building process isn't enough, another reason for buying a business is that, historically, the failure rate is twice as high for starting a business as compared to buying one. So why doesn't everyone buy a business instead of start one? Because there aren't that many good businesses that make it to the auction block. Many of the good ones never hit the market; instead, they are passed on within the family or are sold in private transactions without ever being listed for sale. In the following sections, we discuss reasons why you may prefer to buy an existing business rather than build one from scratch.

Reducing start-up hassles and headaches

Running a business is always a juggling act, but you often have more balls in the air during those start-up years than at any other time in the life of the business. Beyond formulating a business plan, you have to develop a marketing plan, find customers, hire employees, locate space, and possibly incorporate. Although you still need a game plan when buying an existing business, many of these start-up details have already been done.

Consider the learning curve for the type of business you're thinking of purchasing. Buying an existing business makes sense if the business is complicated. For example, purchasing a business that manufactures an intricate product makes more sense than purchasing a house-painting business, which doesn't require much more than the necessary tools and equipment and painting know-how. Also, unless you yourself have built the product the company manufactures, and unless you understand the intricacies of the production process, starting such a business from scratch is quite risky and perhaps even foolhardy.

Lessening your risk

In situations where a business has an operating history and offers a product or service with a demonstrated market, some of the risk in the company is removed when you buy it. Although no investment is a sure thing, the risk should be significantly lower than the risk involved in a start-up. Reviewing past financial statements (see Chapter 13) also helps you make more accurate financial forecasts than you can with a start-up venture that has no history.

As we cover in detail in Chapter 8, you must do your homework, which means carefully inspecting (otherwise known as *due diligence*) the business you're considering buying and its financial statements. You can't take at face value how the business appears on paper or in site visits, because more than a few business sellers have been known to dress up the books and the business to hide problems and flaws.

Increasing profits by adding value

Some business owners who decide to sell their company don't see the potential for growth or don't want to grow their business. They may be burned out, content with their current earnings, lack needed business-management skills, or simply be ready to retire. Finding businesses that have the potential to improve operating efficiency and expand into new markets is difficult but not impossible, if you have the time and the patience to wait for the right one to come along. It's probably easier for a business-minded person to find small companies that are undervalued relative to the potential they have to offer than it is to find undervalued stocks or real estate when investing in those markets.

However, just because you think you see potential to improve a business, never, ever pay a high acquisition price based upon your expectations of being able to add that value. Even if you're correct about the potential, why should you pay the current owner for the hard work and ingenuity you plan to bring to the business? If you're wrong, you could grossly overpay for the business. Always offer a fair price based on the value of the business at the time you purchase it. (We explain how to arrive at this figure in Chapter 9.) Then you can realize the rewards of your improvements after you make them.

A smart seller will do everything he can to convince you that he has under-achieved with the business and all it needs is your energy, enthusiasm, and fantastic business acumen. Don't fall for the compliments; remember that you're buying the present while the seller is trying to sell you the future.

Those people who make their living buying and selling businesses have a saying that every business buyer should remember: "Sellers sell the future, buyers buy the past." What this saying means is that the person who's buying the business shouldn't listen to the seller talking about the grandiose things that can be done with the business, but instead focus on what the business has already done. In other words, the buyer isn't buying the seller's vision; he or she is buying what's in place today.

Establishing cash flow

One of the biggest unknowns involved in starting a business from scratch is estimating the new business's cash flow. (We discuss cash flow in detail in Chapter 13.) Will the business generate cash quickly, or will it take a long time? How long will collecting monies due from customers (receivables) take? How long will selling inventory take? How much will you have to invest in fixed assets? How quickly will your sales be established?

With start-up businesses, estimating these figures is fraught with potential for wide margins of error. Not so when buying an existing business. The previous owners have already answered most of these questions. Assuming that you don't walk in and make immediate, glaring changes to the business's products or operations, the cash flow pattern should continue somewhat as it has been. As a small-business owner, you'll find it reassuring to have a reasonably predictable cash flow. You and your family, your banker, and other investors will deeply appreciate it. Conversely, unpredictable cash flow is troublesome at best and will keep you from sleeping at night.

If you buy a business rather than do a traditional start-up, borrowing money from banks and raising money from investors should be easier for you. Lenders and investors rightfully see more risk with a start-up than with an established enterprise with a good track record. Plus, they have the business's existing assets with which to collateralize their loans. And, for the amount they invest, investors usually demand a smaller percentage of owner-ship in an existing business than in a new business.

Capitalizing on someone else's good idea

We've said it before: You don't need an original idea to go into business for yourself. Plenty of successful small-business people enjoy running a business; whether they sell tires or trim trees doesn't matter.

If you know you want to own a business but you lack an idea for a product or service to sell, chalk up another good reason to buy an existing business. But make sure that you can develop a passion for the industry.

Opening locked doors

In certain businesses, you can enter geographic territories only as a result of buying an existing business. For example, suppose that you want to own a Lexus dealership within an hour of where you currently live. If Lexus isn't granting any more new dealerships, your only ticket into the automobile industry may be to buy an already existing Lexus dealership in your area.

Inheriting an established customer base

Perhaps you're not terribly good at selling (maybe because you dislike it). Buying an existing business gives you a ready-built stable of customers, which means you don't have to recruit them yourself. Then, if you can provide quality products or services and meet customers' needs, you can see your business grow through word-of-mouth referrals.

In the long term, your lack of sales ability could wreck even an established business. All businesses, even those that don't want to grow, need to add new customers if only to replace those who inevitably leave. If you can't sell (or figure out how to sell to new customers), your business eventually may flounder. Be sure your new business has employees on staff with sales skills, or be ready to hire people with the necessary selling skills (see Chapter 15). (Also, check out Chapter 12 for more on keeping loyal customers.)

Knowing When You Shouldn't Buy

Of course, you can find more than a few downsides to buying an existing business. Similar to the advantages, the relative weight of these disadvantages depends largely on your personality and available resources.

You dislike inherited baggage

When you buy an existing business, the bad comes with the good. All businesses have their share of the bad. A business may have problem employees, for example, or it may have a less-than-stellar reputation in the marketplace. Even if the employees are competent, they and the culture of the company may not mesh with your direction for the company in the future.

Do you have the disposition and desire to motivate your employees to change or to fire employees who don't want to change? Do you have the patience to work at improving the company's products and reputation? Do you have the cash to upgrade the technology or remodel the dated offices? All these issues are barriers to running and adding value to a company. Some people enjoy and thrive on such challenges; others toss and turn in their sleep with such pressures. Think back on your other work experiences for clues about what challenges you've tackled and how you felt about them. If you haven't done so, take the quiz in Chapter 1 to help you assess your workplace likes and dislikes.

The wrong reasons for buying a business

Jeff (not his real name) was a successful electronics wholesaler. As Jeff approached the age of 50, he and his wife began to think more and more about where they might spend their retirement. As is typical of many Midwesterners fed up with long and dreary winters, Florida jumped to mind.

During a winter vacation in Naples, Florida, Jeff was idly perusing the classified ads when he noticed a business for sale in the wholesale electronics industry. His curiosity got the better of him; he visited the company and talked at length with the owner. Before you could mutter the words *spring break,* Jeff had purchased the company with one-third of the purchase price in cash and the balance borrowed as a long-term loan.

Jeff's primary reason for buying the business? To give himself and his family a chance to travel to Naples on the company expense account, mixing golf with business during those cold Midwestern winters. "A great way to ease into retirement," he told his friends.

Fast-forward two years. The Naples business was foundering badly. Apparently, many of the company's customers had been *relationship customers* (ones who mainly did business with the company because of their friendship/relationship with the owner), and now that the

previous owner was gone, so were they. (It didn't help that Jeff was only around three months out of the year, and the company's efficiency suffered accordingly.) Additionally, Jeff discovered that managing his new Deep South employees had little in common with managing his old Midwestern employees. Meanwhile, the business was hemorrhaging money.

Six months later, Jeff reluctantly closed the company's doors by transferring the remaining inventory to Minneapolis, taking a $250,000 hit to his bottom line in the process. A hefty price to pay, he admitted, for a few rounds of wintertime golf and some tax deductions.

In the end, Jeff's business failed because he purchased it for the wrong reasons. He didn't purchase it because he had a passion for his customers, or because he had an urge to make a difference for his employees, or because he had a driving need to create something meaningful, or for any strategic business reason. He purchased the business to get away from Minnesota winters and for some meager tax deductions, which, Jeff can tell you in retrospect, isn't nearly enough.

The lesson here? You should have compelling reasons to buy a business. As Jeff learned the hard way, golf in Florida and tax deductions just aren't enough.

You're going to skimp on inspections

If you think buying a company is easy, think again. You must know what you're buying, so you need to do a comprehensive inspection (see Chapter 7). For example, you (or a competent financial/tax person) need to analyze the existing business's financial statements to ascertain if the company really is as profitable as it appears and to determine its current financial health.

After you close the deal and transfer the money or duly record the IOUs, you can't turn back. Unless a seller commits fraud or lies (which is difficult and costly for a buyer to prove in a court of law), it's "buyer beware" with the quality of the business you're buying. In Chapter 8, we cover all the homework you should do before you decide to buy.

You lack capital

Why do a lot of people start a business instead of buying one? Because they simply don't have enough cash — or credit potential — to buy one. Existing businesses have value over and above the value of their hard assets, which is why you generally need more money and credit to buy a business than to start one. Although you may feel like you're more the business-buying type than the business-starting type, if you don't have the necessary dough, and if you can't find investors or lenders to provide it, then your avenue to business ownership may be decided for you, regardless of the avenue you'd prefer.

You can't handle lower potential returns

If you purchase a proven business and run it well, you can make a respectable-or-better return on your investment. (A business should be able to pay for itself in three to five years, assuming profits remain constant.) But you generally (though not always) have less upside and potential for hitting it really big when you buy, rather than start, your own business. Those who have created the greatest wealth from small businesses are those who have started their own, which makes sense — the greatest returns generally accrue to those accepting greater risk.

If you buy a business, you still have plenty of potential profits and wealth to make, just not as much. And, besides, how many millions or billions of dollars do you really need?

You think you'll miss out on the satisfaction of creating a business

Whether it nourishes their souls or simply gratifies their egos, entrepreneurs who build their own businesses get a different rush than those who buy companies. Certainly you can make your mark on a business you buy, but doing so takes a number of years. Even then, the business is never completely your own creation.

Recognizing Pre-purchase Prerequisites

Not everyone is cut out to buy an existing business, and we're not just referring to those who don't have enough cash or credit. In fact, you can purchase a good small business with little or, in rare cases, no money down.

Buying a business requires a lot of work. However, successfully running the business day in and day out is much harder for most people than finding and buying a business. Some succeed wildly at running a business they buy; others fail miserably. So what, then, are the traits common to people who successfully buy and operate an existing small business?

Above all else, being persistent, patient, and willing to spend time on things that don't lead to immediate results pays off. You need to be willing to sort through the rubbish to find the keepers. If you're a person who needs immediate gratification in terms of completing a deal, you may become miserable as you search, or you may end up rushing into a bad deal. Try breaking the process into steps to provide more success points and give yourself time for clear thinking.

Business experience and training

You should have the necessary business experience and background if you want to buy a business. If you were an economics or business major in college and took accounting and other quantitatively oriented courses, you're off to a good start.

If you have worked on business-management issues within a variety of industries, you also may have the proper background. Consultants who work as generalists get such training. However, one danger in having done only consulting is that you're usually not on the front lines where you confront most of the serious day-to-day operational issues. We've seen plenty of sophisticated consultants who didn't have the foggiest idea how to meet payroll or ship a UPS order or read an Accounts Receivable aging report.

If none of these backgrounds apply to you, you won't necessarily fail if you decide to buy a business, but the odds are against you. If you don't have a business background and work experience, you may still succeed. However, you'll probably simply survive (and just surviving isn't what you're after). Plus, your prospects for outright failure are relatively high, as compared to your experienced competitors.

We strongly encourage you to get some hands-on, small-business management experience, which is more valuable than any degree or credential you earn through course work. You'll find no substitute for real-life experiences in marketing to and interacting with customers, grappling with financial statements, dealing with competitive threats, and doing the business of everyday business.

If you want to own a computer repair service, go work in a good one. If you want to run a jet-ski rental business, go work in a successful one. Try to wear as many hats in the business as the boss allows. Consider the experience as paid, on-the-job training for running your own business. You're getting your unofficial MBA, and someone is even paying you for it!

We're not saying that you should avoid academia. You may, in fact, have to get a certain credential to do the work that you want to do. If you don't need a specific credential, taking selected courses, as well as reading relevant business books, can boost your knowledge.

For those of you with a large company or government background, be advised that there's a huge difference between working for IBM or the U.S. Treasury and owning a small business. The skills required simply aren't transferable, plus you must wear every business hat (sales, marketing, shipping and receiving, customer service, and so on) when you own a small business. Too many corporate or government employees have bit the proverbial dust when buying a small business because they made the erroneous assumption that working in a larger organization requires the same skills as running a small one.

Down-payment money

To purchase a business, as in purchasing real estate, you generally must make a significant down payment on the negotiated purchase price. In most cases, you need to put down at least 25 to 30 percent of the total purchase price. Bankers and business sellers who make loans to business buyers normally require down payments to protect their loans. They've learned from past experience that small-business buyers who make small down payments are more likely to walk away from a loan obligation if the business gets into financial trouble.

Succeeding with less money down

We know two people who made hefty profits with businesses they bought with small down payments. We don't want to mislead you into believing that it's easy or that anyone can do it, but it can be done.

First, Ken purchased an off-site file-storage company from an older owner who wanted to retire. The business did about half a million a year in sales and had allowed the owner to earn a decent living. After working for a year at a low salary, Ken gained the trust of the owner, who sold Ken and his partner the business for just $20,000 down, which represented less than 5 percent of the $550,000 purchase price. Ken and his partner had lots of great ideas about how to grow and build the business, and they did just that. Within seven years, after acquiring another area business and opening another location, sales and profits mushroomed, and the partners' stake in the business was worth about $7 million.

The basis for Ken's success here is that he had created trust with the seller by working for him first. This trust then translated into the owner selling Ken the business with a minimal down payment.

If you think Ken's story is extraordinary, check out Kyle's. He worked as an investment banker and discovered how to borrow large sums of money through selling high-yield (junk) bonds. Kyle and a business partner purchased a company that manufactures musical instruments. With $250,000 down, Kyle and his partner bought the business for $95 million. (In other words, they financed $94.75 million of the $95 million purchase price!) In case you don't have your calculator handy, that's a down payment of less than one-half of 1 percent! Kyle's stake in the company is now worth tens of millions of dollars.

Despite pulling off these smashing successes in their early 30s, both Ken and Kyle had excellent backgrounds to prepare them. Kyle, a Stanford MBA, had worked as a management consultant and investment banker. He also loved musical instruments and knew how to structure deals with little money down. Ken, also a Stanford MBA, had a background as a financial analyst and had done a lot of research into the off-site file-storage industry.

For example, consider what happened with co-author Jim's fourth business, which he sold for 33 percent of the sales price in cash and the balance on a ten-year loan. Two years after the sale, the buyers declared bankruptcy, leaving Jim holding the bag on the remainder of the loan, which was still more than 60 percent of the purchase price. Had Jim not required a down payment at all, he would have received no cash from the deal, only a long-term note that he would eventually eat; on the other hand, had he required 50 percent down, he would've received another 17 percent of the purchase price in cash, thereby reducing the amount of the note he would eventually write off.

If you lack a sufficient down payment, try asking family or friends to invest or lend you the cash. (See Chapter 5 for more on bootstrapping options.) You can also set your sights on a less-expensive business or seek out business sellers willing to accept a small down payment.

If you find a business for sale in which the owner wants less than 20 percent down, you may be on to something good. Be careful, though; owners willing to accept such small down payments may be having a difficult time selling because of problems inherent in the business or simply because they've overpriced the business. Smart sellers want to maximize the amount of the down payment. Your intent as a buyer should be to keep the down payment to a minimum (subject, of course, to obtaining favorable loan terms), thereby retaining as much cash as possible to use in operating the business.

Beware of the all-cash deal, even if you can afford it. If the business turns out to be something less than what was presented, you, the buyer, will lose all your leverage to negotiate. He who has the cash has the power — and you don't if you've paid 100 percent cash for the business purchase.

You can purchase many existing small businesses with a loan from the seller. Also, check with banks that specialize in small-business loans. For more financing recommendations, see Chapter 5.

Chapter 7

Finding the Right Business to Buy

• •

In This Chapter

▶ Looking at your business-shopping criteria

▶ Discovering the best resources for generating leads

▶ Surveying franchises and multilevel marketing companies

▶ Sidestepping bad "opportunities"

• •

*A*fter you make the decision to purchase a business, be realistic as you start your search for a worthy business to buy. Give yourself plenty of time; haste makes for lost money if you purchase a business without thinking through what you want and taking the proper steps to buy a quality business for a fair price.

If you limit your search time to nonbusiness hours, finding a good business can easily take a year or two. Even if you can afford to search full-time, you can still expect to spend several months on the prowl. This chapter offers our suggestions for uncovering the best business to buy.

Defining Your Appetite

Many businesses are for sale. To conduct an efficient search, you need to set some preliminary criteria. Although you don't have to define every precise detail of the business you want to purchase, a few well-chosen parameters help focus your search and keep you from spinning your wheels.

Although everyone has a different set of business-shopping criteria, you probably want to nail down the following general issues:

✓ **Type of business:** Businesses to buy come in four major categories:

- Retail (includes restaurants)
- Manufacturing
- Service
- Wholesale

Pick any one, but usually a good manufacturing business is the hardest to find, followed by service and wholesale. Most communities usually have an adequate quantity of retail and restaurant businesses available to buy.

✔ **Industry:** We highly recommend focusing on some specific niches in industries that interest you or that you know something about. Focusing helps you conduct a more thorough search and turns up high-quality companies. In addition to the industry knowledge you bring to the table, the knowledge you accumulate in your search can pay big dividends during your years of ownership.

If you have a hard time brainstorming about specific industries, here's a trick to jump-start your cerebral synapses. Take a walk through your local Yellow Pages. Listed alphabetically are all the businesses known to exist in your area. Remember that a separate Yellow Pages directory exists for businesses that sell mainly to consumers, while a "business-to-business" phone directory lists businesses whose customers primarily are other businesses. Look at either or both, depending upon the types of businesses in which you're interested.

You also may want to buy a business in a sector that is experiencing fast growth so that you, too, can ride the wave. Check out *Inc.* magazine's annual *Inc.* 500 list of the fastest growing smaller companies in America and their *Inc.* 5000 list of fast-growing private companies.

✔ **Lifestyle:** The type of lifestyle you want your small business to provide can narrow your search significantly. If you're going into small business because you'd like to work from home, for example, then you obviously don't want to buy a retail store. Also, consider how large an income you hope to generate, how many employees you want to manage, and whether or not you want to travel.

✔ **Size/purchase price:** Unless you can cleverly craft a deal with a low down payment, the money you have to invest in a business constrains the size of business you can afford. As a rule, figure that you can afford to pay a purchase price of about three times the down payment amount you have earmarked for the business. For example, if you have $30,000 in savings, you should look at buying a business for $100,000 or less.

Because many business sellers overprice their businesses, you can probably look at businesses listed at a price above $100,000 — perhaps even as high as $150,000 — because you can probably negotiate to buy such businesses for less.

Don't invest all your money in the purchase — you'll probably need some money to finance the day-to-day operations of the business until it becomes profitable.

✔ **Location:** If you're rooted to a location already and don't want to move or have a long commute, the business's location further narrows the field. Although you may be willing to consider broader territory — maybe even nationally if you're willing to relocate — evaluating businesses long distance is difficult and expensive. Unless you want a highly specialized type of company, try to keep your search local.

✔ **Opportunity to add value:** Some buyers want to purchase a business with problems that need fixing or with untapped opportunities. For most people, managing an ongoing business is enough of a challenge. As with real estate, most people are happier leaving the fixer-uppers to the contractors with experience in rehab. However, some businesses with correctable problems (lousy employees, inadequate systems and controls, or a shortage of cash, for instance) offer significant untapped potential and can usually be purchased at bargain prices.

After you define your shopping criteria, you're ready to go to the marketplace of businesses for sale. We recommend typing your criteria on a single page so that you can hand it to others who can put you in touch with businesses for sale. (For ideas on who to give it to, see the next section.)

Generating Leads

Break out your Sherlock Holmes cap and magnifying glass. Finding a good business to buy is a lot more like detective work than shopping at the mall. Be prepared to turn over a lot of stones and follow a lot of tracks, many of which will lead to dead ends. The following sections cover some proven resources for generating leads in your search for the right business to buy.

Peruse publications

If you focus on specific industry sectors, you may be surprised to discover all sorts of specialty newsletters and magazines. Just think of the fun you can have reading publications like *Marine Store Merchandising, Piano Technicians Journal,* and *Diaper Delivery Service Business Guide!* Specialty publications get you into the thick of an industry and also contain ads for businesses for sale or business brokers who work in the industry.

A useful reference publication that you can find in public libraries with decent business sections is the *Small Business Sourcebook* (Gale). Organized alphabetically, this enormous reference (which retails for $499) contains listings of publications, trade associations, and other information sources by industry.

Also peruse the classified ads in leading business publications such as *The Wall Street Journal,* where owners wanting to sell small businesses can buy ads in the full-run or regional editions of the newspaper.

Conducting literature searches of general-interest business publications helps identify articles on your industry of interest. Online computer searches can help find the articles. Visit the small-business resources we recommend in Chapter 21.

Network with advisors

Speak with accountants, attorneys, bankers, financial advisors, Chamber of Commerce employees, and business consultants who specialize in working with small businesses. These advisors sometimes are the first to find out about a small-business owner's desire to sell. Advisors can also suggest good businesses that aren't for sale but whose owners may consider selling.

Knock on doors

If you're a homeowner and someone came to your door and said they were interested in buying your home, you'd probably say that you're not interested in selling. If the interested buyer said they really liked the type of property you had and were willing to pay a good price, the person may get a little more of your attention, but you'd still likely turn him away. But if you, as the home-owner, were considering selling anyway, you'd be all ears — especially if you think you can sell directly and save paying a broker's selling commission.

Some business owners who haven't listed their business for sale are right now thinking about selling. So if you approach enough businesses that interest you, you'll find some of these not-yet-on-the-market businesses.

The reason to go to this trouble is that you increase the possibility of finding the right business. You may also get a good deal on such a business. You can negotiate with the seller from the beneficial position of not competing with other potential buyers.

Instead of calling on the phone or knocking on the business's door, start by sending a concise letter of introduction that explains what kind of business you're seeking and what buyer qualifications you possess. This step demonstrates that you're investing some time into this endeavor. By all means, follow up by phone a week or so after you send the letter.

Enlist business brokers

Some sellers list their businesses for sale with business brokers. Just as a real estate agent makes a living selling real estate, a business broker makes a living selling businesses.

Business brokers — or *intermediaries* — provide a number of services:

- Establish a confidential selling process
- Maintain an inventory of businesses for sale
- Assist in determining a fair market value of a business
- Work with potential buyers
- Help clients negotiate and structure their offers
- Assist through the close

You'd hire a business broker for similar reasons that you'd hire a real estate broker:

- **Technical expertise:** Business brokers understand the process. They also understand the pros and cons of most businesses because they've seen a number of similar businesses throughout their career.

  The trick here is to find a broker you can trust. When you've done that, the broker can take a lot of mystery out of the process and a lot of risk out of the purchase.

- **Emotional noninvolvement:** The broker serves as a middleman between buyer and seller. As everyone who has ever bought or sold a business knows, the process can get quite emotional.

- **An ability to see the deal from both sides:** You can bet there will be two points of view!

You can find business brokers by asking tax, legal, and business consultants for good brokers they may know. Ads for businesses for sale may lead you to a broker as well. If you've found a broker you think you'd like to work with, check references from other buyers who have worked with the broker. Be sure that the broker works full-time at his profession and has solid experience. Some business brokers dabble in it part-time and make their living other ways. These brokers may lack focus and experience.

Unfortunately, the pitfalls of working with business brokers are numerous:

- **Commission conflicts:** Brokers aren't business advisors; they're salespeople. That fact doesn't make them corrupt or dishonest, but it does mean that their interests aren't always aligned with yours. Their incentive is to do a deal and do the deal soon — and the more you pay, the more they make.

Business brokers typically get paid 8 to 10 percent of the sales price of the business. Technically, the seller pays this fee, but as with real estate brokers, the buyer effectively pays, too, because the seller will build the commission into the price.

If a broker isn't involved, the seller can sell for a lower price and still clear more money, and the buyer is better off, too.

✔ **Selling undesirable businesses:** Problem and marginal businesses are everywhere, but a fair number end up with brokers. The reason: The owners had trouble selling them on their own.

✔ **Deceiving packaging:** This problem relates to the previous two potential pitfalls. Brokers help not-so-hot businesses look better than they really are. Doing so may involve out-and-out deception, but more typically it involves stretching the truth — that is, omitting negatives and hyping potential. (Owners selling their business themselves may do these things as well.)

You (and your advisors) need to exercise due diligence on the business you're thinking of buying. Never, ever trust or use the selling package a broker (or an owner) prepares for a business as your sole source of information. Unscrupulous brokers, as well as unscrupulous sellers, can stretch the truth, lie, and commit fraud. (See Chapter 8 for more on how to evaluate a business.)

✔ **Access to limited inventory:** Unlike a real estate broker who typically has access, through a shared listing service, to almost all the homes currently for sale in a particular area, a business broker can tell you only about his office's listings. Confidentiality is an issue, as a shared listing service increases the number of people who can find out that a business is for sale and the particulars of the sale, which may hurt future business or cause a key employee exodus.

If you plan to work with a business broker, use more than one. Working with a larger business brokerage firm or one that specializes in listing the type of business you're looking for can maximize the number of possible prospects you see. In some areas, brokerages pool listings to allow access.

✔ **Few licensing requirements:** Unlike real estate agents in most states, the federal government doesn't regulate the business brokerage field and requires no official licensing. The majority of states have no requirements — anyone can hang out a shingle and work as a business broker. Some states require real estate licenses of business brokers who operate in their states. Real estate transactions or leases are part of many business deals. Some states allow those with securities brokerage licenses to operate as business brokers.

Business brokers generally sell smaller small businesses — those with less than $1 million in sales annually. These businesses tend to be family owned or sole proprietorships, such as restaurants, dry cleaners, other retailers, service firms, and small manufacturers and wholesalers. Approximately half of such small businesses are sold through brokers.

Most business brokerage firms sell different types of businesses. Some firms, however, specialize in only one industry or a few industries. If you don't have your heart set on buying a particular type of business — a doughnut shop, for example — one advantage of working with brokers is that they can expose you to other businesses you may not have considered. Brokers can also share their knowledge about some of your ideas — like the fact that you need to get up at 2 a.m. to make doughnuts if you buy a doughnut shop. Still want to buy one?

When evaluating brokers, ask for the names of several buyers the broker has worked with in the past six months. Ask for buyers of businesses in your field of interest so that brokers can't simply refer you to the three best deals of their careers. Also, check with the local Better Business Bureau and any state regulatory department (for example, real estate, attorney general, or department of corporations) that oversees business brokers to see whether complaints have been filed against the brokerage.

Considering a Franchise

Among the types of businesses that you can purchase are franchise operations. Some companies increase the number of their locations by selling replicas, or *franchises,* of their business. When you purchase a franchise, you buy the local rights within a specified geographic area to sell the company's products or services under the company's name and to use the company's system of operation. In addition to an upfront franchisee fee, franchisers typically charge an ongoing royalty (percentage of sales).

As a consumer, you've likely done business with franchises. Franchising is a huge part of the business world. Companies that franchise — such as McDonald's, H&R Block, Subway, and FootLocker — account for about $1 trillion in sales annually. Purchasing a good franchise can be a more-expensive but relatively safer ticket into the world of small-business ownership.

Franchise advantages

Unlike buying other businesses, when you purchase a franchise, you don't buy an existing enterprise. Although the parent company should have a track record and multiple locations with customers, you start from scratch if you purchase a new franchise (unless you purchase an existing franchise directly from owners interested in selling). As the proud owner of a new franchise, you don't have customers. As with starting any new business, you must recruit your customers.

So why would you want to pay a chunk of money to buy a business without customers? Actually, you should consider purchasing a good franchise for the same reasons that you would purchase other solid, established businesses. A company that has been in business for a number of years and has successful franchisees proves the demand for the company's products and services and that its system for providing those products and services works. The company has worked the bugs out, developed marketing programs that work, and hopefully solved common problems. As a franchise owner, you benefit from and share in the experience that the parent company has gained over the years.

Franchises offer two additional advantages that most other small businesses don't:

- ✔ **A larger and successful franchise company has brand-name recognition.** In other words, consumers recognize the company name and may be more inclined to purchase its products and services. Or stated another way, the franchiser has already done the marketing and public relations. When you purchase the franchise, you're buying into the results of those efforts.

- ✔ **A franchise offers centralized purchasing advantages.** As you'd hope and expect from a corporation made up of so many locations, the franchise can buy supplies and accessories at an extremely low price. Such volume-purchasing generally leads to bigger discounts to customers and bigger profit margins to franchise holders. In addition to possibly saving franchisees money on supplies, the parent company can take the hassle out of figuring out where and how to purchase supplies.

Franchise disadvantages

Franchises aren't for everyone. As with purchasing any other small business, pitfalls abound in buying franchises. Some common problems that you should watch for include the following:

- ✔ **You may not be the franchise type.** When you buy a franchise, you buy into a system that the franchiser has created for you. People who like structure and following established rules and systems more easily adapt to the franchise life. But if you're the creative and free-wheeling sort (that is, the typical entrepreneur) who likes to experiment and change things to keep life interesting, you'd probably be an unhappy franchisee.

  Unlike starting your own business in which you may get into the game without investing a lot of time and money, buying a business that ends up not being what you want can be a more expensive learning experience. For example, you may discover that you don't like being on the phone and dealing with the public after shelling out significant money to purchase a travel-agency franchise.

- ✔ **You're required to buy overpriced supplies.** Centralized, bulk purchasing through the corporate headquarters is supposed to save franchisees time and money on supplies and other expenditures. Some franchisers, however, attempt to make big profit margins through large markups on the proprietary items that they contractually obligate franchisees to buy from them.

✔ **The franchise may be unproven.** One of the problems with buying a franchise is that you may not be buying an ongoing, established business complete with customers. If the concept has not stood the test of time and survived the experiences of other franchisees, you don't want to be a guinea pig as an early franchisee. And some franchisers are more interested in simply selling franchises to collect the upfront franchise money. Reputable franchisers want to help their franchisees succeed so that they can collect an ongoing royalty from the franchisees' sales.

✔ **The franchise may be a pyramid scheme.** Unscrupulous, short-term-focused business owners sometimes attempt to franchise their business and sell as many franchises as quickly as possible. Some even have their franchisees sell franchises and share the loot with them. Everything becomes focused on selling franchises rather than operating a business that sells a product or service intended to satisfy customers. In rare cases, franchisers engage in fraud and sell next to nothing, except the false hope of getting rich quick. (See the following section for more on these schemes.)

Evaluating Multilevel Marketing (MLM) Firms

A twist, and in many cases a bad one, to the franchising idea (see preceding section) is a *multilevel marketing* (MLM) company. Multilevel marketing is designed to replace the retail store as a conduit for selling certain products. Advocates of the MLM business model maintain that, when given identical products, the one sold face to face (without the cost of maintaining a storefront and hiring employees and paying insurance) is less expensive than the same product sold in a store. Additionally, MLM advocates believe that buying a product from someone you know and trust makes more sense than buying from a clerk behind a retail counter.

Sometimes known as *network companies,* MLMs can be thought of as a poor person's franchise. For those weary of traditional jobs, the appeal is obvious. Work at home, part-time, with no employees and no experience necessary, and make big bucks. We've heard claims that you can make tens of thousands of dollars per month for just a few hours per week.

Representatives for an MLM, who are treated as independent contractors, work to solicit new customers as well as to recruit new representatives, known in the industry as your *down line.* The big selling point is that you make money not only off your own customers but also off the business that your down-line recruits bring in.

Being wary of pyramid schemes

The number-one trait of MLM that leads to its all-too-frequent excesses is that everyone can get in for little money up front; thus, everyone does get in. And we do mean everyone — hence, MLM's oftentimes shaky reputation.

The problem is that the worst of the MLMs are the equivalent of a pyramid scheme. They offer no legitimate service or product and exist solely to "sign up" as many reps as they can before someone realizes that the castle has been built on a cloud — at which point they take the money and run.

MLMs have been known to offer the pitch that you can make tens of thousands of dollars monthly while sitting on your duff and letting someone else do the work. All you have to do is sign up a few friends and relatives to sell the company's widgets. Then, before you can shout the words "easy money," the big bucks come rolling in. We know many people who have been taken for thousands of dollars in multilevel marketing schemes; all they found was a quick way to lose money and to alienate friends and relatives.

Anyone considering becoming an MLM investor should keep in mind that any network marketing arrangement is really just another form of a job. No company, MLM or otherwise, can offer to pay you money while you're busy watching the soaps. As with any other worthwhile venture, time — three to five years, in most cases — and a lot of hard work are required to create a business that will provide you with a decent living. If the MLM business were as simple as some in the business would lead you to believe, everyone would dive in and get rich.

For sure, some legitimate and successful companies are MLMs — Mary Kay and Tupperware, for example. However, they're the exception rather than the rule, particularly among the types of MLMs that you're likely to have aggressively pitched to you by others.

Finding the better MLMs

Quality MLM companies make sense for people who really believe in and want to sell a particular product or service and don't want to or can't tie up a lot of money buying a franchise or other business. Just remember to check out the MLM company, and remember that you won't get rich in a hurry, or possibly ever. Capitalism has taught us over the years that whatever looks too good to be true usually is. Be sure to check the references of the MLM company that you're considering.

Remember that due diligence requires digging for facts and talking to people who don't have a bias or reason to sell to you. Do the same homework that we recommend in Chapter 8 when thinking about buying into an MLM firm. Assume that an MLM company isn't worth pursuing until your due diligence proves otherwise.

Legitimate MLMs put as much emphasis, if not more, on the products or services they offer, and they don't claim that you'll make a killing without working hard to find new customers. Although not shy about advertising the big earnings its successful salespeople make, Mary Kay doesn't hype the income potential. Local sales directors typically earn $50,000 to $100,000 per year, but this income comes after years, not weeks or months, of hard work. Mary Kay rewards top sellers with gifts, such as the coveted pink Cadillac.

The ingredients for Mary Kay's success include competitive pricing, personal attention, and social interaction, which many stores don't or can't offer their customers. "We make shopping and life fun . . . we make people look and feel good," says one of Mary Kay's sales directors.

Mary Kay encourages prospective reps to try the products first and host a group before they sign up and spend approximately $100 to purchase a showcase of items to sell. To maximize sales, Mary Kay representatives are encouraged to keep a ready inventory because customers tend to buy more when products are immediately available. If reps want out of the business, they can sell the inventory back to the company at 90 cents on the dollar originally paid, a good sign that the company stands behind its product.

If you do decide to buy into an MLM that seems reputable, think twice before signing up relatives, friends, and co-workers in your MLM venture — at least until you're satisfied that the concept is a viable one. The particular danger in doing business with people you care for, and who care for you, is that, in addition to your reputation and integrity, your friendships and family relations are also on the line.

Checking Out Work-from-Home Opportunities

Ads promoting ways to make piles of cash while working out of your home are easy to find these days, especially in the magazines that cater to small-business owners and wannabes and through e-mail spam solicitations. They read something like this:

> "Earn $10,000 monthly! We'll even help you hire agents to do the work for you. . . . FREE! Thirty days is all that it takes!"

"FIRE YOUR BOSS AND DOUBLE YOUR INCOME! Earn $2,000 to $5,000 weekly — starting within 3 to 6 weeks. Own your own business. Control your destiny! Work from home! No overhead; no employees; no commute! 55 to 70 percent + profit margins."

"Work out of your home. Company needs help. Earn $500 to $900 per week. Anyone can do this — will train. Full-time or part-time. Only for the serious — please!"

"Earn $4,000 per month on the new instant information superhighway."

And so the refrain goes. In many cases, these ads are just another form of overhyped multilevel marketing scam and should be avoided. In these and other similar ads, no legitimate company may exist, but rather, you'll find a person or two with a post office or e-mail box somewhere who wants to sell you a package of "confidential information" explaining the business opportunity du jour. This package of confidential information may cost several hundred dollars or more. More often than not, this information ends up being worthless marketing propaganda and is rarely useful.

Our advice? Read this book and tap the other helpful resources we list in it to understand more about legitimate small-business opportunities. You'll find more and better information, and the price will be far lower.

And remember one more thing on such money-making, can't-miss "opportunities": Never buy into one that's pitched over the telephone or that requires a nonrefundable cash outlay — unless, that is, you want to lighten your pocketbook and feel like a doofus.

Myriad opportunities are available in today's fast-paced entrepreneurial economy. The best ones will come from studying your local economic environment, from discovering a niche from within your current job, or from your exhaustive research of the business community as a whole. Beware of those "opportunities" that promise overnight success. And beware of those "opportunities" that promise you something for nothing.

Chapter 8

Evaluating a Business to Buy

. . . .

In This Chapter

▶ Executing a pre-offer evaluation

▶ Analyzing financial statements

▶ Considering the unique issues in franchises

▶ Assessing what needs changing in the business

. . . .

*I*n the American legal system, a person is presumed innocent until proven guilty beyond a reasonable doubt. When you're purchasing a business, however, you should assume, until proven otherwise, that the selling business owner is guilty of making the business appear better than it really is.

We don't want to sound cynical, but more than a few owners out there try to make their businesses look more profitable, more financially healthy, and more desirable than they really are. The reason is quite simple: Business sellers generally seek to maximize the price their business will command. So, don't trust only your gut when evaluating a business, because you could be fooled.

Buying a business can be tricky because the business brokerage market rarely favors the buyer. The following list presents some of the obstacles you're likely to encounter when buying a business:

✔ **The necessary confidentiality of transactions:** You can't publicly investigate a lot of the background information.

✔ **Few listings:** A paucity of businesses for sale means that the seller is in control. For good businesses that are fairly priced, there are usually plenty of potential buyers waiting in the wings.

✔ **Unpublished prices of previous sales:** There are no benchmarks. No templates to follow.

✔ **Emotional circumstances surrounding the sale:** People can get more emotional about selling their business than they do about selling real estate. Blood, sweat, retirement, and yes, egos, are involved. Emotions run high, on both sides.

Buying a business is a long, detail-ridden, and stressful procedure. Don't rush it; be sure to cover your bases. We hit all the key points of consideration in this chapter.

Kicking the Tires

Before you make an offer to buy a small business, you're going to want to do some digging into the company to minimize your chances of mistakenly buying a problematic business or overpaying for a good business. This process is known as *due diligence,* and it is every bit as important as hiring an attorney or signing the purchase agreement.

Smart buyers build plenty of contingencies into a purchase offer for a small business, just as they do when buying a home or other real estate. If your financing doesn't come through or you find some dirty laundry in the business (and you're not buying a laundromat), contingencies allow you to back out of the deal legally. However, knowing that you'll draft all purchase offers with plenty of contingencies shouldn't encourage you to make a purchase offer casually. Making an offer and doing the necessary research and homework is costly, in both time and money.

Before making an offer for a business, you'll want reasonably clear answers to the important due diligence questions discussed in the upcoming sections.

Examining Owners' and Key Employees' Backgrounds

A business is usually only as good or bad as the owners and key employees running it. Ethical, business-savvy owners and key employees generally run successful businesses worthy of buying. Unscrupulous, marginally competent, or incompetent business owners and key employees are indicative of businesses that you should avoid.

Just as you wouldn't (we hope) hire employees without reviewing their resumes, interviewing them, and checking employment references, you shouldn't make an offer to buy a business until you do similar homework on the owners and key employees of the business for sale.

Buyer beware

Consider Katie's unfortunate story. Katie made a gut-level decision when she decided to buy a restaurant from a silver-haired, distinguished-looking gentleman named Max. Well-dressed, well-educated, well-traveled, and well-versed in his wines, Max charmed the socks off Katie, flattering her about how successfully she could run his restaurant. (His French accent didn't hurt either.)

Max's "fact sheet" on the business was also impressive. It showed, over a period of several years, steadily increasing revenue and even more rapidly increasing profits for the restaurant. In the 12 months before the negotiations, the restaurant grossed in excess of $500,000 and had pretax profits of about $150,000.

A wine collector and food connoisseur, Katie had always dreamed of running her own restaurant. But she wanted no part of the grunt work of a start-up: developing a complete menu from scratch, negotiating a lease on a good location, advertising for and interviewing prospective employees, and so on. However, with a recently received inheritance, Katie could now afford to bypass the start-up stage and purchase an established restaurant such as the one Max offered for sale.

After just a couple of offers and counteroffers, Katie slapped down cash for the whole business. Max turned over the restaurant, hailed a cab for the airport, and headed for a retirement cottage in the south of France.

The first few months, business seemed a little slower than Katie had anticipated, but, overall, things seemed to be going okay. However, by the end of the first year, Katie found that she had serious problems.

First, expenses were higher and revenues lower than Max's historic financial statements had indicated they would be. For the first full year

under Katie's ownership, the restaurant grossed around $300,000, which, after expenses, was just barely enough to break even.

Second, Katie ended up with lease problems. In her tenth month of ownership, the owner of the building that housed Katie's restaurant politely informed her that the restaurant's lease was about to expire; when it did, he was going to increase the rent 300 percent. Katie couldn't believe it. Max never mentioned that the lease was about to expire or that he had negotiated a rate well below market value a long time ago and that it was bound to jump up when it did expire.

To make a long story short and to spare you the agonizing details of what Katie discovered in the ensuing months and years, Katie's restaurant eventually dragged her into personal bankruptcy. As it turns out, when Max was preparing the financial statements for Katie, he exercised quite a bit of, how shall we say it, "creative license" — also known as Enroning your financials.

Katie was never able to track Max down in France. If she had found him, she could have tried to sue him for misrepresenting the business's profitability. Of course, that's probably why Max did such a good job covering his tracks.

Although somewhat extreme, problems of the magnitude left hidden in Katie's restaurant aren't that unusual among businesses for sale. Don't expect the business seller to point out the cracks in the foundation; you have to hunt for them yourself. (In Katie's case, Max's financial shenanigans would've easily been discovered with the proper amount of due diligence.)

Until you prove to yourself beyond a reasonable doubt that negative surprises don't exist, you shouldn't go through with a business purchase.

Here's a short list of information we suggest gathering as well as suggestions on how to find it:

- ✔ **Business background:** Request and review the owner's and key employees' resumes, remembering that some people may fabricate or puff up information on that piece of paper. Are the backgrounds impressive and filled with relevant business experience? Just as you should do when hiring an employee, check resumes to make sure that the information they provide is correct. Glaring omissions or inaccuracies send a strong negative message as to the kind of people you're dealing with.

- ✔ **Personal reputations in the business community:** The geographic and work/professional communities to which we belong are quite small. Any business that has been up and running for a number of years has had interactions with many people and other companies.

  Take the time to talk to others who may have had experience dealing with the business for sale (vendors, Chamber of Commerce, Better Business Bureau, and so on) and ask them their thoughts on the company's owners and key employees. Of course, we shouldn't need to remind you that you can't always accept the statements of others at face value. You have to consider the merits, or lack thereof, of the source.

- ✔ **Credit history:** If you were a banker, we hope you wouldn't lend money to anyone without first assessing their credit risk. At a minimum, you should review the seller's credit history to see how successful they've been at paying off, on time, money they've borrowed. Even though you won't be lending money to the business seller you're speaking with, we recommend that you check his credit records. A problematic credit record could uncover business problems the owner had that he may be less than forthcoming in revealing. The major agencies which compile and sell personal credit histories and small-business information are Experian (www.experian.com), Equifax (www.equifax.com), Transunion (www.transunion.com), and Dun & Bradstreet (800-234-3867; www.dnb.com).

- ✔ **Key customers:** The people who can usually give you the best indication of the value of a business for sale are its current customers. Through your own research on the business or from the current owner, get a list of the company's top five to ten customers and ask them the following questions:

  - In general, how is the company perceived by its customers?

  - Does it deliver on time?

  - How do its products or services compare to its competitors' offerings?

  - Does it have a culture of integrity?

  - What does the company do best?

  - What does it need to improve?

✔ **Key employees:** If the employees of the business for sale are aware of the prospects of the impending sale, be sure to interview them and get their insider's take on the condition of the business. You also want to know whether they intend to remain as employees under the new owner-ship. (If Katie, in the earlier "Buyer beware" sidebar, had interviewed the restaurant's employees, she surely would've found out about Max's char-acter and credibility shortcomings, and maybe even gained an insight into the false revenue figures he presented.)

Finding Out Why the Owner Is Selling

After you locate a potentially attractive business for sale, the serious work begins. First, try to discover the reason the owner is selling. Small-business owners may be selling for a reason that shouldn't matter to you (they've reached the age and financial status where they simply want to retire), or they may be selling for reasons that should matter to you (the business is a never-ending headache to run, it isn't very profitable, or competition is changing the competitive landscape).

If an owner wants to sell for some negative reason, that shouldn't necessarily sour you on buying the business. If the business has a low level of profitability, it isn't necessarily a lemon — quite possibly the current owner hasn't taken the proper steps (such as cost management, effective marketing, and so on) to boost its profitability. You may well be able to overcome hurdles the current owner can't. But before you make a purchase offer and then follow through on that offer, you absolutely, positively should understand many aspects of the business including, first and foremost, why the current owner wants out.

Here's how to discover why the current owner is selling (where appropriate, get the current owner's permission to speak with certain people):

✔ **Chat with the owner.** Okay, so this isn't a terribly creative, Sherlock Holmes–type method, and yes, we know that many sellers aren't going to be completely candid about why they are selling, but you never know. Besides, you can verify the answer you get from the owner against what other sources tell you about the owner's motivations to sell.

✔ **Talk with the business owner's advisors.** As we explain throughout this chapter, in the course of evaluating the worth of a business, you should be speaking with various advisors, including those you hire yourself. Don't overlook, however, the wealth of information and background that the cur-rent owner's advisors have. These advisors may include lawyers, accoun-tants, bankers, and/or the business's own board of advisors or directors.

✔ **Confer with industry sources.** Most industries are closely knit groups of companies, each one knowing, in general, what's going on with the other businesses in the same industry. Most importantly, the vendor salespeople or manufacturers' representatives who call on the industry can be a terrific source for information. Sure, they may not be completely candid, but your job is to read between the lines of what they have to say. (They generally won't out-and-out lie to you either. They're aware that you could be their next customer.)

- **Seek out customers.** The business's current customers usually have a good idea of why a business is for sale; they can provide you with the information you need to determine whether the current owner is selling from strength or from weakness.

- **Discuss with employees.** Some employees probably know the real answer as to why the business is for sale. Your job: Find out what they know.

Knowing how to tell whether a seller is motivated

Imagine that you're in the market to buy a home. In the course of touring houses for sale in a neighborhood you'd like to live in, you discover two houses — one on Elm Street and the other on Oak Street — that meet your wish list of criteria. Both houses have the right amount of space and good-sized yards and are located on quiet streets. In all other respects, the two houses are similar, and your analysis of comparable house sales in the neighborhood indicates that each house is worth about $240,000.

The Elm Street house is priced at $299,000, and the Oak Street house is priced at $249,000. The owner of the Oak Street house has already had the house inspected, has provided a copy of the inspection report, and has offered to correct the problematic items in the report at his cost. You also notice that the Oak Street house has been cleaned up both inside and out and looks ready to move into.

Now, assuming that you like both houses equally well, which house would you be more interested in making an offer on? It should be no contest. Clearly, the Oak Street house owner is more motivated and serious about selling. You can tell this not only from the more realistic asking price put on the house but also from all the time, effort, and money put into getting the house ready to sell.

So, when you're shopping for a small business to buy, you should be looking for similar ways to identify a motivated seller. Just as with real estate, a significant portion of small-business sellers aren't serious or motivated about selling. And just as with some house sellers who don't need to sell, some small-business owners stick a high price on their business and are willing to sell only if some salivating pushover comes along and is willing to (over)pay.

Other small-business owners aren't really emotionally ready yet to part with their "babies." If you follow our advice in this chapter, you won't be anyone's fool because you'll know how to value a business for sale and how to identify whether the owner is motivated to sell.

In your discussions with and investigations about the current owner, also reflect upon these final, critical questions: How important is the current owner to the success of the business? What will happen when he or she is no longer around? Will the business under new management lose key employees, key customers, and so on?

Surveying the Company Culture

When you buy a small business, you're adopting someone else's child. Depending on the strength of its already-formed personality and how it meshes with yours, you may or may not be successful in molding that business into your image.

Larry was an MBA from one of the nation's top business schools. He thought he could make a bundle of money buying a small manufacturing company and running it better than its current owners. With his blue-chip credentials, he thought running the company would be a snap. So, Larry purchased the company with a 35 percent down payment of the purchase price, with the seller carrying a note for the balance.

Larry's first task was to clean house of the "deadwood," firing key employees so that he could replace them with people who would better measure up to his high standards. Larry made his downsizing decisions after just a couple of weeks on the job. Larry didn't seem to know (or perhaps didn't care) that the company had a history and culture of respect for its employees. Even during slow economic times, previous management hadn't let people go but instead scaled back hours of operation.

Not surprisingly, after nearly 20 percent of the staff was gone, Larry had earned himself the reputation as the "grim reaper" because many of Larry's new hires couldn't do the jobs as well as the previous job holders who had been fired. The original staff that remained, not surprisingly, feared for their jobs; thought Larry was callous, incompetent, and uncaring (all of which were probably true); and worried about the future of the company. Many of the best remaining employees had updated their resumes and were actively seeking employment elsewhere. Gradually, most of the good employees who had survived Larry's initial bloodlettings quit as the company went into a financial tailspin. Eventually, Larry himself had to move on.

What is the point of this story? What should Larry have done differently?

 ✔ **Before buying the company, Larry should've taken the time to understand the company's culture.** Changing employees may not be impossible in the company you buy, but attempting to change the culture, especially in such a short period of time, is a too-often-fatal endeavor. Cultures are a sensitive business asset and should be treated accordingly. Larry should've spent more time both before he bought the business as well as after his purchase in assessing and considering the company's culture.

✔ **Larry should've known that preconceived notions rarely withstand the scrutiny of day-to-day operations.** Buying and running a company isn't as easy as people like Larry may think. An MBA from a top business school and specific work experience don't come close to guaranteeing success when buying and managing a business. Larry should have maintained the company as it had been run until he studied and learned its real strengths and weaknesses, knew the business well enough to recognize the skills of the employees, and could formulate an informed plan to move the company forward.

Inspecting the Financial Statements

We explain in Chapter 13 the ins and outs of the various financial statements — including the balance sheet and income statement, also known as the profit and loss statement. If you're unfamiliar with those statements, you're going to be at a huge disadvantage in evaluating businesses for sale. The following sections explain what to look for and what to look out for in the income statement and balance sheet.

Interpreting the income statement

A company's *income statement* details profits, which are simply revenues minus expenses. *Revenues* are the money that the company receives from its customers as payment for its products or services.

Expenses are the company's costs of doing business. Just as much of your personal income or revenue goes toward income taxes, housing, food, and clothing, company expenses use up much and sometimes all of a company's revenue.

When considering buying a business, take the time to examine the following issues on the company's income statement:

✔ **The owner's salary and bonuses:** Of utmost importance when computing the profitability of any business is the determination of how much money the current owner is (or has been) taking out of it. The profitability of the business may look large at first glance, but the owner may be paying himself little in order to fatten the bottom line. Or the owner may be taking out excessive salary and bonuses, minimizing the business's profitability in the process.

✔ **Change in revenues over time:** Examine at least the last three years of income statements. Do you see a steady or increasing rate of growth in a company's revenues? If a company's revenues are growing slowly or shrinking, that raises the important question, "Why?" Is it because of poor service or product performance, better competitor offerings, ineffective marketing, or an owner who is financially set and unmotivated to grow the business? Before you buy is the time to find out.

✔ **Revenues by product line:** For companies with multiple divisions or product lines, ask for the revenue details of each product line. Find out what's spurring, or holding back, the company's overall growth. One red flag is businesses that were acquired but don't really fit with the company's other business units. Some larger small companies that are struggling to build revenues sometimes try to "enter" new businesses through acquisition, but then they don't manage them well because they don't understand the keys to success in those businesses.

✔ **Revenues by individual stores:** With retail stores, such as a picture-framing enterprise that has multiple locations, examine the revenues on a store-by-store basis. If the business has been opening new sites, also determine the change in revenues that has resulted from opening new locations versus the change at existing locations. A company can show overall revenue growth by simply adding new stores while the existing locations may actually be experiencing declining revenues.

✔ **Expense detail:** To help you identify which expense categories are growing and which are shrinking over time, take a look at the expense categories for the past three years and calculate what percentage each category is of the company's revenue. As a well-managed and financially healthy company grows, expenses as a percentage of revenues should decrease. Not all expense categories necessarily decrease. Research and development, for example, may be expanding in a company awash in revenues.

✔ **The bottom line:** The net result of revenues increasing faster than expenses is a fatter *bottom line* (the last line of the income statement that indicates net profits or losses after taxes). When you examine how a company's profits change relative to total revenue received, focus on *operating income,* which is net income from operations before one-time write-ups or write-downs. (Sometimes companies experience one-time, revenue-enhancing events that can change profits temporarily.)

Even healthy, growing businesses can get into trouble if their expenses balloon faster than their revenues. Well-managed companies stay on top of their expenses during good and bad times. Unfortunately, it's easier for companies to get sloppy during good times. So, don't be fooled into thinking that all is well financially just because a company's revenues have been increasing.

✓ **Other expenses:** Thoroughly examine other expense items — such as automobile expenses, club memberships, and travel and entertainment — for insight as to how the business has spent its money in the past. You may unearth fat that, if you're successful in cutting, could almost immediately improve your bottom line as the new owner.

A term you may come across when you're dealing with attorneys, accountants, business brokers, or sophisticated buyers is EBITDA. *EBITDA* is an acronym that stands for Earnings Before Interest, Taxes, Depreciation, And Amortization. Many business sales will be made on the basis of EBITDA earnings rather than net income. Be sure to be aware of which of the two methods you'll be using in determining the value of the business.

Reviewing the balance sheet

A *balance sheet* is a snapshot-in-time summary of a company's assets and liabilities. This report is typically prepared as of the last day of the company's fiscal year-end, which for most companies is December 31. (Some companies have a fiscal year that ends at a different time of the year.)

Audited and unaudited financial statements

In your initial evaluation of a potential business to purchase, you will be handed (at your request) the company's financial statements. Some business owners will be reluctant (usually due to concerns about confidentiality or because they may not be convinced yet that you're a serious buyer) to release too much financial data.

You may be asked to sign what's called a *nondisclosure agreement* (NDA), which legally binds you to keep confidential any information that the company shares. NDAs are fine as long as signing one doesn't tie your hands from evaluating similar businesses for sale, including those that compete with the one under consideration. Don't sign an NDA without your attorney's consent.

If the financial statements you're handed haven't been independently audited by a reputable accounting firm, be extremely cautious

in assuming accuracy and honesty in the statements. In the "Buyer beware" sidebar earlier in this chapter, had Katie demanded that Max's financial statements be audited by a reputable accounting firm, either she wouldn't have bought the company or she wouldn't have paid the high price that she did. And don't take the financial statements at face value simply because they're audited. The accountant who did the audit could be incompetent or chummy with the seller.

An excellent way to uncover inflated profitability as reported on the financial statements that the current business owner shares with you is to ask the seller for a copy of the business's income tax returns. Owners are more likely to try to minimize reported revenue and maximize expenses on their tax return to keep from paying more tax.

The assets section of the balance sheet summarizes what the company holds or owns that is of significant value. The liabilities section details what the company owes to others.

Here are several key things to look for and to look out for when reviewing a company's balance sheet:

✔ **Accounts receivable (also known as *receivables*):** This is money that's owed to a company for products or services already sold but not yet paid for. As companies grow, so, too, do their receivables (typically). Be on the lookout, however, for accounts receivables growing at a faster rate than the company's revenues. (In other words, its receivables are becoming a larger portion or percentage of the company's revenues.) Bloated receivables may indicate that the company is having problems with the quality of its product or pricing. Dissatisfied customers pay more slowly and/or haggle for bigger discounts. Out-of-proportion receivables may also indicate that the company's customers are having financial problems of their own. Be sure to ask for the business's *accounts receivable aging* — a listing of the monies owed the company accompanied by the length of time the bills have gone uncollected.

If the business doesn't maintain an aging, it's a red flag unless all its customers are paid to date.

✔ **Property and equipment:** All companies require equipment, such as office furniture, computers, and so on, also known as *fixed assets*. Manufacturing companies also own machinery for making their products. Equipment becomes less valuable as it becomes more obsolete over time. This *depreciation of fixed assets* is charged against profits by the company as a cost of doing business each year. Thus, even if a company ceases buying new equipment, its balance sheet will continue to show fixed asset charges — not for purchases but for depreciation of the value of property and equipment. As depreciation is subtracted from the value of the equipment, the amount shown for fixed assets on the balance sheet will gradually decrease.

If a company hasn't been periodically upgrading its equipment, you could get stuck buying a company needing a lot of costly new equipment. When a company's balance sheet indicates a continual decline in the bookkeeping value of the company's equipment, beware that the company may simply be deferring new equipment purchases. Inspect the company's equipment and talk with others familiar with the type of business so that you can understand how out-of-date the equipment in the business really is and how much you're likely to expend on replacement equipment down the road if you buy the business.

✔ **Inventory:** The balance sheets of manufacturing and retail companies should detail *inventory,* which is simply the cost of the products that have not yet been sold. As a business expands over time, inventory should follow suit. However, beware if you see inventory increasing faster than revenues because it may signal several problems, including customers scaling back on purchases, poor management, or an obsolete or inferior product offering. Inventory is the most dangerous asset of all because a swollen inventory often represents cash that can't be redeemed.

✔ **Accounts payable:** When companies purchase supplies, equipment, or products for resale for their business, they generally have some time to pay the bills. Similar to inventory and accounts receivable, accounts payable (which is on the liability side of a company's balance sheet) usually increases in tune with a company's increasing revenues. If accounts payable is growing faster than revenues, it may or may not indicate financial trouble. The increase may simply be good financial management (the slower a company is with paying bills, the longer the funds are in the corporate accounts drawing interest). On the other hand, if the company is struggling to make ends meet, an accumulation of accounts payable can occur and can be an early warning sign of financial trouble.

✔ **Debt:** *Debt,* both short term and long term, is money that the company has borrowed and must someday pay back. Footnotes to the financial statements generally detail the terms of the debt, such as when the debt is to be paid back. In Chapter 13, we explain important ratios and calculations that can assist you with sizing up the amount and type of debt a company is carrying.

✔ **Other assets:** This catchall category is for the other assets of the company and can include stuff that will make your eyes glaze over. For example, companies keep a different (yes, this is legal) set of books for tax purposes. Not surprisingly, companies do this because the IRS allows, in some cases, more deductions than what the company is required to show from an accounting standpoint on its financial statements. (If you were a company, wouldn't you want your shareholders, but not the IRS, to see gobs of profits?) The benefit of deferring taxes is treated as an asset until the IRS gets more of its share down the road.

Even if you're competent in reading financial statements, never purchase a business without involving a good tax advisor to help you evaluate the value of the business and the financial terms of the transaction. Buying a business isn't the time to be relying on your own trial and error; be sure to involve someone in the buying process who can bring his or her experience to the table.

What are the "off-balance-sheet" assets worth?

The value of a company's assets includes not only tangible items, such as inventory, accounts receivable, furniture, fixtures, and equipment, but also *soft assets,* such as the firm's name and reputation with customers and suppliers, customer lists, patents, and so on. These soft assets are also known, in accounting jargon, as *goodwill.* In many cases, the value of this goodwill is greater than the value of the hard assets.

If you're seriously interested in making an offer to buy a particular business, you should assess whether the current customers of the business will continue to buy from the business after you take it over. You should also evaluate the quality of the key employees. How about the business's relationships with suppliers? In addition, check out the competition — does it seem formidable?

Ask key employees these questions:

✔ What do you like the most about your company? What do you like the least?

✔ How do you see the future of the company?

✔ Can the products or services be improved?

✔ What would be the first improvement you'd make if you owned the business?

Ask suppliers these questions:

✔ Does the company pay its bills on time?

✔ Do you get an inordinate amount of returns from them?

✔ Compared to other companies in the industry, how does the company treat its suppliers — as partners or as a necessary evil?

✔ If you could change one thing about the company, what would it be?

Some final points about goodwill: Companies work hard through advertising, product development, and service to attract and retain customers. Companies can't put a value on the goodwill they've generated, but when they purchase (acquire) another firm, some of the purchase price is considered goodwill. Specifically, if a company is acquired for $100 million yet has a net worth (assets minus liabilities) of just $50 million, the extra $50 million is considered to have gone to goodwill. This goodwill then becomes an asset, which, similar to equipment, is amortized (depreciated) over the years ahead. (Goodwill is amortized over 15 years while equipment is usually depreciated over 4 years.)

Uncovering Lease Contract Terms

A soon-to-expire lease at a low rate can ruin a business's profit margins. With a retail location, the ability to maintain a good location is critical as well.

Check *comparables* — that is, what similar locations lease for — to see whether the current lease rate is fair and talk to the building owner to discover his plans. Ask for and review (possibly with the help of a legal advisor) the current owner's lease contract. Pay extra careful attention to the provisions of the lease contracts that discuss what happens if the business is sold or its ownership changes.

Evaluating Special Franchise Issues

As we discuss in Chapter 7, buying a reputable franchise can be the right ticket into the small-business world. No matter what type of franchise you're buying, do plenty of homework before you agree to buy. The following sections describe steps to take and questions to ask when evaluating a franchise.

Don't skip any of these steps when evaluating a franchise opportunity. You may be most tempted to cut corners when reviewing a franchise from a long-established company. Don't. You may not be a good fit for the specific franchise, or perhaps the "successful" company has been good at keeping its franchisee problems under wraps.

Thoroughly review regulatory filings

The Federal Trade Commission (FTC) requires all franchisers to issue what's called the Uniform Franchise Offering Circular (UFOC) at least ten days before a prospective franchise buyer writes a check or signs a document to purchase. We recommend that you ask for this valuable document well before that deadline if you're seriously interested in a particular franchise.

Don't be put off by the size of the UFOC. Read the document cover to cover. The UFOC contains such valuable information as

✔ **The names and addresses of the ten geographically closest franchisees to the one you may buy, as well as a list of franchises that were terminated, not renewed, or bought back by the company.**

Speaking with franchisees for whom things didn't work out may help you uncover aspects of the business that are turnoffs for you. Now is not the time to stick your head in the sand about possible problems or drawbacks of a given franchise — finding out those downsides now is better than finding out after you've plunked down a chunk of your money, borrowed even more, and gone through a lot of work to buy a franchise.

✔ **Disclosure of pending or settled litigation, as well as a detailing of potential or actual troubles between franchisers and franchisees.**

✔ **The employment background of the senior management of the franchiser.**

✔ **The costs to the franchisee of purchasing a franchise, as well as required inventory, leases, and other costs.**

Evaluate the franchiser's motives

A good franchising company will want to check you out as much as you should want to check it out. Successful franchisers don't want to sell a franchise to someone who is likely to crash and burn and tarnish the reputation they've worked so hard to build. These companies know that their interests are aligned with yours — they make more money from ongoing royalties if they sell franchises to solid franchisees who are determined to be successful. At the outset of your investigation, ask yourself whether the franchisers are looking for a long-term business partner or simply the fast sale of another franchise.

Observe closely how the franchising company interacts with you. Be wary if the franchiser seems more interested in selling franchises than in finding and helping the most qualified franchisees succeed. Obviously, franchising representatives will be generally enthusiastic about their company. But a fine line exists between enthusiasm and a hard sell.

Run in the opposite direction if a franchiser tells tales of great riches from just a small investment of your time and money. Run extra fast if the franchiser is pressuring you into making a quick decision to buy and is evasive about providing detailed information about the business. And if the franchiser doesn't want to give you the UFOC, sprint!

Interview plenty of franchisees

Interview as many of the company's franchisees as is practical — both current owners as well as those who quit or were terminated (who should be listed in the UFOC). Skip the list of references eagerly provided by the franchise company and go to the lists of franchisees provided in the UFOC. Ask the franchisees what their experiences, both good and bad, have been with the parent company. Those franchisees for whom things didn't work out are generally more forthcoming about the warts of the system, but you should also try to identify whether some of these people were poor fits.

Conversely, active franchisees are more likely to see things through rose-colored glasses, if, for no other reason, than to reassure themselves on their decision to buy a franchise. If active franchisees are dissatisfied, steer clear. Observe which franchisees are happiest and most successful and see whether you share their business perspectives and traits.

Understand what you're buying and examine comparables

Most reputable franchises require you to plop down a chunk of cash to get started. Home-office-based service businesses may charge a $25,000 upfront franchise fee, compared to the several hundred thousand to a million dollars required for the bricks-and-mortar locations of established franchisers, such as McDonald's. Additionally, ongoing franchise royalties can range from 3 to 10 percent of gross revenue. The UFOC should detail all the upfront costs.

You should be asking the following questions: What are you receiving for these payments? Is the system and brand name really worth this fee? What kind of training will you receive? What kind of corporate headquarters management assistance is provided? What programs are in place to foster communications with other franchisees?

Few franchises are unique. Compare the cost of what a franchise is offering to the cost of purchasing franchises from different companies in the same business. For example, if you're considering the purchase of a franchise from Wendy's, compare the terms and offerings to those of McDonald's and Burger King.

If you look at the "best" franchises in a particular business and think, "Hey, I can do this as well or better and at less cost on my own," remember that you don't *have* to buy a franchise. Consider the start-up alternative. Be realistic, though, because many hidden costs — both out-of-pocket financial costs and costs in the form of time and energy — are involved in starting a business from scratch (see Chapter 3). And the franchise has a head start in name recognition and customer base.

Check with federal and state regulators

Franchises are generally regulated at both the federal and state levels. The FTC regulates nationally (877-382-4357; www.ftc.gov/bcp/menus/consumer/invest/business.shtm), and the state-level regulatory agency is usually called something like the "Department of Corporations" or the "Attorney General's Office." Check with these regulators to see whether complaints about a franchiser are on file.

The UFOC should also detail pending litigation against the company by disgruntled franchisees. For lesser-known franchises, you may also want to check with the Better Business Bureau in the city where the franchising company is headquartered to discover whether anything is on file.

Investigate the company's credit history

Just as you have a personal credit report on file, every business has a credit report that shows how the company has dealt with payments and debts owed to suppliers and creditors. The franchiser's credit report is a good indicator of how well they maintain its business relationships and how financially stable the franchiser is. Where the franchiser is publicly owned, obtain a copy of the company's annual report and Form 10-K. Examine the company's stock price over recent years.

Analyze and negotiate the franchise contract

If your digging has made you feel more, rather than less, comfortable with the franchise purchase, to move forward you'll need to get down to the nitty-gritty of the contract. Franchise contracts are usually long, tedious, and filled with legalese. Read the contract completely to get a sense of what you're getting yourself into. It's imperative that you have an attorney experienced with franchising agreements review the contract as well.

In addition to the financial terms, the franchise contract should specify how disputes are to be handled, what rights you have to sell the franchise in the future, and under what conditions the parent company can terminate the franchise. Make sure that you can live with and be happy with the nonfinancial as well as the financial terms in the contract.

Almost everything is negotiable. This is especially true with the lesser-known franchisers that are in the early stages of their business growth. Although some companies offer their best deal up front and refuse to engage in haggling, others don't initially put their best terms and conditions on the table, hoping that you'll simply sign and accept the inferior terms and conditions.

There is a saying that every buyer or seller of a business should remember: "You name the price, I'll name the terms." What this saying means is that the terms can be more important to the deal than the price. What if, for example, you buy a business that is somewhat overpriced, but you have to pay only 10 percent down, the interest rate on the balance is 2 percent, and you don't have to pay off the note for 30 years? In this example, the terms are much more important to the deal than the price.

Chapter 9

Negotiating Terms and Sealing the Deal

Ask yourself this important and hopefully revealing question: "How many businesses have I purchased in my lifetime?" If you're like most people we know, the answer is a big, fat zero.

Now, you're an intelligent and discerning person, as evidenced by the fact that you bought this book in order to help fill the gaps in your small-business knowledge! And we, as your humble authors, have high hopes that you'll gain a wealth of practical insights and knowledge by reading our book. However — and this is a most important however — we think that you'll benefit from retaining the services of experts with extensive small-business deal-making experience. (See Chapter 10 to find out how to track down good experts.)

Negotiating is a skill that improves with experience. Experienced advisors can help you inspect what you're buying and look for red flags in the company's financial statements. Advisors can also help structure the purchase to protect what you're buying and to gain maximum tax benefits. To get the best deal, you need to do a number of things well, the first of which is to put a value on the business you intend to buy. This chapter starts there and then moves on to cover deciding on the purchase price, doing your due diligence, and starting off strong after you become the owner.

Valuing the Business

When you begin exploring businesses for sale, you won't know what a given business is really worth. Thus, you'll risk overpaying for a given business, considering your lack of knowledge. However, with time and the right resources combined with investigative work, you can get a good handle on what a given business is worth, which may or may not be close to the owner's asking price. (For more on the search process, see Chapter 7.)

You can start by taking a cue from smart home buyers and real estate investors: In order to find out how much a property is really worth, consider *comparable sales* — that is, what other similar properties have sold for. Compared to business buyers, however, home buyers have it relatively easy. Real estate transactions are a matter of public record; small-business sales are not. You'll have to do extra sleuthing to find the specific price and terms of comparable businesses that have sold.

In the end, however, after you've done the math and developed a dollar value for the business, remember one thing: Similar to buying a house, the real worth of a business is what you, or someone else, will pay for it. A business isn't a car with a factory sticker price; it's a multidimensional, complicated organization of people, assets, and systems. Its true value is in the eyes of the beholder, and the beholder is you.

Exploring valuing methods: Multiple of earnings and book value

Many methods exist for valuing a business. Some are unnecessarily complicated; others won't provide you with sensible answers. For example, some advisors and business brokers advocate using a multiple of revenue to determine the value of a business — that is, if a business has $300,000 in revenues, it may be valued at $450,000 (a multiple of 1.5). However, revenue is a poor proxy for profitability. Two businesses in the same field can have identical revenue yet quite different profitability due to the efficiency of their operations, the pricing of their products and services, and the types of customers they attract. Also, the multiple varies depending upon what industry the business is in. For example, the multiple for a manufacturing business is higher than the multiple for a retail establishment or a restaurant.

Other measures are more exact. Here are our preferred valuation measures for small businesses:

- ✔ **Multiple of earnings:** When you compare the sales data for comparable companies to the one you're interested in buying, determine what *multiple of earnings* these businesses sold for. Divide the price the business sold for by its annual earnings (profits) to arrive at a figure that will give you the *multiple of earnings* (also known as the *price-earnings ratio*) of that transaction.

  When the multiple is low, say 3 to 1 (meaning if the business had earnings of $50,000, it sold for $150,000), it means that the buyer and seller don't have great expectations for the business's future earnings. However, when the multiple is high, say 12 to 1 (earnings of $50,000 and a selling price of $600,000), the buyer's and seller's expectations of future earnings are correspondingly high.

  Future earnings are what will provide the return on the buyer's investment; therefore, the higher the buyer expects those potential earnings to be, the more he or she is willing to pay for the business. (In general, a business should be able to pay for itself in three to five years. If the time period is any longer than that, you're probably paying too much for the company.)

  Small, privately held businesses, however, typically sell for a lower multiple of earnings than larger companies in the same line of business. The reason: Small companies are less well established and are riskier from an investing standpoint. Plus, your investment in their stock will be *illiquid* (that is, even in good times, the stock generally can't be converted into cash within a reasonable period of time).

- ✔ **Book value:** In addition to looking at the sales price of other businesses relative to earnings, you can also consider the value of a company's assets. The *book value* of a company is the company's assets minus its liabilities, which is the same as the net worth of the business that comes from its balance sheet (assuming that the values for the assets and liabilities on the balance sheet are accurate; see Chapter 13 for more on balance sheets). The figures that go into determining book value should be checked carefully to ensure that the underlying asset values and liability accounts are correct.

Of the two approaches, each of which has advantages as well as imperfections, the multiple-of-earnings approach is generally considered to be far superior to the book-value method. After all, what you're purchasing when you buy a business is not primarily its assets but rather its ability to generate profits (earnings). Some businesses, such as a consulting firm, have little in the way of tangible assets — the personnel may be the firm's greatest asset, and valuing that is difficult. Because the determination of a price-earnings multiple figure is based on an income-generating formula, it is generally a better indicator than the book-value approach, which simply measures the difference between assets and liabilities.

Also, be sure to remember that when using the multiple of earnings approach, the figure you come up with represents the *goodwill* portion of the business only and doesn't include the value of the business's assets. (Goodwill is, in essence, the value of the business's reputation and existing customer list.) Thus, you'll have to add to the goodwill number the value of the assets. The assets involved in a typical small business purchase include accounts receivable (make sure that they're all collectable), inventory (make sure that what you're buying is merchantable), and equipment, furniture, and fixtures (the fair market value thereof).

Getting a professional appraisal

Business appraisers make a living estimating the value of businesses. If you want to buy a business and your initial investigation suggests that the seller is committed and serious about selling the business, consider hiring an appraiser. Although the fees they charge vary depending on the size and complexity of the prospective business, for the typical small business you can usually figure somewhere north of $5,000 for a professional appraisal.

Tax advisors, lawyers, and business consultants who specialize in working with small businesses may be able to refer you to a good business appraiser if they can't do it themselves. The Institute of Business Appraisers (954-584-1144; www.instbusapp.org) can provide you with a list of association members in your area. Also, check the business-to-business Yellow Pages in your area under "Appraisers — Business."

Tracking businesses you've explored that have sold

If your search for a business to buy lasts months or perhaps years, keep track of similar businesses you've considered that eventually sell. These sales provide valuable comparables because you've seen the business up close and obtained details about the company's financial position that give you a valuable perspective in assessing the eventual sale.

Obtaining the final selling price of a small business can be challenging. You can try asking the ex-owner. Other options include speaking with advisors who are involved in such deals and business brokers. For more details on these sources, see the next section.

Tapping the knowledge of advisors who work with comparable companies

Business consultants, attorneys, and tax advisors you work with can assist you with pinning down sales data for companies comparable to the one you're considering buying. The challenge is to find advisors who have knowledge of and experience with both small businesses in general and businesses similar to the one you're thinking of buying.

If you do end up buying a small business, you'll benefit from having competent advisors on your team who have worked on comparable deals. Ultimately, when you're going to hire an advisor for tax, legal, or business advice, be sure to check references. Also ask the advisor for a comprehensive list of business deals (including purchase or sale price and industry) that he or she has been involved in over the past year.

Don't be deterred by the cost of such advisors, especially tax advisors and attorneys. The terms you agree to in the purchase of a business will be with you for a long, long time.

Consulting research firms and publications

Because finding the details on similar companies that have sold can be difficult, wouldn't it be helpful if a service compiled such information? Well, you may be happy to know that some companies do publish comparable sales information or conduct searches for a fee. Some public libraries with extensive business sections carry some of the following publications:

✔ *Bizcomps* is an annual publication that provides sales price, revenue, and other financial details for businesses sold. This compendium of sales information is available for different major regions of the United States (Western, Central, and Eastern editions). A national edition provides sales information for larger manufacturing, wholesale, and service businesses. Call 702-454-0072 or visit www.bizcomps.com for a sample of this publication. Each directory sells for $145. The company also offers online access to business sales data through an annual membership fee (which varies).

✔ *Financial Studies of the Small Business* is an annual directory published by Financial Research Associates (FRA). It provides balance sheet and income statement comparisons for small companies. Call 863-299-3969 to receive a background package on this directory, which sells for $136 (software version is $167). This company also maintains a bare-bones Web site at www.frafssb.com.

Turning to trade publications

Trade publications can help you find out more about a particular industry and how to value companies within that industry. Most publications are willing, typically for a small fee, to send you past articles on a topic. Or, you may be able to access them for free from the publication's Web site.

Enlisting the services of a business broker

If you're already working with a *business broker* (a salesperson who lists small businesses for sale and who works with buyers as well) or looking at businesses listed for sale through business brokers, the broker should be able to provide a comparable market analysis of similar businesses that the broker's office has sold.

We'd like to think that we don't need to say this, but such an "analysis" may be less analytic and more sales oriented than you want. Business brokers earn commissions based upon a percentage of the selling price of the business that you may buy through them. The commissions generally range from 6 to 10 percent, depending on the size and complexity of the deal.

Also, understand that business brokers generally have access to sales data only on the small number of similar businesses that their particular office has sold. Unlike real estate agents, business brokers who work for different brokerage firms in a given community don't share their sales data with one another.

Before enlisting the services of a broker, be sure to check his or her references carefully — especially given the fact that business brokers are in a virtually unregulated industry requiring no specific credentials or educational training to enter. Involve your own attorney when the closing comes around. Having your own attorney will take the broker's bias out of the equation and help assure that what you get is best for you.

Developing Purchase Offer Contingencies

When you make an offer to buy a home, you should make your purchase offer contingent upon obtaining mortgage loan approval, satisfactory inspections, and the property seller holding clear title to the home. When you make an offer to buy a business, you should make your purchase contingent upon similar issues, including the following:

✔ **Inspections and due diligence:** Your purchase offer for a business should be contingent upon a thorough review of the company's financial statements and interviews of key employees, customers, and suppliers. You should be allowed to employ whomever you like to help you with these evaluations. The typical period of time allowed for due diligence is 30 to 60 days, and more if the business is large.

✔ **Financing:** Unless you're paying cash for the full purchase price of the business, another condition of your purchase offer may be an acceptable seller-provided loan. Sellers can be a great financing source, and many are willing to lend you money to purchase their business. Seller financing is quite common in small-business purchases — about 90 percent of all small business sales include seller financing.

Be sure to compare the terms that the seller is offering to those of some local banks that specialize in small-business loans. (See Chapter 5 for your best financing sources.) In the purchase offer, you should specify the acceptable loan terms, including the duration of the loan and the maximum interest rate. If interest rates jump before your loan is finalized, you don't want to be forced to complete your deal at too high an interest rate.

✔ **Noncompete clause:** You don't want to buy a business only to have the former owner set up an identical one down the block and steal his previous customers. To avoid this unpleasant possibility, be sure that your purchase offer includes a *noncompete clause,* which should state something along the lines that the seller can't establish a similar business within a certain nearby geographic area for a certain number of years.

You may also consider asking the owner, as part of the deal, to make himself available to consult with you, at a specified hourly rate, for 6 to 12 months to make sure that you tap all his valuable experience, as well as to transition relationships with key employees, vendors, and customers. To further align the selling owner's interests with yours, also consider having a portion of the total purchase price dependent on the future success of the company.

If the transaction includes seller financing, most sophisticated sellers will want to continue to work with you for a period following the sale. Beware of those who don't want to hang around. Restaurant owner Max from a story in Chapter 8 illustrates this concern; he couldn't get out of Dodge fast enough when his deal was done. There was a reason: too much dirty laundry in his hamper.

✔ **Limited potential liabilities:** When you buy a business, you buy that business's assets and usually (but not always) its liabilities. Some potential liabilities aren't going to show up on a company's balance sheet and could become a thorn in your side. Make sure that the seller is liable for environmental cleanup and undisclosed existing liabilities (debts). Conduct legal searches for liens, litigation, and tax problems. (Your attorney should do this for you as a part of the closing process.)

Allocating the Purchase Price

When you pay $300,000 for a business, you're not simply paying $300,000 for the business. You're paying $60,000 for the inventory, $40,000 for the accounts receivable, $50,000 for the company equipment, $100,000 for goodwill, and so on.

No matter how you determined the purchase price, it must always be broken down, or *allocated,* among the assets of the business and other categories. This requirement applies whether you set the price of the business by determining the value of its assets (such as the multiple-of-earnings method, described earlier in this chapter) or by some other method. Although allocating assets is the kind of stuff that makes accountants giddy and may cause your eyes to glaze over, snap to attention when the subject comes up, because how you structure the purchase can save you tens of thousands of dollars in taxes.

Experienced tax advisors will tell you that you'll generally want to allocate much of the purchase price to specific assets of the business. Some assets are what their numbers make them out to be (such as accounts receivable) while others can be negotiable (such as equipment and goodwill). The reason for the negotiation is that different assets can be written off (or *depreciated*) over different periods of time. For instance, equipment can be depreciated over as little as 4 years, while goodwill takes 15 years.

The purchase of the business and allocation of the purchase price among business assets must be reported on IRS Form 8594 (Asset Acquisition Statement). Make sure that you do so because if you don't, the penalty is stiff — up to 10 percent of the amount not reported.

Doing Due Diligence

After spending months searching for the right business to buy and finding one that fits your fancy, you may well spend weeks negotiating an acceptable deal. Now, just as you're about to stumble across what you think is the finish line, you realize you have plenty more work left to go.

Time to get out the microscope and really pick nits. Time to play devil's advocate and assume that you have problems to uncover. Before you go through with the deal and fork over the dough, you have one last chance to discover hidden flaws. All businesses, of course, have their warts, but better for you to uncover them now so that the purchase price and terms reflect those warts.

Is the business as profitable as the financial statements indicate? Will the business's customers remain after a change in ownership? What lease, debt, or other obligations will you be assuming when buying the business? You should answer these and other important questions through a process known as *due diligence.* Due diligence typically lasts for 30 to 60 days.

You should be working on your small-business purchase with experts who can assist you with putting together a good deal. These same experts also will form your due-diligence team. For more on choosing your experts, see Chapter 10.

In addition to the homework we recommend in Chapter 8, read the following sections, which list some additional due-diligence steps for you to perform before making an offer.

Think about income statement issues

What could be more important than the profitability of the business? That's why we suggest the following steps to deal with income statement concerns:

- ✔ **Have an experienced small-business tax advisor review the company's financial statements.** He or she will know what to look out for. Just be sure to agree on a budget for the cost of services (and, therefore, the time he or she will spend).

- ✔ **Adjust for one-time events.** If necessary, factor out one-time events from the profit analysis. For example, if the business got an unusually large order last year that is unlikely to be repeated and hasn't been the norm in the past, you should subtract this amount from the profitability analysis.

- ✔ **Check the owner's compensation.** Examine the owner's salary to see whether it's too high or low for the field. Owners can pump up the profitability of their company in the years before they sell by reducing or keeping their salary to a minimum or by paying family members in the business less than fair-market salaries.

- ✔ **Consider how the building expense will change.** You should also consider whether the rent or mortgage expense will be different after you buy the business. This change clearly affects the profitability of the business.

- ✔ **Factor in financing costs.** Calculate what will happen to profits when you factor in the financing costs from borrowing money to buy the business.

- ✔ **Pay attention to trends.** How are the sales and the profits trending? If this year's profits were, say, $80,000, and last year's were $100,000, the trend is unfavorable. On the other hand, if this year's profits were $70,000, and last year's were $50,000, it constitutes a good trend. Knowledgable buyers are generally willing to pay a higher multiple for favorable trends.

Consider legal and tax concerns

You should do the following homework to research legal and tax issues:

- ✔ **Look for liens.** Check to make sure that no liens are filed against assets of the business, and, if you're buying real estate, that the property title is clear. A competent attorney can help with this tedious and important legal task.

- ✔ **Get proof that taxes are all paid.** Get the seller to provide proof certifying that federal and state employment, sales, and use taxes are all paid up.

Moving Into Your Business

If you've made it through the searching, researching, negotiating, and closing phases, you're now a bona fide small-business owner. Congratulations and welcome to your new business! You've completed a lot of challenging and important work and should feel proud of yourself.

After your deal is closed, be sure to take care of the following tasks as soon as possible:

- ✔ **Disclose ownership transfer.** Notify creditors of the transfer of ownership. In counties where the company does business, you should publish a transfer-of-ownership notice in a general circulation newspaper. If you omit this step, unsecured creditors can come after your business if the previous owner had outstanding debts.

- ✔ **Write a business plan and mission statement.** Having researched the industry and evaluated in detail the business you bought, writing a good business plan should be relatively painless. Doing a quality business plan, however, will take some time and thinking, which will benefit you and your business in increased sales, reduced costs, and happier employees. If you ever seek outside capital from a banker or investor, you'll also need a good business plan. We explain how to write your business plan and mission statement in Chapter 4. An ideal time to begin work on this business plan is during the due diligence phase.

- ✔ **Plan the company's finances.** Going forward, you need to have a good handle on the revenue, expenses, and cash flow of your business. Your business should have a budget in place, and you should forecast future needs for capital, both of which should be included in the business plan. See Chapters 5 and 13 for details.

- ✔ **Consider the entity/legal form of organization.** Just because the business you bought was structured as a sole proprietorship or corporation doesn't mean that such a legal entity makes the most sense for you. We provide the framework for you to think through this important decision in Chapter 5. Your attorney and tax advisor should be part of this decision.

✔ **Spend time thinking about your customers.** Without good customers who buy profitable products and services and who pay their bills on time, you won't have a viable long-term business. Even the best of businesses will lose customers for a variety of reasons beyond the business owner's control. So, don't skimp on understanding your customers' needs, what makes them buy your company's wares, and what their ongoing customer service needs are. Completing your business plan should help clarify many of these vital issues, as will reading Chapters 11 and 12. Get to know your best customers as soon as the ink is dry on the sales agreement.

✔ **Get to know your employees.** Employees who liked the previous owner(s) will take time to warm up to you. Some employees will fear for their jobs or may worry about a change in ownership leading to reduced job satisfaction. Err on the side of doing more listening to your employees rather than always being the one jabbering about all your grand plans. The employees contain a wealth of knowledge about the business from which you can learn, and the better you listen, the more the employees will grow to respect and like you.

Also be sure to evaluate the employee benefits package and compensation structure (see Chapters 15 and 16). Don't make rash changes in this area, especially if you're thinking about reducing benefits and/or compensation. Early, negative changes can have ugly long-term consequences. (See Chapter 15 for more on handling your employees.)

✔ **Walk, don't run.** Don't make huge changes your first day, week, or even month at the helm. Take your time to discover the culture of the business, the needs of its customers, and the idiosyncrasies of its vendors before you attempt major changes. Employees, customers, and vendors don't like quick change, especially when the person behind the change is new and relatively unknown.

✔ **Consult the prior owner.** Don't expect that you'll know everything there is to know about running your new business. No matter how much better a business manager you may think you are than your predecessor, he or she has certain knowledge and skills that you don't have. Don't let your ego stand in the way of asking the previous owner for advice.

✔ **Work with a good tax advisor.** You don't want to fall behind in your taxes or the required filing of myriad tax forms, or you'll have a nasty surprise in the form of an unexpectedly large tax bill. The tax advisor who helped you with evaluating your business purchase may be able to recommend a tax advisor you could work with at least during your first year of business ownership. You'll also want to make sure you come out of the starting gates with well-organized and accurate financial statements. See Chapter 18 for more details.

Much like a first-time home-buyer moving into a newly purchased home, your euphoria at owning your business may quietly slip into anxiety when you more fully realize that your work is just beginning. Relax, take deep breaths, and use the time-tested method of breaking a big task into many smaller manageable ones. Also, rest assured that if you take our advice from Chapters 6, 7, and this one, and you do your homework before buying your business (see Chapter 8), you should end up purchasing a company that doesn't have major problems and one that you have the skills to run well.

Part III
Running a Successful Small Business

In this part . . .

Small-business ownership is a never-ending exercise in problem solving. This part is designed to help you resolve a small business's most compelling challenges, including "the care and feeding" of customers, improving sales and increasing profitability, using advertising and publicity, developing strategies for pricing and distribution, and keeping tabs on the all-important profit and loss statement.

Chapter 10

Owners as Jack-of-All-Trades

* *

In This Chapter

▶ Handling the details of a start-up

▶ Determining which tasks you want to outsource

▶ Establishing a bookkeeping system that works best for you

▶ Managing your expenses

▶ Maintaining relationships with vendors and other people outside your business

* *

*I*n the beginning, you as owner will perform all your start-up's chores, or at least you will personally see to it that they get done. Well, you'll personally take care of all the *important* tasks at least — those responsibilities that will, down the road, either make or break your enterprise if they aren't done correctly.

More often than not, however, much of those early-stage duties are grunt work — the not-so-exciting-to-entrepreneurs stuff that doesn't involve dealing with customers, creating new products, or generating much-needed cash. Instead, the duties are yawn-inducing things like appeasing the government, developing a bookkeeping system, and covering your behind in the event of adversity — you know, the kind of stuff that, if it doesn't get done, will come back to haunt you.

In this chapter, we walk you through the many hats you wear as you navigate these sometimes mundane details.

Dotting Your i's and Crossing Your t's: Start-Up Details

We're assuming here that you've completed the big-picture tasks of the start-up (such as writing a business plan, finding a mentor, determining the legal entity that works best for you, locating financing, and developing the product or service), many of which we discuss in earlier chapters of this book. Now you must dive into the nitty-gritty details.

Buying insurance

One of the first things you need to do when you start a business is buy insurance. We're talking here about liability insurance — auto, fire, theft, business interruption, and so on — and workers' compensation insurance. Insurance is an expense that never goes away and generally increases every year.

Making things worse is the fact that, if you're like most entrepreneurs, after the original policies are signed, you'll file the policies away and won't consider reshopping them to get a better price for long periods of time because you're so busy running your business. This means that the expenses related to insurance policies will be etched on your profit and loss statement for long periods of time as a fixed cost when the expenses should be a variable cost — in other words, reviewed every year.

Don't even think about entrusting the creation and negotiation of your initial insurance package (and the creation of the costs related to it) to anyone else.

Liability insurance

In most cases, insurance is a necessary expense, not unlike a host of other necessary expenses, such as rent, telephone, and salaries. In some cases, the justification for insurance is the owner's logic; in other cases, the insurance is required by an outsider — a bank or a property-leasing company. For example:

- ✓ **Theft insurance:** Sooner or later, someone is going to steal something of value from you. (Statistics show that this someone is likely to be an employee.) *Our recommendation:* If you're in the high-ticket retail or wholesale business (automobiles, appliances, and the like), buy theft insurance. Otherwise take your chances until you're profitable, especially in the early stages of your business.

- ✓ **Property damage insurance:** In addition to the physical property you own, rent, or lease, property damage insurance covers your inventory. Similar to homeowner's insurance, property damage insurance is often required by the terms of a lease or bank loan. *Our recommendation:* If you're in a service business with little expensive equipment and you're leasing or renting in an office building, take your chances if your lease will allow it (until you're profitable). Otherwise, buy it.

- ✓ **Liability:** No telling what may happen on your business premises in these litigious times. *Our recommendation:* Buy enough liability insurance to protect at least twice your net worth.

- ✓ **Business interruption:** This insurance covers the possibility of your business being halted by any number of random events, most of them natural disasters. Business interruption insurance reimburses you for the profits you don't make during your downtime. *Our recommendation:* In a business's early stages, there usually isn't much business to interrupt. Spend your scarce money elsewhere. However, this situation (hopefully) will change. When it does, business interruption insurance is a must-buy.

Workers' compensation insurance

Workers' compensation is payment for insurance that provides benefits — in the form of medical expense reimbursement and replacement of lost wages — to employees injured on the job. Workers' compensation is a state-mandated, no-fault insurance system, and, when you have employees, appears as a hefty expense on your profit and loss statement.

Shop around for a trustworthy insurance agent (use referrals from satisfied small-business customers), set up a meeting with him or her along with a representative of the state (your prospective insurance agent can tell you how to locate that person), and find out what it will take to keep your *experience modification factor* to a minimum. The experience modification factor is a numerical expression of a company's accident and injury record compared with the average for the firm's industry. The higher experience modification factor, the higher the cost.

In addition to the experience modification factor, job classification also plays an important role in determining the cost of your workers' compensation insurance. Each employee (or job) in your small business is assigned by the state a particular rating — and subsequently a particular premium — based on the estimated level of risk involved in the performance of that job. (The higher the job classification, the more it will cost you; the lower, the less. Argue for the lower; the classification criteria often are fuzzy.)

Myriad job categories exist to choose from, and you'll find a lot of overlap between various job categories. Your business will waste a bunch of insurance money if your employees aren't properly classified. Don't take this classification process lightly.

Because workers' compensation insurance is a state-run program, for further questions on the subject, ask your insurance agent for the telephone number and address of the applicable state agency. Or click the link to Department of Insurance Web Sites at the National Association of Insurance Commissioners (NAIC) Web site (www.naic.org).

Paying federal, state, and local taxes

Federal taxes (income, Social Security, unemployment, and excise) come in a mind-boggling array, as do state and local taxes (income, real estate, sales, and assorted other special levies depending on your industry). For more on the nuts and bolts of taxes affecting your small business, see Chapter 18.

When short on cash (don't kid yourself; sooner or later, it's bound to happen), make sure that you pay any taxes you owe the government first, even if you have to put off paying your private vendors. Governments, especially the federal one, have an enormous array of collection tools at their disposal, and they have the right to extract a dear price (in the form of onerous penalties and interest rates) from those who don't follow the letter of the law. We strongly recommend you faithfully pay your taxes on time.

Negotiating leases

When leasing space as a start-up, aim for two-year leases, or three years as an absolute maximum. If you think you'll want the space for a longer term, consider negotiating and adding to your lease agreement an escalation clause that stipulates upfront how much the rental rate will increase should you choose to extend the lease for a subsequent year or multiyear period.

Unfortunately, reading, understanding, and creating a lease is for lawyers, not laypeople. Pay the legal fees and don't get locked into any long-term leases with the lure of free rent or equipment use.

Long-term leases are a no-win situation for the small-business owner: If your business grows, it will outgrow the long-term lease, and you'll pay a higher price for its cancellation; if your business doesn't grow, you'll pay an even greater price to get out of the lease.

Leases for more than two years can be considered long term. Many landlords will offer you long-term leases (three to five years) with all sorts of exotic discounts; don't be lured into taking them unless you can afford to pick up the final years out of your own pocket should the business no longer want, need, or be able to pay for the space.

Maintaining employee records

The day you hire your first employee is the same day you must create and begin maintaining your first employee-personnel folder. Maintain a running written record for every employee, covering such issues as employment agreements (including salary history), performance reviews, business goals, commendations, and, of course, reprimands.

These records come in handy when managing and motivating your employees. Such key managerial and motivational tools as goal-setting and performance reviews require that you keep detailed employee records for these instruments to work. (For more information on these two subjects, see Chapter 15.)

Also, assuming that you employ living, breathing human beings, you can also count on the fact that, sooner or later, you'll have a conflict with one or more of those living, breathing human beings — a conflict that in the worst case can end up in court. When a legal battle occurs, the party who can back up his or her claims with the most information usually prevails. Don't be the one who's handicapped by poor record-keeping and documentation.

Some states are *at-will* employment states, which simply means the employer has the right to terminate employees "at will." In effect, the reason for termination doesn't have to be clarified; all you have to tell the terminated employee is that "things just aren't working out." Other states aren't so lenient or understanding. Find out where your state stands on the issue by calling your state's Employment Department. It will have a long list of rules that will determine the employee records you should maintain.

Getting licenses and permits

Almost all businesses require filing certain licenses and obtaining particular permits. We cover all this in detail in Chapter 17.

Signing the checks

Remember, checks represent cash, and from the day you hang out your shingle until the day you close your doors, cash will be the lifeblood of your business. The annals of small business are filled with stories of $12-an-hour bookkeepers running off with a hardworking entrepreneur's cash.

If you have a spouse as your bookkeeper, you can rest easy. But what do you do when your bookkeeper isn't your spouse? You guard your cash like it's your life, because it is (well, your business life anyway). Following is a list of tips on how to do exactly that:

- ✔ Schedule an audit at the end of every year. It doesn't have to be a full-fledged, expensive, cover-every-detail audit. Simply ask your CPA to spend half a day reviewing your books. Your CPA knows the sensitive areas.

- ✔ Make sure your bookkeeper takes a vacation every year. Most bookkeepers who are siphoning off their employers' cash don't want anyone else probing their books, even for short periods of time.

- ✔ Review and approve every invoice yourself.

- ✔ Balance the bank statement yourself.

Outsourcing: Focus on What You Do Best

We define *outsourcing* as delegating services you don't want to do, or don't have time to do, to someone outside your company (not an employee) who can usually do them better and faster. Outsourcing is a buzzword that has surfaced more in the past decade, but the concept itself isn't new. Businesses have been outsourcing, in one form or another, for many years. We outline the basics in the sections that follow.

Knowing which tasks get outsourced

Take a look at this list of small-business functions that are most frequently outsourced:

- **Accounting and bookkeeping:** *Accounting* (the beginning-to-end process of collecting financial data, generating financial statements, and preparing tax forms) and *bookkeeping* (the collecting-of-financial-data function only) provide the gamut of outsourcing opportunities. You can, for example, hire someone to do all your accounting and bookkeeping, or you can hire someone to do only your payroll, only your financial statements, or only your tax returns. Because the typical entrepreneur is not usually well versed in accounting and bookkeeping skills, our suggestion here is that these functions be among the first you consider for outsourcing.

- **Human resources:** As your company grows, the various functions of human resources should be next in line for outsourcing consideration. Human resources includes a wide variety of nonproduct-, noncustomer-, and nonsales-related issues, such as

   - New-employee hiring procedures

   - Policies and procedure manuals for employees

   - Payroll and related information-gathering systems

   - Employee training on human resource issues

   - Employee training on a wide variety of sensitivity issues, such as ethics and sexual harassment

- **Manufacturing:** The manufacturing process for most products is expensive, time consuming, and extremely detail oriented. For many entrepreneurs, especially the creative and/or sales types who typically gravitate to this career, the outsourcing of the manufacturing function makes a lot of sense.

   Even if your core business is manufacturing, some elements of your product may lend themselves to outsourcing their manufacture to subcontractors. Even behemoth manufacturers such as General Motors subcontract a good deal of their work.

- **Sales:** Outsourcing sales is certainly the most potentially dangerous of the outsourcing options but one that's used by some businesses, including those that employ manufacturers' reps. We say "potentially dangerous" because it's difficult to impart to outsiders the enthusiasm and knowledge necessary to most effectively sell your business's product or service. Sales is definitely the last of the responsibilities to consider outsourcing, although doing so works well for some small businesses. (For more on the subject of manufacturers' reps, see Chapter 11.)

Figuring out what to outsource

Here's the $64,000 question: How do you determine which services to out-source and which ones to retain in-house? Each business and owner is different, of course, but you need to answer these questions before making the decision:

- ✔ **Can I better manage my available cash if I outsource?** The answer here will primarily depend upon how much cash you have. For example, by outsourcing the manufacturing process, you avoid the costs associated with maintaining an inventory of raw materials and hiring manufacturing employees. Or by outsourcing your sales functions, you avoid the costs associated with maintaining a sales force.

- ✔ **What do I do best?** Because your time is finite, why spend a lot of time doing the things you don't do well (such as bookkeeping) when you can farm out those duties, thereby leaving you with more time to do the things you do well?

- ✔ **Will the cost of the outsourcing tasks include a product (or service) whose quality is better than what I can produce at that same cost?** The answer to this question is often yes given the fact that the best outsourcing sources are almost always specialists in their areas of expertise. Of course, you shouldn't outsource until you find a competent specialist.

- ✔ **What do I enjoy doing the most?** We can guarantee you this: If you choose to keep your bookkeeping or human resource functions in-house, you will, over the years, end up spending no small amount of time dealing with issues related to these functions. Think about it: Is this the way you want to spend your time?

  In the final analysis, the decision whether to outsource will be primarily based on what you enjoy spending your time doing.

Simplifying Your Accounting

If this were a perfect world, you wouldn't need an accounting system — you'd simply let your business checkbook do the talking. You'd pay your bills and deposit your receipts, and whatever was left over at the end of the year would represent your profit. How simple (and inexpensive) such a procedure would be.

Alas, this isn't a perfect world, and your checkbook does the talking only when measuring one of your assets (cash). Furthermore, your checkbook only measures today's cash; it doesn't give you the foggiest idea of what tomorrow's or next month's cash balance will be. Will you have enough cash in the bank to pay the month's bills, to meet next Friday's payroll, or to pay the quarterly tax payments that come due in 30 days? Who knows? The checkbook isn't talking.

The problem is that your business's checkbook can't do any of the following things:

- ✔ Keep score (of anything but cash)
- ✔ Give you the information you need to pay your income taxes
- ✔ Provide you with the percentages and ratios you need to help you manage your business
- ✔ Provide you with the trends you need to determine the direction of your business
- ✔ Present you with the information you need to value your business

Like it or not, accounting is one of the most important functions of running your business. Whether you intend to eventually outsource your accounting or do all the work yourself, at the start-up stage, accounting demands your undivided attention. One of the most common mistakes we see entrepreneurs make in the start-up stage is to not learn the basics of accounting and how they apply to the business. Learn the basics early, or you'll never take the time.

Introducing some common systems

You have three options to consider when determining which accounting system to employ:

- ✔ Outsourcing of the accounting services (this decision is to be made before opening your business's doors)
- ✔ An in-house manual bookkeeping system
- ✔ An in-house computer-based accounting system

A discussion of the manual and computer-based options follows. In Chapter 18, we provide advice on how to hire good tax and bookkeeping assistance.

Manual bookkeeping systems

Maintaining a manual bookkeeping system is certainly the quickest and easiest of the two in-house options. All you have to do is visit your local office-supply store, purchase one of the many manual bookkeeping ledger and journal systems available (the entire package should cost $25 or less), and — voilà! — before you can mutter the words *green eyeshades,* you're a bookkeeper. You won't need to buy an expensive computer or the software to go with it; the only accessories required are a #2 pencil or a pen and, depending on the complexity of your business, no small amount of your (or someone else's) time.

In addition to the low cost of a manual bookkeeping system, another advantage of such a system is that you learn the basics of the standard double-entry accounting systems from the ground up — a skill that will hold you in good stead as your business grows. (See the "A collection of accounting definitions" sidebar if you need more information about double-entry accounting.)

The downside of the manual-entry system, especially when your business has a lot of activity, is that it can be extremely time consuming, and time is money in the small-business world. Also, the information that you collect manually won't always provide you with the depth of financial data you need for making important business decisions. Finally, manual bookkeeping is more prone to human error than are computer-based systems.

After you purchase your manual system, follow the step-by-step directions inside the ledgers and journals to perform a relatively uncomplicated, connect-the-dots bookkeeping process. During the course of your fiscal year, make your entries in the general journal pages (*journals* are where you make the entries; *ledgers* are where you total the journal entries). The manual system you buy will include definitions of each of the following categories along with examples:

- ✔ Your disbursements according to their expense and/or capital account category

- ✔ The receipts (income) of your business

- ✔ Various period-ending adjusting entries designed to record such items as depreciation, accrued taxes, and accrued payroll

At the end of the year, complete your journal entries summarizing the year's activity. Then, if you prefer, you can turn over your journals to a tax advisor or certified public accountant (CPA), wait a few weeks, and be rewarded with a professionally prepared profit and loss statement, a balance sheet, and the balance due for your year-end tax payment (see Chapter 13).

If, on the other hand, you're that special entrepreneur who actually enjoys the bookkeeping process, you can expand the manual bookkeeping process to include the year-end preparation of your profit and loss statement, as well as the balance sheet, leaving only your taxes to be computed by a tax practitioner.

Finally, in those cases where your business is a relatively uncomplicated sole proprietorship or partnership (see Chapter 5), you may make the determination to carry the manual process through the preparation of Schedule C of IRS Form 1040 and on into the preparation of your personal income tax return.

When it comes to how much of your own bookkeeping and taxes you perform yourself, the only limits are your time and patience. The primary issue to consider when determining how much, or how little, of your accounting you should do is how best to utilize your time.

In addition to the general ledger and journal functions previously described, most manual bookkeeping ledger and journal systems also include the forms you need to maintain such subsidiary records as monthly payrolls, schedule of accounts receivable, schedule of accounts payable, and inventory worksheets.

Simple accounting can work!

A Greek restaurant owner in Cleveland had his own bookkeeping system. He kept his accounts payable in a cigar box on the left-hand side of the cash register, his daily cash returns in the cash register, and his receipts for paid invoices in another cigar box on the right. When his youngest son graduated from Harvard with his MBA, he was appalled by his father's primitive accounting methods. "I don't know how you can run your business that way," the son scolded. "How do you know what your profits are?"

"Well, son," the father replied, "when I got off the boat from Greece I had nothing but the pants I was wearing. Today your brother is a doctor, you are an MBA, your sister is an investment banker, and your mother and I have two nice cars, a city house, and a country home. We have a fine business, and everything is paid for. Add that together, subtract the pants, and there's your profit."

Computer-based systems

If you already have a computer (in the event you don't, you're going to have at least two strikes against you as you work to grow your business), using it to accomplish your bookkeeping and accounting functions probably makes sense. Although the least expensive computerized software package available is a tad more expensive than a comparable manual system, the computerized system, if you use it properly, should save you time, provide you with more information, and establish a base for you to grow into a more sophisticated system as your business (hopefully) expands.

You can consider four categories of computerized systems when shopping for your first accounting package, remembering that the system you ultimately select should depend upon the size and complexity of your business. A description of the four categories follows, along with several basic questions and a collection of tips intended to help you make the final choice.

Category #1: Quick and easy

Category #1 includes those quick-and-easy accounting systems used by many families, as well as by small businesses. The cost of these systems is usually about $50. They are basically an electronic checkbook register with the capacity to categorize expenses and generate both profit and loss statements and balance sheets. Most Category #1 systems also include the capability to electronically pay bills.

Examples of Category #1 accounting software packages include Quicken and Microsoft Money.

The primary shortcoming with Category #1 systems is that the software allows for the deletion of bookkeeping entries, so if you're interested in providing an audit trail for you or your accountant, you shouldn't purchase a Category #1 package. An *audit trail* enables you to track every dollar of income and expenses, thus making theft much more difficult. (Audit trails are required in all publicly held companies.) For this reason, most accountants don't recommend Category #1 systems to small-business owners who have prospects of future growth — these owners will eventually require the security that audit trails provide.

When your business is small and you know it's going to remain small, and you'll be the only person writing the checks, Category #1 systems may be satisfactory for you.

Category #1 systems don't include payroll systems. If you plan on eventually having employees and don't want to figure your payrolls or write your checks manually, your next choice would be to spend another $50 to $100 and upgrade to Category #2.

Category #2: Plus payroll and inventory

For about $100, Category #2 systems provide a number of services that Category #1 systems don't. For example, Category #2 systems can perform the following functions:

- ✓ **Compute, write, and compile employee payroll.**

- ✓ **Track and age** *receivables* **(monies your customers owe you) and** *payables* **(monies you owe to your vendors).** *Aging* means determining the amount of time your receivables have been due to you or your payables have been due to your vendors.

- ✓ **Establish customer receivable ledgers.** These ledgers are, in effect, your customer's statements.

- ✓ **Maintain a basic inventory system.**

The primary disadvantage to Category #2 accounting software programs is that, similar to Category #1, the system doesn't provide an audit trail.

Examples of Category #2 accounting software packages include QuickBooks, Cash Flow, and Manage Your Own Business (MYOB).

Category #3: Marching the audit trail

Category #3 programs provide their owners with all the benefits that Category #2 systems provide, as well as the audit trail necessary to the business in which someone other than the owner will be writing checks and maintaining the books. Additionally, Category #3 systems allow for multiple users: the bookkeeping department, the accounts receivable department, the inventory department, and so on. Prices vary, depending on the horsepower required, but they're generally in the range of $200 to $700.

Examples of Category #3 accounting software packages include Business-Works, AccPac, BPI, Peachtree Accounting, and QuickBooks Pro (an upgraded version of QuickBooks).

A collection of accounting definitions

If you're interested in mastering a manual system (or if you just want to understand the basics of accounting, no matter what system you use), here are definitions of key accounting terms you need to know:

Fiscal year: A fiscal year is the specific 365-day period that you have chosen to begin and end your accounting period. Most businesses must choose a calendar year as their fiscal year; in other words, their year begins January 1 and ends December 31. (All personal service businesses are required to use a calendar year, as are all partnerships and sole proprietorships.) Some corporations, LLCs, and subchapter S Corporations may decide to use a fiscal year other than the standard calendar year; for example, many retailers choose not to end their fiscal year on December 31 because they're still too busy winding up their holiday season. As a result, they may select a non-calendar fiscal year of February 1 through January 31 (or any such 365-day period).

Double-entry accounting and bookkeeping: All accounting and bookkeeping systems are double-entry. For each entry made on the expense side, an offsetting entry must be made on the income side. Or, for every entry on the asset side, an offsetting entry must be made on the liability side. Every plus must be accompanied by an offsetting minus, or in accounting-speak, every debit to one account must be offset by a credit to another. For example, when a retail business sells goods for cash from its inventory, a credit is made to cash, and a debit is made to inventory. Because of this double-entry aspect, such systems are always self-balancing. (The total debits will always add up to equal the total credits, hence the term *balance sheet.*)

Single-entry record-keeping: Single-entry bookkeeping can best be illustrated by the example of your personal checkbook — one entry, and the transaction is completed. Single-entry record-keeping systems aren't self-balancing. (Your checkbook doesn't balance until you've reconciled it to your statement.) Cash register tapes and the maintenance of internal ledgers are other examples of single-entry record-keeping systems.

Cash-basis accounting: A cash-basis bookkeeping system records income at the time it's received and deducts expenses at the time they're paid. In effect, the date of the check and/or the deposit determines the date of the applicable bookkeeping entry. Most sole proprietorships and partnerships use the cash-basis accounting system because it's easier to understand and requires fewer year-end adjusting entries. However, you get much less useful information with which to manage your business.

Accrual-basis accounting: Accrual-basis accounting records income at the time it's earned (at the time a sale is made as opposed to when cash changes hands) and deducts expenses at the time they're incurred (which may not necessarily be when cash changes hands). The IRS requires that businesses that have inventory use the accrual system. As a result, nearly all corporations use the accrual system.

If you have a choice for your business, consult with a tax advisor for advice as to which system will work best.

Category #4: Modular power

Unlike the software packages described in Categories #1, #2, and #3, which are purchased in a single package, Category #4 systems are purchased in modules. A few of the #3 programs come with modules, thus making the choice between the two even more complicated.

Separate Category #4 modules include these components:

✔ Basic system manager (the module that manages all the other modules)

✔ General ledger (otherwise known as the *chart of accounts,* which is the list of all the account titles that are tracked by every accounting system, including assets, liabilities, equity, and expenses)

✔ Financial reporting (profit and loss statement, balance sheet, and so on)

✔ Accounts receivable

✔ Accounts payable

✔ Payroll

✔ Inventory

✔ Job costing (a system that allows you to compute the exact cost of each of your products or services for pricing purposes)

The cost of each module is approximately $500, but the total price for a complete system can begin at $2,000 and run all the way up to $10,000, depending on the bells and whistles you select. Good programs in this category are flexible and can support many types of accounting issues and business processes.

Examples of Category #4 accounting software packages include Great Plains, Dynamics, AccPac Plus, Intuit's Enterprise Solutions, and MAS-90. Category #3 and #4 programs overlap to some degree.

Choosing the system that's right for you

When deciding which software package to purchase, ask yourself the following questions:

✔ **What characterizes your business?** Will you have inventory? Do you expect your business to significantly grow within the next year? Who will be maintaining the books and writing the checks? And the most important question of all: Do you intend to follow our advice on using financial reports to manage your business? Or is your bookkeeping solely for the purpose of collecting information to later complete your taxes?

✔ **How many employees will you have on your payroll?** Do you expect this number to expand significantly within the first two years?

✔ **Do you intend to sell your products on the Internet?** If so, look at Category #4 systems that have the capability to handle these electronic commerce transactions.

The answers to these questions should help you narrow your choice. The following collection of tips should assist you in making the final decision:

✔ **Don't waste your time purchasing and figuring out a system that you're going to outgrow in six months or a year.**

✔ **Don't buy a system that you think will take you three years or more to grow into.** That's too far out to accurately project. Buy a system that you believe will work for you for the next two years.

✔ **When purchasing software, in addition to considering the system itself, consider the company behind the package you're buying.** Criteria should include the support that the company provides, the history of its program updates (as a general rule, better companies provide more frequent updates), and the future of that company (will it be around to provide upgrades in future years?).

✔ **In the likely event that you can't answer these questions yourself, call the company (most have a toll-free number on the package) and ask direct questions yourself.**

✔ **Find out whether someone locally is trained to provide implementation and support services for the product you're considering.** Look in the Yellow Pages, ask an accountant, or call the manufacturer.

✔ **If you suspect you're a Category #3 or Category #4 customer, buying several hours of computer accounting consulting is usually a worth-while investment.** Rates begin around $50 an hour and escalate from there.

Companies grow. Even if you think you want a Category #1 software package now, chances are you'll be in the market for an upgrade soon enough. The additional investment required to switch software packages is not really the issue. The real damage comes from the time and staff retraining required to switch.

The lesson here? When in doubt, buy the highest category that you can afford and that you can picture yourself using within the next two years. Consult a computer software professional if you're still unsure which programs would work best for you. Also include your tax advisor in the decision.

Controlling Your Expenses

You have only three ways to increase your business's profitability:

✔ Increasing sales (in which case, those increased sales may or may not have a positive impact on profitability)

✔ Increasing prices (in which case, the entire amount of the increase will have a positive impact on profitability, assuming that you don't lose customers due to the price increase)

✔ Decreasing expenses (in which case, the entire decrease will have a positive impact on profitability, assuming that you don't lose business due to the expense reduction impact on your product or service quality)

In other words, you'll find a one-to-one leverage factor at work on your bottom-line profits when you increase prices or cut expenses. This is why the successful small-business owner always looks to the expense and pricing categories first when in a profitability crunch: Results can be instantaneous, and the impact is usually dollar on dollar.

Whether starting a new company or running an existing one, you must always remember that controlling expenses is a cultural issue, and cultural issues begin at the top. This means that many of your employees are going to emulate you. If you have overstuffed chairs in your office and idle secretaries in your foyer, your employees are likewise going to demonstrate a penchant for spending unnecessary money. We're talking about the old practice of leading by example.

Whenever we walk into a business's lobby or reception area and we're greeted by the gurgle of cascading waterfalls and the sight of bronze sculptures, we're reminded again of Sam Walton and Wal-Mart. Linoleum floors and metal desks were the order of the day at Wal-Mart's corporate headquarters in Bentonville, Arkansas. No wonder they could underprice and outperform such longtime competitors as Sears, Montgomery Ward, and J.C. Penney, whose overhead included the cost of maintaining plush corporate offices in the towering skyscrapers of Chicago and Dallas.

Looking at fixed and variable expenses

Two kinds of expenses need controlling: fixed and variable. *Fixed expenses* don't fluctuate with sales; they're usually negotiated in the start-up stage and then left to their own devices until the original negotiations lapse and it's time to renegotiate them. Such periods may be anywhere from one year to five years.

Effective control of these fixed expenses, which include such categories as insurance, rent, and equipment leases, requires the small-business owner's skillful negotiation, because after they're established, renegotiation time probably won't come around for a while. That cost is then fixed, and you can do little about it.

Variable expenses are those expenses that fluctuate with sales — as sales go up, variable expenses go up as well (and vice versa). You can delegate the determination of the prices to be paid for variable expenses, as long as you remember that the responsibility for controlling them, in the early stages of a business anyway, should always rest with you (the owner). You should approve all purchase orders and sign all checks that relate to variable expenses.

As the company grows, you may choose to delegate the responsibility for controlling expenses to other responsible individuals inside the company. Or you may still choose to maintain control by signing the checks and questioning the invoices that support those checks.

A key to controlling expenses is keeping your employees cost-conscious: If the employees know that you or other key managers are cost-conscious and will question unreasonable or unnecessary expenses, then they, too, will be motivated to contain them. Incentives are also an often-used tool for cutting costs — give your employees a reason (bonus, perks, recognition) to look for unnecessary costs, and they're sure to find them.

Always be aware that the 80-20 rule is alive and well when it comes to managing your expenses. In this case, the 80-20 rule says that 80 percent of your wasted expense dollars can be found in 20 percent of your expense categories. For businesses that have a number of employees, the wages and salary account is usually the largest expense category and, thus, the most often abused.

We don't mean to say that expenses shouldn't be challenged in every category. Quick and easy dollars can usually be found by rooting around in such expense accounts as utilities, travel, insurance, and, of course, the compost heap of them all, the "miscellaneous" expense account.

Effective expense control isn't only a profitability issue; it is also an important element for controlling cash flow (see Chapter 13). Because lack of cash is usually the number-one warning signal of a small business's impending failure, how better to begin building a solid foundation than by controlling your company's expenses?

Understanding zero-based budgeting

Budgeting (also known as *forecasting*) is the periodic (usually annual) review of past financial information with the purpose of forecasting future financial conditions. If you've completed your business plan, you, in effect, prepared your first budget when you forecasted your profit and loss statement for the upcoming year. The only difference in preparing a budget for your ongoing business is that you'll now enjoy the advantage of having yesterday's figures to work with.

The process of budgeting is one that should apply not only to your business, but also to your personal finances, especially if you have trouble saving money. If you aren't currently budgeting your personal revenues and expenses, what better way to prepare yourself for running a business than to first begin at home?

In your small business, you have two ways to budget expenses from year to year. The first — the easy way — is to assume a percentage increase for each expense category, both variable and fixed. For example, say that you decide that your telephone expense (a variable expense) will increase by 5 percent next year, your rent (a fixed expense) will remain the same, and your advertising and promotion (a variable expense) will increase by 10 percent. Whoosh, a few multiplications later, and you've budgeted these expenses for the course of a year. How easy can budgeting get?

Zero-based budgeting, on the other hand, makes the assumption that last year's expenses were zero and begins the budgeting process from that point. For example, the zero-based formula assumes that your supplies' expense account begins at zero; thus, you must first determine who consumed what supplies last year, who will be consuming them this year, and how much will be consumed. Then you must determine what price you'll pay for this year's supplies. In this manner, zero-based budgeting forces you to annually manage your consumption at the same time that you're annually reviewing your costs.

The effect of zero-based budgeting is that you'll no longer include prior years' mistakes in the current year's budgets. For example, when budgeting telephone expenses for the year, instead of increasing it by a flat percentage, zero-based budgeting demands that you make sure that your prior year's bill was the lowest it could be. This assumption forces you to determine who's using your phones for what kind of activity and also to reprice your rates with telephone carriers. Instead of forecasting a 5-percent increase, you may well end up projecting a 5-percent decrease. The zero-based method also assumes that you'll check out prices with vendors other than those that you're presently using.

 Far too many small businesses don't budget expenses at all. Furthermore, of those small-business owners who do, few use zero-based budgeting, despite its many advantages. Not budgeting is truly one of the most expensive mistakes you can make as a small-business owner. Sure, zero-based budgeting may take more of your time, but it can pay big dividends in increasing bottom-line profitability — at home or at your business.

Managing Vendor Relationships

A small business's most underrated priority is its vendors (suppliers). Think about it. Without a good vendor, what would happen to your business? You own a computer retail store? Where would you be without Compaq and Hewlett-Packard and Microsoft on your shelves? You run a restaurant? Where would you be without a reliable baker, meat supplier, and fresh vegetable resource to depend on? Every successful business owner has learned the importance of having a cadre of loyal vendors standing behind his or her business.

Yet few small businesses have the muscle or the clout to demand any significant degree of vendor loyalty, which means that they must build strong vendor relationships the old-fashioned way — by earning them. The following tips provide information on how to earn favored relationships with your vendors:

✔ **Don't nickel-and-dime your vendors.** Agree on the details of your business arrangement (price, delivery, and terms) and then try to work within those parameters for the agreed-upon period of time. (Occasional exceptions will exist.) And whatever you do, don't use the lowball pricing of the latest vendor on the street as leverage against the longtime reliable vendor unless you're prepared to lose or greatly annoy the longtime reliable one.

✔ **Pay your bills on time.** Paying your bills in the designated period of time helps maintain favored-customer status. After all, isn't prompt payment what you expect of *your* customers?

✔ **Save your special favors for when you need them.** Don't cry wolf on requests for out-of-the-ordinary service; save those requests for crunch time.

✔ **Treat your vendor's representatives (sales or customer service employees) as you want your own employees to be treated.** The Golden Rule is alive and well when it comes to maintaining vendor relationships.

✔ **Remember that relationships matter.** Everyone these days is preaching "relationships, relationships, relationships" when dealing with customers, right? Well, the same thing applies with vendors. Work to build a solid relationship with yours. If your vendor is a national supplier, build that relationship with its local or regional salesperson or representative or person at the other end of the phone line. If your vendor is a local supplier, get to know him or her personally, just as you would a local customer. And remember, bankers are vendors, too (perhaps the most important one of all)!

Vendors, incidentally — especially the good ones — can provide you with more than just a product or service. Vendors can be a great source of new business referrals. They can also provide training to both your employees and, on some occasions, your customers — a form of assistance that the typical small businesses can never get enough of. For example, in co-author Jim's sporting-goods business, the manufacturers of many of the products the company sold (fitness products especially) offered both on-site and off-site training programs at no charge. Be sure to ask your vendors what training programs and/or sales aids they offer and make use of them.

Not every prospective vendor will measure up to your standards. Be sure to check out your new vendors carefully, especially when they don't have a reputation or a track record. You can accomplish this inspection by touring their facilities, requesting customer references, or asking for financial statements.

The overriding point here is that creating a successful business takes a unique combination of human beings: you, your employees, your customers, your vendors, and a variety of outsiders (see the next section for more information). No matter which of these you consider the most important, the others all have their roles in building your successful business.

Dealing with Bankers, Lawyers, and Other Outsiders

In earlier chapters of this book, we discuss the loans bankers make, the entities lawyers initiate, the government agencies that interact with entrepreneurs, and the financial statements that accountants generate. But we haven't discussed the people themselves who are behind all that activity.

This section is intended to help you understand the outsiders you must deal with, with the intention of helping you successfully manage the relationships that evolve.

Bankers

Ask the typical small-business owner what he thinks about bankers, and you'll usually get a reaction somewhere between a roll of the eyes and a hair-tearing tantrum. Bankers get a bad rap from the small-business community.

When bankers say no, they're only doing what they're trained to do — protect their depositors' money. For example, we know of a banker who will, as part of his spiel to would-be borrowers, say, "I treat my bank's money as if it belonged to my parents." What this banker is really saying here is, "If there's a hint of a risk, you'll have to find your money elsewhere." After all, most of a typical bank's depositors are *someone's* parents or grandparents.

What this translates to is that bankers don't like to take big risks; that's a key part of their job description. Think about it: If bankers were creative and optimistic and prone to take risks, they'd be entrepreneurs, not bankers. We all have our roles in a capitalistic system. Being safe and conservative just happens to be theirs.

Make no mistake about it; start-ups are the riskiest of risks, which is the reason bankers don't usually consider financing them, unless the collateral is right. Meanwhile, especially in recent years, a variety of small-business below-market lenders have appeared on the scene, and today a number of viable alternatives exist for finding start-up capital.

Although bankers may not play an important role in the start-up, after the business is up and running, their role can become more crucial, especially when the small business experiences rapid growth. Expansion often requires operating capital in the form of outside financing, which is where the bankers come in. (On occasion, of course, the entrepreneur may go back to his original source for that operating capital; more typically, however, it is provided by bank loans.)

Here's how we recommend that you work with bankers:

- **Help your banker do his job.** Call him more often than he calls you — not with just the good news, but also with the bad. Bankers don't like surprises, especially bad ones.

- **Always ask for more money than you think you need.** A little insurance never hurt anybody, and you usually won't get everything you ask for anyway. Besides, going back to the well a second time can be difficult, as well as embarrassing.

- **Prepare in advance for your banker's visits.** These aren't social calls your banker's paying on you; she's kicking your tires. Include an agenda and a tour of your facilities, and then review your financial results *before* she asks you for them. Finally, follow up your banker's visit with a letter outlining your discussion and thanking her for her time.

- **Recognize that you're probably going to have to *personally guarantee* (legally obligate your personal assets as collateral) your business's loans.** After all, you're asking your banker to, in effect, deposit his firm's money into your business. If you were in your banker's shoes, wouldn't you ask for such a guarantee? Remember, however, that your guarantee is only one of many issues that is up for negotiation when you're borrowing money. Try to use your guarantee to get an offsetting concession (something in return for your benefit) in the lending agreement.

- **Don't lose sight of the fact that a bank's interest rate, the collateral it requires, and the terms it outlines are negotiable.** What you settle on will depend on the strength of your bargaining position. Don't blindly accept everything the banker offers; shop around among various banks that do small-business lending.

- **Be prepared to answer the bank's tough questions, especially where your assets are concerned.** The banker will want to know more about such hard assets as inventory, receivables, and equipment than you ever thought possible. But remember, that's the bank's insurance. It needs to know those answers, and the better your business's assets look to the bank, the better your negotiating position will be when the time comes to work out the terms of the loan.

Bankers and their conservative, close-to-the-vest ways are a fact of life. You can either learn to live with them, or you face life without being able to borrow their money.

Look at the community banks first because they have historically taken the lead in small-business lending.

The problem with bank committees

Several years after co-author Jim purchased General Sports Corporation, the largest bank in Minneapolis granted his business its first line of credit. The relationship between Minneapolis's biggest bank (at the time) and its scrawniest entrepreneur (at the time) proceeded smoothly for the next several years, thanks to General Sports's profitable operations and the bank's capable account executive who handled the account. The account executive, who had become Jim's friend, knew everything that went on inside the business — Jim saw to that.

One day, the account executive stopped by unexpectedly to say good-bye (he had been promoted) and to pass on the news of a new bank policy: Jim's loan application had to be approved by "the committee." It seems that General Sports's borrowing needs had exceeded some magic level and now required three loan-officer signatures instead of one. Jim was assured that this new procedure was only a formality.

A year or so later, the inevitable happened. "The committee regrets to inform you," the voice on the telephone began. And so ended the relationship between Jim and the biggest bank in town.

Jim and General Sports eventually survived, thanks to hard work and a relationship with a neighborhood community bank. And as Jim's companies have grown over the years, he has learned to live with banks' committees. Although the formula is simple (you depend on facts and figures and not on trust), the enactment is difficult and usually runs against human nature (against Jim's, anyway).

The problem, as Jim sees it looking back on the incident, is that committees don't spawn relationships; individuals spawn relationships. Jim found out the hard way that he would rather do business with a living, breathing human being than a committee, anytime.

Lawyers

Lawyers used to be like FBI agents: You were aware that they existed, and sometimes you even met one, but you rarely had occasion to deal with one. They practiced their trade on someone else — never on you.

Today, lawyers are like pets. Everybody seems to have one. If you worked for General Motors, for example, lawyers would be part of the overhead — a fixed expense, similar to rent and depreciation and the CEO's limousine driver.

 But small-business owners don't work for General Motors. To you, lawyers are a large, additional expense. Lawyers' fees redirect your hard-earned cash, resulting in capital expenditures that you must put on hold, new employees that you can't hire, or trade shows that you must skip. Additionally, spending time with them takes time away from work and results in lost productivity on the job.

All that said, consulting a lawyer has a time and a place. Lawyers provide protection (often against other lawyers) and force you to make plans to guard against the downsides that your entrepreneurially optimistic nature may overlook.

Yes, lawyers definitely have a time and a place. The place is always in the lawyer's office — you can't afford to pay a lawyer to travel to your office — or on the phone, and the times are as follows:

- ✔ When forming your corporation or LLC
- ✔ When taking in a partner or partners
- ✔ When creating shares of stock in your company — for you and for others
- ✔ When signing a lease, contract, or binding agreement
- ✔ When buying or selling a business
- ✔ When dealing with someone else's attorney on a conflictive issue
- ✔ When creating an employee handbook
- ✔ When designing employee bonus programs that result in company ownership for the employees
- ✔ When dealing with a situation that could result in expensive litigation (such as terminating a longtime employee)
- ✔ When (we hope this never happens) considering bankruptcy

No matter how much you want to avoid the expense of consulting with a lawyer, you should hire one at the start-up stage and on the preceding occasions throughout the life of your business. When these occasions present themselves, we suggest you follow these suggestions on how best to find and utilize your lawyer:

- ✔ **When you absolutely, positively have to find a lawyer, don't shop price; shop quality *and* price.** As with cars and quarterbacks, lawyers differ greatly in the way they perform, and that difference usually translates into winning or losing. Check references closely, just as you would when hiring a key employee.

- ✔ **Get a quote on your prospective lawyer's hourly fees and ask for an estimate of the total tab in advance.** The estimate may not hold up, but the lawyer will know that you're watching.

- ✔ **Always ask for your invoices to be itemized.** A lump-sum invoice includes only time and rate, while an itemized invoice includes the date and time of each segment of work, the specific subject of each charge, and then the hourly rate. An itemized invoice also indicates work that was done by others — paralegals, for example — along with their hourly rates and charges for related materials.

- ✔ **Don't let lawyers chitchat about golf and football if their meters are running.**

✔ **Keep in mind that lawyers are human beings, too, which means they aren't always right.** They work in a gray profession, not a black-and-white one. The power of logic — theirs and yours — working in unison with their knowledge of the law will play a significant role in your business. You're capable of logic, too. Don't be afraid to use it in their presence. If your lawyers won't listen to you or ask for your input with important decisions, ditch 'em.

✔ **Don't be afraid to fire lawyers when they fail to perform up to your expectations.** They're no different from employees, accountants, and anyone else you hire to provide a service.

Lawyers aren't the only resource for settling disputes. Many small businesses today are mediating to resolve issues with customers, suppliers, or employees. Mediation is significantly less expensive than litigation and can take a fraction of the time (no court dates, no judges, and no miles of red tape). Nationwide providers of mediation services include the American Arbitration Association (800-778-7879; www.adr.org) and JAMS (800-352-5267; www.jamsadr.com), or you can look in the Yellow Pages under Mediation.

Tax advisors

Tax advisors, like lawyers, are professionals, too. The services they provide aren't rooted in conflict, but hiring and paying them can be equally annoying and almost as expensive.

The role of tax advisors, in essence, is to provide you with the information you need to pay your taxes, make tax-wise business decisions, keep score of your progress, and help you manage your business. We cover the hiring of tax advisors/CPAs in Chapter 18.

Consultants

Hiring a consultant is akin to playing wild-card poker, meaning that fate will be a factor in determining whether you select the right one. That is not to say your success or failure is entirely in fate's hands, because the more effort you put into the hiring process, the better your chances will be to do the job right.

Consultants can provide a wide array of services. Several of the areas where consultants can help the most include computer and information systems, tax issues, human relations, sales, and marketing.

You'll find more than one way to use and pay consultants. Some consultants offer their clients advice only; other consultants dive head-first into their client's business and get their hands dirty. Some consultants are paid by the hour, others by retainer (a fixed fee every month). It all depends on what you want and what you can afford.

We've collected these tips on how to get the most out of your consultant:

- ✔ **Engage a consultant as if hiring a key staff employee.** Network to find the best one and always check references carefully. Avoid consultants who have had only big corporate (as opposed to small-business) experience. Despite what they'll tell you, most don't understand what running a small business is like. Hire only consultants with plenty of small-business experience.

- ✔ **Whatever you do, don't hand over to your consultants the responsibility of making key decisions.** Also, never bet the house on the suggestions they make. Make your consultants prove themselves on smaller issues before you make the bigger changes they're recommending. And never forget that you're in charge.

- ✔ **Offer no long-term contracts.** Build in a quick-exit option in the event that you don't get what you expected. And don't hesitate to show consultants the door when they aren't doing the job. Or, as the old adage goes, "Hire them slowly, fire them quickly."

- ✔ **Understand that the ultimate cost of engaging ineffectual consultants can be measured only in part by their fees.** Add misdirection, upset employees, and time lost, and consultants are capable of running up monumental tabs in surprisingly short periods of time.

Governments

If only entrepreneurs would understand that the government is often an uncontrollable random event, like a fire or a flood or a competitor moving next door. This is especially true of the federal government, where the small-business owner may find it quite difficult to so much as talk to those officials who are the actual decision-makers, let alone to get their problems resolved.

Come to terms with the fact that you'll sometimes have to comply with the government's unwieldy and often unfriendly rules and regulations. Don't antagonize government employees — they can make your life miserable. Do what needs to be done to satisfy the sometimes disagreeable government employees (you'd probably be disagreeable, too, if you had to spend your life in their environment), treat the agreeable ones like you'd want your own employees to be treated, and don't shoot the messenger — most government employees are only trying to do their jobs. In Chapter 17, we offer helpful advice for dealing with government regulations.

Chapter 11

Marketing: Product, Pricing, Distribution, Promotion, and Sales

- -

In This Chapter

▶ Defining marketing and developing products or services

▶ Determining a price and pricing strategy

▶ Setting up a distribution system

▶ Promoting your products or services

▶ Creating buzz with publicity

▶ Getting your products and services sold

- -

*C*lose the door, turn off the phone and stereo, and put on your thinking cap. It's time to discuss the topic of marketing and the process that defines it. After all, marketing is the facet of your business that will separate your product or service from the hundreds (or thousands) of competing products or services in the marketplace. And yet, marketing typically is either number one or number two on the small-business owner's list of the most difficult skills to master. (Managing employees is the other; see Chapter 15.)

Most small-business owners don't understand the process of marketing. Being a successful marketer requires a number of make-it-or-break-it skills that, more than any other, separate the mediocre (or failed) companies from the long-lived or fast-track ones. For proof of the importance of marketing as a business skill, look no further than those less-than-stellar products and services that are quite successful thanks to first-class marketing efforts (McDonald's certainly doesn't have the best hamburgers in the world). On the flip side, rarely are first-rate products successful through inadequate marketing efforts.

Lucky for you, this chapter explains the five key elements of marketing to get you up to speed and on your way to a long, healthy business life. Along the way, we include tips and suggestions aimed at helping you develop your marketing skills.

Marketing in a Nutshell

You aren't alone if you can't readily identify the difference between marketing, sales, and distribution. The definitions of these key terms (ones you'll hear over and over in the business world) are as follows:

- **Marketing:** The manner in which product development, sales, promotion, distribution, and pricing are bundled together to create an overall plan designed to communicate and deliver your company's products or services to the marketplace and, hence, to the ultimate customer.

- **Sales:** The manner in which your company either directly or indirectly connects with, convinces, and contracts with customers to purchase your products or services. Sales represent one component of the marketing process.

- **Distribution:** The channels (such as retailers, wholesalers, or catalogs) that you use to deliver your product or service to your customers.

In large corporations, the senior executive in charge of marketing carries the burden; the work he or she does is pivotal to the success or failure of the business. In a small business, however, the marketing function usually rests on the shoulders of the owner.

These five key components, which we discuss in detail in the following sections, make up the marketing process:

- Product and service development
- Pricing
- Distribution
- Promotion
- Sales

Tackling Product and Service Development

For most entrepreneurs, product and service development is the most enjoyable part of building a business. Whether refining an existing product or service or inventing a brand-spanking-new one, many entrepreneurs hang out their shingles in the first place because they believe they have valuable products or services to offer or have identified an unmet demand in the marketplace. They love the nuances of their products or services and are forever looking for ways to redefine and expand them.

Co-author Eric is an excellent example of how product and service development can define the direction of a small business. From his work in the corporate world, Eric understands the financial services industry from the inside, and he sought to take that knowledge to help people improve their personal financial situations. Eric's initial service was personal financial counseling. Because he enjoys teaching, he soon began teaching personal finance courses through the University of California. He also began writing for a variety of newspapers and magazines and was hard at work on a book proposal. Today, somewhat to his surprise, Eric's writing takes most of his time; in the early stages of the business, Eric had envisioned reaching more people and growing his business through his financial counseling practice.

Co-author Jim's second business had a similar growth pattern, resulting from the development of new products. His retail and wholesale sporting-goods company spawned a screen-printing operation as he strove to add new lines of products. (He wanted to be able to number and letter the athletic jerseys that his company sold to teams.) Fifteen years later, his simple product development idea had grown into a stand-alone, $25-million business.

Despite the fact that too many small businesses go about product and service development in haphazard ways, a defined process exists. That process goes something like this:

1. **Get an idea.**

   Someone (not necessarily you, the entrepreneur) hatches the idea. No matter where it comes from, though, you, the business owner, are always the one to *champion* (or support) the idea.

   New product and service ideas can come from a variety of sources, including vendors, trade publications, and, of course, employees. Unquestionably, however, the majority of new product ideas result from talking with and listening to customers, both current and potential. After all, customers are the people who are most familiar with the use of the product or service, and customers are, in most cases, the same people who ultimately purchase new products. Your ears should always be open to customer ideas, no matter how off-the-wall they may seem.

2. **Together with the people responsible for product development, you evaluate your idea.**

   Pay particular attention to issues such as profit potential, ease of manufacturing (where applicable), competition, and pricing.

   Not every idea turns into a workable or profitable product or service. You need to be critical and tough during your evaluation. Be sure to ask the following questions:

   • Do you have the staff and the cash (or can you assemble the resources) necessary to back the idea?

- Does the idea fit your current product line, mission statement, and the values of your business, or can you build a new business or business unit around the idea?

- Is the competition already offering a comparable product or service? If so, is your idea distinctly better or more competitive?

Make sure that you can answer "yes" to these three questions before moving on to Step 3. The product development process is expensive; you're better off cutting your losses early in the process rather than later.

3. **Analyze your opportunity.**

   You present the product or service concept to a few, select customers in an attempt to determine the size and scope of the potential market.

4. **Develop your product or service.**

   At this stage, if the project is still a go, you develop the product or service. Time to dot the *i*'s and cross the *t*'s in preparation for the next step.

5. **Test the market/conduct market research.**

   Test the (hopefully) completed product or service with a few prospective customers, with the intent of working out any bugs, in preparation for the product's introduction to the marketplace.

6. **Introduce your product or service to the marketplace.**

   Begin an advertising program, send the press releases, and commence the training of the salespeople responsible for selling the new product or service.

Because not every idea will turn into a workable or profitable product or service, you need to be tough as you proceed through these steps — especially when you reach the evaluation process (Step 2). Make sure that you thoroughly evaluate before moving on to the opportunity-analysis stage. The product development process is expensive, and you're better off cutting your losses early in the process rather than later.

Pricing: Cost and Value

Someone once made the observation that pricing is two-thirds marketing and one-third financial. This statement goes against the grain of common sense, which suggests that nothing could be more financial than price. But if your pricing isn't right, your marketing plan, no matter how well crafted, won't get off the ground. Prices too high? Your product won't sell. Prices too low? Your product may sell but your company won't be profitable. The price, as the television game show proclaims, must be right.

To properly understand the role of pricing, you must first understand the word margin. *Margin* is the difference between how much it costs you to produce your product or service and the price for which you can sell it. If your widget costs your company $2 to manufacture, for instance, and you sell it for $3, your margin is $1. Presented in terms of percentages, you have made a profit of $1 on that $3 sale, in the process providing you with a margin of 33 percent ($1 divided by $3).

Margins vary widely depending on the industry, so we can't give you guidelines about what margins to expect for your specific business. The margins on grocery items, for example, are relatively low, ranging typically from 5 to 10 percent. Meanwhile, the margins on clothing are relatively high, typically averaging 50 percent. What we can do is help you craft your pricing strategy and decide on a price that suits you.

Developing your pricing strategy

Every business needs an overall strategy to guide it in making its pricing decisions. This means you need to plan your pricing strategy, as opposed to letting it evolve. Pricing shouldn't be a decision you make on a day-to-day basis, but rather an extension of an overall plan.

For example, you may decide (by planning) to be the lowest-priced company in your niche, thus attracting customers who think they're getting a bargain by frequenting your business. Or you may want to have the highest prices in your niche — high prices send messages of quality and distinction to some customers (witness art galleries, fine wines, or Brooks Brothers shirts). You may even want to sell some of your products at a low price (these products are referred to as *loss leaders*) in order to attract customers who will then buy other products at higher prices.

As a small-business owner, you have the flexibility to determine your price points any way you see fit. Keep the following five factors in mind as you consider your pricing strategy.

Your marketing objectives

Marketing objectives vary with the product or service you're selling. If, for example, you have a new product to introduce, your short-term objective may be to gain market share and preempt competition, in the process making your product well known to the consumer. So, you may discount your normal prices over the short-term in order to achieve these long-term objectives, with profitability being shunted to the background. Discounted prices can't go on forever, however, because your business won't survive without profits.

Another marketing objective may be to sell slow-moving inventory in order to generate cash. Similar to the example of new-product introduction, this objective also dictates short-term discounted pricing.

Be careful, however, not to get in the habit of continually discounting prices — unless, that is, you want to be perceived as a discount retailer. One business maxim states that if you *lowball* (discount prices) in the beginning, you're likely to lowball forever.

Most of the time, your marketing objective should be to maximize profit on your products without losing (too many) sales in the process. This is the objective that should dictate your long-term pricing decisions.

The cost to produce the product or service

Cost is the total of all the expenses involved in generating your product or service — not only direct costs, such as wages and salaries directly involved in the product, materials, and freight-in, but also indirect costs, such as administration, accounting, and sales.

Knowing the direct and indirect costs of your product or service is important in determining its *break-even point,* or the price below which you can't sell your offering without incurring losses.

Cost is one barometer of your break-even point, but should never be the primary determinant in the pricing process.

The process of determining your break-even cost is quite simple — assuming, that is, that your accounting system is capable of gathering the necessary figures (see Chapter 13 for more on accounting systems).

Here's how you can determine your break-even cost:

1. **Determine the direct-cost allocation for each product or service.**

   To do this, add all the direct costs (those directly involved in its manufacture — wages specifically involved in the product or service, materials, and incoming freight) associated with that particular product or service during a specific accounting period (preferably one month, and no more than one quarter).

   Divide the total amount of direct-cost dollars by the total number of products manufactured or services provided during that period.

2. **Determine the indirect-cost allocation for each product or service.**

   Add the total dollars of your indirect costs (those indirect general and administrative costs that can't be specifically tied to a product or service) for that period. Divide that number by the total number of products or services you provided in that period.

3. **Add the direct-cost allocation to the indirect-cost allocation.**

   The result is your break-even cost.

Amounts above the break-even cost represent your profit on that product or service; amounts below it represent your loss. If you offer more than one product or service, the process of determining a break-even point for each product or service can become complicated. The sophistication of your accounting system will determine whether you succeed in arriving at an accurate break-even cost for each product or service.

Customer demand

The relative ease or difficulty of selling your product or service to the customer should play an important part in the pricing decision. What's the ratio of product on the market to supply available? You see this factor at work as you watch gasoline prices at the pump fluctuate due to murky supply-and-demand factors. Although the price pressures in other industries may not be as readily apparent to the public as they are in the gasoline business, the price points in all industries are subject to similar supply-and-demand factors.

Comparative value to the customer

Just as beauty is in the eyes of the beholder, so is the value of a product. In addition to knowing what your product is worth in your eyes, you need to understand how much your product is *perceived* to be worth in the eyes of your customers. Set your prices at a level where your desired customers feel that they're getting their money's worth.

Competition

Who is your competition, and what's the price point of their products? How comparable are those products to yours? What are their products' perceived values compared to yours, and what factors affect their perceived values?

To determine the answers to these questions, you must first kick your competitors' tires by visiting the stores where their products are sold, or by picking up the phone and asking the right questions. Ask buyers of their products such questions as the following:

- Why they purchased the product
- What their perception of the relationship between value and price is
- Whether they would pay more for it if they had to
- What they like most about the product, and what they like least about it

Be sure, when comparing your product to that of your competitors, to include all the criteria involved, not just the price. Additional criteria can include but isn't limited to delivery, strength of brand name (image), packaging, quality, after-sales service, guarantees, and return and trade-in policies. The rest of this chapter helps you decide what to do with this competitive information, such as changing your prices, better promoting why it's worth paying more for your products and services, and so on.

Deciding on price

After you understand the factors that go into making your pricing decisions, and you've done your comparative shopping (see the previous section), you need to pull all the pieces together to make the pricing decision. We explain in this section how to make pricing decisions both for introducing a new product or service and for updating your price list for existing products or services.

Pricing new products or services

When introducing new products or services, you have three pricing options. You may choose any one of the following three, depending on your predetermined pricing strategy:

- ✔ **Premium pricing:** Premium pricing is when you set your price higher than the competition or, in the event that you have no competition, higher than what's typical within the industry for that particular product. In this way, you skim the market, in effect appealing to the customers who are most motivated to pay a high price for products based on perceived value. Premium pricing may limit your unit sales, but it will also increase your profit margin.

  This strategy is most successful if you offer unusual, one-of-a-kind products (art galleries, collectables, and so forth) or provide hard-to-get services where your pricing strategy can be to create a high perceived value.

- ✔ **Market penetration:** This choice involves lowering your price to undercut competition, with the intent of gathering dominant *market share* (the percentage that you own of the total available market). This pricing strategy is designed to help maximize your company's name recognition in the marketplace and is frequently used by start-up businesses that want to attract low-cost buyers. Generally speaking, this is a short-term tactic that you can't maintain over the long term.

- ✔ **Meeting the competition:** This pricing decision is, as the name implies, designed to meet the price of your competition, thus encouraging the customer to compare your product or service to your competitor's — feature by feature, benefit by benefit. Before adopting this pricing decision, however, you must make sure that your product or service can withstand the comparison and that you can offer a competitive price and value without threatening your survival.

Updating prices of existing products or services

Reviewing and altering prices on existing products or services is an ongoing procedure, not a once-a-year occurrence. Prices must never be cast in stone; they can and should change as market conditions change (think of gasoline prices, as noted earlier in the chapter). You can't always change prices — for instance, in those cases when you have to generate an "official price list" — but remember that pricing is primarily a marketing strategy; as markets change, so must your strategies for capturing those markets.

Channeling to Customers: Distribution

Distribution is how you get your product or service to the ultimate consumer. Distribution channels vary within the same industry and apply to all businesses. No one right or wrong way exists to distribute your products or services; you can, however, almost always find a way that works best for you.

Two basic categories of distribution exist, depending on whether a middleman comes between the manufacturer of the products (or the provider of the services) and the consumer: *Direct distribution* occurs when no middleman is involved; *indirect distribution* involves a middleman.

Each distribution channel has evolved for a reason, and each has its strengths and weaknesses. Following is a discussion of the various distribution options and how you decide between them.

Direct distribution of products

The *direct distribution* of products involves establishing one-on-one relationships with the buyers, without passing any middlemen along the way. The following sections present the various channels of direct distribution.

Retail

What better way to avoid a middleman and be close to your customers than to physically interact with them in a retail environment? Knowing your customer is crucial to any small business's success, and a retail distribution system offers a perfect vehicle for doing just that. Retail chains like The Gap and The Body Shop have chosen to sell their products through a direct distribution channel. The same person-to-person sales tools that make these big players successful can help small businesses succeed, too.

Another advantage of retail distribution is that you retain the entire markup on your products. Still another advantage is that, in most cases, you don't have the expense of maintaining accounts receivable (as in, "Put it on my tab"), because these days retailing is primarily a cash — or credit/debit card — business. Although credit-card charges — Visa, MasterCard, American Express, and others — may not represent immediate cash, they do represent a dependable stream of cash, and you don't have to worry about collecting the funds. You do, of course, pay fees — up to 2 percent or more — for these privileges.

The disadvantage of retail distribution is that the costs of maintaining and staffing a retail store are high. Also, because you can't have your eye on the till and the door all the time (in most cases), retail is susceptible to theft of both cash and products. Finally, in most cases, you're required to sign a lease, a document which legally binds you to pay a landlord for a specified period of time, regardless of whether or not your store remains in business.

Direct mail

Direct mail refers to the mailing of flyers and advertisements directly to a specific audience. The success or failure of any direct-mail campaign is usually tied to the quality of both the mailing list and the promotional piece itself.

One of direct mail's advantages is its capability to directly target and reach qualified prospects with the demographics that you choose. Looking for a list of potential customers with two or more children, who own their own homes, and who have annual incomes in excess of $100,000? No problem. You can purchase a list and do the mailing yourself. Or you can hire a firm that will do it all for you.

One disadvantage of direct mail is the relatively high cost per contact. The cost-per-thousand of direct mailings is significantly higher than the cost-per-thousand to reach newspaper or magazine readers via advertising. The difference, of course, is that if your mailing list is good, every recipient represents a *qualified prospect* (someone who fits your demographic projections of who's most likely to want your product or service), whereas only a fraction of your advertising contacts may be qualified. A second disadvantage of direct mail is that many consumers simply don't like businesses that use the direct-mail medium — so you can end up alienating potential customers if you use it.

Here's how to successfully develop your own direct-mail program:

- ✔ **Collect existing direct-mail pieces that you like and use them as examples for your own design.** Contact the business behind the materials that appeal to you the most and inquire how it was done and who did it.

- ✔ **Concentrate on solving your customers' problems, not on selling them products.** Decide what offer you'll make to move your target prospect to take the action your mailer invites. People don't want to pop pills; they want to increase their energy, so if your vitamins can help them do that, tell them so.

    This tactic is commonly known as *selling your product's benefits* and not its features and is possibly the #1 rule of marketing!

- ✔ **Purchase or rent a mailing list by interviewing several different list companies.** Look in the Yellow Pages under Mailing Lists or call trade magazine reps and inquire about their subscription lists. Costs should vary from $25 to $75 per thousand names. Make sure you've defined the target market for your product or service and obtain a mailing list that includes only those who match the profile of your target.

- ✔ **Consider using a self-mailer where possible, thereby saving the cost of an envelope.** More people throw away junk mail in sealed envelopes.

- ✔ **Stick with it; don't give up after the first mailing.** Many consumers need to see the same message several times before they react.

> ✔ **Follow up your mailings with phone calls.** When you intend to follow up the mailing with a phone call (which often helps to ensure better results), stagger your mailings so you don't have to make too many calls during a short time period.

Finally, be sure to maintain a complete record of the results of your mailing, detailing the number of responses and the number of orders that result. Don't set your goals overly high — a 2- to 3-percent response rate on a first-time direct mailing is usually considered good.

Mail-order catalogs

Mail-order catalogs, along with Web sites, have enjoyed a leap in popularity as the American shopper does more and more of his or her shopping from the comfort of home. Make no mistake about it, however: Catalog selling is an expensive channel for businesses, especially for start-ups. Creating and mailing a top-notch catalog — if you can't afford a top-notch catalog, you probably don't belong in this distribution channel — can be off-the-charts expensive, depending on the size of the mailings you want to do.

Initial outlays include the charge for obtaining mailing lists, the costs of creating and developing the catalog, and the mailing expenses. And don't forget the additional cost (and risk) of maintaining sufficient inventory to be able to ship your orders within a reasonable amount of time.

Internet sales

Certainly the newer kid on the block, Internet selling (also known as *e-commerce*) is the most exciting development since the wagon trains headed west. In essence, Internet sales are another form of catalog sales. Customers simply connect to your company's Web site, click around until they find the items they're looking for, plug in their credit-card numbers, and wait for the packages to arrive by mail. Distribution via the Internet is easy on the shopper (no dodging traffic or fighting crowds) and easy on the vendor (no mall rent or expensive mailing lists).

Incidentally, this relatively inexpensive way of reaching customers also allows Internet prices for most products (except for those that are quite costly to ship) to be competitive. If you have any doubts, try undercutting Amazon's prices on anything it sells (which includes a lot more than books).

Internet selling works best for the small business when you have an off-the-beaten-path product that customers can't find anywhere else. Customers who are having trouble finding good products easily turn to Internet searches to locate alternative suppliers. For instance, one company we know sells, via the Internet, car-mounting brackets for carrying fly rods on the top of automobiles. And a national magazine recently published an article about a man who successfully sells emus over the Internet! Bottom line: You can't compete with the Amazons, the Wal-Marts, or the eBays, who are offering thousands of products.

Trade shows

You may be in an industry that allows you to use trade shows to purchase your products from your vendors or to sell your products to your customers. Trade shows also provide the opportunity to network with other people who do the same thing you do and to check out the competition (see Chapter 14). Most of all, the information you glean from successfully working a trade show will allow you to keep a pulse on your industry. (Don't overlook the training classes that are usually included with most trade shows.) Yes, trade shows can be expensive by the time you factor in travel and time away from the job, but they're usually a justifiable marketing expense.

Check out `www.tsnn.com` for an excellent resource that lists trade shows, seminars, and conventions all over the world for a wide variety of industries and organizations. The site covers everything from helping you find the best trade shows, conventions, and seminars to offering related travel information.

Indirect distribution of products

Indirect distribution is the process in which consumer products or services first pass through a middleman before reaching the consumer. The following sections outline the channels you may use for indirect distribution.

Reaching your customers through other retailers

Traverse the aisles of a Wal-Mart or Target store and you'll find that every product on its shelves is from a manufacturer somewhere that has opted for the secondhand retailing method of indirect distribution. Meanwhile, Wal-Mart and Target are left to do what they do best: Sell directly to the consumer.

The advantage of selling to retailers is that you have to deal with only one, or a few, customers — the retailer's buyer(s) — which simplifies the distribution process immensely. This one-stop selling process enhances the *relationship selling* process — that is, the establishment of a relationship between the vendor and the customer. (For more on relationship selling, see "Sales: Where the Rubber Hits the Road" later in this chapter.) In this case, the relationship is between the manufacturer's salesperson and the retailer's buyer.

One distinct disadvantage of selling your products to retailers — especially those with multiple stores — is that they often use the size of the orders they place as leverage to become extremely demanding on such issues as price, payment-related issues, delivery, and packaging. Retailers, especially the larger ones, can keep their prices low for a reason, and more often than not, that reason comes at the expense of their vendors — especially the smaller ones that don't have the leverage the bigger guys have.

Relying on wholesalers or distributors

Wholesale distribution is a perfect example of how the middleman process works. The typical wholesaler/distributor buys large quantities of products from manufacturers, breaks them down into manageable quantities, sometimes repackages them, and then offers them to the consumer in manageable, bite-sized pieces. Examples of wholesalers include plumbing- and electrical-supply businesses, whose primary customers are contractors, and grocery wholesalers, whose primary customers are grocery and convenience stores. Many manufacturers don't want the hassles associated with selling to consumers and smaller customers; after all, their expertise is in manufacturing.

Repackaging

Another common example of indirect distribution is *repackaging:* selling your products to another manufacturer or a developer of related products who offers them to their customers in another form. You often see examples of repackaging in the grocery business, where a grocery store chain includes on its shelves products that bear the store's own name (the process is known as *private labeling*) on the containers of products someone else has manufactured. Many juices, frozen foods, and health and beauty products have been repackaged.

An advantage of repackaging is that, in most cases, the sales and marketing functions are left to your customer, allowing you to concentrate on the manufacturing part of your business. The disadvantages are that your profit margins are sure to suffer and you're likely to be overly dependent on one customer — the company doing the repackaging.

Deciding on distribution

No easy answer exists to the question of which distribution channels are best suited to your business. To set about determining the answer to this question, list the distribution channels that

- ✔ Your competitors are using. Rank the list with the most successful businesses at the top.
- ✔ You can afford.
- ✔ Your research and intuition tell you will be successful in your industry five years from now.

Now compare the three lists, add a pinch of common sense, and determine the distribution channel(s) that you prefer. Then gear up to meet the needs of that channel.

Whatever you do, don't lock yourself into one distribution channel forever. Land's End, for instance, started in the catalog business, but today it also has consumer retail and Internet channels. Ditto L.L. Bean. Today's technologies are changing distribution channel options at warp speed. Small business is about staying flexible — whatever distribution channel(s) you select should be subject to ongoing review.

Spreading the Word: Promotion

Promotion is the process of informing potential customers about your company and its products and services and then influencing them to purchase what you're selling. Promotional activities include word-of-mouth advertising, networking, media advertising, online communications, and publicity. You'll undertake some promotional efforts to generate sales; other tactics you use will aim to educate, inform, and plant the seed for future sales.

Before you invest in any promotional effort, you must first determine the target market you want to reach and the objective you want to achieve. If you want prospective customers to call or visit your Web site, your ad better give good reasons to, and it better have a prominent presentation of your phone number and Web site address. If you want to create foot traffic, you have to put forward a time-sensitive, compelling reason to visit your business, such as a one-time discount or the appearance of a VIP.

To put it in one sentence: Know your audience and your objective and craft your messages accordingly. The following sections show you the way through the scope of possible promotional activities.

Networking (It's not what you know . . .)

Networking is connecting with people in order to make good things happen. Networking offers a host of benefits to those who partake in it, the two most obvious being the opportunity to promote your products or services and the opportunity for you to learn from your peers. These two benefits are the primary reasons that organizations such as the Chamber of Commerce, the Rotary, and Toastmasters exist.

But wait. Before you run out and join your local business organizations (see Chapter 14), think about using the networks you already have. Your friends, your relatives, your alma mater, your church, your children's school, your neighborhood, and the social organizations you belong to are all viable networks. With a little priming (being proactive), many of your existing networks will be happy to give your product or service a try. All you have to do is initiate the priming.

This priming can come in many forms — a telephone call, a flyer in the mail, an e-mail, or even a casual mention during a conversation following a school event. All these are viable parts of the network priming process and all are available at little cost.

Be thoughtful and careful when networking with the people you know. People are busy and bombarded daily (aren't you?) with tons of advertising, solicitations, and spam e-mail. The last thing most people want is to be accosted by a pushy salesperson in what they thought were the friendly and safe confines of a school or church. Start with a low-key approach: Assemble a one-page summary or a simple flyer of your company's products or services, and mail or e-mail copies to people you know.

You can improve your network priming with these additional tips:

- ✔ **At the beginning of every year, make a goal for yourself to add one more network to your current stable of contacts.**

- ✔ **Make sure that you have a professional-looking business card, and don't be shy about handing it out.** Folks should be able to discern exactly the business you're in through the combination of your company name and your tag line, both of which should appear on your business card.

- ✔ **Be sure to follow up every networking opportunity.** A telephone call or a letter the next day will remind your networking prospects of your business and will show them that you manage it professionally.

- ✔ **Remember that networking works both ways.** Help another small business within your network, and you can usually expect that the other business will eventually help you. Such is the basis for successful networking.

Recognizing the power of referrals

What do you think when you hear a radio spot that says the Greasy Spoon Café serves the best burgers in town, but five minutes later, a friend tells you that it's Danny's Diner that really serves the best burgers? Who are you going to believe — the radio ad or your friend?

If you're like most people, you'll believe your friend — unless you know that he has doughnuts and soda for breakfast. After all, radio ads are scripted and paid advertising. Not so with friends; they have no script and generally no agenda, which makes them a credible resource. Such is the power of *word-of-mouth referrals.*

The problem, of course, is that you can't dictate the script of a referral the way you can with a radio ad. If Danny's hamburgers aren't up to snuff, Danny's would be better off if its customers kept their mouths shut. Word-of-mouth referrals tell it the way the customer sees it, not as the owner would like him to see it; so, make sure your product or service is up to snuff before people start talking.

You don't have to hire an ad agency or media consultant to make word-of-mouth promotion work for you; you can do it yourself. The price is right. If you take care of your customers in the early stages of your business's life and provide an easy feedback mechanism, the referrals from satisfied customers should take care of you and your business in the future.

Every time you serve a satisfied customer, follow up the sale by calling the satisfied customer or asking her to fill out a feedback card (making sure the transaction went to her satisfaction). Ask for one referral. Additionally, whenever a new customer does business with you, ask how he heard about your company. When the customer replies that he has been referred to you by, say, Harry, make sure that the next time Harry stops by, he gets a sincere thank you and possibly a discount or some other offer of value. You're thereby rewarding Harry's behavior — not necessarily a new trick in the motivational game, but an effective one.

Marketing with permission via e-mail

The Internet is the greatest direct-mail medium of all time, and e-mail is the engine that delivers the advertising message of Internet direct mail. We're not talking about the endless delivery of unrequested and unwanted e-mail — called *spamming* — you see too much of these days. (That kind of e-mail is annoying more often than not, and it's often illegal.) Instead, we're talking about sending targeted e-mails to lists of current and potential customers who have given you permission to communicate with them via this medium. You get such permission through personal contacts generated by phone conversations, sales calls, networking requests, and so on.

Small-business owners use the Internet for a number of reasons, including but not limited to gathering information and purchasing products. Communication, however, leads the list, with more than 80 percent of Web users listing it as the main reason they go online. Research by The Direct Marketing Association (www.the-dma.org) indicates that the average advertising cost per sale of an e-mail campaign is $2. (This compares to a direct-mail cost per sale of $71 and a banner-ad cost per sale of $100.)

Using e-mail allows you to do a number of marketing-related tasks that are directly related to building relationships with both current customers and potential customers. You can

- Invite response to your e-mail so that you can e-mail the recipient back.

- Invite the recipient to visit your Web site, thereby saving the cost of mailing a brochure.

- Provide information that will be noteworthy to the recipient.

- Simply keep in touch with your customer, as long as the content of the message is relevant to the permission you've been granted.

- Use e-mail to process a customer's order in the most efficient way possible.

We can name at least three more reasons why e-mail is such a rapidly growing direct-marketing tool and will continue to be for the foreseeable future:

> ✔ **Postage and printing are free.** Compare e-mail to the cost of creating (and then mailing) a brochure.
>
> ✔ **Frequency is free.** You can talk with your prospect over and over again.
>
> ✔ **Contact is fast.** Hit the Send button and your message is delivered.

Used in such a wide variety of ways, e-mail, when targeted and based on previously granted permission, can build solid customer relationships. And relationships lead to sales.

Media advertising

Our definition of *advertising* is a program of paid messages designed to inform large numbers of prospective consumers on the features and benefits of your product or services. Although the ultimate long-term purpose of advertising is to persuade the consumer to think well of your business and to purchase your product or service, some short-term advertising strategies may focus on the achievement of specific objectives. For instance, you may want to attract attendance at events, win sales within a certain time period, or gain name recognition for a new business.

Good advertising is about repetition. Mention Federal Express, and people remember "When it absolutely, positively has to be there overnight." M&M's are remembered for the slogan "Melts in your mouth, not in your hand." Neither of these slogans became implanted in your mind via a one-shot advertising blitz or a slogan-of-the-month effort. Those brands became well known, in part, because they invested heavily in oft-repeated advertising and then they kept their messages focused and consistent.

View advertising as an important investment rather than a dreaded expense. When you budget money to put your message in front of prospective customers with effective frequency, it's an investment in your future success.

Because you're not a large company, you can't afford to spend buckets of money on media advertising. That's why we highly recommend that, in the early stages of your business — when cash is generally scarce — you focus on networking and referrals as well as other low-cost, highly targeted advertising tools (such as e-mail) to get your first customers in the door. Then, when you're ready to venture out into the world of paid advertising, use one of these three methods of developing your advertisements to get the best results in a cost-effective manner:

> ✔ **Create your ads in-house, either by writing them yourself or by utilizing an employee who has advertising and creative talent.** Make sure, however, that serious editing is performed on everything that goes out your door. Mistakes or misspellings in advertising materials reflect poorly on the advertiser and will turn off some buyers.

✔ **Work with freelance copywriters, designers, media buyers, or other resource professionals.** Contract projects on an as-needed basis, and maintain responsibility for continuity, accuracy, and timeliness.

✔ **Hire an advertising agency to handle all your advertising needs.** This way, instead of calling a designer when you need a trade booth, a copywriter when you need an ad, or a direct-mail house when you want a mailing, you turn to a single resource for all projects. A good agency should review your entire communications needs, create a single campaign, and produce all the materials that you need to prepare the message that works best for you.

Yes, you'll pay handsomely for the expertise and service, but you free yourself for other activities. Also, assuming the agency you select is a reputable and qualified one (check references carefully), your advertising program will give you the bang for your buck that you're seeking.

To find the advertising resource that's right for you, watch, read, or listen to media (radio, television, magazines, newspapers), select the ads you like, and then call the business that's doing the advertising and find out who produced or assisted in producing the ad. Or you can simply network with other small-business owners who have advertised and ask questions to determine who and what worked for them. Also, network with your vendors, your customers, or within your business organizations. Be sure to check your prospective advertisers' credentials and get firm quotes on the cost of their services.

The following media options are the most widely used by small businesses for spreading the message.

Successful advertising requires focus, especially when dealing with the issue of consumer demographics. If, for instance, you're selling opera star Placido Domingo recordings and advertising on a country-and-western radio station, you're focusing on the wrong audience.

Yellow Pages

The Yellow Pages were largely created for, and belong to, hometown retailers and service suppliers. Looking for a hardware store or somewhere to rent a tux? Many prospective customers head for the Yellow Pages first.

Generally speaking, if your small business is looking to advertise, and if your clientele is primarily local, consider the Yellow Pages first. The relatively low cost of ads in the Yellow Pages allows smaller businesses to compete with the bigger ones. Best of all, ads in the Yellow Pages have an extended shelf life; they can be found next to most people's telephones for at least a year.

Be creative with your ad, and remember that bigger (which the Yellow Pages sales rep will push for, thanks to the commission) isn't necessarily better. In the Yellow Pages, your ad will be placed right there with all your direct competitors, so your ad needs to set your product or service apart from the rest. Often, your product or service may fit in more than one category. Suppose that you sell screen-printed T-shirts. For an extra fee, you could be listed under T-shirts, Advertising, and/or Screen Printing.

Be sure and track new customers and find out how they heard about your business. You won't know whether your Yellow Pages option (or any other medium you've selected) is working unless you ask.

If your primary customer audience comes from outside your local area, chances are you have little or no need for Yellow Pages advertising. Opt for a one-line entry, because you don't need any more. Yellow Pages ads can be expensive, especially when they aren't generating customer traffic.

Newspapers

Newspaper advertising generally requires less cash outlay than other forms of advertising. Most ads are black and white, so production costs are low. Newspaper ads are excellent for specific geographic targeting (such as *zoned advertising,* in which areas of town are targeted for specific advertising content in news sections tailored to them). Most large metropolitan newspapers offer community sections with advertising targeted at local customers, as well as placement of ads on their Web sites.

Newspaper ads have a relatively short life span, don't offer the same quality of reproduction that other print advertising tools do, and are oftentimes quickly scanned (as opposed to read in detail) by readers.

Radio

Radio, along with magazines (see the upcoming section), can better target a specific demographic group. Also, similar to newspapers, radio focuses on a specific geographic area. Want to sell acne cream in Albuquerque? Buy commercial time on the local hard rock station.

Additional advantages of radio advertising include the following:

- ✔ It allows for short *lead times* (the time between when you decide to advertise and when your ad is heard by prospective customers).

- ✔ It reaches people when they're working, traveling in cars, and otherwise going about their daily activities.

- ✔ It's a proven answer for speedy reaction. Studies indicate that approximately 75 percent of the responses to radio advertising occur in the first week after air time.

That same immediacy, however, is also the downside of radio advertising. If your prospects aren't tuned in at the exact moment that your ad airs, you're out of luck. That's why radio advertisers use the term *frequency* when planning their schedules. They aim to have the same ad run over and over, often on several stations in the same market area, hoping to catch the attention of prospective customers at least a few times.

Television

Television takes radio advertising one step further, adding video to the audio, and thus making more impact on the listener. TV also adds prestige to the business doing the advertising, although with significant costs. Finally, similar to radio ads, good TV ads can evoke a speedy response.

TV ad *buys* (another name for the buying of time to present your ads) come in two packages:

- **Network buys:** These involve running your ad on the entire network (think about the ads run during the Super Bowl) — a very expensive proposition.

- **Spot buys or local time buys:** These are the ad time slots the network makes available, even during the Super Bowl, for use by local stations. These ads are priced based on the size of the audience reached by the local station and the time of day the ad runs.

As with buying radio ad spots, TV ad buys, especially those on a local basis, usually involve a frequency strategy — that is, the ad is intended to be viewed frequently over relatively short periods of time. TV ads also work best when the message is clear, simple, and entertaining.

The cost for producing a television ad can run the gamut. You can have the local station assemble a simple 30-second ad relatively inexpensively; you can have an ad agency produce the ad (the same freelance professional or ad agency that does your print advertising); or you may be able to produce the ad yourself. Look at what comparable companies in your category are doing, and be sure that your ad ranks right up there with the best of the kind.

After your ad is produced and you're ready to buy time slots on the local station, approach the scheduling process with your facts in hand. Know the age, gender, and programming preferences of your customer prospects. Then either your station representative (the salesperson reprcsenting the TV station) or your media buyer (the ad agency that's putting together your ad program) can show you the viewer demographics and other viewing patterns for various programs to help you select a schedule that will target the right audience. Discuss your overall strategy with your media buyer, making sure that he or she also understands your budget constraints.

Local and national magazines

The primary benefit of magazine advertising is that the advertiser can target specific audiences, as opposed to newspaper ads, where anyone and everyone may be the reader. Run an ad in *Scientific America,* for example, and you'll attract one kind of audience; place an ad in *GQ,* and you'll reach another.

An additional advantage of magazine ads is that they have a longer life than the other forms of advertising media, because magazines are often passed from reader to reader. Compare this longer-life benefit to radio or television, whose ads are gone after their broadcast cycle.

If you're a manufacturer, for example, a magazine for your trade can offer a rare degree of consumer-targeting potential. Readers of trade magazines are more than likely potential consumers; in many cases, readers peruse a trade magazine with the specific intent of studying its ads. Check out a reference book entitled *Small Business Sourcebook* (Gale), which includes lists of trade publications for all types of businesses.

The downside of magazine advertising is that it's a high-budget item relative to other media, especially if you use high-profile publications. The cost of a full-page, full-color ad in a national magazine can easily hit five figures.

Here are a few other interesting notes on magazine advertising:

- ✔ **You must plan your magazine ads well in advance.** Often, magazine ads must be submitted more than two months before the publication hits the mailbox or newsstand.

- ✔ **Cross your fingers when it comes to placement of your ad.** Everyone wants front-of-the-magazine, right-hand-page placement, but at some magazines, those prime locations usually go to long-standing, multiple-page advertisers who have built up clout over the years. If you're an infrequent advertiser, you may be placed in a less-desirable space.

- ✔ **The more upscale the magazine and the bigger its audience, the more expensive the space.** Plan accordingly.

Online advertising

An increasingly viable advertising option for many small businesses today is a company Web site. Web sites — particularly those intended to be "brochure-ware" only (and not interactive) — are relatively inexpensive to establish (several hundred dollars and up) and maintain.

One distinct advantage of online advertising is that it levels the playing field. Even without massive monetary outlays, smaller companies can compete with the big boys by building professional Web sites and maintaining them diligently.

As with other advertising media, the success of your online strategy will be determined by how many people are introduced to your company and how frequently your message falls on their eyes. Following are several tips on how to build a strong Web presence and keep your Web customers coming back for more information:

- ✔ **Provide up-to-date content.** Your Web site information should be updated on a regular basis (at least monthly and preferably weekly) so your visitors have an incentive to come back. You're looking for repeat visitors here.

✔ **Commit to functionality.** A wide variety of Internet tools are available to take your business beyond a basic brochure-ware-intended Web presence — enabling you to communicate and collaborate with both customers and potential customers. Ask a local Web-site designer for a list of these tools.

✔ **Allow for easy navigation.** Keep the look and the layout clean. If information is difficult to come by, if the flow of your site isn't intuitive, or if the font or the background makes information difficult to read, visitors will move on to the hundreds of other choices on the Web.

✔ **Differentiate your site.** Your site needs to stand out by being creative, with both the text and the graphics. When visitors arrive, you need to make sure they understand what it is that makes your site (and your products or services) different from the crowd.

✔ **Promote your site.** Just because you build a site doesn't mean that consumers will visit it. You need to let people know your site address and why they should visit your site. Promote your site via your traditional communication efforts and online communication strategies.

Other advertising vehicles

A wide range of other, usually less-expensive advertising options are available. That range includes such media as billboards and bus ads (and other transportation-oriented media), as well as less-professional advertising tools such as flyers, posters, and handbills. We recommend you research the various media options carefully, making your decisions methodically after studying the alternatives. Ultimately, the description of your target market, the nature of your message, the depth of your pocketbook, and your own expertise will determine the medium that's best for you.

Measuring the results of each of your advertising tools is important in order to make sure that you're using the medium that works best for you. Be sure to devise a form or a procedure to track where your new business is coming from. This way, you'll know which of your advertising tools are working and which ones aren't.

And remember, if you don't measure it, you can't manage it. *Measuring,* in this case, means tracking the results of your advertising efforts.

Publicity

Publicity is especially effective as a promotional tool because people (specifically, prospective consumers) give more credibility to what they read or hear when it comes from news sources, whereas their belief in advertising messages is often tainted with varying degrees of suspicion (understandably). And unlike advertising, you don't pay for publicity. You will, however, spend time and money to generate it. Typical examples of publicity include feature stories and product (or service) announcements distributed via print, broadcast, or online media.

The downside to publicity, of course, is that, similar to word-of-mouth advertising, you can't control what's said about your company or your product or service. Make sure that what you're about to publicize can withstand media scrutiny. After all, members of the media know that to maintain their credibility, they must present the facts as they really are, not as you say they are. By nature of their profession, they tend to be suspicious.

Media resources that can offer publicity you're looking for include newspapers, business periodicals, television and radio stations, magazines, and Web sites — including online magazines and newsletters as well as links to and from sites that serve those in your target audience. And don't limit your search for publicity to only the business-oriented outlets; oftentimes, exposure in the news or human-interest stories will be of more benefit.

The following tips can help you develop "free advertising" for your business:

- ✔ **Write an article for your local newspaper on a subject that relates to you or your business.** If the article is well written and has a special hook, it could bring you the publicity you seek.

- ✔ **Give talks or teach classes about your profession or business (or hook — see "Creating a hook," later in this chapter) to local groups.** You can go to places such as the Chamber of Commerce, Rotary Club, civic associations, and other groups.

- ✔ **Hire a public relations firm.** PR firms are to publicity what ad agencies are to advertising. (Their fees are similar, too!)

Whenever appropriate, send a professional-quality photo of yourself (and of your event, if there is one) along with any publicity requests. Photos personalize the request, and many papers will use them. A start-up business owner should always have a high-quality photo of him or herself available, in the event that a sudden PR opportunity should present itself.

Sending a news release

One frequently utilized tool of publicity is the news release. A *news release* is a notification of something newsworthy that you send to appropriate newspaper, magazine, and radio and television editors and/or reporters. News releases are appropriate for such occasions as the opening of a new store, the introduction of new products and services, or the procurement of an important new customer or key employee.

You send most news releases about your business to the business editor or business reporter; in some cases, however, you can send them to the editor of a specific area, such as sports or lifestyle.

The best way to determine the appropriate editor or reporter is to look at the bylines on newspaper or magazine public-interest articles that are about companies similar to yours, or listen for the name of the reporter on public-interest radio or TV stories.

Work diligently to build a relationship with the employee who's the gatekeeper of the kind of publicity you're looking for. Try to make his or her job easier. Prepare the news release carefully, make sure all the relevant data is included, and write it (and then rewrite it) until you're sure it's as professional as you can make it. Also, don't abuse this relationship after you've established it — make sure that whatever it is you're submitting is newsworthy and factual.

Creating a hook

In most cases, you need some sort of hook to attract publicity. A *hook* is the characteristic that makes you or your product or service unique and of publicity value. Examples of hooks include an excellent Italian restaurant where the waiters are intentionally rude to patrons or an antique shop with goats in its lobby for visitors to feed. (Visit Las Vegas if you're looking for examples of hooks. Every hotel, for instance, has a hook, from belching volcanoes to golden Sphinxes.)

A secondary advantage of having a hook is that it makes your attempts to find publicity easier. A bona fide hook, which of course need not involve rudeness or something bizarre, will interest some reporters, because a media writer will perceive it as something of interest to the readers or viewers.

How about your business — what exactly is your hook? If you can't think of a hook, perhaps you need to do some thinking about your overall approach to marketing. If your business doesn't have a hook, develop one.

Sales: Where the Rubber Hits the Road

Co-author Jim spent the majority of his business career in Minneapolis. One of that city's most successful entrepreneurs, the late Curt Carlson (known for Radisson Hotels, TGIF Restaurants, and Carlson Travel), coined a phrase years ago that Minneapolis business veterans know by heart: "Nothing happens until a sale is made." What Curt was saying here is that a product or service, no matter how good it may be, will live or die based on the ability of the sales and marketing staff to generate sales. (Of course, even the best salespeople can't overcome a crummy product, an overpriced offering, or any number of other factors that contribute to the buyer's decision.)

Pitting in-house versus outsourcing

Face it: Someone has to sell your products or services. As good as they may be, they simply can't sell themselves. The question then becomes: Who should that selling-someone be?

- ✔ Should the seller be you, an employee hired by you, or a team of employees hired by you? (These are examples of an *in-house* sales force.)

- ✔ Should the seller be an outsider — someone who's already calling on your potential customers with related products? (This is *outsourcing,* and the people who do it are typically known as *manufacturers' representatives.*)

The following sections are designed to help you make the decision about whether to sell in-house or outsource.

Using an in-house sales force

An *in-house sales force* is comprised of employees of the company whose products they sell. In-house salespeople are usually hired, trained, and compensated by the company itself. Thus, their mission is to sell only the company's offerings.

The advantage of hiring and maintaining your own sales force is that you can exert direct control over your salespeople, and they, in turn, can direct all their energies toward selling your products or services. The disadvantage of hiring an in-house sales force is that you're picking up 100 percent of the expenses involved in employing and deploying your salespeople; therefore, you must be able to find enough sales potential within any given geographical area to support the salesperson assigned to it.

Most in-house salespeople today are compensated on a commission basis, and you can find a wide variety of ways to pay those commissions. (For more on this subject, see Chapter 15.)

Using manufacturers' representatives

Manufacturers' reps (also called *independent agents*) are independent salespeople who carry a "line of products" from different manufacturers and get paid a percentage of every sale they make. The collection of products they choose to sell usually is aimed at customers within a given industry. For example, the sales rep who calls on photography stores will pitch products from varied manufacturers, such as film, tripods, and scrapbooks. A varied bag, to be sure, but all are designed for the photography shop customer. The collection of products from any one manufacturer is called a *line,* and a rep may have anywhere from 1 to 30 lines of products in his or her bag.

Always ask how many lines the rep you're considering is carrying; the more lines in his or her bag, the less attention yours will get.

Some reps are part of a larger rep agency; others work on their own. Manufacturers' reps are paid only for what they sell (in other words, straight commission), and they often cover, depending on the density of population, a large geographic territory. The commissions they charge vary with the product and the areas they cover; a commission can range anywhere from a low of 5 percent (on big-ticket sales) to as much as 25 percent on small-ticket, difficult-to-sell items.

The primary advantages of using manufacturers' reps include the following:

- ✔ You don't have the out-of-pocket expense of maintaining a sales force: no salaries, benefits, or travel expenses. Because the reps are paid solely on commission, if they aren't selling your products or services, they aren't getting paid — period.

- ✔ Because reps can spread their costs over a number of manufacturers' lines, they can cover a wide geographical area for minimal expense. Networks of manufacturers' reps, both individuals and firms, cover every state in the nation; you can pick and choose until you find the combination you need. Thus, you can have nationwide distribution without the corresponding high expenses.

- ✔ Reps also can make *small-ticket* (low-price-tag) sales as a result of their ability to spread their time and expenses over a number of products. This means that, when you have a small-ticket product, your reps can afford to sell it to customers in outlying areas, whereas an in-house sales staff, with only one manufacturer's product in their bag, can't afford to make the sales call in the first place.

The primary disadvantages of hiring manufacturers' reps include the following:

- ✔ You lack control over your reps' activities. After all, you aren't employing them; they're employing themselves. As a result, a rapid turnover rate between reps and their manufacturers exists.

- ✔ Due to the reps' distance from and non-involvement in your day-to-day business, they can't possibly know your product as well as an in-house sales staff — especially if your product is technical in nature.

- ✔ Manufacturers' reps, like all salespeople, have limited time in front of each customer. The products the reps choose to sell during that designated time depend upon their perception of how easily they can sell a given product, as well as how much commission they can generate from the transaction.

If your product or service is well established and relatively easy to sell, and your customer base is widespread, a manufacturers' rep may work well for you. In these cases, the reps will be sure to pull your product out of the bag during the course of a sales call. On the other hand, if you have a relatively new product or one without an established customer base, manufacturers' reps may not give your product the time or attention it needs.

Where do you find manufacturers' reps? Look in your industry's trade magazines or visit a trade show within your industry, and ask for the manufacturers' rep bulletin board. Or contact the Manufacturers' Agents National Association (877-626-2776; www.manaonline.org) for the latest directory containing the names of manufacturers' rep organizations around the country. (Your library may also have this directory.)

Making the decision

In short, you sacrifice control for expense when you employ a manufacturers' rep in lieu of an in-house sales force. Neither right nor wrong, the decision depends on your situation. The following "equations" can help you decide what will work best for you:

> Easy products to sell, limited finances = manufacturers' reps
>
> Difficult products to sell, adequate finances = your own sales staff
>
> Small-ticket item, wide territory = manufacturers' reps
>
> High-ticket item, small territory = your own sales staff

Becoming a sales-driven company

Today's owners and leaders of sales-driven companies know that to be truly sales driven, every employee — from the person who answers the telephone to the one who drives the delivery truck — must understand the overriding principles of a sales-driven company:

- ✔ **Sales-driven companies sell solutions, not products.** Product-driven companies focus on the product, which is only a part of the solution. Sales-driven companies focus on the entire solution, which is what the customer is really seeking. The result is that the company that provides solutions builds relationships with its customers, while the company that sells products only sets itself up to be undersold by its competitors.

- ✔ **Sales-driven companies sell benefits, not features.** The sales-driven company's sales force sells the benefits that a product provides, not the product's features. It doesn't matter how light the razor is, or what color it is, or how easy it is to change blades. What matters is the ease and quality of the shaving experience.

- ✔ **Sales-driven companies respect their sales force.** One sure sign of a sales-driven company is the manner in which its salespeople are perceived by the other employees. Because salespeople are the voice of the customer, and because they're responsible for making the sale — without which "nothing happens" — salespeople in sales-driven companies are held in high esteem. They're perceived as the leaders and movers and shakers of the business team — the rainmakers, the people who make things happen. And yes, they're usually paid more than the other employees.

Understanding the Business Triangle

To be a successful sales-driven company, you must first create a mindset within your company that everyone needs to be a winner in the sales transaction, the customer included. To understand how to develop this concept within your company, consider the Business Triangle model.

Visualize a triangle with three equal sides. This triangle represents the relationship among the three principals of the business: the company itself, its employees, and the company's customers. When the three sides of the triangle are equal and stable, a balanced triangle results. However, when one side is significantly longer or shorter than the other two, the triangle — and thus the relationships among its principals — becomes unbalanced and precarious.

The length of each side of the triangle is determined by the benefits that each party derives from the relationship. Because those benefits are measured against expectations, take a look at what each of these three parties expects from a business relationship:

- ✔ **The customer expects:** Solutions to problems and promises kept regarding quality, delivery, and pricing.

- ✔ **The employee expects:** Fair wages, reasonable job security, and courteous treatment.

- ✔ **The company expects:** Fair profit, good professional reputation, and opportunity for continued growth.

Your job as a small-business owner is to make sure that you and your employees understand how this Business Triangle works and then see to it that the three legs remain balanced. The overriding principle here is that, in the long term anyway, everybody wins.

✔ **Sales-driven companies build relationships; they don't just sell products or services.** It used to be that the typical business's primary sales goal was to get the order. Everything that the company did was in response to that goal. If the salesperson wrote the order, the sales call was a success; if she didn't, the call was a failure. And so it went throughout the company — the emphasis on getting the goods out of the door.

Today, the sales-driven business's primary sales goal is to establish an ongoing relationship with the customer. Relationships come from employees understanding the value of the relationship with the customer, and doing whatever they can to foster that relationship. If it involves the customer returning a product that was ordered incorrectly, so be it. This is how relationships are built and maintained.

It matters not, incidentally, whether it's you, your employees, or your manufacturers' reps who are dealing with the customer. Every employee in the business chain — from customer service to the shipping department — must be in tune with the relationship-building principle.

Today's successful companies have learned this lesson well: You can put a price on a product or service, but you can't put a price on a relationship.

If you're looking for a resource that will pick up where we leave off and deliver the best marketing advice available from a small-business perspective, we recommend Barbara Schenck's *Small Business Marketing For Dummies* (Wiley).

Chapter 12

Keeping Your Customers Loyal

· ·

In This Chapter

▶ Knowing that satisfied customers are long-term profitable customers

▶ Examining customer defections

▶ Practicing good customer service before, during, and after the sale

▶ Communicating with unhappy and difficult customers

· ·

A huge factor in your business's long-term success is not only attracting but also satisfying and retaining customers. As a small-business owner, you may well be on the front lines of dealing with your business's customers. However, if you have employees, they'll be dealing with customers as well. Therefore, the importance of providing excellent customer service must be clear to all people in your organization who have any impact on customer satisfaction. This includes, directly or indirectly, everyone from the receptionist to the accounts receivable clerk to the delivery truck driver.

Although it has been said that the level of customer service in many American businesses leaves much to be desired, only a foolish business owner would assume that unhappy customers will continue to tolerate poor service or buy products that don't perform. Consumers today have too many choices; if you and your employees don't satisfy your customers' needs, you'll likely face some of these unpleasant results:

▰ **Competitive threats:** Now more than ever, customers have many options for buying what your firm has to offer. For the vast majority of businesses, competition is intense at the global, national, state, regional, and local levels. It's only a matter of time before your unhappy customers become your competitors' newest customers.

▰ **Negative word-of-mouth:** Even worse than losing dissatisfied customers to the competition is "negative word-of-mouth," whereby unhappy customers talk and tell other consumers not to buy your products and services. Furthermore, your competitors will happily recount the negative stories they've heard from your disgruntled customers. All this talk will certainly tarnish your business's reputation.

✔ **Potential lawsuits:** And, if losing customers and tarnishing your business's reputation aren't enough, disgruntled customers can initiate (gasp!) lawsuits. Even if those litigious customers don't prevail in court, they can cause you to face large legal bills, and your business can suffer further damage to both its profitability and reputation.

In this chapter, we include helpful advice for providing excellent customer service. You discover many strategies for keeping your current customers, both satisfied and dissatisfied.

Retaining Your Customer Base

As the owner of a small business, you need to keep your customers happy. You have an enormous impact on your customers' satisfaction with your company's products and services and how you present them. This section provides you with the keys to keeping your customers satisfied. Of course, not all customers will stay satisfied and loyal to your business. In this section, we also explain how you can learn from customer defections so they don't keep happening.

Getting it right the first time

As a small-business owner, if you don't get your product or service right the first time, you may not have a second chance with customers. Large companies usually have enough cash reserves built up to weather a storm, but the typical small-business owner does not. Customers aren't stupid, and if you continually sell them inferior merchandise — especially when better merchandise is available from other sources — they won't come back the next time they're in the market for the products and services you offer. What's more, they'll tell others of their lousy experience with your company.

Think back to the 1970s and 1980s, when the big U.S. auto manufacturers (Ford, Chrysler, GM, and AMC) made a major mistake: They ignored the competitive threat of foreign automakers. Despite having a relatively small market share in the early 1970s, the foreign auto manufacturers had intensely loyal customers. Why? Because the best foreign automakers made quality cars that rarely had problems. And, when the rare problem did occur, they generally provided excellent service.

Domestic automakers, on the other hand, were upsetting customers by producing subpar cars. Sure, their cars looked nice on the auto dealer's lot, but after a short time in use, many of them developed problems. And, to add insult to injury, U.S. auto customers didn't get particularly good customer service when they brought in their cars for needed tune-ups and repairs.

Focusing on good customers

Some small-business owners believe that all they have to do is build a quality product or develop a quality service, entice someone to purchase it, and then deliver the goods, whereupon — poof! — the party on the receiving end immediately becomes a customer. But, what you should be looking for are *good* customers — people who enable you to make a profit, who purchase repeatedly, and who refer others to your business.

You've perhaps heard the expression, "The customer is always right." Well, we would modify this expression to say that the customer is always right as long as that customer is a good customer, as previously defined. If, on the other hand, the customer isn't a good customer, he or she may *not* always be right.

Remember: You aren't engaged in business to generate sales volume. You're engaged in business to generate profits!

The bottom line is that the chief bean counters and the management of the major U.S. automakers weren't considering the bigger picture when they analyzed their companies' financial statements. They were too focused on short-term profitability and weren't considering the after-sales service that was required as a result of their initially shoddy products. This put them in bad shape against the up-and-coming foreign automakers, who worked on getting their cars right the first time.

Continuing to offer more value

Getting your product or service right the first time isn't enough in the long run. As with life itself, the business world keeps changing. Due to the ever-present threat of competition, resting on your laurels is foolish — and perhaps fatal. In addition to initially developing a top-notch, quality product or service, you must regularly examine how you can offer even more value — improved products or services at the same or lower cost. If you don't, competitors who faithfully keep up with market forces will gradually eat your lunch.

Suppose that you're a dry cleaner. A new dry-cleaning technology has been introduced in the marketplace; it allows dry-cleaning establishments to get their work done 20 percent faster and 30 percent cheaper. If you fail to take advantage of this improvement in your industry, you may discover the hard way that your customers are seeking this value when competitors have implemented this new technique. As your competitors cut prices and reap greater numbers of customers and profits, you lose business and experience shrinking profit margins. (For more on how technology can aid your small business, head to Chapter 21.)

Remembering that company policy is meant to be bent

Flexibility is paramount in any organization, but it's especially important in a small business, where responsive and personally tailored service can set you apart from the larger companies. One place you should be flexible is in your company policy. If a customer has a problem but you have a rule or regulation preventing you from resolving that problem, forget the rule or regulation. Bend it. Skirt it. Find a loophole in it.

Put yourself in the following situations:

> You're an electrical contractor who needs material to complete a job. Your electrical wholesaler tells you that he has a backlog in the order-entry system and can't process your order right now, so you'll have to come back tomorrow to place your order.

> You're a regular customer at a dry cleaner. It's Wednesday and you need your tuxedo dry-cleaned by Friday night. The dry cleaner informs you that it won't be ready until Saturday because of the firm's three-day turnaround policy. Sorry!

What are the common threads here?

- The first common thread is that the electrical wholesaler and the dry cleaner apparently have cast-in-stone sets of rules and regulations that dictate the way they do business, and they won't bend those rules to solve a customer's problem.
- The second common thread is that the two businesses are in danger of alienating a customer.

How can these business owners become more flexible to satisfy the customer? The electrical wholesaler should give the contractor the material today and run the transaction through his order-entry system tomorrow. The dry cleaner should put the customer's tuxedo in front of someone else's order, no matter what the company's operations manual dictates (the customer is, after all, good, as stated earlier in this chapter).

These are the moments of truth in any business — the times when what the business says it will do conflicts with what the business actually does. These times differentiate the business that *says* the customer is king from the business that *acts* as if the customer is king.

We're not saying that you should always provide extra service casually or for free. In some situations, you may want to charge more for a special service. Consider the special favor, the one-time transaction, when you set your pricing strategy (see Chapter 11). Also, you don't want to tell your employees to feel free to break any rule at any time; that's the road to chaos and lack of profitability. But flexibility helps keep customers happy and coming back. Let your managers and employees know that you stand behind this philosophy, and you'll empower them to always provide good customers with top-notch service.

Learning from customer defections

The costs of acquiring a new customer are huge. After spending the marketing effort and dollars needed to secure a new customer for your business (see Chapter 11), you want to keep that customer loyally patronizing your business for many years to come. If you experience much customer turnover, your cost of doing business will rise significantly as you try to attract replacement customers. Take action quick. Customer turnover can indicate major problems with your company's products or services and customer service.

A popular action within a business is to celebrate successes rather than examine failures. However, as a small-business owner, you'll stick around much longer if you examine your failures and make positive changes to correct them. Take the time to examine customer defections and their underlying causes. The following sections dig deeper into this topic.

Examining the value of customer loyalty

Frederick Reichheld is a management consultant who specializes in understanding, and working with corporations on, customer loyalty. He's the author of several books on customer loyalty. Reichheld's research and work have produced the following powerful insights and facts:

- The average company today loses half of its customers in five years.

- The typical *Fortune* 500 company has an average annual *real growth* (that is, growth in excess of the rate of inflation) of 2.5 percent. If such a company retained just 5 percent more of its customers each year, its real growth would triple to 7.5 percent.

- A 5-percent increase in customer retention in a typical company generally translates into an increase in profits of more than 25 percent. In some industries, good, longstanding customers are worth so much that reducing customer defections by 5 percent can double profits.

Clearly, retaining customers — particularly your best customers — has an enormous bottom-line impact. Given how important and valuable retaining customers is, you may think that if a business were losing many of its customers, it would seek to understand why and to correct the underlying problems. Well, if that were the case, customer loss wouldn't be as high as it is in many businesses.

Short-term profit concerns can harm long-term profitability

In business schools and economics courses all across the world, eager business students are taught to maximize profits. However, in the quest for higher and higher profits, some people are inclined to cut corners. In addition to perhaps lessening the quality of their products and services, the people at these companies do things that clearly aren't in their customers' best interests.

Just as the major U.S. automakers got into trouble by not producing high-quality cars in the 1970s and '80s, some major U.S. investment brokerage firms did significant long-term damage to their businesses by engaging in short-term profit-maximizing behavior.

Prior to May 1, 1975, retail brokerage firms (companies that act as brokers in the buying and selling of securities such as stocks, bonds, and mutual funds for their customers) had their commissions regulated. Regulation was great for the industry (but not for their customers) because the commission rates were high and brokerage firms didn't have to compete with one another on price as companies do in nearly all other industries.

The world changed for these firms and their customers when the Securities and Exchange Commission (SEC) deregulated brokerage commissions in 1975. Interestingly, many of the old-line brokerage firms, such as Merrill Lynch, Prudential, Smith Barney, and E.F. Hutton, gradually raised their prices.

Upstart discount brokers, on the other hand — such as Charles Schwab and Quick & Reilly — offered big commission discounts. These firms paid their brokers on salary rather than commission, which not only saved the brokerage firm money (a savings that could be passed on to customers), but also eliminated the conflicts of interest inherent when securities brokers work on commission.

During the late 1970s and 1980s, the discount brokers chipped away at the old-line brokerage firms' share of the marketplace. Some of the old-line brokers responded by finding a short-term solution to the profit pressure they were feeling: Jumping on the bandwagon of selling newfangled investments, such as limited partnerships (LPs), to their customers. The appeal to the brokerage firms of peddling LPs was the huge upfront commissions — 8 to 10 percent or more of the amount invested. Never mind that the customer who bought an LP had little chance of earning a decent return, due to the high commissions and the levying of high ongoing management fees.

In the short term, sales of LPs boosted the brokerage firms' profits. In the long term, however, as customers learned for themselves what crummy investments LPs were, the old-line brokerage firms that sold a lot of LPs began losing customers. And to make matters worse, the most disgruntled LP owners participated in lawsuits against the brokerage firms.

By viewing their association with their customers as a one-night stand rather than a long-term relationship built on trust, the old-line brokerage firms tremendously damaged the long-term health and profitability of their businesses — all in the pursuit of short-term profits. The leading discount brokerage firms and mutual fund companies reaped the benefits by capturing a huge portion of the dissatisfied customers who left the old-line firms.

In the small-business world, you need to take a long-term view on your customer relationships. Doing so will not only maximize your profits over the long haul, but also ensure that your business will be around in the long term.

Tracking customer defections

Reichheld also has found in his work that, not surprisingly, many businesses don't learn from their customer losses. He says,

> Psychologically and culturally, it's difficult and sometimes threatening to look at failure too closely. Ambitious managers want to link their careers to successes; failures are usually examined for purposes of assigning blame rather than detecting and eradicating the systemic causes of poor performance.

The good news for you, the small-business owner, is that you don't have to be concerned with bosses and organizational politics when addressing the problem of customer defections. You're The Boss. However, it's a natural human tendency to spend more time chasing and celebrating success rather than stopping long enough to investigate and learn from failures and losses.

Make a commitment to track the customers that you lose and ask why. (This is the customer equivalent to the exit interview that you should always perform with departing employees; see Chapter 15.) Knowing that you've lost customers isn't enough; you must find out *why* you lost them. Many businesses don't even know what customers they've lost, and it's rare that a business takes the time to discover why customers defect. But doing so can help keep you in business and help keep your business growing (see Chapter 19).

Consider, for example, the automotive oil-change business that co-author Eric used to frequent about 5 minutes from his home. The business boasted that you can get your oil changed within ten minutes and be on your merry way. On one visit to the establishment, Eric pulled into the entrance and got out of his car. He was then ignored for the next ten minutes — and not because the business was too busy. The people who were checking in new customers moved at a snail's pace, and one employee even spent several minutes on a personal phone call.

When it was Eric's turn, the employee who checked him in was rude. Eric left during the oil change to do some shopping nearby rather than sit in the poorly ventilated, exhaust-infested garage. Upon his return, he had to wait another ten minutes because, although his car had finally been serviced, the paperwork wasn't completed. The same employee who checked Eric in took another 15 minutes to get the paperwork done, and kept his unfriendly and surly attitude all the while.

Throughout this poor-service experience, Eric didn't utter a word of complaint, but guess which oil-change shop he bypassed the next time his car needed an oil change? A gas station just two minutes from Eric's home started offering oil changes, which were about 20 percent less costly than the last place. The attendant who checked Eric in at the service station was friendly and polite, and his car and paperwork were ready when promised.

You need to make it part of your company's culture that you don't expect employees to be perfect, and that making mistakes won't necessarily lead to an employee's immediate firing. However, you should show little tolerance toward employees who repeatedly drive away good customers from your business. (For more employee tips, head to Chapter 15.)

Recognizing customer service

All businesses have products or services to sell. And sometimes businesses get too focused on those products and services, giving short shrift to the accompanying customer service that customers expect.

Maybe you can't readily define the term *customer service,* but we bet that you know what it is when you get it or don't get it. For example, you surely recognize customer service in a company you do business with when

- ✔ Its telephone operator (or at least its telephone system) connects you with your party quickly and efficiently.

- ✔ Its bookkeeper politely answers a question you have about an invoice.

- ✔ Its shipping clerk quickly traces your order and tells you exactly when to expect it.

- ✔ Its salesperson gets back to you quickly with the quotes and delivery schedules you requested.

In each of the situations just described, the company is solving your problem or addressing your need in a manner that meets or exceeds your expectations, which is, after all, the definition of customer service. Customer service = solving your customers' problems or meeting their needs.

When you ask an employee for help in a business that you frequent, have you ever felt that his or her behavior was essentially saying to you, "That's not my department/responsibility"? In a business — large or small — that recognizes the value of customer service, the correct response to a customer question is, "Let me find the solution for you." The solution may ultimately rest in the hands of another employee, another department, or even another business, but the employee has accepted responsibility for solving your problem.

Some larger companies have distinctly identified *customer service departments* — a person or group of persons whose sole purpose is to solve customer problems. In such a company, all customer telephone calls requiring information are routed through to the customer service department. In smaller companies, however, many — perhaps even all — employees are involved in customer service. In the examples from the previous list, the telephone operator, the bookkeeper, the shipping clerk, and the salesperson are providing customer service. If you, the boss and Grand Poobah, get involved in solving a customer's problem, you, too, are focused on customer service. The same is true for the janitor or the night watchman.

The challenge is for your employees to understand that they're on the job to solve your customers' problems. Instead, they may believe (because this is the way their job descriptions read) that their role is simply to answer the telephone, keep the books, ship products, or sell services. Although each of these functions accurately describes an employee's assigned *activities,* these functions don't define the employee's assumed *responsibilities.*

You and your employees are on the job — just as your entire company exists — for one reason and one reason only: to solve your customers' problems.

Smart business owners know that customer service (and the accompanying problem solving) begins before a sale is made, continues during the sale, and continues long after the sale is complete. Remember that customers aren't just coming to your business for your products and services. The attentiveness to your customers' needs — before, during, and after the sale — that comes with what you sell also is an integral part of the package. Treat your customers as you would a good friend. The following sections break down the stages of customer service.

Customer service before the sale

When a customer goes to buy a product or service, part of what can close the sale or blow the deal is the quality (or lack thereof) of customer service before the moment the customer decides to buy. When a customer schedules an appointment, he or she is buying not only the service provider's expertise, but also "proper care and handling" before the service is provided. And when a potential customer enters your store for a product, he or she wants the store clean and well maintained and conveniently arranged. It's all customer service.

Consider the last time you bought something, whether a car, groceries, a medical exam, or a haircut. With each of these purchases, you interacted with the business provider before you committed to buy the product or service.

If you're like most people, you probably have some bad memories about slick salespeople who accosted you the moment you walked onto an auto dealer's lot. Many car salespeople spend more time selling rather than listening and educating. The salesperson isn't trying to solve *your* problem — figuring out which car to purchase. He's trying to solve *his* problem — how to make a fat commission in order to meet his next mortgage payment. Because of poor customer service at the point of sale in the car business, many people turn around, checkbooks in hand, and take their business elsewhere.

Now consider a medical exam. When scheduling an appointment with a doctor, you may enjoy how politely and flexibly you're treated when arranging a time for you to come in. But when you arrive for your appointment, you're greeted and asked to wait before you see the doctor — and the wait stretches on and on. Although people are less likely in this circumstance to walk out before a checkup, we know people who've walked out of a doctor's office, never to return again, after waiting more than 45 minutes beyond the scheduled appointment time without a word from anyone.

Customer service during the sale

After a customer commits to buy a product or service, the customer service must continue. Never halt your efforts to satisfy customers. When a customer forks over the dough for your wares and you don't meet the customer's service expectations, even if the sale is finalized, you may lose repeat business, and you may lose the opportunity for referrals to other customers.

For example, after your doctor arrives in the examination room, you'll pay close attention to how well she listens to you and her demeanor toward you. If the doctor is abrupt, a poor listener, and arrogant in asserting her opinion — rather than showing a willingness to discuss options and consider your needs — you may choose to find another physician.

Likewise, after you decide to buy a car, you won't be overjoyed if it takes several hours to complete the transaction. Even though you may be happy with the selection of the car, the hassle in getting on your way may make you less glowing in your recommendation to others.

Customer service after the sale

After a customer has purchased your company's products or services, your relationship with that customer, at least as it relates to that transaction, isn't over. The customer may have follow-up questions that need to be answered or problems down the road with your products or services.

Some customers, of course, begin complaining at the drop of a hat. Many are justified in their complaints, but others complain simply because that's the type of people they are. Know how to tell the difference (the following section helps you deal with dissatisfied customers).

If you or your employees treat your customers as if they're bothering you, and you aren't attentive to after-sales service, you could turn off customers from making more purchases and referring others to your business. Poor after-sales service will communicate to your customers that after you have their money, you don't really care what happens to them.

In addition to being attentive to all your customers' questions and concerns, be sure to solicit feedback (possibly from a formal survey) from your customers as to the quality of the customer service that your business offers them.

Showing that you care, the old-fashioned way

In this age of technology, you may be tempted to discard some of the personal touches that today's customers still appreciate. Although technology certainly answers many of your business needs, it will never replace the following personal touches in the eyes of customers:

✔ **Handwritten notes:** A handwritten note is always the best way to say "thank you."

✔ **Personal thanks:** The owner of a company calling and saying "thank you" (as opposed to an assistant or salesperson sending out an e-mail) makes a positive impression.

✔ **Handling mistakes:** Don't waste one second trying to cover your tracks after mistakes are made. Come clean, fess up, and solve the problem. Provide personal customer service representatives — not voicemail boxes that allow you to avoid dealing with problems. Approached correctly, mistakes can provide an opportunity to improve your business, impress your customers, and reward their loyalty.

In some businesses, you must be careful not to give away valuable support that you can and should charge for. For example, if follow-up exams or appointments are expected, you should build the cost of those expected services into your upfront pricing or set a pricing schedule for the cost of the follow-up. Be sure that at the time customers buy from you, they know the cost of such follow-up work. Customers don't like negative surprises, especially when they affect their pocketbooks.

Dealing with Dissatisfied Customers

You can have the best products and services, offer the fairest prices, and provide terrific customer service and you'll still end up with the occasional unhappy customer. How you handle complaints — both justified and unjustified — is vital to the long-term reputation and health of your business. The following sections contain our time-tested advice for dealing with your unhappy and sometimes troublesome customers.

And here's a tip to help you maintain your sanity: Keep in mind that you have your own way of doing things, that yours isn't a perfect product or service, and that you can't meet *all* your customers' needs and expectations *all* the time.

Listen, listen, listen

Most people like to believe that they're terrific listeners. The reality is that most of them aren't. And even if you *are* a good listener, you have moments when, for any of a variety of reasons, you don't listen well. You get busy and stressed out with the competing demands on your time from work, family, friends, daily chores, and obligations. You also have days when you're tired, not feeling well, or have been on the receiving end of bad news or bad experiences.

Another impediment to good listening is that you may be convinced that an upset customer is simply being a troublemaker. As with all personal relationships, however, your preconceived notions (dare we call them *prejudices*) about others can keep you from hearing legitimate and real concerns and reasons for being dissatisfied.

Before you (or one of your employees) lose your temper with a complaining customer, take a deep breath. Try to set aside all your personal issues, your opinions about the situation, and your preconceived notions about the customer and his or her right to be unhappy. Stop and listen. Try to ask about and care about discovering what the customer is unhappy about and why. Different people, not surprisingly, get upset about different things. You have no way to know and understand what's upsetting a particular customer until you take the time to ask and truly listen.

To ensure that you've really heard what your upset customer has said, paraphrase the concerns you've heard and tell the customer that you're sorry that he or she is unhappy. (Keep in mind that this isn't an admission of wrongdoing or guilt on your part, especially if you're worried about landing in court and being sued for product liability.) Then work on developing a solution with the customer (see the following section).

The absolute worst thing that you (or your employees) can do to a customer with a complaint is to interrupt and argue when he or she is trying to convey dissatisfaction with your products or services. And, don't be defensive. We realize that this is easier said than done, but you'll do far more long-term damage to your business reputation by further upsetting an already unhappy customer. Even if you're 100-percent certain that the customer is the biggest jerk you've ever dealt with and that you don't want him or her as a customer, treat the concerns with respect and try to solve his or her problem. Otherwise, you may end up with negative word-of-mouth advertising and possibly a lawsuit.

Develop a solution

When a customer complains, remember that he or she is complaining because of dissatisfaction with the deal that he or she received. The next step, after listening to the customer's complaints, is to develop a solution that addresses the complaints.

You have two ways to arrive at a solution:

✔ **You can ask the customer what solution he or she would propose and then see how it compares to what you can do.**

The advantage of asking the customer for a solution is the same as with any other form of negotiation (which, after all, is what's going on in this situation). If you let the dissatisfied customer make the opening offer, you know exactly where you stand and what you have to do to satisfy him.

Imagine the benefit you can derive when the customer's solution is less costly than what you were about to offer. In such a circumstance, the opportunity suddenly exists for you to take an unpleasant situation and turn it into an opportunity to strengthen the complaining customer's loyalty to your business.

✔ **You can propose a solution yourself and then wait for the customer to counter with a solution that he or she thinks is better.**

Only when the customer doesn't have, or refuses to come up with, a solution is it time for you to propose one.

For example, suppose that you run a professional service business and you're responsible for missing a customer's appointment — either because of a scheduling mistake or because you're behind schedule and the customer simply couldn't wait any longer. You quickly determine that the customer is really angry about having been stood up after he had taken valuable time out of his workday.

Your solution to ease the customer's unhappiness could go something like this:

1. Apologize for the time he wasted.

2. Ask for his recommended solution.

3. If he doesn't have a solution, offer a discount (perhaps 15 or 20 percent off the appointment price when he reschedules).

4. When the customer returns for the rescheduled appointment, be absolutely certain that he's seen on time and provided with the best possible service.

The key to understanding your customers' complaints (and your employees' complaints, really) is your ability to put yourself in the complainer's shoes. After you've made this transition (figure out how to view your business through the eyes of a customer), you'll find that you can solve problems the vast majority of the time.

Now suppose that your company sells products, and a customer comes in to say that a product you sold her broke and isn't worth the packaging it came in. In this case, you could offer a replacement product, fix the broken one, or offer the customer a refund. But if you're certain that the customer misused the product, and her mistake subsequently led to the breakage, you have a dilemma on your hands. You have to decide whether this person adheres to your definition of what a "good" customer should be.

Even in those situations in which you determine that this person isn't what you consider to be a good customer, try to make the parting of your ways as harmonious and conflict free as possible.

It's okay if an unmanageable customer doesn't do business with you anymore. Just do everything you can to ensure that he or she doesn't go away angry and tell others that your business offers a lousy service or product.

If you want to delve into more details about what makes for good customer service, we highly recommend reading *Customer Service For Dummies,* by Karen Leland and Keith Bailey (Wiley).

Chapter 13

Managing Profitability and Cash

. . . .

In This Chapter

▶ Grasping the concept of cash flow

▶ Reading and interpreting P & Ls and balance sheets

▶ Reviewing the key ratios and percentages of profitability

▶ Overseeing your accounts receivable and inventory

▶ Controlling your costs

. . . .

*A*lthough people drive the business of doing business, money fuels the engine. That money can be counted, compiled, and presented in a number of different ways — ways that, in the right hands, can provide a steady flow of financial information with which to accomplish a number of key business functions, such as the following:

✔ **Maintaining bookkeeping information:** This includes keeping records of physical inventories, monies due from others (accounts receivable), and monies due to others (payroll and accounts payable).

✔ **Paying taxes:** Federal, state, and local governments not only require that the business pay taxes, but also that it keeps records to back those payments (see Chapter 18).

✔ **Keeping score:** In order to know whether you're going to be able to meet next month's expenses or if your business's profitability and cash is trending in the right direction, you need to keep track of the results of doing business.

✔ **Providing a management information tool:** Information fuels the decision-making process, and the more information you have as a small-business owner, the better your decisions can be.

This chapter is about collecting and using financial information. It should be noted that you don't need to be a tax and financial expert to understand the numbers. (Do you need to understand how a thermometer works to take your temperature?) A thorough review of this chapter, some time spent with your tax advisor, and several months of reviewing your own statements, and you'll figure out how to properly use the financial information your accounting system generates.

Although we discuss three of the four previously mentioned key business functions in this chapter (we deal with the subject of taxes in Chapter 18), our primary emphasis is on the use of financial information as a management tool. Specifically, we focus on information that you can use to manage your cash flow, increase your profitability, and improve your chances of staying in business for the long haul.

Cash Flow: The Fuel That Drives Your Business

In order to pay your bills, you need to manage the money/cash you have both going out and coming in — your *cash flow*. Before you can have cash flowing out, you must first have cash flowing in. When your cash keeps flowing out in excess of what flows in, your business is inviting trouble.

To understand the basic concept of cash flow, you need first to distinguish between two oft-confused terms: cash flow and profitability:

- ✔ **Cash flow:** An operating term describing the movement of money (cash, checks, electronic debits, and credits) in and out of your business.

- ✔ **Profitability:** An accounting term meaning the capability of your business to generate more sales dollars than the cost of operating expenses.

Now, to fully understand the difference between cash flow and profitability, you need to understand that when a business is profitable, profits don't necessarily accumulate in the form of cash. Instead, they can take the form of an increase in other noncash assets such as inventory, accounts receivable, equipment, or real estate. Yes, those profits may once have been in the form of cash, but somewhere along the line, the owner made the decision to shift that cash into another asset — purchasing additional inventory or buying a piece of equipment, for example. In this manner, a business can be profitable in accounting terms but short of cash in the checkbook.

Although an increase in cash is only one of the many possible results of profitability, it is by far the most important result, because cash fuels the day-to-day operation of your business. If you've chosen to spend too much cash on purchasing inventory and equipment, or you've been slow in collecting your accounts receivable, you may not have enough cash to pay your vendors and compensate your employees. After all, you can't pay them with inventory or equipment! Sorry, vendors and employees want cash.

Ironically, some profitable (in accounting terms) businesses have gone bankrupt because their owners made the wrong choices when allocating their cash. Instead of accumulating it, they (knowingly or unknowingly) accumulated other nonliquid assets, and then, lo and behold, the bills came due and the cupboards were bare.

Your business's bank account (or money market fund) is the obvious measure of today's cash. Do you have enough money in it to pay today's bills and meet today's payroll, and will you still have money left over when the day is done?

The difficulty comes in projecting tomorrow's cash flow. Because every business has to be concerned with more than just what's happening today in terms of cash availability, projecting tomorrow's cash flow is an important task. To do that, you should consider questions like the following:

- ✓ Will you have enough cash to meet next Friday's payroll?
- ✓ Will you have enough to pay that big vendor invoice that's due the following Monday?
- ✓ Will you have enough to pay the bank-loan payment, the upcoming utility bills, and the real-estate taxes that come due at the end of the month?

Questions like these, and the answers they beg, point out the need for preparing *cash flow projections* — forecasts of how much cash you'll have over a given future time frame. Some businesses project cash flow for 30 days out, some for 180 days, and some for an entire year in advance.

To project cash flow accurately, you need to polish up the old crystal ball, because you're about to make a number of important predictions. For example, you must predict

- ✓ Your future sales
- ✓ The rate at which you'll collect the money that's due you
- ✓ The dollar amount of your upcoming payrolls
- ✓ The dollar amount of vendor invoices to be paid in the next day, week, month, six months, or even year

The better your predictions, the more accurate a forecast you can prepare.

Table 13-1 shows a sample format for making cash flow projections.

Table 13-1	Sample Cash Flow Projections
Period of time (days, weeks, months, and so on)	_____
Current cash (checking, money market, and petty cash accounts)	$_____
Add expected cash sales for time period	$_____
Add expected receivable collections for time period	$_____
Subtotal	$_____
* Less disbursements	
Payroll	$_____
Taxes	$_____
All other Accounts Payable	$_____
Total = Expected cash balance at end of time period	$_____

You can prepare your cash flow projections for the next day, next week, next month, next year, or any combination thereof. Predictions for longer time periods, although more useful, are likely to be fuzzier and less accurate than your predictions for shorter time periods. We recommend that you make your cash flow projections for at least six months out and then update them at least once each month, always staying six months out. That way you'll spot problem periods earlier and be able to adjust to them more quickly.

Although most start-up small-business owners keep their cash-flow projections in their head and won't go to the trouble of generating documented projections from one day to the next, you need to understand the concept behind measuring cash flow. No matter how small or uncomplicated your business happens to be, cash is key. We can guarantee you one thing: At some point in your business career, you *will* have cash-flow problems. When that time comes, be prepared.

Most accountants have a preformatted cash flow projections worksheet available for their clients to use. Whatever you do, be sure you understand the concept of cash flow, because it's one of the most important (and least understood) financial concepts that a small-business owner must know.

Don't let cash flow intimidate you. The concept is as simple as the concept behind maintaining a checkbook. Cash flow is nothing more than a few new wrinkles on an old, familiar face.

Making Sense of Financial Statements

Whether manual or computer based, the accounting system you use should ultimately generate two financial statements: the profit and loss statement (also known as the income statement) and the balance sheet. Both of these statements are produced at the end of a business's accounting period, usually monthly, quarterly, or annually.

We recommend that you prepare (or have prepared) your financial statements as frequently as possible, with monthly statements usually being the most useful. If your accounting system allows you to generate your financial statements internally, we suggest you generate your statements monthly. If monthly statements are impossible for some reason, quarterly statements will do, but don't fall into the trap that many small businesses do by generating your statements only once or twice a year.

Financial statements function primarily as a management tool, and you can't go 365 days without paying attention to the information they provide.

The following sections discuss in detail the profit and loss statement and the balance sheet.

The profit and loss statement

The *profit and loss statement* (P & L) adds all the revenues of your business and subtracts all the operating expenses, thereby providing you with a figure representing what's left over: the profits. (If the total expenses exceed the total revenues, your business would have a loss rather than a profit.) The P & L measures the results of operations of your business over a given period of time — typically a month, a quarter, or a year.

Choosing a P & L format

When you sit down with your bookkeeper and/or tax advisor to design your financial statement format, always remember the cardinal rule of business numbers: Any given number is only meaningful when compared to another number. For instance, if you're the CEO of IBM and your company showed a profit of $500 million this year, that may sound like a positive result to most outsiders, but if IBM showed a profit of $1 billion the previous year, a $500-million decline spells big trouble. And so it shall be with your business. You need to compare the current year's figures to other numbers — last year's actual performance or this year's budget — or, preferably, both.

In Figure 13-1, we show a sample P & L to help you understand how to construct one and how to effectively use it in managing your business.

Big Spenders Corp.
Profit and Loss Statement
For the year ending December 31, 2008

	Prior Year	Budget	Current Year	Percent Change Compared to Prior Year
Sales (revenues)	$450,000	$475,000	$500,000	11%
– Cost of goods sold	$200,000	$210,000	$225,000	12.5%
= Gross margin	$250,000	$265,000	$275,000	10%
Expenses				
Wages and salaries	$75,000	$77,000	$97,000	29%
Rent	$50,000	$52,000	$54,000	8%
Selling expenses	$55,000	$58,000	$61,000	11%
Telephone	$10,000	$11,000	$11,000	10%
Utilities	$10,000	$11,000	$11,000	10%
Total expenses	$200,000	$209,000	$234,000	17%
Net income (pretax)	$50,000	$56,000	$41,000	(18%)

Figure 13-1:
A sample four-column profit and loss statement.

You can use a wide variety of formats in presenting a P & L statement. The four-column format that we use in Figure 13-1 is the one that we recommend for both the profit and loss statement and the balance sheet. This four-column format allows you to quickly and easily compare each of the three key figures: Prior Year, Budget, and Current Year. The fourth column measures the percentage increase or decrease (in parentheses) between the current year and prior year.

The process you can use to arrive at a P & L's net income conclusion isn't difficult to understand. Follow its construction through these two easy steps:

1. **Subtract from the gross sales (in Figure 13-1, $500,000) the cost of the goods that were included in those sales (in Figure 13-1, $225,000).**

   What's left is the gross margin on those sales — the gross income before subtracting operating expenses. Our example shows this figure to be $275,000.

2. **Subtract from that number all the operating expenses incurred during that accounting period — including all selling and administrative expenses.**

   You see $234,000 as this figure in the example. The number left over is — how easy is this? — the net income. Ta-da! $41,000!

As you can see, the trick is not so much in assembling the P & L. Instead, the trick is in retaining and retrieving all the figures that go into it. In essence, the better your accounting system, the easier this process will be. (See Chapter 10 for more on accounting systems.)

Deciphering P & L information

Deciphering important information from an income statement (formatted like the one in the previous example) is easy:

- ✔ Go to the net income figure under the Current Year column — the P & L number that every small-business owner is most interested in. Using the percentage in the adjacent column, you can quickly determine how profitable Big Spenders Corporation is compared to the previous year. (Profits are down by 18 percent.)

- ✔ A quick glance at the top of the statement reveals that the profitability decrease isn't due to falling sales, which are up by 11 percent, nor is it due to a declining gross margin, which is up by 10 percent. Recalling our discussion on profitability earlier in this chapter, you can then assume that the problem must be related to expenses.

- ✔ Moving down the expense column, you see that wages and salaries are up by 29 percent. This means that, although sales have increased by 11 percent, and the gross margin is up by 10 percent, the whopping increase in wages and salaries has caused the problem. A quick comparison to the wages and salaries budget column reveals that the 29-percent increase wasn't budgeted; therefore, whatever has happened wasn't planned for. You can then delve into your wages and salaries account to determine what caused the problem.

Some companies may include an additional three columns on the P & L. These three columns represent the percentage of the total for the Prior Year, Budget, and Current Year categories. For example, using the sales total as 100 percent, every figure in each column would represent a percentage of that total. Thus, continuing with the Big Spenders Corporation example from Figure 13-1, the percentage of the Total column for the Current Year column would reveal a gross margin of 55 percent ($275,000 divided by $500,000), wages and salaries to sales of 19 percent ($97,000 divided by $500,000), and net income to sales of 8.2 percent ($41,000 divided by $500,000). The only disadvantage of adding these three columns is that it clutters up the P & L and makes it more difficult to read.

After you have your P & L prepared in an easy-to-read, four-column format, you'll find it relatively easy to determine what your business has done and where it currently needs to improve. For example, as a result of comparing the three columns, the P & L allows you to quickly answer the three questions that define any business's profitability:

- ✔ **Have you controlled your costs?** For Big Spenders Corporation, the answer appears to be no.

- ✔ **Have you maintained or improved your *gross margin* (the difference between what it costs you to produce your product or service and the price you charge for it)?** In this example, the answer is yes.

- ✔ **Have you maintained or increased sales?** In this example, the answer is yes.

Although the answers to these three questions provide significant help in managing your business, the answers aren't the only information the P & L provides. See "Turning the Numbers into Action," later in this chapter, for even more uses of the figures generated by the profit and loss statement.

The balance sheet

The second of a small-business's important financial statements is the *balance sheet,* which provides a snapshot of a company's financial position at any given point in time. As with the P & L, the concept behind a balance sheet isn't complex. Quite simply, the balance sheet is a list of what your business owns *(assets)* minus what your business owes *(liabilities),* with the resulting difference being what your business is worth *(net worth).* This net worth figure is also commonly referred to as *book value.*

The P & L is designed to analyze profitability issues: sales, margins, and expenses. The balance sheet, on the other hand, answers an entirely different question: How did you allocate your resources? Did you decide to allocate your dollars to inventory, to paying off loans, or to accumulating cash? The small-business owner makes many asset-allocation decisions over the course of the year; the balance sheet provides a year-end snapshot that summarizes the history of those decisions.

In Figure 13-2, we reproduce a sample balance sheet to help you understand how this important financial statement works.

We've prepared this example in the same four-column format that we use in the P & L. This format is designed to make easy the comparison of the Prior Year, Budget, and Current Year figures. Although we suggest that you consider this format when preparing your own balance sheet, we should note that the vast majority of businesses don't budget their balance sheets but still operate successfully.

Big Spenders Corp.
Balance Sheet
For the year ending December 31, 2008

Assets	Prior Year	Budget	Current Year	Percent Change Compared to Prior Year
Current Assets				
Cash	$25,000	$35,000	$5,000	(80%)
Accounts receivable	$50,000	$55,000	$55,000	10%
Inventory	$50,000	$55,000	$85,000	70%
Total current assets	$125,000	$145,000	$145,000	16%
Fixed Assets				
Land, buildings	$100,000	$95,000	$95,000	(5%)
Furniture & fixtures	$50,000	$47,000	$47,000	(6%)
Equipment	$50,000	$47,000	$47,000	(6%)
Total fixed assets	$200,000	$189,000	$189,000	(5.5%)
Total Assets	$325,000	$334,000	$334,000	4.9%
Liabilities				
Current liabilities				
Accounts payable	$75,000	$69,000	$80,000	6.7%
Short-term notes payable	$10,000	$10,000	$10,000	-
Total current liabilities	$85,000	$79,000	$90,000	6%
Long-term liabilities				
Mortgages payable	$70,000	$65,000	$65,000	(7%)
Long-term notes payable	$45,000	$0	$20,000	(55%)
Total long-term liabilities	$115,000	$65,000	$85,000	(26%)
Total Liabilities	**$200,000**	**$144,000**	**$175,000**	**(12.5%)**
Owners' equity (net worth)	$125,000	$190,000	$159,000	27%
Total Liabilities & Net Worth	**$325,000**	**$334,000**	**$334,000**	**4.9%**

Figure 13-2:
A sample balance sheet.

In our example, Big Spenders Corporation completed its 2008 fiscal year with an increase in net worth of $34,000 ($125,000 to $159,000) over the prior year. This is the same amount of profit reported by the profit and loss statement in the earlier example. By comparing the Current Year column on the balance sheet with the Prior Year column, you can readily determine what has happened to the mixture of assets and liabilities during the course of the year — in other words, how Big Spenders Corporation's management decided to allocate the company's resources.

To give you a further example of how easy it is to glean information from this four-column balance sheet format, take a look at the Percent Change Compared to Prior Year column. Note that although the total current assets didn't change appreciably, two of the categories within the current asset category — cash and inventory — did. The cash account, as of December 31, is only $5,000, while inventory has ballooned to $85,000. Sometime during the course of the year, a larger inventory has built up, depleting the company's cash reserves in the process.

An examination of the Budget column confirms the fact that this inventory accumulation was unplanned and unbudgeted. (Incidentally, this is a classic example of how a company can be profitable and still get into financial trouble.) As evidenced by this balance sheet, Big Spenders Corporation currently has $90,000 in short-term liabilities, but only $5,000 available in cash. As a result, despite being profitable, Big Spenders is in a classic cash crunch.

The only other percentage on this sample balance sheet that should attract immediate attention is the 55-percent decrease in long-term notes payable. Sometime during the course of the year, management decided to pay off a portion of its long-term debt — a decision that, in light of the company's present cash shortage, they would now probably like to reverse.

Turning the Numbers into Action

Here's an exercise that every small-business owner should attempt: Try figuring out exactly how much money it costs to produce your financial statements every year. Go ahead, we dare you! Add up the wages and salary costs of the people responsible for collecting the data, the depreciation of the accounting hardware and software involved, and the cost of any outside services you contract (tax preparers and advisors and so on). Now add the figures together and what do you have?

You probably have one costly process for determining how much income tax you have to pay — especially if that's all you use your financial statements for (see Chapter 18)!

On the other hand, if you use your financial statements as a management tool to guide and direct your business, the picture changes. In some cases, your financial statements may even pay for themselves if the actions you take because of the lessons they provide result in increased profits and/or cash flow.

For example, in the Big Spenders Corporation profit and loss statement (see the previous section), if the business owner had plugged the salary increases into the budget before making them and been fully aware of the impending negative impact on the company's profitability, he or she may have given a second thought to this decision. Ditto with the balance sheet example, where the owner made the decision to increase inventory and pay down his or her long-term debt. Had the owner plugged those figures into the balance sheet budget, he or she would've understood the impact these decisions would have on the company's cash account and would probably have altered those decisions.

Such is the power of using financial statements and budgets. They allow you to see the results of your decisions — before you make them! Every small-business owner should use the numbers and statistics that the business generates to help make important decisions.

Understanding Key Ratios and Percentages

Before you can take the numbers generated by the P & L and balance sheet and turn them into meaningful management tools, you need to consider two overall points about the numbers, ratios, and percentages that come from those financial statements:

- ✔ **Comparisons work best.** As explained earlier, numbers, ratios, and percentages are most useful when compared to other numbers, ratios, and percentages. Your company may have what appears to be a respectable percentage of net profit on its sales, but if that percentage is less than it was during the same period the preceding year, danger may lie ahead. Numbers are most effective when they can be used to identify trends — and identifying trends always requires a comparison of numbers over time.

- ✔ **The industry matters.** Acceptable numbers in one industry may not be acceptable in another. Industries vary widely in the numbers they generate. For example, if you're in the software business, you may be disappointed with a 15-percent profit return on your sales dollar (we explain what that means later in this chapter). If you're in the grocery store business, however, you'd probably be ecstatic with a 5-percent profit return on sales.

If you don't know the acceptable ratios and percentages in your industry, contact your appropriate trade association. Most trade associations can give you the benchmark ratios and percentages that you need to know to compare your own business to industry averages. The *Small Business Sourcebook* (Gale) should list the trade associations applicable to your profession.

We strongly suggest that you figure out how to extract the key ratios and percentages from your financial statements by yourself, rather than depending upon your bookkeeper or tax advisor to do so. The process of doing it yourself gives you a better idea of where the numbers come from and how to use the financial statements for other ratios and percentages that may be meaningful to your individual business. Although any ratio or percentage alone won't give you all the information that you need to become a sophisticated financial manager, the knowledge of how they all work together will make you much more effective.

In the following sections, we explain the most commonly used percentages and ratios a small-business owner should consider.

Return on sales (R.O.S.)

Return on sales (R.O.S.) is a percentage determined by dividing net pretax profits (from the P & L) by total sales (also from the P & L). The resulting figure measures your company's overall efficiency in converting a sales dollar into a profit dollar. R.O.S. very much depends upon what type of business you operate.

The R.O.S. is an excellent figure on which you and your employees can focus. It's relatively easy to track, understand, and explain. Some businesses use this percentage as a company-wide scorecard to help their employees understand how the businesses make money, motivating them in turn to do their part in assuring and improving profitability. (Most employees think their businesses make much, much more money than they really do.)

Return on equity (R.O.E.)

Return on equity (R.O.E.) is a percentage determined by dividing pretax profits (from the P & L) by equity/net worth (from the balance sheet). The resulting figure represents the return you've made on the dollars that you invested in your business (your equity).

Over several years, if your return on equity isn't higher than 5 percent or thereabouts (which is the average return on money invested in such secure investments as short-term, high-quality bonds), you may want to consider selling your business and investing the proceeds in bonds. Your return would be similar, your risk and the work much less.

TRUE STORY

Financial ignorance isn't bliss

Ed owned a successful construction company. In business for 15 years, Ed's company employed 20 people, did several million dollars in yearly sales, and provided a comfortable living for Ed. During the course of a meeting between Ed and co-author Jim, who was a consultant with Ed's company at the time, Ed confided that he had been embarrassed by a question the bank had asked when he recently inquired about a loan.

"They asked what my current ratio was," Ed said sheepishly. "And I not only didn't know the answer, I didn't know where on my financial statements to find it."

As it turned out, that wasn't all Ed didn't know about his financial statements. He also didn't know where to find his return-on-sales, how to

determine his days-in-accounts-receivable, or how to compute his debt-to-equity ratio (see the following sections of this chapter). And he didn't have year-to-year comparison figures with which to properly compare his profit and loss statement and balance sheet line items. In short, Ed didn't know how to read his financial statements, much less utilize the information that was on them.

Unfortunately, Ed is typical of many small-business owners who use their financial statements for little more than keeping score and paying taxes. Ironically, Ed employed a well-paid controller to maintain his books, keep score, and pay the business's taxes. Not much of a return on a $75,000 expense!

This assumes, of course, that you're in business to make money. If, however, you're motivated by something else — creativity, growth, independence — or if you simply like owning your own business, you may be content with miniscule earnings despite the fact that you could make a similar or better financial return elsewhere.

Note: Both R.O.S. and R.O.E. are impacted heavily by the amount of money the owner decides to take out of the business in the form of salaries, bonuses, and benefits. Obviously, the more taken out, the lower the R.O.S. and R.O.E. percentages will be.

Gross margin

Gross margin is a percentage determined by subtracting your cost of goods sold (from the P & L) from total sales (also from the P & L). This figure represents your business's effective overall markup on products sold before deducting your operating expenses.

How good your gross margin is depends upon your industry, your business, and what you're selling. Trend is especially important here. Over a period of time, you want to see an increasing rather than decreasing gross margin.

Quick ratio

Quick ratio is a ratio determined by dividing current assets (from the balance sheet) by current liabilities (also from the balance sheet). The resulting figure measures your business's *liquidity* (the ability to raise immediate cash from the sale of your assets); thus, this ratio is of great interest, especially to your lenders.

The higher the quick ratio, the more liquid your business. As a general rule, quick ratios in excess of 2-to-1 are considered healthy; anything less is questionable. Again, trend is especially important here. Over a period of time, you want to see an increasing rather than decreasing quick ratio.

Debt-to-equity ratio

The *debt-to-equity ratio* is a ratio determined by dividing equity/net worth (from the balance sheet) by debt/total liabilities (also from the balance sheet). The resulting ratio indicates how much of the business is owned by the owners (represented by equity/net worth) and how much is owned by its creditors (represented by debt/total liabilities).

As a general rule, a 1-to-1 ratio is considered healthy; anything less is questionable. To further illustrate this point, refer to the Big Spenders Corporation balance sheet from an earlier section. Note that Big Spenders owes its creditors and debtors $175,000 (its total liabilities), while the company's net worth is $159,000 (the owners' equity). This means, in effect, that as of the date that this balance sheet was assembled, Big Spenders Corporation's creditors and debtors had $16,000 more dollars working for the company than the owners did (the difference between $175,000 and $159,000); therefore, its debt-to-equity ratio was slightly less than 1-to-1. If the owners needed another loan to make ends meet, they'd have a hard time showing that their financial stake in the company justified another loan.

Keeping the debt-to-equity ratio within the 1-to-1 parameter, as outlined here, is of paramount importance. For example, when the debt-to-equity ratio falls below 1-to-1, such cash-draining options as adding inventory, hiring new employees, and buying new equipment should be put on hold until the ratio becomes more banker friendly.

Inventory turn

Inventory turn is the number of times your inventory turns over in a year. You determine the number by dividing your cost of goods sold (from the P & L) by your average inventory (beginning + ending ÷ 2). If your beginning inventory (on Jan. 1) was $100,000, and your ending inventory (on Dec. 31) was $150,000, your average inventory would be $125,000.

The figure that results from calculating inventory turn shows how well you're managing your inventory. The higher the number, the more times your inventory has turned, which is always preferable.

The number of times your inventory turns is highly dependent upon the industry (manufacturer, wholesaler, or retailer) and your role in it. Typical inventory turns can range anywhere from 5 to 20 times a year (see the section "Managing Your Inventory" for more).

Number of days in receivables

You determine the *number of days in receivables* — that is, the average length of time between selling a product or service and getting paid for it — by first computing your average sales day. Divide your total sales for the period (from the P & L) by the number of days in that period (for a year, use 365).

After you've computed the average sales day, you divide that number into your current accounts receivable balance (from the balance sheet). The resulting figure gives you the number of sales days in your receivables.

Generally speaking, less than 30 sales days in receivables is considered excellent; between 30 and 45 days is acceptable; and over 45 is cause for concern. (See the later section "Collecting Your Accounts Receivable" for more advice on this topic.)

Managing Your Inventory

The opportunities to improve profitability by the efficient handling of inventory are endless. Inventory isn't gray, like marketing, or in the future, like sales; it is here, today, on your shelves, available to touch and feel and count. As a result, if you improve your efficiency at handling inventory, your business can have a double financial benefit:

- ✔ **Profitability:** The less inventory you write off, the more profitable you will be.
- ✔ **Cash flow:** The fewer dollars you have invested in inventory, the more cash you'll have in your bank account.

Aside from driving with your eyes closed, the accumulation of excess inventory is the quickest and easiest way we know of to get into trouble. Excess inventory and its long list of hidden horrors have turned many a healthy small business into an ailing one.

Unlike getting rid of employees who aren't performing, you can't give inventory that isn't performing a pink slip and send it out the door. Nor can you step up your collection effort with your inventory, as you'd do with slow-moving receivables, and expect it to turn into cash. Nonperforming inventory just sits there, collecting dust, at the same time that you're paying interest on the money you've invested in it.

Yes, sometimes inventory disappears, but not always in the manner intended and not always in exchange for a customer's money. Inventory can disappear in a number of unsatisfactory ways, including internal theft (by your employees), external theft (by your customers), and at the hands of the most virulent scourge of them all — obsolescence.

If inventory is an integral part of your small business, use the following tips to effectively manage it:

- ✔ **Gather information on past purchasing and sales transactions.** Prevention of inventory accumulation starts with the person doing the purchasing. The more information on past purchasing and sales transactions that person has, the better his or her future purchasing decisions can be:

  - Make sure that you buy the best inventory-tracking software you can afford, because inventory's past performance is usually the best indicator of how it will perform in the future. A good small-business tax advisor should be able to counsel you on which software choice is best for you. (If you aren't computerized, ask your accountant to help you develop a manual system.)

  - For those considering entering the retailing business, make sure that you include a *point-of-sale program* (a system that makes adjustments to inventory as a result of cash-register transactions). The system should be sophisticated enough to capture the information needed for you to accurately track your inventory.

- ✔ **Divide your inventory into small, manageable pieces.** Pay especially close attention to those pieces where you have the most financial exposure. Remember, inventory is subject to the 80-20 rule: You usually get about 80 percent of your sales from 20 percent of your inventory units. Pay special attention to tracking that 20 percent. And start considering which of the slow-moving 80 percent you may want to stop selling.

- ✔ **Make sure that you have a workable system and qualified employees in place at the inventory-handling corners: shipping and receiving.** Most inventory disappearance problems can be identified at one of these two positions. If your inventory system is manual, ask an experienced tax practitioner to help you establish a workable system.

- ✔ **Take frequent physical inventories.** To determine whether you're having inventory-shrinkage problems and, if so, how significant they are, count the items in your inventory and compare your physical count to your financial records. (If you divide your inventory into small, manageable pieces, you can more readily determine where the shrinkage is occurring.) Taking a physical inventory is the only way you can be assured that the gross margin figures on your profit and loss statements are correct. We suggest that most businesses take a thorough physical inventory at least twice a year, and preferably four times.

✔ **When selecting suppliers, don't simply settle on the supplier with the lowest price.** Include delivery time and shipping dependability at or near the top of your criteria. After all, the shorter the delivery time and the more dependable the vendor, the less of that vendor's inventory you'll have to carry.

Some vendors will even take returns on inventory you've purchased from them, oftentimes charging a restocking charge of some sort. If so, give such a company a long, hard look as your vendor of choice.

Collecting Your Accounts Receivable

Banks aren't the only institutions in the business of lending money; most small businesses lend money, too. The primary difference between the two, however, is that when banks lend money (known as _loans_) to their customers, they charge interest; when small businesses lend money (via _accounts receivable_) to their customers, it's usually interest free.

Think about it. When customers buy your product (unless your business deals only in cash), you usually give them 30 days to pay the invoice. That's 30 days when the customer not only has your product but also retains the cash that's due you — the same cash that you could otherwise use to reduce your debt, pay your bills, or invest for your benefit.

Today's business culture places the customer on a pedestal, and well it should. After all, someone has to purchase your products or services. But that word _customer_ is incomplete; the correct phrase should be _paying customer_. Today's successful entrepreneurs know that a customer isn't a desired customer until he or she has paid the bills.

Finding paying customers

The following list presents our time-tested collection of tips on how to find, and do business with, paying customers:

✔ **Understand that not everyone is a desirable customer.** Only those customers who pay their bills within a time frame that allows you to make a profit are desirable customers. Don't bet the house on a hot-shot customer who promises big sales; make sure that the customer can pay.

✔ **Use a credit application.** Design and use your own credit application. Ask one of your vendors if you can use its application as a sample. Make sure that every potential customer fills one out before you ship an order or provide your service. And be sure to check the references provided in the application.

✔ **Evaluate every applicant.** Ask yourself these questions about every prospective customer who submits a credit application:

   • Does this applicant have the ability to pay?

   • Has he or she indicated by his or her past actions a willingness to pay on time?

   • Can you make a reasonable profit on sales to this account?

   If the answer to any of these questions is no, feel free to wave good-bye to the prospective sale.

✔ **Ask for a financial statement.** Don't be afraid to ask for a financial statement before shipping to a first-time customer. Can you imagine a bank lending you money for your business without first asking for a financial statement?

✔ **Check credit.** You can bet that your good vendors checked on your credit; you should check on your customers' credit, too. Remember that the granting of credit is a privilege; in effect, you're lending money to the person requesting it. Grant credit like the banks do — with great care.

✔ **Establish terms.** No sale should be made without first establishing credit terms. Terms should work for both parties, but remember that when a customer wants you to carry his or her receivables for long periods of time, that's your signature on the bank's guarantee. Your bank won't back off its terms — why should you?

Managing your accounts receivable

Every successful small business needs someone dedicated to the collection of accounts receivable. In the early stages of the business, that someone is almost always the entrepreneur or founder. In later stages, that responsibility may be delegated to a bookkeeper, controller, or Chief Financial Officer (CFO). But whoever that person happens to be, he or she must be passionate about collecting the monies due the business.

After you've properly established your accounts receivable record-keeping functions (see Chapter 10 for more on bookkeeping systems), you need to figure out how to manage them. Use this collection of suggestions to help you do just that:

✔ **Bill promptly.** If you wait until the end of the month, you've already lost a number of days before you'll receive the cash. Bill the same day you ship or, in the case of a service business, the same day you fulfill the customer's order or the terms of the contract.

✔ **Measure.** Outstanding receivables should be *aged* (the process of computing the number of days that every receivable has been outstanding) at least once a month. (Companies where money is tight will run agings every day.) Creating an aging list reminds you who's in control of a large amount of your company's cash. An acceptable age of a receivable (in most industries, anyway) is 30 days; danger signals should appear after a receivable exceeds 45 days.

✔ **Begin collections promptly.** Don't wait until your receivables are over 90 days old to kick in your collection procedures. Do it while the invoice is still warm (no more than 45 days).

✔ **Utilize a carrying charge or interest charge.** Why shouldn't you charge interest on overdue balances? After all, you're expected to pay a carrying charge when you exceed your payment terms (review your credit-card agreement if you have any doubts on this one). Don't charge anything less than 12 percent. A relatively high interest rate will assure that you get the overdue account's attention.

✔ **Don't ship to nonpayers.** Don't continue to ship to customers who don't pay in accordance with your terms. Your good vendors won't ship to you if you don't abide by their terms, will they?

✔ **Involve the boss.** Pick up the phone yourself when the bill-paying stalling becomes noticeable. A call from the owner or boss will always be more effective than a call from the bookkeeper.

✔ **Use a collection agency only as a last resort.** Collection agencies are expensive, charging up to 50 percent of the receivable for their services. Also, collection agencies aren't known for their consideration and politeness. Be sure that you're willing to kiss your customer good-bye forever if you choose to hand your slow-paying account over to an agency.

Finally, remember that your accounts receivable represent cash, and cash is the ultimate measure of your business's liquidity. Liquidity is the first place lenders and investors look when appraising the health of a business. Make sure that your receivables are current before showing your financial statements to people who have a reason for reading them.

Using Three Ways to Improve Profits

Every small-business owner spends a significant amount of time trying to increase the business's *profitability* — the difference between revenue (the money you take in) and expenses (the money you pay out). No one succeeds in increasing profitability all the time, no matter how hard he or she tries. Some succeed often enough to grow a small business into a larger one. Some succeed just often enough to survive. And, unfortunately, some don't succeed at all.

There are only three ways for you to increase your business's profitability:

- ✔ Decrease expenses
- ✔ Increase margins

   Margin is the difference between sales price and the cost of the goods or services sold. You can increase margins by raising prices, lowering the costs of the goods or services sold, or both.

- ✔ Increase sales

You can do all three at the same time — that is, if luck and the small-business gods are with you.

Instead of proceeding by trial-and-error, you can use a thorough understanding of how these options work to know exactly what to do when your profits aren't what they should be. In the sections that follow, we explain what you need to know about each of these three options.

#1: Decreasing (or controlling) expenses

The biggest advantage that comes from controlling your expenses is that appropriate expense cuts have a direct short-term impact on the bottom line. For every dollar you save by eliminating an expense, you may earn an extra dollar of profit. (Sure, increasing sales is another way of increasing profits, but an extra dollar in sales may bring in only 25 cents of profit. We explain more about that shortly.)

Of course, there's a world of difference between reducing the expense of your phone bill, for instance, by switching to a company with a lower cost but comparable long-distance service and reducing the cost of your product by switching to a supplier that offers lower cost *and* lower quality. Higher returns from disgruntled customers — or, worse, lawsuits stemming from harmful products or services — can do more harm than good to your business's long-run profitability.

So, although we're strong advocates of operating a lean business, you must be thoughtful about where and how to reduce your expenses. You should consider all the effects of cost cutting, not just the short-term, bottom-line effects.

Controlling expenses is a cultural issue, which means that it's a lead-by-example issue that begins with you, the business owner, and carries over to your employees (presuming that you've hired the right ones; see Chapter 15). From the day you open your business's doors, you must pay close attention to managing its expenses, being careful not to spend money carelessly and being tactfully critical of those who do. If the boss sets the right example, the rest of the company is certain to follow. That's how a company culture flourishes.

The following sections give you guidelines for successfully controlling expenses.

Zero-based budgeting

After you determine what kind of expense-controlling culture you want (and make the commitment to act accordingly), your next step is to introduce a zero-based budgeting program. *Zero-based budgeting* requires that you begin each year's annual budget process by setting each expense category to zero. In other words, you don't assume that the dollar amounts in the preceding year's expense account were legitimate; you question every dollar that went into that expense account — hence, the term *zero-based*.

This zero-based budgeting approach contrasts with the manner in which many businesses budget expenses. Most businesses add a percentage increase to the preceding year's expenses, with the rate of the prior year's inflation increase being the most frequently used common denominator. If last year's inflation rate was 3 percent, for instance, just plug in 3-percent increases to arrive at this year's budget and move on to something more exciting.

The primary advantage of budgeting by the percentage-increase method is that it's quick and easy. The primary disadvantage is that it means that last year's fat is destined to be carried forward into this year's menu. And ditto with next year's menu, and so on, forever — unless that particular expense category is eventually purged through the zero-based budgeting technique.

Here's an example of how zero-based budgeting works: Suppose it's time to budget your telephone expense for the year. The quick-and-easy solution is to take the preceding year's telephone expense figure, add 3 percent (or whatever inflation is), and move on to the next line item on the profit and loss statement. However, the zero-based budgeter's job is to examine the firm's business — determine what kinds of calls need to be made in the course of business and then call alternative carriers, collect quotes on their services, and award the business to a less-expensive but comparable-quality provider.

More often than not, the additional time you spend budgeting will be rewarded with a decrease in expenses, as opposed to an inflation-based increase.

Trimming costs

In addition to zero-based budgeting, effective control of expenses requires understanding the 80-20 rule as it applies to expenses. The *80-20 rule* maintains that you usually can find 80 percent of wasted expense dollars in 20 percent of the expense categories.

Challenge expenses in all categories, large and small. You can usually find quick-and-easy dollars to save by rooting around in such overlooked expense categories as utilities, travel and entertainment, insurance, and the compost heap of them all, the miscellaneous category.

The following important tips provide a framework in which you can effectively control your expenses:

- **Avoid overstaffing.** Finding and hiring a good employee is costly, and after you've hired one, unhiring him or her is not only difficult but also expensive. Use outside contractors, temporary services, and part-timers if you're on the fence about the need to hire a full-time employee.

- **Automate where possible.** Technology is usually cheaper than people (and it can be depreciated). When possible and where it won't compromise the quality of your products or services, purchase software in lieu of hiring additional employees. Functions such as accounting, inventory control, accounts receivable, and payroll lend themselves to automation. Let technology do your detail work.

- **Don't wait until a crisis arrives to do something about your expenses.** Institute an expense-control program when things are going well; you don't have to wait until the roof caves in. Be motivated by efficiency, not by fear.

- **Put the responsibility for controlling expenses where it belongs — in the hands of the employees who spend the money.** Also, make them accountable for their actions. Reward them when they meet their goals, and provide corrective feedback when they don't (Management 101!).

The preceding tips are intended to provide you with an overview of how to control your expenses. Following are several cost-controlling measures, intended not only to give you specific ideas, but also to put you in the frame of mind for getting specific on all your expenses:

- **Ask for price quotes before you obligate yourself to services.** This is true for everything from lawyers, accountants, and financial advisors to computer repair people, plumbers, and consultants. (Often the quotes won't hold up, but they'll give you a basis on which to negotiate subsequent charges.) Also, always ask for itemized invoices.

- **Don't pay unnecessary bank charges.** Question the fees on your statements. Shop around if your bank is charging more for services than competitors. Some banks today are aggressively pursuing small businesses. Just about everything is negotiable, including bank charges.

✔ **Shop your telephone service every year or so.** Everyone is discounting telephone services as technology and deregulation make prices more competitive.

✔ **If you have employees, review your experience ratio with your insurance agent.** Your *experience ratio* is the factor that determines your workers' compensation payment (see Chapter 10).

Speaking of insurance agents, how long has it been since you've shopped for insurance, both liability and health? So, what are you waiting for?

We're not suggesting that price should be your only consideration or that after you've found a lower price you should automatically wave good-bye to your current supplier. Rather, we're suggesting that you be aware of the going rate in the marketplace and, where appropriate, either change suppliers or press your current supplier to reassess the prices it's charging you. Squeaky wheels get the grease, and the effective control of expenses is no exception to this rule.

The preceding tips are a few of the many possible ways for you to control your business's expenses. Remember that effective expense control isn't a one-time event; it's an ongoing occurrence whose success or failure lies entirely in your hands. You can read this entire book for smart business ideas that are cost effective.

#2: Increasing margins

Gross margin represents the difference between the selling price and the cost of the product or service in question. If your product sells for $15 and the cost of that product (including shipping charges) is $10, your gross margin is 33 percent — the $5 in margin or markup divided by the $15 gross sales price. Your gross-margin dollars are $5 (the difference between the $10 cost and the $15 sales price).

The magic of increasing margins is that, similar to decreasing expenses, every dollar of income derived from the margin increase, assuming no reduction in sales, ends up as additional profit. In the preceding example, if the price of the product is raised to $16, the margin jumps from 33 percent to 37.5 percent, and the gross-margin dollars increase from $5 to $6. Because increasing prices generally costs very little, nearly all the $1 of the price increase will be realized as profit, again assuming no reduction in purchasing from customers.

Consider the case of the small business doing $500,000 in sales in a year. If the owner, at the beginning of the year, decides to increase the prices of his products by an average of 1 percent, that would mean an additional $5,000 in profits at the end of the year. An average increase of 2 percent would add another $10,000, and 5 percent a solid $25,000 (again, all this assumes that the price increases don't reduce sales).

Generally speaking, small-business owners are more reluctant to raise prices than they should be. So many times, your humble authors have witnessed reluctant small-business owners tremble in the course of reasonably raising prices, only to learn that their customers don't care as long as the quality of the relationship endures.

The tolerance of your customers to accept price increases will depend on such issues as competition, alternative products, and, most of all, the customer relationships you maintain. (See Chapter 12 for tips on keeping your customers happy.)

We strongly recommend that every small-business owner review the margins on every product or service offered at least once a year. Determine a time of the year when raising prices makes the most sense (usually at the beginning of the business's fiscal year), mark that date on your calendar in indelible ink, and when the time comes, start with your lowest-priced item and work up. Analyze the percentage of price increase on each individual item. Don't simply increase prices by using an across-the-board percentage increase. Also, be sure to aim for higher margins on the lower-priced items (those that aren't as likely to be price-shopped by your customers) and on those products that don't need to be as competitively priced.

However, you don't have to wait until the end (or the beginning) of the year to consider increasing your prices. You may want to consider a price increase when the demand for your product suddenly increases. Perhaps a competitor has raised its prices, or perhaps the law of supply and demand is hard at work — in other words, maybe more demand than supply for the product in question can provide a perfect scenario for raising prices. Don't feel guilty for taking advantage of such situations — you'll encounter plenty of occasions when the law of supply and demand works in reverse, and you'll be forced to cut your prices.

#3: Increasing sales

After you have zero-based your expenses and increased your margins, it's time to do what every entrepreneur worth his or her weight in loan guarantees loves to do: increase sales.

After all, increasing sales is what most of us are born to do, and besides, offense (increasing sales) is always more enjoyable than defense (cutting expenses). We love to roll out a new product, hire a new salesperson (it's always more fun to hire a salesperson than it is a bookkeeper), or develop a new sales promotion. What's more, you can easily measure the results of a plan to increase sales. Please see Chapter 11 for loads of advice on how to increase sales.

Chapter 14

Learning from Others' Experiences

- -

- -

All right, here's an important question: What's the number-one cause of small-business failure?

All hands shoot up.

What's that? No, it isn't a lack of money. Sorry, not lousy location. Nope, not poor distribution either. Give up?

All heads nod.

The answer is isolation. As in the small-business owner's isolation.

A lack of money, a lousy location, and poor distribution aren't causes of small-business failure, they're only symptoms — symptoms of that dreaded disease, Owner's Isolation Syndrome. The symptoms of the syndrome affect every small-business owner at one time or another, but if you commit yourself to preventing the disease, you can avoid many of the symptoms.

In light of our status as charter members of the Never-Bring-Up-a-Problem-without-an-Accompanying-Solution Club, we present a collection of options in this chapter that will help you do away with the trial-and-error method of small-business management. We recommend that you sail away from your island and make room for all these options in your repertoire.

Utilize Mentors

We know two things for sure:

- ✔ If we had our small-business careers to live over again, the first thing we'd do is find more mentors.

- ✔ Somewhere within your reach, you can find a veteran small-business owner who will agree to be *your* mentor if you approach him or her correctly.

Mentors are basically consultants — usually working for free — in the experience business, and experience is the best teacher of them all. You can go to a mentor to deal with strategic issues — the long-term, fundamental, and always critical issues. (Most mentors prefer to focus on the strategic as opposed to the operational issues — short term, day-to-day, and often temporary dealings.)

So, get the help of a mentor. Simple right? But most small-business owners don't know how to find the veterans who will agree to become mentors and provide that experience, and they don't know how to cultivate that relationship after they have it.

Finding your mentor

Here's our three-step "Mentor Search Plan:"

1. **Compile a list of prospective mentors.**

   Ask your banker, your accountant, your lawyer, and folks around town who are wired into the small-business community (people at the Chamber of Commerce, Service Corps of Retired Executives, and Small Business Development Centers) for the names of veteran small-business owners who may be interested in helping you succeed.

2. **Contact the person that your research and intuition indicate may be the best mentor for you.**

   The best mentor is someone who (currently or previously) has experience within your chosen industry, but this isn't a prerequisite. (General business knowledge, however, *is* a prerequisite.) Oftentimes, a good mentor is retired and thus may be motivated to help others as a way to stay involved in business.

    The best way to approach a prospective mentor is to write him or her a letter introducing yourself, your business, and the reason for your interest. Follow up the letter with a phone call. Don't use e-mail for the initial contact; it's too informal and doesn't send the message as to how important the mentorship is to you.

3. **Persuade your prospective mentor to sign on.**

   Proceed as follows:

   a. "Mr. (or Ms.) Veteran, my name is Wanda Wannabe. Mr. Legal Beagle, a mutual friend of ours, suggested I call you."

   b. "Mr. (or Ms.) Veteran, I'm not looking for your money, but I am looking for your advice. Would you agree to spare a small amount of your time each month to meet with me if I promise not to waste one nanosecond of it, if I provide you with a complete agenda in advance of every meeting, if I follow up on the suggestions you make, and if you can name the place and time of our meetings, along with your price?"

   c. "Mr. (or Ms.) Veteran," you conclude, with just a touch of a plea in your voice, "As you have probably surmised, I am looking for a mentor. Would you consider being that person?"

Don't rush into the relationship; have a lunch or a dinner together first. (You buy, of course!) Remember, this is a relationship you're seeking here; you want to make sure that you and your mentor will be compatible.

This pitch usually works. We should know — it has been successfully used on both of us and on other business owners we know.

Building the mentor-business owner relationship

When you've found a mentor who matches your needs and requirements and is willing to work with you, work at fostering your relationship. Here are several tips that will help you retain your mentor and make the most of the relationship:

- ✔ **Understand that mentoring is a personal experience, not a business one.** If the chemistry is right, the relationship works well. If the chemistry doesn't work, the relationship won't work either. A mentoring experience may endure for one day, one month, one year, or the lifetime of your business. The only determinant is how well the relationship works for both parties involved.

- ✔ **Follow up.** Drop your mentor a note after your meetings. Or, the next time the two of you talk, let your mentor know how implementing her advice turned out and how much you appreciate the help.

- ✔ **Be honest with your mentor about the problems and issues you face.** No sugarcoating allowed. Your mentor will see through the fluff anyway, and he won't hang around for long if he thinks you aren't being truthful with him.

✔ **Leave your thin skin at home.** Good mentors speak their minds and aren't shy about shooting down poor ideas.

✔ **Don't blindly follow all your mentor's advice.** Your mentor may have different priorities, ethics, and needs than you do. So, in the end, follow your heart as well as your head in making decisions based on your mentor's input. Just be sure to show respect and consideration in your disagreements.

Network with Peers

Nobody knows the business of small business better than a retired veteran (see the previous section), but finishing a close second in the antidote-to-lonely-decision-making competition is the current small-business owner — a peer who faces the same day-to-day issues that you face.

Imagine the power of putting a dozen or so current small-business owners in the same room. Imagine the wealth of solutions that may appear when one of the members presents a nagging problem or a thorny issue and asks for help. Do you have a problem with an employee who can't seem to get to work on time (see Chapter 15)? Surely, another business owner has had the same problem before — discover from your peer what has worked for him. You say you don't have a personnel manual yet? A peer has already gone to the trouble of assembling one and could lend hers to you to use as a template.

Peer networking works because, as we say throughout this book, a small business's problems are generic — that is, they're not unique to the industry or niche. Thus, the solutions to common problems are generic, too.

Second only to what a good mentor can offer, peer networking is the best of the small-business owner's learning devices — *if* you can locate the right networking resource. (Sorry, we're not talking Rotary Clubs or Chambers of Commerce here, although these are steps in the right direction.)

Some cities already have for-profit or nonprofit peer-networking programs up and running and are spreading word of the value of the concept. You can ask at your local Chamber of Commerce or your city's or state's small-business magazine or newspaper to find out what and where these programs are. These organizations include

✔ Vistage (formerly The Executive Committee), San Diego, California

✔ American Women's Economic Development Corp. (AWED), Washington, D.C.

✔ The Alternative Board (TAB), St. Louis, Missouri

✔ President's Resource Organization (PRO), Chicago, Illinois

✔ Opportunity Knocks (OK), Bend, Oregon (co-author Jim founded this organization)

One or more of these organizations (or another with a similar agenda) may surface in your city if one hasn't set up shop already. Keep your eyes peeled.

Form a Board of Advisors

Boards of advisors are like breath mints; almost everybody could benefit from one, but too few people partake.

Similar to a mentor, a board of advisors provides you with an affordable, outside perspective. Boards replace trial-and-error with experience and knowledge. They act as sounding boards, rebound boards, and boards of inquiry. They open needed doors and close unnecessary ones, while giving you an inside look at the outside business world.

Incidentally, we're not talking about a board of *directors* here; we're talking about a board of *advisors*. Directors are responsible for directing the company; advisors are responsible only for advising the president or Chief Executive Officer (CEO) — that's you!

Because directors, by virtue of accepting their positions, assume the *fiduciary responsibility* (the responsibility to the shareholders for the financial state of the business) of directing the company, they're legally liable for its direction. Because directors can be sued, companies that use a board of directors must also carry expensive "directors and officers insurance packages" on their positions. For these reasons, most privately held small businesses use boards of advisors instead (while most public companies utilize boards of directors).

Reaping the benefits of a board

The primary benefits of having your own board of advisors include the following:

✔ **Credibility:** Having a board is an indicator that your business is serious about its direction. Also, board members with solid reputations can bring additional credibility to your organization.

✔ **Lead generation:** Your board can play an integral role in networking sales leads.

✔ **Connections:** Your board will open a variety of doors that you can't open.

✔ **Advice:** You can diversify the skills of your board and then look to your board members for advice in their specialties.

There aren't many valid reasons not to have a board of advisors. Yes, a board does take time to organize and coordinate, but that time will be repaid many times over if your board is a good one. A board also is inexpensive. Most board members will gladly donate an hour or two of their time every three months or so for the price of a lunch.

Of course, you can reap these benefits only if your board meetings are well organized, if the board members feel that their time isn't being wasted, and if they feel that their advice is being heeded.

Forming your advisory board

Most small-business advisory boards consist of three or five members, excluding the owner. (If you're a home-office business or a truly small, small business, you may select the three-board-member size.) Here are some tips on how to assemble, utilize, and treat your board of advisors:

- ✔ **Select advisors from outside your company.** No board of employees here, all nodding their heads in unison. Besides, you want knowledge and perspectives that don't already exist in the company.

- ✔ **Balance your skills with the skills of the board members.** If your strengths are sales and marketing, make sure that you cover the finance and operational bases through your other advisory board members. Could you use a banker on the board? A lawyer? An accountant?

- ✔ **Include a customer as a board member.** No viewpoint can equal the viewpoint of a customer — especially one who knows your industry, pays his or her bills on time, and considers vendors to be partners. Never go to a board meeting without that viewpoint.

After you've selected the banker, lawyer, accountant, and/or customer, and you still have a slot or two left over, feel free to include someone from your industry — someone with potential mentoring skills and/or someone with financing contacts that may eventually aid your growing business.

- ✔ **Schedule meetings regularly and well in advance.** Give at least one month's notice, maybe more. Quarterly meetings usually are the best; anything more frequent is asking too much from your board members.

- ✔ **Limit the meetings to two hours.** Keep them meaty, and keep the advisors interested.

- ✔ **Avoid surprises.** Send out an agenda in advance of the meeting and then stick with it, unless an emergency prompts some last-minute changes. Board members, like bankers, don't like surprises.

- ✔ **Focus on strategic and overview issues.** Don't discuss operations. What's the difference between operations and strategy?

- *Strategic issues* are issues of business direction and positioning; they include such subjects as distribution systems, marketing plans, and sales initiatives.

- *Operational issues* include specific problems such as administrative snafus, shipping and receiving roadblocks, and invoicing issues.

And what about the biggest issue of them all, cash flow? Although a shortage of cash really is an operational problem, it always results from a strategic problem — not enough sales, inadequate margins, or out-of-control expenses, for example.

✔ **Be truthful.** Lose your credibility, and you lose your advisors. Be candid — no sugarcoating or truth bending allowed.

✔ **Follow up on suggestions.** Follow up on your board's recommendations, and not just those you consider to be valid. You don't have to *implement* every recommendation; you should, however, have the courtesy to *respond* to all seriously considered recommendations and ideas.

✔ **Pay the board.** If you can afford it, you should pay board members anywhere from $50 per meeting on up. If you're a start-up and money is tight, at least buy the members lunch until you can afford to compensate them.

 After your advisors get comfortable with you and your business, you can ask to use their credibility and contacts to help you gain new customers, new vendors, and new sources of financing.

Get a Partner

Here's a fact that not everyone knows: According to studies, partnerships outperform sole proprietorships by a wide margin. We're not talking rocket science here; this statement is nothing more than simple math at work: One plus one equals at least two. Sometimes, one plus one equals significantly more than two if the partners can blend their skills and talents. (Google, Apple Computer, and Hewlett Packard are examples of companies that began as partnerships.)

So, why may a partnership make sense? Here are some reasons:

✔ **Complementary skills:** Although you're probably aware of your own strengths, your human nature lets you more easily overlook your weaknesses. Ask those who know you well — family, friends, and current or previous co-workers — what complementary skills you should seek in a business partner. And try to do some honest introspection to answer that question for yourself.

✔ **Additional capital:** Two savings accounts are better than one.

- ✔ **Greater problem-solving capacity:** Two heads are (usually) better than one.

- ✔ **More flexibility:** One partner goes on vacation or gets sick, the other one minds the store.

- ✔ **Ease of formation:** Partnerships are easier and less expensive to form than corporations (but not as easy or inexpensive as sole proprietorships; see Chapter 5).

- ✔ **Less risk:** Profits aren't the only thing partnerships share.

For sure, you may have plenty of reasons not to want to take a partner (or multiple partners) into your business, however. Everyone knows juicy horror stories about business partnerships that turned sour and even ended up in court, destroying the business in the process (assuming anything was left to destroy). And warring partners seldom go down alone.

Well, a partnership is just another example of how the risk-reward equation works. Sure, partnerships present an additional risk that doesn't exist when you go it alone. After all, partnerships really are nothing more than organized relationships — and we all know what can happen to relationships, organized or not. Even the good ones are difficult to maintain.

We can tell you that the success ratio is highest when the two partners have complementary skills. You're a salesnik? Find an operations type for a partner. Your skills are in product development? Find someone who has experience in getting the product to the marketplace and subsequently sold. You're a mover and shaker? Find someone who can count the beans that you'll be moving and shaking.

How do you find a partner (or partners)? The same way you locate a key employee, a consultant, or a mentor (see the first section of this chapter): Identify what it is that you need (in this case, the skills you're looking for) and then network your available resources.

When forming a partnership, you're beginning what you hope will be a long-term relationship — a long-term relationship that oftentimes rivals a marriage in terms of complexity. If you're smart, you'll determine a way to test the chemistry of the partnership before you get so far involved that you can't get out. Otherwise, you may learn the same lesson that too many marriages teach — a lifetime can be a long time. (See the nearby sidebar for more on testing your partnership chemistry.)

The number-one rule of a partnership? Don't enter into one without first consulting an experienced small-business lawyer. The attorney should advise you and your prospective partner about the many obstacles that lie in the path of a successful partnership. Then the lawyer will assist you in drawing up an ironclad, airtight, cast-in-stone, buy-sell partnership agreement to overcome those obstacles — an ironclad, airtight, cast-in-stone, buy-sell partnership agreement, by the way, that will be tested many times over the life of your business, if not by you then by your next-of-kin or your partner's. (For much, much more on partnerships and partnership agreements, refer to Chapter 5. For more on legal issues, head to Chapter 17.)

Join a Trade Association

Thousands of trade associations exist in the United States, and we recommend that you join one. No matter who you are or what industry you're in, a trade association is probably available for you. The best trade associations offer a wide range of potential benefits — everything from business contacts to skill-building workshops to industry-specific information to group insurance programs. In addition, most trade associations host industry-wide trade shows at least once a year, during which you can mingle with suppliers and peers.

Two kinds of trade associations exist: industry-specific trade associations and small-business-specific trade associations. The following list breaks down the options:

- **Industry-specific trade associations:** Consult your local library to find the trade association or organization that caters to your industry. The *National Trade and Professional Associations of the United States* (Columbia Books) lists more than 7,500 associations in the United States today. Your local library should have a copy of this $269 annual publication. Or, you can search the Web by opening a search engine and keying in the name of the specific industry you're in, followed by the word *association* — as in "sporting-goods association."

- **Small-business-specific trade associations:** These trade associations include the following:

  - **National Small Business Association (NSBA):** This association watches congressional action and reports on issues affecting small businesses. Call or visit its Web site (202-293-8830; www.nsba.biz) for details.

  - **National Association for the Self-Employed (NASE):** NASE offers resource materials and a monthly magazine. Call 800-232-NASE for details, or visit its Web site at www.nase.org.

  - **National Association of Women Business Owners (NAWBO):** This association brings together women entrepreneurs for support and assistance. Call 800-55-NAWBO for more information, or surf its Web site at www.nawbo.org.

  - **National Business Association (NBA):** The NBA assists small-business people in achieving their personal and professional goals. Call 800-465-0440 for details, or visit its Web site at www.nationalbusiness.org.

> • **National Federation of Independent Business (NFIB):** The NFIB is the largest lobbying organization for small businesses in the country. Call 800-NIFB-NOW for details, or visit its Web site at www.nfib.com.

Trade associations aren't without their warts. First, don't assume that products and services marketed to the association's members are necessarily the best of what's out there. Many associations, for example, offer insurance programs to their members — programs that the members could purchase at a lower cost elsewhere. Remember this: The programs a trade association offers are only as good as the people who determine what that association will and won't offer its members.

Don't limit yourself to providing a product or service only in the manner that people in the trade association recommend to provide it. For example, when co-author Eric began offering personal financial counseling services, he chose to do so exclusively on an hourly basis, even though most other financial advisors worked on commission or managed money for fees. Eric knew that their way wasn't the only way, and the path he chose reflected his belief that a financial counselor should have no personal financial stake dependent on any of the products or services that he or she recommends. This policy worked well for him.

Find a Business Incubator

Business incubators provide new small-business owners with a friendly location to set up shop. An incubator offers its start-up customers a mixture of the following benefits:

✔ Below-market rent

✔ Free or discounted access to a variety of office services

✔ Discounted administrative services

✔ The opportunity to network with other entrepreneurs who are in the same knee-knocking, start-up boat

Because entrepreneurs are most inclined to trust the advice of their peers, what better place to receive your advice and locate your business than within an incubator?

For more information on incubators, log on to the National Business Incubation Association (NBIA) Web site at www.nbia.org, or call the association at 740-593-4331.

Testing the partnership waters

How can you test a partnership before you get in so far that you can't get out? First, ask your attorney or accountant for the names of partners who currently own a business together. Meet with them (without your prospective partner) and ask questions to find out the pros and cons of partnering. Ask your attorney or accountant for the names of people who have been involved in failed partnerships, too. You can learn just as much from failures as you can from successes.

We also suggest that you give your partnership a trial run before you open your business. For starters, write your business plan together;

doing this will give you an immediate insight into whether you're capable of working side by side. Next, investigate your financing options together; meet with probable vendors, interview potential customers — do everything just short of hanging out your combined shingle for business. Sure, the time involved in testing a partnership may cost you a month or two of doing business. But we can guarantee you this: No matter how time-consuming and messy the formation process may be, it will never be as time-consuming and messy as the dissolution of a failed partnership.

Locate a Small Business Development Center

Small Business Development Centers (SBDCs) are cooperative programs designed to provide current and potential business owners with advice and information on running their businesses. SBDCs are sponsored by a partnership between the Small Business Administration (SBA), a local college or university, and, often, your state's Economic Development agency. Every state has a central SBDC, and the United States has nearly 1,000 service centers, most of which are located on college or community college campuses.

Most SBDCs have an abundance of material on starting and running a small business, so you'll want to be sure to check out their libraries and resources. Also, most offer training courses on just about every business subject imaginable — including their specialty, the small-business start-up. Finally, most SBDCs offer one-on-one counseling.

As with any type of consultant, the quality of SBDC counseling varies widely from one SBDC office to another. Tread slowly and don't bet the farm on their advice.

To locate the SBDC nearest you, call 800-8-ASK-SBA or visit www.sba.gov/sbdc.

Give SCORE a Try

The Service Corps of Retired Executives (SCORE) is affiliated with the SBA and offers one-on-one counseling through its 10,000+ experienced counselors across the country. SCORE is a wonderful concept, whose offerings sometimes fall short of its potential.

 SCORE volunteers (usually *Fortune* 500 graduates) will probably be most helpful to you if you're trying to determine whether to leave your day job and make the risky leap to business ownership.

The quality of SCORE's advice varies widely and depends on the individual counselor. Similar to the SBDCs, proceed cautiously when accepting advice from SCORE volunteers, and make sure your volunteer is knowledgeable and on-target. If you find the right volunteer, however, you could find a great candidate to be your mentor (as mentioned in the first section of this chapter).

SCORE offices are easy to locate. Log on to `www.score.org` and find the chapter closest to you.

Tap Into Small-Business Information

Magazines and books (and associated videos, audiotapes, and CDs) focused on helping the small-business owner abound. Where small business is concerned, you name it and a book has been written about it — including this one! Read your industry trade publications (which you can often find through your industry's trade associations, a topic we discuss earlier in this chapter). Also, we suggest you check out the *Small Business Sourcebook* (Gale), a huge two-volume reference that you can find in most public libraries.

And on the technological front, DVDs, podcasts, and Webinars are often produced and offered by larger companies that service your industry, or by technology vendors that sell products within the small-business space. Intuit and Microsoft are two examples of companies that offer a wide variety of technology-based informational offerings.

The number of Web sites and small-business blogs available online have grown to a near-infinite number. Put the online medium to work to keep up to speed on new trends and offerings under the small-business category. (See Chapter 21 for our top Internet resource recommendations, and check out Chapter 3 for helpful government resources, such as the Small Business Administration.)

Part IV
Keeping Your Business in Business

The 5th Wave   By Rich Tennant

©RICHTENNANT

Paul's Petsitting

"I have read your resume, Ms. Cotham.
Now please, come...sit...speak."

In this part . . .

After you start your business, the real fun begins — staying in business and growing your business. This part puts you through your paces, covering employee issues including hiring and benefits, government regulations, taxes, and special issues for fast-growing businesses.

Chapter 15

Finding and Keeping Superstar Employees

- -

In This Chapter

▶ Executing the hiring process

▶ Motivating your employees through training

▶ Handling pay and performance issues

▶ Terminating an employee when all else fails

▶ Assembling an organization chart and an employee manual

▶ Examining the traits of successful employers

▶ Determining whether to lease employees

- -

*I*f you're like most small-business owners we know, you may work without any employees at all for a period of time as you transition through the start-up stage, and then, after you decide to hire employees, you may find that you need or want to hire only one or two. However, if you have ambitions to really grow your business, you'll probably end up hiring many employees. After all, employees mean *leverage* (increased means of accomplishing your mission) in the world of business, and leverage opens up the opportunities for growth.

The concepts and suggestions in this chapter are designed to help you hire top employees and keep them happy and, in the process, exactly where they belong: working for you, not for your competition.

Every business has a number of *gamebreaker* positions (key positions that will make or break your company). When you're just starting out, that position may be yours alone, because you may be the only employee. In larger, established small businesses, those gamebreaker positions may include the president/CEO/Grand Poobah (that's you), the financial person, the sales manager, the marketing manager, the production manager, the office manager, the purchasing agent, the art director . . . well, you get the point. Select these people carefully.

Every successful, growing small business must have superstars filling its gamebreaker positions. A superstar is an employee who

- ✔ Is capable of taking on increasing responsibilities and contributing to the company's continued growth.
- ✔ Is loyal to your vision.
- ✔ Shares your ethics and principles.
- ✔ Is creative within his or her area of expertise.
- ✔ Adds to the synergy of the team — superstars aren't superstars unless they can work effectively with other team members.
- ✔ Welcomes positive change.

Assuming you follow the hiring guidelines as suggested in this chapter, you should have no trouble recognizing a superstar when you see one. The trick, of course, is finding them in the first place and then keeping them.

Assembling your team of superstars is a three-part process — hiring, training, and motivating. Unfortunately, in the process of hiring people you hope are superstars, you'll sometimes stumble and hire someone who doesn't work out. Sadly, that calls for a related process that's equally as important: firing.

Assembling a Top Team

The best employees go to the entrepreneur who's willing to go to the most trouble to find them. Hiring is mostly science, not art. It's methodical, it can be repetitive, and it's usually a drawn-out, brain-dulling process.

You must first collect a roster of worthwhile applicants for the position, likely through one of the following methods:

- ✔ By running an ad
- ✔ By putting out a sign or a Web site posting
- ✔ By encouraging referrals from employees, vendors, and customers

Referrals are almost always the best of the options, because referrals are more likely to be skilled applicants (those doing the referring don't want the embarrassment of referring a weak applicant). Referrals cost next to nothing — just get the word out that you're looking and then let your employees, vendors, or customers do the talking.

You may, on occasion, when hiring for a part-time position or a minimum-wage job, receive applicants who don't have resumes. Be sure you have an application form ready for them to fill out (ask your accountant or any active business for a copy of the form it uses). Never accept an applicant for a responsible position (one responsible for managing employees, for handling money, for dealing with customers, and so on) without a professionally prepared resume. If the applicant hasn't taken the time to create such a resume, that alone tells you all you need to know about his or her potential for the position.

The tough part comes after you've collected the resumes: You must interview, then reinterview, and then reinterview again. You must check those often-camouflaged references, whose primary function, you soon discover, is to tell you as little as possible about a candidate's faults in between glowing adjectives.

Taking hints for hiring

Following is a list of hiring tips to help you locate and hire that elusive superstar:

- ✔ **When running an ad, remember that you're selling an opportunity, not just offering a job — write the ad accordingly.** You want (we're assuming) to attract a career-minded employee who wants to grow with your company, so you need to paint your company, and the position, in a similarly attractive light. Review a large number of existing ads carefully, and then use bits and pieces of the best ones.

- ✔ **Establish a reward system to encourage your employees to introduce qualified candidates.** The best candidates often come from inside-the-company referrals. Rewards can include anything from cash to vacation days.

- ✔ **Always prepare a job description (see "Writing performance expectations" later in this chapter) in advance.** Good applicants want to know exactly what the job entails and what's expected of them. Include the job definition, performance expectations, salary, expected bonus, perks, and the chain-of-command, as it relates to the position being offered.

- ✔ **Review the applicant's resume, looking for the names of businesses or people you may know who aren't listed as the candidate's official references.** The most informative references may be those the applicant doesn't list. Such third-party references are usually more candid with their comments than the official references are.

✔ **Try to open the door to more candid conversations when you're talking to the applicant's references.** Look for areas of commonality in order to put the person at ease. Tune in for the little things as you listen. Ask about the applicant's weaknesses, and then multiply — most references are prone to sugarcoating. If the reference is reluctant to provide information on the applicant, that doesn't necessarily mean that the applicant has problems — the reference may simply be protecting him or herself.

✔ **Have every applicant complete a job application in addition to submitting a resume (even if applicants note "see information on resume").** Resumes + applications = more information on candidates. Most applications ask questions about topics that aren't found on a resume, such as citizenship, green card, felony arrests, and so on.

✔ **Look for the applicant's ability to listen.** If he doesn't listen well now, he's unlikely to listen well after you hire him and he's on the job.

✔ **Find out what research the applicant has done on you and your company.** If she comes to the interview unprepared and devoid of knowledge about your company and industry, you've discovered something about either her work habits or the depth of her desire for the job.

✔ **Remember that the hiring process usually requires you to wear two hats:**

- The detective's hat, as you interview and separate potential superstars from the rest of the pack.

- The salesperson's hat, to be donned after you find the superstar. Most superstars will have other options than yours, so part of your job is that of a salesperson.

Don't forget to prepare for the second role, and don't incorrectly assume your company is the only, or the best, opportunity in town. And, like any good salesperson, remember to sell the benefits of the job as opposed to its features; you want to show your prospective superstar how working for you will make her life better.

Considering the employee leasing option

More than 2,000 employee-leasing companies — also known as *professional employer organizations* (PEOs) — exist in the United States today, which means that at least one is probably near you. The employee-leasing company's primary customer is the small-business owner — because most large businesses develop a wide variety of human-resource services in-house.

Employee leasing means that the leasing company assumes the paperwork and administrative responsibilities of dealing with employees, allowing you to concentrate on their operational activities. Thus, in effect, you're simply outsourcing your human-resource needs. In this way, you and your employee-leasing company become "co-employers" of the employees.

In return for the services the employee-leasing company provides, it charges its customers an administrative fee (in effect its markup over costs) of anywhere from 2 percent to 8 percent, depending upon the dollar amount of the transaction.

We aren't advocating employee leasing for every small business — whether to lease or not is a gray area. Leasing employees makes sense for a number of reasons:

✔ Employee-leasing companies do what they do best (hire and handle the administration of employees), and you do what you do best (run your business). You can focus on developing your product, selling your product, servicing your customers, and concentrating on profit.

✔ You write one check and the employee-leasing company does all the rest.

✔ Employee-leasing companies can serve as unofficial employment agencies. You hire the best and send back the rest.

✔ By pooling employees, employee-leasing companies can cut costs in such areas as insurance rates.

✔ Employee-leasing companies worry about regulatory compliance. The Fair Labor Standards Act, the Civil Rights Act, the Discrimination in Employment Act, the Occupation and Safety Act, and a half dozen more obscure and troublesome acts are plenty of reason to let someone else keep up with the letter of the law.

At the same time, leasing has the following disadvantages:

✔ When an employee-leasing company goes under, it can take your payroll cash (including tax payments) and prepaid insurance along with it. This leaves you, the employees, or both holding the bag.

✔ If you can provide comparable employee services at the same cost, you are, in effect, cutting your expenses by hiring your own employees. Remember that every dollar saved by not paying a leasing-company fee results in an extra dollar of profit.

If you decide to lease your employees, be extremely careful in selecting the company you use as your "co-employer." Check references thoroughly and remember that everything is negotiable when signing a leasing contract. You may even want to customize the leasing agreement to meet your specific needs. Also, you may want to check with the Employer Services Assurance Corporation in Little Rock, Arkansas (call 501-219-2045 or log on to www.esacorp.org), to verify that you're dealing with an accredited PEO. This self-regulating industry group has accredited PEOs representing workers in 50 states. When in doubt as to where to look for a PEO, this is a helpful resource.

In the final analysis, most small-business owners make the decision to lease employees based on whether they think they can save all or part of that 2 to 8 percent administrative fee by taking care of the hiring process themselves. They also evaluate how much of their time and energy they want to spend dealing with human resource issues. The fact that the employee-leasing industry is growing at a rapid rate indicates that increasing numbers of small-business owners have made the decision that the 2 to 8 percent charged in fees is worth the expense.

Hiring right brings you an endless list of benefits. The biggest is that the better the employee you hire, the less time you have to spend managing him. Instead, you can spend your time on product (or service) development; business-building activities, such as marketing and sales, hiring more employees, and supervising the production floor; or doing the other things you enjoy most.

Mastering the interview process

Yes, the interview process is time consuming and will take you away from other projects that may appear to be more meaningful and are certainly more enjoyable. But remember, the price you'll pay for doing a second-rate job of hiring is that you'll have to do the costly and time-consuming process over again — sooner rather than later.

The process of hiring superstar employees (any employee who isn't either part-time or in line for a minimum-wage position) should proceed along these lines:

1. **Interview #1:** This interview takes place in your office with you asking probing questions and the interviewee doing about 90 percent of the talking. (If he isn't doing that much of the talking, *you're* talking too much.) Immediately following the interview, assuming it went well, begin the reference-checking process while the details are still fresh in your mind.

2. **Interview #2:** Meet on neutral turf this time, maybe for breakfast or lunch. Relax the interviewee, loosen him up, and get a look at his social and personal side. Ask any puzzling questions that may have emerged as a result of the reference checks.

   Be careful here — simply observe the behavior; personal questions may get you into areas that you legally can't enter. You shouldn't ask the applicant's age, race, religion, nationality, or political persuasion. And you shouldn't inquire about his or her marital status, parental status, or wealth. Doing so could land you in court.

3. **Interview #3:** If all has gone well, have the applicant go through the interviewing process with other key employees who have a stake in the hire. Ask for their opinions. Compare. If the applicant isn't going to mesh with your key employees, finding out now is better than finding out later.

4. **Interview #4:** Review, negotiate, and close — if the applicant still passes muster. Then cross your fingers — employees don't come with guarantees, no matter how thorough a job you do. (Your odds will improve with experience, however.)

Ask open-ended questions in the interview. *Open-ended questions* are those that can't be answered adequately with a simple yes or no; the questions are designed primarily to get the interviewee talking.

Following are a few of our favorite open-ended questions that help you discover those superstar job applicants:

- ✔ **What's the number-one trait that differentiates you from other applicants?** Look for something measurable here — specific accomplishments, specific skills, or specific prior jobs. Get inside the general statements such as, "I'm a people person" or "I meet my deadlines" or "I'm a hard worker" by asking specific questions: "What makes you a people person? Give me an example." Watch out for egotistical and egocentric responses; large egos usually get in the way of becoming a team player.

- ✔ **What's your most significant business achievement?** Again, look for specifics. If this is the person's first job, ask for her most significant achievement in whatever else she has done — schooling, homemaking, and so on.

- ✔ **What was your biggest failure and what did you learn from it?** Look for honesty here. Everyone has had failures. Promising applicants have no trouble admitting theirs and are quick to tell you what they learned from them. Insecure applicants have trouble admitting failure and, thus, may have a difficult time learning from it.

- ✔ **What are your weaknesses?** Everyone has weaknesses. The honest and mature applicant readily admits his or hers. Where the applicant can't come up with any, soften the question to, "What kind of work do you dislike?" or "What aspects of this job will you enjoy the most and what will you least enjoy?"

- ✔ **What are your strengths?** Specifics again. Ask for examples. Do the candidate's strengths match the needs of the position?

Hiring for attitude

Thanks to Southwest Airlines, a new hiring paradigm was introduced to the business world: "Hire for attitude, you can always teach the skill."

What Southwest was saying when it introduced the mantra is that skills are taught but attitudes are not. Skill levels change, but attitude styles stay the same. A new employee's positive, team-building attitude can quickly be complemented with the skills needed to perform the duties at hand.

How did Southwest practice what it preached? Southwest trained its interviewers to watch the nuances of the person being interviewed, focusing on body language, eye contact, and a wide variety of reactions that give away important tips indicating character traits, people skills, and, of course, attitude.

Why the big emphasis on employees and their attitudes when everyone knows that the customer is what makes the world go 'round? Because, as Southwest Airlines learned and the rest of the business community has since adapted, an employee's attitude, not an employee's skills, leads to building and maintaining cohesive teams.

✔ **Who's the best boss you've ever worked for and what made him or her so good?** The answer to this question will give you an insight into what it takes to motivate the interviewee. Also, it should indicate whether he should, and could, work for you.

✔ **What do you want to be doing five years from now?** The "right" answer to this question is determined by the position you're hiring for and your own personal goals for the company. For gamebreaker positions in a growing company, for instance, you may look for an answer signifying that the candidate wants increasing responsibility over the next five years.

On the other hand, if you're hiring someone into, say, a truck-driver position from which you don't anticipate promotion possibilities, you may hope that the candidate's response is that he wants to be doing the same thing five years from now that he'd be doing today — driving a truck.

Training: An Investment, Not an Expense

Training is the most-efficient and least-expensive answer to employee improvement. Unfortunately, however, training remains close to the bottom of too many small-business owners' priority lists. Too often, small-business owners view training as an expense and not as an investment.

Think about it. The money you spend on leasing an automobile and buying a mahogany desk represents money gone forever. Meanwhile, the money you invest in training good employees is money that comes back to you in the form of increased productivity.

We've heard small-business owners complain about the cost of training, especially when that training results in the employee moving on to greener pastures — and taking her knowledge with her. Although such occurrences definitely do take place, part of the reason that employees move on is because they don't get the training they need. Besides, as the saying goes, "If you think training employees and watching them leave is expensive, try not training them and watching them stay!"

Training comes in many forms and from various sources. Unlike many large companies, which generate much of their training from in-house sources, small-business training usually comes from the outside. We list the major options here:

✔ **Consultants** have perhaps the most potential as trainers, but they're also the most expensive and risky (see Chapter 10).

✔ **Vendors** can also be an excellent resource for training, and they're less costly than consultants. Some vendors provide free training on their products or services (see Chapter 10).

✔ **Seminars** can be expensive in both dollars and time, and their potential value is difficult to predict. Good seminars are great bargains; bad ones are outlandish scams. Potentially the best seminars, and usually the least expensive, are those put on by your trade association at its annual trade shows (see Chapter 14).

✔ **Schooling** (universities, colleges, night schools, and vocational training), although probably more dependable than seminars, is also difficult to predict. The benefit of the course depends largely on the quality of the instructor.

Consider offering a tuition-reimbursement program, whereby you reimburse employees' expenses for outside studies related to the business. The benefits to the company from such a program include goodwill, the development of a self-improvement culture, and the infusion of new ideas in its employees. Require a B grade (or better) for reimbursement, to be paid after the course is completed.

✔ **Books** are a great value. In fact, a good book is the ultimate training bargain. Read it (or have your employees read it) between projects, put it down when you please, and refer to it always. Keep it forever or pass it on to a friend or another employee. If you extract and implement one good idea, no matter how small, the $20 you've spent is quickly repaid, many times over. Every good idea after the first one is a bonus. (Audio and video courses fall into this same category.)

✔ **The Internet** is becoming an increasingly valuable training tool for both small-business owners and employees. More and more training classes are appearing on the Internet — some are for pay and some are for free. Be sure to investigate the agenda of the course sponsor. Is the organization, in truth, trying to sell you something? Is it interested in improving your business?

Motivating: Pay and Performance Issues

People who study such things tell us that the typical employee is motivated by the following (in this particular order):

✔ Recognition or appreciation

✔ Interesting work

✔ Wages

✔ Awareness of what's going on in the company

✔ Good working conditions

✔ Job security

✔ Feeling that management cares about the employee

Meanwhile, the typical entrepreneur is motivated by one or more of the following (in no particular order):

- ✔ Creativity or growth
- ✔ Money
- ✔ Power
- ✔ Freedom
- ✔ Survival

Although the two lists have some overlap, what motivates you, the employer, is in most cases quite different from what motivates your employees. So, if you expect your employees to perform as you want them to, you must figure out how to motivate them differently than you motivate yourself.

To be a successful employer, you must adjust the way in which you envision the motivational process. The biblical Golden Rule needs its own special twist for employees; you should amend it to state, "Do unto your employees as they would have done unto themselves."

The following sections discuss the tools that play a primary role in the motivational process: compensation, goal-setting, performance expectations, and performance reviews. Look for the differences between you and your employees as you read.

Designing a compensation plan

Compensation (wages) is, according to the previous list, number three on the typical employee's list of key motivators. Although this news may be encouraging to the U.S. economic future, as well as to that of your own business, it becomes irrelevant when salary-review time comes around — Pee Wee Herman suddenly turns into Mike Tyson when his wages are on the line.

The next time the annual salary-setting time comes around in your company, try saying no to a few expected (and deserved) raises among your employees. Or try cutting the salary for a few of your good employees. Number three on the list suddenly becomes number one!

Nothing is more important than compensation on *that* particular day — the day you tell your employee whether he's getting a raise and how much it will be. Compensation is a black-and-white issue — your employees can look at it, compare it, and show it off to their loved ones. Compensation states what that particular employee is worth, in your eyes anyway. Oh yes, and compensation can also be the first foot in the door when competitors come snooping around

TRUE STORY

Finding out what employees really want

Employees are like spouses: Just when you think you have them figured out, they do or say something that leaves you scratching your head. Here's what we mean.

An acquaintance of ours is the local manager of a small wholesale business with 20 employees. One day, the home office sent a consultant to his branch to conduct an employee survey. It seems that the home office wanted to delve deeper into its employees' wants and needs, to find out what they liked and didn't like about the company and to determine ways to improve the workplace environment. "A waste of time and money," our friend groused, as some managers (and owners) are prone to do when consultants come bearing suggestions. "I already know what my employees want: more money, more benefits, more vacation, and longer coffee breaks."

Well, the results from the survey came in and guess what? The employees asked for more of only one thing: training. That's a pleasant commentary on human nature, if you ask us — a commentary that says most people want to discover more about their jobs, improve their skills, and be better off tomorrow than they are today. Most thinking employees (especially your potential "superstars") recognize that ongoing training is what gives them the opportunity to realize their goals.

Our friend went on to increase training, whereupon his company's 15 percent growth in profits doubled to 30 percent. And then, because the company paid its employees monthly bonuses (that's right, monthly!) based on profits, each employee received a healthy bonus.

Training — it's a win-win situation, if ever there was one.

to hire away your best employees. (A healthy salary increase is usually used as the opener for negotiations between an employee and a prospective new employer.)

In the following sections, we dig deeper into the types of compensation you can provide and the best plans you can create for your company and employees.

Reviewing the types of compensation

You can compensate employees in a number of proven ways:

- ✔ **Hourly:** The original tool of the "paying for time" compensation method. It works for Honda and Wal-Mart, and it can work for you, too, especially for your part-time and entry-level employees.

- ✔ **Salaried:** The long-term version of "paying for time." Salaries usually come with annual cost-of-living raises and bonuses, typically ranging anywhere from 3 percent to 25 percent of base salary. (These bonuses should be based on performance and/or achievement of goals.) Salaries, as a rule, represent security to their recipients, and most employees value security.

✔ **Commission:** Always the best compensation method for the hungry, hard-charging, sales types. Security isn't important to these folks; open ends and opportunity are.

✔ **Pay-for-performance:** Also called *gain-sharing* or *success-sharing,* this method is an increasingly popular alternative to the traditional "paying for time" compensation plans. Pay-for-performance usually involves a relatively small base salary — often without annual cost-of-living adjustments — with all other compensation based on either individual or team performance (or a combination of both). Specific pay-for-performance plans are as varied and creative as the small business itself, and they always require an efficient measuring system to back them up.

✔ **Hybrids:** A mix of annual salary, pay-for-performance, annual bonuses, stock-option plans (see Chapter 16), and whatever else you can devise.

Creating compensation plans that work

The subject of compensation is one of those eyes-of-the-beholder kinds of issues. If you view compensation as an expense when you establish a plan for your business, that's exactly what it will turn out to be — an out-of-pocket, painful expense, with all the downsides that term implies. On the other hand, if you view your compensation plan as a motivational tool, you won't be creating an expense account; you'll be developing an instrument to increase your employees' performance.

Think about it. The best employees are those who believe they're valued and being treated fairly. The best *measurable* (key word here!) method of that valuation is their salary. If they believe the money is consistent with the value they deliver to your business, you won't have to motivate them — they'll motivate themselves. Poof! The salary expense account suddenly becomes a salary investment account. A huge difference!

The following list outlines our advice for devising a compensation plan that will work for *your* business:

✔ **Be sure to design your compensation plan before you hire your first employee.** This will assure that you have a defined plan in place and won't set precedents for your first employee that will later have to be reset.

✔ **Make sure that your employees thoroughly understand whatever method you use to compensate them.** Paying for performance may make all kinds of motivational sense, but only if the employee understands the concept behind the performance formula being used and how he or she can impact the results.

✔ **Make sure that you can measure whatever needs measuring before you agree to pay for it.** Measurement is always easier said than done.

- ✔ **Be consistent within employee groups.** For example, with your salespeople, have one compensation method and be consistent within that group.

- ✔ **Remember that benefits are an important part of the compensation package — important to your employees' security and to your bottom line.** Consider them carefully and be sure you (and your employee) know what they're worth (see Chapter 16).

- ✔ **Keep the time between bonus payments as short as possible.** Rewards, financial and otherwise, lose their impact when stretched out too long.

- ✔ **Contact your industry trade association.** It may have information on what similar-sized businesses are paying employees in comparable positions if you're unsure of how much to pay your employees.

- ✔ **Make any period-ending bonus meaningful in size.** We suggest at least 3 percent of the employee's annual salary. We also recommend that you give it to the employee personally.

Solve your employees' problems to solve your own

Joe, the owner of a small machine parts business, tells the following story:

> Fred, my shipping and receiving supervisor, had been unusually quiet — bordering on morose — for the past several weeks. The rest of my employees started doing whatever they could to avoid communicating with him. Fred was also making an unusual number of mistakes, and whenever I corrected him, Fred shrugged his shoulders and made the same mistake again. Finally I called Fred into my office.

> "Fred," I began, "you've worked for me for four years now, and I know the quality work you can do. What you've been doing lately isn't up to your usual standards. This can't continue."

> Fred's shoulders slumped, but he didn't argue. "I know," he whispered, his eyes gazing at the floor. "I'm sorry Joe, but I can't keep my mind on my work."

> "Okay, Fred, 'fess up. What's the trouble?"

> "It's the IRS. I owe them $1,200, and I don't have the money. I don't know what they're going to do if I can't pay them by Friday."

> I briefly excused myself, walked into the adjoining office, and returned with a check for $1,200 made out to Fred.

> "Fred, here's an interest-free loan," I said, handing him the check. "I'll deduct $25 a pay period until the loan has been repaid."

> That was six months ago. Fred went back to being a great employee and enjoying his job again. Best darn investment I ever made.

"Hey, it was a no-brainer," Joe laughed, explaining why he decided so quickly to write Fred the check. "$1,200 is a small price to keep a good employee. Aside from the fact that I owe Fred for his past performance, think how much I would spend hiring and training a new supervisor to replace him."

Your employee compensation plan is one area in which you don't want to be the early adopter. Make sure that the compensation plan you're contemplating has been successfully adopted by other small businesses. Changing compensation plans midstream can be quite detrimental to a team of employees; be sure, by asking others, that the change is going to accomplish your objectives.

The bottom line? You can willingly spend a fortune compensating your employees, but if the dollars don't help motivate the people you pay them to, your compensation plan may be less than effective. The possibility exists, too, that you hired the wrong employee for the position. If that's the case, see the earlier section on hiring for tips on upgrading your hiring skills, as well as the upcoming section on firing.

Get SMART: Goal-setting that works

Everyone can use goals as a motivational tool, and not just when relating to the workplace. You can also use goals in raising kids, pursuing financial security, and improving your golf game. And we're not talking lighthearted New Year's resolutions here — we're talking *goals,* as in commitments to objectives.

Although the purpose of this section is to assist you in working with your employees to set goals that will motivate them, these suggestions can also help you with your own personal goals.

LIFO, FIFO, CRM, TQM — acronyms are everywhere these days. Even goal-setting comes with its own acronym — SMART — and here's how it works:

- ✔ **S = Specific.** Goals must be clear, direct, and definable.

- ✔ **M = Measurable and meaningful.** Goals must be measurable, in the sense that employer and employee can assess whether the goal is achieved. And, of course, goals must be meaningful to both parties.

- ✔ **A = Appropriate.** Goals should be appropriate to the employee's experience, training, potential, and responsibilities.

- ✔ **R = Realistic.** Goals should challenge but be achievable. Eighty percent of the goal should be relatively easy to meet, 20 percent a stretch.

- ✔ **T = Time limit.** Goals should be achievable within a specified time frame.

The two biggest mistakes business owners make when setting goals for themselves, their businesses, or their employees are creating goals that aren't measurable and including a nonspecific time frame for the goals. Consider the following examples:

- ✔ **Non-SMART goal:** "Increase sales and increase profitability by working smarter and harder." Nothing measurable here, and no time frame to measure it in.

✔ **SMART goal:** "Increase sales by 15 percent and increase profitability by 20 percent by the end of this fiscal year." Are these goals measurable? Yes. Is a workable time frame given? Yes. Are they achievable? You make the call.

The following list outlines how you and your employees can set and achieve SMART goals:

✔ **Never set goals without first planning how to reach them.** For instance, wanting to increase sales by 15 percent isn't enough; you must have a game plan for how to do so.

✔ **Don't wait until the end of the goal-setting period to do the measuring.** Check progress informally as the mood strikes and formally at defined time intervals between now and the end of the goal-setting period.

✔ **Allow for the unexpected.** Changing goals midstream is acceptable if the reasons are right. Because the success of a small business is in part due to being able to make changes faster than your larger competitors, the likelihood of change should always be built into your goal-setting procedures.

✔ **Make a public announcement within the business (occasionally outside of the business when the goals reached are extraordinary) as soon as your business or your employees have achieved goals.** Let the celebration begin, let it be spontaneous, and let it be loud.

✔ **Understand that an employee may come up short on his goals occasionally.** What's not okay is for an employee to consistently come up short. In that event, something is wrong with either the employee or the goal-setting process.

Effective goal setting should be a communal, bottoms-up process. The more involved the employee is in establishing her goals, the more committed she'll be to achieving them. Ask her to prepare her goals first, and then review them together, hone them together, and be sure to write them down, giving one copy to the employee and adding a second to her personnel file. Documenting goals makes the goal-setting process official and minimizes potential misunderstandings when the employee's performance-review time comes around.

Writing performance expectations

Many years ago, this section would've been entitled, "Writing job descriptions," but no longer. In these days of empowered and enlightened employees, the term *job description* is a remembrance of the past. Today, the correct term is *performance expectations*.

Although some companies may get by without using performance expectations (or the old-fashioned job descriptions), we think that most small-business owners would agree that employees need some degree of structure in their jobs. Performance expectations provide just that — used correctly, they provide a loose but reliable framework to help the employee focus on the *results* of his activities, not on the activity itself. And that's the key difference between job descriptions and performance expectations: Job descriptions focus on the activity of the position; performance expectations focus on the anticipated results.

An example? A typical job description would state that a salesperson is responsible to sell the company's products at the published prices, to write sales orders correctly, and to make sure that the sales orders are submitted within a specified time. On the other hand, a performance expectation for the same position requires the salesperson to represent her company professionally (it should define the word *professional*), to build ongoing relationships with customers and buyers, and to assist the entire business team in realizing the specified departmental goals.

You write the performance expectation, the employee reviews it, and the two of you either sign off on it or suggest revisions. Writing a performance expectation isn't as difficult as you may think. Here's how the process works:

- ✔ Include a brief explanation at the beginning of the performance expectation of the position's objective (or mission) and how it relates to the business's overall mission.

- ✔ Describe the position's location on the organization chart (which we discuss later in this chapter in "Designing Flexible Organization Charts"). Include the immediate supervisor's title and the positions (if any) of those being supervised.

- ✔ Define the performance evaluation process. Who will perform the evaluation, when will it be done, and on what basis will the employee's performance be appraised?

- ✔ Concentrate on output, not on activity, and be careful not to limit the ways in which the job can be accomplished. Define the responsibilities and allow the employee the freedom to make the job work.

- ✔ Be flexible. The world changes. So do expectations.

Employees are not robots; the biggest mistake you can make is to develop performance expectations that restrict the employee's options. You should write the performance expectation before you advertise for the position, and then after you've hired the new employee, you and she should review the performance expectation together and agree on the expected results. Then, you must avoid most employees' number-one headache: micromanagement. You should give the employee the leeway to achieve those results.

Reviewing employees' performance

How important is the performance review? How important is anything that assigns a value to someone's existence in a place where he likely spends more than 50 percent of his waking hours during the work week? If performance reviews aren't important, breathing isn't either!

The biggest problem with performance reviews is that the typical entrepreneur perceives the review to be an opportunity to criticize the employee's performance rather than to improve it. Sure, criticism of past performance may be involved in the review process, but so is the positive critique of performance — both are necessary elements of the process. Also, keep in mind that the intent of that criticism should be to improve future performance, not to punish or complain about past performance. Everything you do in the performance review (including increases in compensation) is a means to improving performance.

Ensuring a successful review process

Good performance reviews don't just happen. They evolve, as a result of a well-defined review process. Take a look at the basic components of a successful review process:

- ✔ **Setting goals:** Working with the employee, you must establish — and agree upon — applicable SMART goals. These goals should be developed as soon as the employee is comfortably settled in her new job. (See the section on goal-setting earlier in this chapter.)

- ✔ **Writing performance expectations:** You must also have written, meaningful standards by which to measure performance (see the preceding section for more information).

- ✔ **Creating critical-event memos:** Critical events in an employee's day-to-day performance should be written and filed in the employee's personnel file at the time they occur. Extract them at review time to add objective support to your otherwise subjective observations.

These critical-event memos should include occurrences of positive as well as negative behavior. Because reviews are intended to improve performance, you can earn more motivational mileage by pointing out the employee's successes than you can by itemizing his or her failures.

- ✔ **Providing interim feedback:** In between performance reviews, you should informally and regularly give employees feedback. Thus, by the time the next performance review comes around, the employee shouldn't have any surprises. If you're consistent in providing feedback to your employees, you'll give them plenty of time in between reviews to work on improving their behavior.

✔ **Conducting the annual performance and salary review:** At last, the main event — the time when you compare actual performance with expectations and goals; the time when you review critical-event memos, assign new wages, and agree on bonuses and perks; all the while discussing goals and expectations for the future (all of which, lest you forget, are intended to motivate the employee to improve his or her performance in the upcoming period).

✔ **Scheduling the follow-up review:** The follow-up review should be held quarterly or semiannually. Or, if the situation is dire enough, you can review monthly until the employee's performance has improved to your expectations. These follow-up reviews should be informal but well prepared, intended to provide feedback on progress since the annual review.

Holding effective reviews

The employee evaluation process is a natural progression that begins with performance expectations and setting goals and ends with the performance and salary review and necessary follow-up review. The performance review itself is but one piece of the process; without the other pieces, the evaluation is incomplete. Don't expect earth-shattering results from performance reviews if you don't adopt the entire process.

Following are guidelines for providing effective performance reviews:

✔ **Hold the official review once a year.** Conduct the review on the employee's hiring anniversary or sometime around the beginning of your business's fiscal year.

✔ **Schedule the review well in advance, giving both parties plenty of time to prepare.** No phones, no interruptions. Go off-site if you expect the review to be stressful.

✔ **Prepare for the review with the same thoroughness as you would for any important business meeting.** Keep in mind that reviews are benchmarks in the employee's career.

✔ **Begin each review with a generous helping of compliments, citing specific accomplishments and good work.** Get things off to a positive start. Reinforce the intent of the review early — to improve the employee's performance.

✔ **Evaluate the employee based on the past year's performance, not just the past month's.** We're talking careers here, not trends.

✔ **Back up subjective comments with objective facts and stories.** These should come from the critical-event memos you've filed in the employee's personnel file.

✔ **Keep it a performance review, not a character review.** Keep personalities out of it.

✔ **Discuss changes in compensation after your critique of the employee's performance but before soliciting feedback from the employee about the company.** Ask how she feels about the way the company is being run and what things may be better managed.

The order here is important. You won't get frank feedback from most employees until they have the assurance — in the form of a pay change commitment from you — that negative comments won't get in the way of their pay increase. If you discuss pay changes first, the employee may not be in a mood to listen well to the review.

When no pay increase is coming, make sure during the course of the review that the employee knows exactly why an increase will not be forthcoming, and then conclude the review by asking the employee if he understands why. Also, be sure he knows when the next opportunity for pay increases will come and what he must do to get his performance up to the level where he can expect an increase.

Dealing with failure

The best way to judge the immediate results of a performance review is by observing and asking how the employee feels about the review and change in compensation. If the employee is visibly upset and goes away angry, the review is a failure. If he or she goes away appearing to be motivated, the review is a success.

If the review is a failure — if you perceive that the employee doesn't go away motivated — one of two things may have happened:

✔ **You didn't conduct the review correctly.** If this is the case, we recommend you try it again a week or so later — after upgrading your presentation and explaining to the employee that you made some mistakes you'd like to correct. Yes, bosses and owners are human; they make mistakes, too!

✔ **You performed the review correctly, but the employee falls into the category of people who simply can't take criticism, constructive or otherwise.** If this is the case, the employee may not be the right person for the job. Observe the employee's performance over the next few weeks to watch for signs of improvement. If you don't see any, you may need to schedule a formal follow-up review or start considering termination (see the following section).

Parting Company: Firing an Employee

Firing an employee, as much as you'd like to avoid it, has its place in the growth of a successful business (though if you hire right, train right, and motivate right, it won't happen frequently). As long as employees are people, you'll occasionally have the need to fire someone. As a matter of fact, if you *never* fire an employee, you're bound to have a handful of nonperforming employees on your payroll — a financial burden few small businesses can afford and a condition that won't be acceptable to the rest of your employees who *are* performing.

The fear of the dismissal process is usually worse than the event itself. After all, most employees know when they're not performing, and they're usually as unhappy in their jobs as you are in having them there. Yet, they're too afraid or insecure (or motivated by unemployment compensation laws) to make the first move, leaving the difficult work to you.

Having to let an employee go is a fact of business life and in the end can be justified by your obligation to your business's existence and to those employees who *are* performing. After all, you have an obligation to them to build a team that's as good as it can be, and you can't meet that obligation when nonperforming employees are included on your team.

You're not passing judgment on the person being dismissed; you're passing judgment on the performance of the employee in that particular job. His or her talents, which may be many, may simply lie elsewhere — within or outside of your company.

Here's our advice to help you get through the unpleasant task of firing an employee:

- ✔ **Explore all the alternatives before settling on dismissal.** Alternatives include demotion, grace periods, personalized retraining, and consultant contracts (hiring the employee as a consultant to do only specific, one-time jobs) outside of the business. When the alternatives won't work, record the reasons why. The employee may ask.

- ✔ **Do the firing as soon as possible after you make the decision to terminate.** The longer you wait, the more likely it is that word will leak out to the soon-to-be-fired employee.

- ✔ **Know the laws of your state.** For example, do you need to provide documentation? Check with your attorney before firing a longtime employee or a member of a minority group if the reasons for the termination may appear vague to the person being terminated. Attorneys should also be involved when the firing is for an offense (sexual harassment, fighting, and other such incidents) that may wind up as a lawsuit.

- ✔ **Prepare the firing package in the same organized and documented manner you would the hiring package.** Include, where applicable, severance pay, continuance of health insurance, duration of benefits and perks (memberships, subscriptions, and so on), and returning company assets (computers, for example).

✔ **Plan the firing meeting as you would any other important business meeting.** Organize in advance, outline your presentation, and have handouts prepared if necessary. Make the dismissal as businesslike as possible, and, above all, avoid sentimentality and reminiscing. Keep emotions subdued; they only make matters worse.

✔ **Perform the termination first thing in the morning.** Doing so allows the employee to leave the company and have the rest of the day to gather his composure. At a minimum, pay the employee through the end of that day and perhaps even the rest of the week or month to help him stay on his feet financially.

✔ **Don't argue.** State the reasons and the facts surrounding the termination. Show the supporting documents. Arguing will only serve to further incense the person being fired. Let the employee rant and rave if he chooses — he may feel better when he's done, and, as the result of your listening, you may find out something about how to be a better manager for the future.

✔ **Arrange for outplacement services.** Small businesses can learn this lesson from watching their *Fortune* 500 cousins perfect the ritual of downsizing. You can soften the firing by helping the employee get back on his feet again.

Using exit interviews to gain fresh perspective

Inevitably, your company will have employees who quit their jobs for one reason or another. These employees can be a valuable resource for you to tap into before they leave. During an *exit interview,* as the name implies, you interview the departing employee to gain insights into the company that a current employee may be reluctant to provide. Exit interviews can be an excellent tool for seeing your business through the eyes of others, especially because you — the person at the top — have a unique perspective that may be narrow or skewed.

Be sure to include at least the following questions in an exit interview:

✔ What was the main factor in your decision to quit?

✔ What did you like the most about our company?

✔ What did you like least?

✔ How do you rate such issues as working conditions, cooperation and teamwork, on-the-job training, supervision, opportunity for promotion, and communication?

✔ If you could change one thing about this company, what would it be?

Always interview employees who quit of their own volition. Where possible, also give employees you fire an exit interview, remembering that the terminated employee may exaggerate your and your business's shortcomings. Never exit-interview an employee at the same time you're firing him — wait until later, when he returns to pick up a severance paycheck or personal belongings. Not every terminated employee is a candidate for an exit interview, of course; select only those who leave under circumstances that aren't overly combative.

Firing an employee plays a role in the process of building a company, but it will never be an enjoyable part, no matter how much practice you may have at it. When you're feeling especially sorry for yourself because you have to fire an employee, keep in mind that the situation is a heck of a lot tougher on the person on the opposite side of your desk.

Designing Flexible Organization Charts

Some say that *organization charts* — a graphic depiction of your company's chain of command — are out of style. All you have to do, these people tell us, is empower your employees and then step aside while the jobs get done. No layers, no politics, no people caught in the middle — or so the story goes. Today's empowered employees don't require management, they conclude; they simply need a flexible and lenient work environment.

We respectfully disagree. We are firm believers in organization charts and in the chain of command, but only when the person at the top of the chain is worthy of the position. We further believe that someone must manage employees, motivate them, and help them improve their performance. Someone must also promote them, demote them, and, on occasion, fire them. Employees, we believe, have to work for somebody, like it or not.

Organization charts, however — especially in small business — don't have to be carved in stone. You don't want to live or die by the constrictions of your organization chart. It should serve as a structural guideline for making decisions and assigning responsibility — nothing more. So use it administratively, but bend it and mold it to fit the skills of your employees and the everchanging needs of your company. For instance, feel free to assemble creative and temporary secondary charts from time to time to accomplish those complicated projects and one-time jobs.

Here's how to construct your business's organization chart and use it effectively:

- ✓ **Construct the organization chart for the employees, not for the "organization."** For instance, if one person is particularly knowledgeable about the project-du-jour, give her the senior responsibility for that job. (This structure means that your sales manager may be working on a project headed by a computer clerk — if the computer clerk knows more about the project than the sales manager.)

- ✓ **Pay by the quality of the employee's performance and his or her contribution to the team, not the position on the organization chart.** So, although the sales manager and the operations manager may be on the same tier of the chart, they may be compensated quite differently based on the relative importance of sales and operations to the overall success of the company.

✔ **Determine how many employees one person can supervise.** The answer depends on the quality of the team you've assembled. One is plenty if that one is like some people we've seen over the years. On the other hand, eight employees may be a snap to manage if those eight are good ones.

Flatter organization charts (those with fewer tiers) are better, especially when you have the right employees.

Valuing Employee Manuals

In terms of excitement, the employee manual ranks right up there with ordering toner cartridges for your copy machine. Most entrepreneurs don't rank it in the top-ten list of Things We Can Hardly Wait to Do.

However, as soon as employees are on the payroll, employee manuals should be a part of your business's preventive medicine kit. A well-prepared manual can save its user pain later. The employee manual is important because of the varied and important functions it fulfills. Behold what a well-prepared employee manual can do for you:

✔ **The employee manual provides the first opportunity to define your corporate missions and goals to your employees and sets the tone for what's to come.** Imagine the message that a well-prepared employee manual sends to the recently hired employee when his or her questions are succinctly answered in an organized and thorough manner. (And imagine the message you send when those questions *aren't* answered!)

✔ **The employee manual saves time — time spent on resolving problems that established policies would've resolved in the first place.** And, the employee manual saves time spent explaining the basics of the job — such basics as hours of work, vacation and sick days, and termination policies.

✔ **The employee manual saves time, effort, and money spent on lawyers by establishing company policies for all to see.** By stating company policies publicly and in writing, potential problem employees are quickly and succinctly alerted that they must either find a way to work within your policies or seek employment elsewhere.

The best way to assemble your employee manual is to use someone else's as a template — a neighboring small business or a vendor or small business that you've frequented over the years. Worthy employee manuals tend to make the rounds from small business to small business, and with good reason, too. The ones that have survived have already been tried and tested and can serve as a guide for constructing yours.

When compiling your employee manual (whether you prepare it yourself or use someone else's as a template), be sure to do the following:

✔ **Include a statement of your company's mission and goals.** Keep it brief, make it specific, and put it at the beginning of the manual where you know it will be read.

✔ **Include an *employment-at-will statement* (which says that you aren't restricted to firing only for cause) if you reside in a state where it's applicable.** An attorney experienced in small-business management can advise you of the laws of your state.

✔ **Declare early on that the employee manual isn't a contract and that it can, and undoubtedly will, change.**

✔ **Include an equal-opportunity statement.**

✔ **Spell out the benefits you offer, such as health insurance, maternity leave, profit sharing, company-reimbursed education, and so on.** Where applicable, include the details of the insurance plans in attachments.

✔ **Define policies concerning the workday.** Also include policies regarding overtime pay, time off, and breaks, as well as those concerning performance reviews, promotions, and wage increases.

✔ **Develop and define a drug and alcohol policy, including pre-employment screening and post-accident testing (if any).**

✔ **Define standards of conduct such as dress, timeliness, and consideration of others.** Include causes for disciplinary actions and termination, along with severance pay policies.

✔ **Keep the employee manual current as you go, assuring that your employees are kept abreast of the changes.** Post any changes on the bulletin board at the same time you hand out or e-mail revision attachments for your employees' manuals. You may also consider posting a copy online in a portion of your Web site accessible only to employees.

Before you distribute the completed manual to employees, have an attorney experienced in working with small businesses and employee handbooks review and edit it. That review, while potentially costly, could save you a great deal of grief and money down the road.

Turning the Tables: Characterizing Successful Employers

No two small businesses are alike. The reasons behind one small business's success are often greatly different from the reasons behind a second one's success. One succeeds because of its marketing, another because of its product or service quality. One focuses on customers, another on employees. One has an awesome in-house sales force, another utilizes an eye-catching catalog to sell its products.

However, every successful small business (one that includes employees, anyway) has three identifiable characteristics, no matter its niche, product, or service: flexibility, accountability, and follow-up.

Flexibility: The bending of rules

Consider the following examples of small-business stakeholders and issues that should be managed flexibly:

- **Employees:** You say you have a good employee who needs additional time off to resolve a family situation? Nuts to the rules. Give him the time off, and help him solve his problem. You say you have a good employee who needs a flexible work schedule in order to honor her responsibilities at home? So what are you waiting for? Create a flexible work schedule, and help her solve her problem.

- **Loyal, paying customers:** Rules are always meant to be bent when it comes to loyal, paying customers. You say you have a good customer who needs an additional 30 days to pay an especially large invoice? Then 30 more days it is. You say you have a good customer who needs his products individually shrink-wrapped rather than bulk-wrapped? Then shrink-wrapped it is. (Yes, you may have to adjust your price to cover the additional cost.)

- **Organization charts:** As we say earlier, organization charts are to be used for administrative and structural purposes only. If you look at your business as providing solutions rather than merely following rules, you'll be better able to meet the demands of today's ever-changing business life.

Don't get us wrong; we're not saying that everything in your business should be managed flexibly. To the contrary, a small business does need a number of inflexible rules and regulations included among its management tools. For instance, you need inflexible rules and regulations to manage such things as

- **Ethics and principles:** If ethics and principles aren't inflexible and inviolate, they aren't ethics and principles.

- **Expense controls:** The best small businesses are those that are as aware of their expenses as they are of their sales. Expenses need to be controlled inflexibly.

- **Quality:** Quality can't be flexible. The product or service is either fit for your most-demanding customer or it's unfit for any of your customers. There is no middle ground.

But where people enter into the picture, flexibility is the order of the day, because people are different and unique and, well, flexible. One employee's reward may be another employee's punishment. Just as no two people are alike, no two responses to management are the same.

Accountability: So the buck doesn't get passed

Your employees really have two options when you ask them to perform a task: Either they do it or they don't. When they don't perform the designated task, the next question you must ask is, "What was the reason they didn't do it?"

The answers to that question can include the following:

- ✓ **The employee is incapable of performing the task.** Your options are to reassign the task, reassign the employee, or replace the employee.

- ✓ **The employee isn't properly trained.** In which case, you must train the employee.

- ✓ **The task and its priority weren't clearly communicated.** It's your job to communicate the task more clearly.

- ✓ **The employee saw no good reason to accomplish the task and, thus, elected not to do it.** In this case, either your company doesn't include accountability as part of its culture or you made a serious hiring mistake.

Accountability — being responsible for your own actions — is a cultural issue. It begins with you holding those employees working for you accountable, which results in the same behavior trickling down through your organization. In the process of creating an accountable culture, you must provide a system of rewards when employees perform.

In order to determine whether your small business has an accountable culture, answer the following four questions:

- ✓ Do your employees have the motivation to achieve what you want them to achieve?

- ✓ Does achievement make a difference in the success of the team, and do you and your employees know how to recognize that difference?

- ✓ Can the other members of the team tell when an employee has achieved or not achieved?

- ✓ Do your employees know that they have to achieve, or is achievement only one of their options?

In the process of answering these questions, you'll quickly recognize the four elements required to differentiate an accountable culture from a non-accountable one:

- ✔ Employees have to have a reason to achieve.
- ✔ Achievement has to be recognized throughout the company.
- ✔ Employees should receive rewards when they do achieve.
- ✔ Consequences have to be in place when employees don't achieve the goals you've agreed upon.

Put these elements together and you can, within a relatively short period of time, create a culture that promotes accountability. Although the manner in which business owners install these elements may vary, your culture and elements have one thing in common: They begin at the top. With you.

Follow-up: The more you do it, the less you need it

Why should you follow up? After all, you've already gotten whatever-it-was off your desk the first time. Why must you do it all over again? After all, if *you* were an employee, you sure wouldn't have to be followed up.

But (and this is the last time you'll hear this) you aren't an employee, you're an entrepreneur, and if you don't remember the difference, you may not be in business for long. If you don't follow up with your employees, missions and goals won't be missions and goals anymore, they'll be hopes and wishes — and hopes and wishes don't build businesses, they only create dreams.

The good news is that when your employees know that follow-up is coming, the need for it decreases. Translation: When an accountable culture is firmly in place, you won't have to follow up as much anymore.

In the beginning, when your culture is being established, every commitment made, large or small, must be followed up. A simple notation on the calendar followed by a transfer to the to-do list on the appropriate day should complete the process.

And never stop trying to collect that team of superstars we mention earlier in the chapter. After all, superstars don't need to be rigorously followed up (if they do, they're not superstars!), which means that employing them will allow you to spend more time doing the things you want to do (like growing your business; see Chapter 19).

Chapter 16

Providing Employee Benefits

· ·

In This Chapter

▶ Selecting a retirement plan for you and your company

▶ Exploring the option of sharing equity with your employees

▶ Designing and securing a quality health-insurance plan

▶ Making sense of disability, life, and other insurance plans and benefits

· ·

*W*hat do you think is the most valuable benefit an employee can receive from an employer? If you answered health insurance, you have plenty of company. According to the Employee Benefit Research Institute (EBRI), by a 3:1 margin, American workers view their health insurance as their most prized employee benefit in comparison to retirement benefits.

However, if you examine the monetary value of all benefits that employers offer, retirement plan benefits are actually the most financially valuable.

This chapter is all about benefits and which ones may make sense for your company to offer.

Underappreciating Retirement Plans

For sure, other benefits such as life and disability insurance may be important to many employees. These benefits, however, are far less valuable (and far less costly) than retirement plan benefits, and employees often can easily purchase them on their own as long as they don't have a pre-existing medical condition. Although health insurance is usually more costly to replace than disability or life insurance, employees can purchase it, too, as long as they don't have a pre-existing condition.

So, if retirement benefits are so valuable, why do so few workers think so? Several reasons may explain why people value their health benefits more than their retirement benefits:

✔ **The absence of health benefits can be financially catastrophic if a major illness arises.** If you do have a pre-existing health condition, being able to jump into an employer's group plan without a health evaluation can mean the difference between getting health-care coverage and going without.

✔ **Younger employees view retirement as something far in the future and not tangible.** Consider this testimonial from a baby boomer named Alice: "I personally believe in the importance of retirement savings and wish I had started sooner. While some younger employees may not value these benefits, eventually they probably will and will be grateful."

✔ **Employees often don't know what retirement benefits are worth because many companies do a poor job educating and promoting such benefits' values.** For example, with a pension plan, an employer is setting aside money separate from an employee's salary to fund the monthly pension payment to be paid during the employee's retirement years. Unlike with a retirement savings plan, such as a 401(k) — where you can see your current account value — employers generally don't prepare individual pension statements showing the total amount contributed for each employee and the investment returns on that money.

The lesson here: If you aren't getting the bang from your benefit dollars, it's probably because you aren't communicating the value of those benefits properly. After all, most employees don't come armed with the basic knowledge they need to understand the value of the benefits you're offering — they need to be educated.

So, if you're still dreaming about starting your own business, don't view your current employer's benefits package as a ball and chain tying you to your current job. As a small-business owner, you can replace the benefits provided by your former employer on your own, and you can establish a SEP-IRA or Keogh retirement plan to tax-shelter your self-employment earnings. SEPs and Keoghs, which we discuss in this chapter, may allow you to shelter far more money than most corporate retirement plans do.

Getting the most value from your plan

Retirement plans are a terrific way for small-business owners and their employees to tax-shelter a healthy portion of their earnings. If you don't have employees, regularly contributing to one of these plans is usually a no-brainer. With employees, the decision is a bit more complicated, but contributing is still often a great idea because of the value in attracting and retaining good employees.

Self-employed people may contribute to Keoghs or Simplified Employee Pension Individual Retirement Accounts (SEP-IRAs). Small businesses with a number of employees should also consider 401(k) and SIMPLE plans.

With SEP-IRA and Keogh plans, if you have employees, you're required to make contributions on their behalf that are comparable to the company owners' contributions (as a percentage of salary) under these plans. Some employees who are part-time (working fewer than 500 or 1,000 hours per year) and newer (with less than a few years of service) may be excluded. Small-business owners often set up plans for themselves but fail to cover their employees because either they don't know about this requirement or they choose to ignore it. Be forewarned — the IRS and state tax authorities may discover that you've neglected to make contributions for eligible employees, sock you with big penalties, and disqualify your prior contributions. Because self-employed people and small businesses get their taxes audited at a relatively high rate, don't take risks in this area (see Chapter 18 for more).

Also, don't avoid establishing a retirement savings plan for your business just because you have employees and you don't want to make contributions on their behalf. In the long run, you build the contributions that you make for your employees into their total compensation packages, which includes salary and other benefits like health insurance. Making retirement contributions need not increase your personnel costs.

Several valuable retirement plan tax-law changes that took affect in recent years benefit small businesses and their employees, including the following:

- ✔ Eligible small businesses that establish a new retirement plan can gain a tax credit of up to $500 per year for three years. This credit covers up to 50 percent of the costs of the employer's setting up and maintaining the retirement plan.

- ✔ Contribution limits for all types of plans have risen dramatically in recent years. (See the various retirement plan sections that follow for details.)

- ✔ Lower-income employees get a special federal tax credit for retirement plan contributions. In addition to the upfront tax break employees get for retirement plan contributions, as well as the ongoing tax shelter such accounts provide, a new federal tax credit sweetens the reward of retirement-account contributions. The credit applies for single taxpayers with adjusted gross incomes under $25,000 and married couples filing jointly with adjusted gross incomes below $50,000, and can annually be as much as 50 percent of the first $2,000 saved in a retirement account.

SEP-IRAs

Simplified Employee Pension Individual Retirement Account (SEP-IRA) plans, which are geared to owners, require minimal paperwork to set up. They allow you to sock away up to 20 percent of your self-employment income (business revenue minus expenses) up to a maximum of $46,000 (for 2008) per year. Each year, you decide the amount that you want to contribute — the plan has no minimum requirement. Your contributions to a SEP-IRA are deducted from your taxable income, saving you on federal and state taxes. As with other retirement plans, your money compounds without taxation until withdrawal.

Keoghs

Keogh plans require a bit more paperwork to set up and administer than SEP-IRAs. The main difference, and attraction, of Keogh plans now is that they allow you, the small-business owner, to maximize contributions relative to employees in two ways that you can't with SEP-IRAs:

- ✔ **Vesting schedules:** Keogh plans allow vesting schedules, which require employees to remain with the company a specified number of years before they earn the right to their full retirement account balances. *Vesting* refers to the portion of the money in a retirement account that's owned by the employee. After a certain number of years, employees become fully vested and, therefore, own 100 percent of the funds in their retirement accounts. If they leave prior to being fully vested, they lose the unvested balance, which reverts to the remaining plan participants. Thus, you've given employees a good reason to stay rather than leave.

- ✔ **Social Security integration:** Keogh plans allow for *integration,* which allows high-income earners at your company (usually you and the other owners or executives) to receive larger percentage contributions for their accounts than the less-highly compensated employees. The logic behind this idea is that Social Security taxes top out after you earn more than $102,000 (for 2008). Social Security integration allows you to make up for this ceiling.

Defined-benefit plans

Defined-benefit plans are for people who are able and willing to put away more than $46,000 per year currently allowed (as of 2008) with SEP-IRA and Keogh plans. As you can imagine, only a very small percentage of people can afford to do this. Consistently high-income earners older than age 45 or so who want to save more than $46,000 per year in a retirement account should consider these plans. If you're interested in defined-benefit plans, you need to hire an actuary to crunch the numbers to calculate how much you can legally contribute to such a plan.

401(k) plans

Many for-profit companies offer 401(k) plans. The silly name comes from the section of the tax code that establishes and regulates these plans. The 401(k) plan allows you to stash away up to $15,500 per year (for 2008). (An individual plan's contribution limits may be lower, however, if not enough employees save enough in the company's 401(k) plan.) Those 50 and older may put away an additional $5,000 per year.

Your contributions to a 401(k) are generally excluded from your reported income and, thus, are free from federal and, in most cases, state income taxes, but not Social Security and Medicare taxes. An employer may make contributions to an employee's accounts as well. Similar to the employee's contribution, these contributions are tax deferred until retirement.

Because of the costs of establishing and maintaining a 401(k) plan, such plans generally make the most sense for larger (20 or more employees) and consistently profitable small companies. You may want to make employees wait a year following employment before contributing to a 401(k) plan to ensure that you have adequate time to educate them about the virtues of your plan and so that they'll view it as a valued benefit. To encourage participation, you may also consider matching a portion of employees' contributions.

The best investment companies through which to consider establishing a 401(k) plan are the bigger and better mutual fund companies, such as T. Rowe Price (800-492-7670), Vanguard (800-662-2003), and Fidelity (800-343-0860). In some cases, your company may need to work with a separate — usually local — plan administrator, in addition to one of these investment firms. These excellent investment companies can also recommend an administrator to help you with all the tedious aspects of 401(k) plan paperwork and accounting.

403 (b) plans

If you happen to be running a nonprofit organization, you can offer a 403(b) plan to your employees. As with a 401(k), contributions to these plans are federal and state tax deductible. Unlike a 401(k) plan, a 403(b) plan includes virtually no out-of-pocket setup expenses or ongoing accounting fees. The only requirement is that the organization must deduct the appropriate contributions from employees' paychecks and send the money to the investment company handling the 403(b) plan.

Nonprofit employees generally are allowed to contribute up to 20 percent or $15,500 (for 2008) of their salaries, whichever is less. Employees 50 and older can contribute more — up to $20,500 in 2008 — and employees who have 15 or more years of service may be allowed to contribute a few thousand dollars beyond these limits.

The best place to establish a 403(b) plan is through the leading mutual fund companies mentioned in the previous section — Vanguard (800-662-2003), Fidelity (800-343-0860), or T. Rowe Price (800-492-7670) — all of which offer terrific mutual funds and 403(b) plans to invest in.

Don't invest through tax-sheltered annuities, the name for insurance-company investments that satisfy the requirements for 403(b) plans. Such plans have higher fees and worse investment performance than the better mutual fund company 403(b) plans.

SIMPLE plans

If you think that the people in Congress have nothing better to do with their time than to keep tinkering with our tax laws and cooking up even more retirement plan options, you may be right! Yet another retirement plan, the SIMPLE plan, was introduced in the late 1990s. SIMPLE stands for Savings Incentive Match Plans for Employees.

SIMPLE-IRAs have a contribution limit of $10,500 per year (for 2008). Older workers (age 50 and over) can put away even more — $13,000 in 2008. Relative to 401(k) plans, SIMPLE plans offer somewhat easier reporting requirements and fewer administrative hassles.

Employers are required to make small contributions on behalf of employees. The employer can either match, dollar-for-dollar, the employee's first 3 percent contributed or contribute 2 percent of pay for everyone whose wages exceed $5,000.

Interestingly, if the employer chooses the first option, the employer has an incentive not to educate employees about the value of contributing to the plan because the more employees contribute, the more it costs the employer. And, unlike a 401(k) plan, greater employee contributions don't enable higher-paid employees to contribute more.

Persuading employees that retirement plans matter

The single biggest mistake that people at all income levels make with regard to retirement planning is not taking advantage of retirement accounts. In your 20s and 30s (and for some even their 40s and 50s), living for today seems a whole lot more fun than saving for the future.

But, assuming that you don't want to work your entire life, the sooner you start to save, the less painful saving for retirement will be each year, because your contributions have more years to compound. Each decade that you delay approximately doubles the percentage of your earnings that you need to save in order to meet your goals. For example, if saving 10 percent per year in your early 30s would get you to your retirement goal, waiting until your 40s may mean putting away about 20 percent of your pretax (gross) earnings.

The longer you wait, the more of your income you'll need to save for retirement and, therefore, the less you'll have left over to spend during your earning years *and* your retirement years. As a result of not starting soon enough, you may not meet your retirement-savings goal, and your golden years may be more tarnished than golden.

We use the preceding brief economics lesson to emphasize the importance of considering now the benefits that you and your employees can reap by saving and investing in some type of retirement account. These benefits include the following:

> ✓ **Contributions offer immediate tax savings.** Retirement accounts should really be called "tax-reduction accounts." If you're a moderate-income

earner, you probably pay about 35 percent in federal and state income taxes. Thus, with most of the retirement accounts described in this section, for every $1,000 you contribute into them, you save yourself about $350 in taxes in the year that you make the contribution.

✔ **Investment earnings accumulate tax-deferred.** Inside a retirement account, contributions accumulate interest, dividends, and appreciation without being taxed. You get to defer taxes on all the accumulating gains and profits until you withdraw the money, presumably in retirement. Thus, more money is working for you over a longer period of time. Even if your retirement tax rate is the same as your tax rate during your employed years, you still come out ahead by contributing money into retirement accounts. In fact, because you defer paying tax and have more money compounding over more years, you can end up with *more* money in retirement even if your retirement tax rate is higher.

As we mention earlier in the chapter, most people don't value retirement plan benefits for the simple reason that they don't understand them. So, as an employer, to get the most employee appreciation from your retirement plan, do the following:

✔ **Educate your employees about the value of retirement savings plans.** For example, people, on average, need about 75 percent of their preretirement income throughout retirement to maintain their standard of living. Personal finance primers, such as the latest edition of Eric's book *Personal Finance For Dummies* (Wiley), offer helpful background information about why people should be planning ahead financially for the golden years. Get your employees to understand and appreciate your investment in their financial futures.

✔ **Use your plan as an incentive to retain employees.** Many small businesses have trouble with employee turnover. With particular types of Keogh plans, for example, employees must stay a certain number of years to become vested in their contributions. (For more on vesting, see "Keoghs" earlier in this chapter.)

✔ **Select the plan that best meets your business needs.** Consider offering a 401(k) or a SIMPLE plan, which allow employees to contribute money from their paychecks.

Deciding Whether to Share Equity

As we discuss in Chapter 5, one decision that all small-business owners must confront in the early days is whether to go it alone or take on partners. If you decide to have partners, you probably will be sharing ownership with some or all of those partners. And even if you go solo, over time you may benefit from sharing equity with key employees or even all your employees.

Naming beneficiaries on retirement accounts

With any type of retirement account, you're required to name beneficiaries who will receive the assets in your account when you die. You usually name primary beneficiaries, your first choices for receiving the money, and secondary beneficiaries, who receive the money in the event that the primary beneficiaries are also deceased when you pass away.

The designations aren't cast in stone; you can change them whenever and as often as you desire by sending written notice to the investment company or employer holding your retirement account. Note that many plans require spousal consent if you want to name a beneficiary other than your spouse. You can even designate charities as beneficiaries.

If you want to reduce the amount of money required to be distributed from your retirement accounts annually, name beneficiaries who are all at least ten years younger than yourself. The IRS allows you to calculate the required minimum distribution based on the joint life expectancy of you and your oldest-named beneficiary. However, you can't use a difference of greater than ten years for a nonspouse. If you name a nonspouse as the beneficiary and he or she is more than ten years younger, for tax purposes of calculating required withdrawals, the nonspouse is considered to be just ten years younger than you.

The reason to consider sharing equity with key employees or perhaps all your employees is that it aligns their incentives with yours. After all, one of the reasons that you may have started a small business is to benefit from the economic rewards of your work. Sharing equity allows others to benefit along with you. If your employees are simply drawing a paycheck, they have less incentive to work toward boosting the short- and long-run profitability of your business.

Not surprisingly, sharing equity also has downsides. One is that some small-business owners end up giving away too much, too quickly and too easily. And, if you give away too much ownership to employees or outside investors, you may find yourself a *minority shareholder* (owning less than 50 percent of your business) and no longer in control of the destiny of your enterprise or your own job security.

Additionally, minority shareholders have, as a result of their ownership, rights that may not always align with yours. (The extent of their rights depends upon the state in which you live.) This disparity in interest is especially true when a minority shareholder leaves the company either on his own or with help from you.

In Chapter 15, we discuss the importance of hiring the best people that you can into key positions in your company. In order for you to attract and retain star employees for the critical positions in your company, you may need or want to offer some equity to those employees. Be sure to use a lawyer whenever creating an ownership position (no matter how small) within your business, and be sure to consider the downsides of sharing ownership. For more tips on types of equity and how to handle them, keep moving into the following sections.

Stock and stock options

Shares of ownership in a company are known as *stock.* The number of shares of stock in a company is an arbitrary item. Suppose, for example, that your company is *capitalized at* (viewed to be worth) $500,000. You could have 1,000 shares of stock, 10,000 shares of stock, 100,000 shares of stock, or any number of shares of stock your heart desires. If you have 1,000 shares of stock, the price or value per share will be $500, whereas if you have 100,000 shares, the price per share will be $5.

When hiring a key employee, you can simply grant that person a certain number of shares of stock that he or she will receive after staying with you for a certain period of time. Alternatively, you can grant *stock options,* which allow the key employee to buy a specified number of shares of your company's stock at a predetermined price within a defined future period.

Continuing with the previous example, suppose you have 100,000 shares of stock in your company and the price is $5 per share, for a total value of $500,000. You've been interviewing a prospective star marketing manager, and you want to offer her some financial upside if she's able to help you expand your company. After some conversations with her, you decide that you'll offer her stock options to purchase up to 5,000 shares of your company's stock (5 percent of the total company stock) within the next five years at a price per share of $5. Five years from now, if your marketing manager and other key players have done their jobs, your company should be worth a whole lot more than it is now, and your stock should be worth much more than $5 per share, thus enriching the stock-option holder's compensation.

Here are some tips for offering stock and stock options to key employees:

- ✔ **Make sure that the employee is a keeper.** Just as you should want to date a person before marrying, make sure that you've had ample opportunity to observe firsthand an employee's abilities and shortcomings before you offer him equity. Just because someone has an impressive resume and comes across well in a job interview doesn't mean that he'll work well in your company and is worthy of equity from day one.

- ✔ **Make 'em earn it.** In most cases, vesting your key employee(s) in a certain portion of the stock per year makes good sense.

- ✔ **Get expert help.** Issuing stock and granting stock options can get complicated fairly quickly and, once consummated, lasts unless you take your company private. You want to have good tax and legal advisors on your team (see Chapter 10).

Employee Stock Ownership Plans (ESOPs)

The Washington, D.C.–based ESOP Association defines an *ESOP* as "an employee benefit plan which makes the employees of a company owners of stock in a company." ESOPs are most often used when the owner of a privately held small business readies for retirement, has no family successor, and wants to pass on the company to the employees. The federal government encourages small-business owners to consider ESOPs through granting tax breaks. The only big expense is the eventual cost to the company of buying out retiring employees.

ESOPs only work when a company has a sustainable record of being profitable and also has a strong balance sheet. ESOPs aren't for the start-up or for the small business that isn't performing.

You can obtain more information on this up-and-coming, unique, equity-sharing tool by contacting The ESOP Association at 1726 M Street N.W., Suite 501, Washington, D.C. 20036; 202-293-2971; or www.esopassociation.org.

Buy-sell agreements

In the event that you and a minority shareholder have a dispute (and you can bet that eventually you'll have one — especially if you have more than one minority shareholder), a buy-sell agreement is a vital legal document for your business. *Buy-sell agreements* specify the terms under which owners/shareholders must sell their stock upon separation from the company. At the same time, they establish a method to determine the price of the buy-back. Buy-sell agreements also make provisions for the death of a shareholder.

As we say earlier in this book, you need to involve a lawyer several times in the life of a business — and making equity decisions is certainly one of those times. Never create a minority shareholder without one!

Including Insurance and Other Benefits

A variety of insurance and related benefits are tax deductible to corporations for all employees. If the business isn't incorporated, with the exception of health-insurance plans, a business owner can't deduct the cost of the insurance plans discussed in this section for himself, but he can deduct these costs for his employees.

Health insurance

Employees usually value their health-insurance coverage over other traditional employee benefits (see the earlier section on retirement plans for more). Of course, not all your current and prospective employees will value health-insurance coverage the same. For example, some married employees may already be covered through their spouses' plans and may neither need nor want health coverage through your small business. Also, as we mention earlier, younger, unmarried employees, who think they're still indestructible, may place a greater value on flexible work time.

Thanks to tax law changes, 100 percent of your health-insurance premiums are deductible for yourself and your covered family members.

We cover the ins and outs of providing a health-insurance plan for your business in the sections that follow.

When you try to enroll with a particular health-insurance plan, you may have trouble securing coverage if any employees have health problems, also known as *pre-existing conditions.* Try health-insurance plans that don't discriminate — some plans will sometimes take you regardless of your condition. Also, some states provide plans for people with pre-existing conditions who are unable to find coverage elsewhere. Contact your state's insurance department.

Establishing a health-insurance plan

Shopping for a quality health-insurance plan requires patience and time to understand the myriad attributes of plans, as well as to address your needs and those of your employees. Here are some issues to consider when establishing a health-insurance plan:

- ✓ **Commitment of the insurer to its health-insurance business:** Some insurance companies have their fingers in various pots — they may dabble in many lines of insurance including health insurance, for instance. One problem with choosing such insurers for your company's health plan is that the insurer may pull the plug on your coverage. In the worst case, your employees with pre-existing medical conditions may be unable to secure new coverage.

  So, although you receive no guarantees that any particular insurer is going to stay in the health-insurance business for the long haul, we suggest that you choose among the biggest plans in your area. Besides increased likelihood of staying in the business, larger players can negotiate better rates from providers.

- ✓ **Comprehensive, catastrophic coverage:** So-called major medical coverage pays for potentially large expenses such as hospitalization, physician, and ancillary charges (such as lab work). Health-insurance plans specify the maximum total benefits ("lifetime maximum benefits") that they'll pay over the course of the time that you're insured by their plans. With the high cost of health care today, a plan that has no maximum or that has a maximum level of benefits of at least several million dollars is preferable.

✔ **Choice of health-care providers:** Increasing numbers of health-insurance plans contract with specific health-care providers, which restricts your choices but helps to keep costs down. Health maintenance organizations (HMOs) and preferred provider organizations (PPOs) are the main plans that restrict your choices.

The major difference between HMOs and PPOs is that PPOs pay the majority of your expenses if you use a provider outside their approved list. If you do this with an HMO, you typically won't be covered at all.

If you and your employees want to be able to use particular physicians or hospitals, be sure to find out which health-insurance plans they accept as payment. If you can't use their services in the restricted-choice plans, ask yourself if the extra cost of the open-choice plan is worth being able to use preferred services.

✔ **Guaranteed renewability:** Only consider health-insurance plans that will keep renewing your coverage without you and your employees needing to take more physical examinations to prove your continued good health.

Selecting higher deductibles and copayments

As with other insurance policies, the more you're willing to share in the payment of your health-insurance claims, the less you'll have to pay in premiums. To reduce your health-insurance premiums, choose a plan with the highest deductible and copayment that you and your employees can comfortably afford. Most policies have annual deductible options, such as $250, $500, or $1,000, as well as copayment options (typically 20 percent or so).

Note: A 20-percent copayment doesn't mean that you would have to come up with $10,000 for a $50,000 claim. Insurers typically set a maximum out-of-pocket limit on your annual copayments of $1,000 to $2,000 and then cover 100 percent of medical expenses over that cap. With HMO plans, most insurers offer copayment options such as $5, $10, or $20 for a physician's office visit. Again, the higher the per-visit charge you're willing to accept, the lower your health-insurance premiums will be.

Sharing costs with your employees enables you to provide better policies at a fair price for all. We suggest that you, as the employer, pay half the cost of the health-insurance premiums and have your employees pick up the other half (to attract and retain employees, you may want to pay a greater portion if your competitors are doing so).

Utilizing health savings accounts

A terrific way to slash your health-care costs is to establish and utilize *health savings accounts* (HSAs). Like many types of retirement accounts, when you contribute to an HSA, you gain an upfront tax break because the amount contributed reduces your taxable income. Also, the money compounds free of tax over time. If you use the funds to pay health-care costs, withdrawals are also free of tax.

To be eligible to have an HSA, your health plan must have a high deductible, which is defined as at least $1,100 for individuals and $2,200 for families (in 2008). The contribution limits are $2,900 for individuals and $5,800 for families (in 2008).

The list of eligible expenses generally is quite broad — surprisingly so, in fact. You can use HSA money to pay for, among other things,

✔ Out-of-pocket medical costs not covered by insurance

✔ Prescription drugs

✔ Dental care (including braces)

✔ Vision care

✔ Vitamins

✔ Psychologist fees

✔ Smoking cessation programs

IRS Publication 502 details permissible expenses.

In the pleasant event where you don't need to tap the HSA to pay health-care costs, the money can compound without taxation over time in the investments you've selected (mutual funds are a good choice). After age 65, you may withdraw HSA funds to use toward non-health-care costs and simply pay income tax at that time on the withdrawal.

Making sure you shop around

Most health-insurance plans are sold through insurance agents, but some are sold directly by the insurer. If a plan is sold both ways, going through an agent shouldn't cost you any more. Start by getting plan proposals from the larger health insurers in your area. Also, check with professional or other associations that you may belong to. A competent independent insurance agent who specializes in health insurance can help find insurers willing to offer you and your employees coverage.

Also, in most cases, you should shop around at least every two years. Health-insurance costs have risen dramatically in the last decade or more, and the affect on your bottom line is significant. You should zero base your health insurance, just as you do liability insurance and any other of your larger expense categories.

Health-insurance agents have a conflict of interest common to all financial salespeople working on commission: The higher the premium plan they sell you, the bigger the commission they earn. So, an agent may try to steer you into higher-cost plans and not suggest some of the available strategies to reduce the cost of your company's coverage (see the previous sections).

Disability insurance

The purpose of disability insurance is to protect your income and that of your employees from being lost in the event of a disability. Anyone who's dependent upon his or her own income should have disability insurance. If you suffer a total disability, you probably won't be able to earn an income or as much income, but you'll have the same or higher living expenses.

As an employer, you may be required by your state to pay into a state disability or workers' compensation program (the latter only covers injuries and disabilities suffered on the job). Additionally, through the Social Security system, you and your employees have minimal disability benefits. Although coverage through government disability programs often isn't sufficient, it's better than nothing, so you as the employer shouldn't beat yourself up for not offering disability coverage to your employees.

One good reason to offer disability coverage to your employees, however, is that your competitors offer their employees coverage, and/or you can afford to pay for such coverage. As with health insurance, we strongly encourage you to have you and your employees share in the cost of disability coverage — perhaps you could pay 50 percent.

If you're in the market for disability protection for you and your employees, here's how to get the best coverage at a competitive price:

- **Replace about 60 percent of income.** A person generally needs enough disability coverage to provide him or her with sufficient income to live on until other financial resources become available.

  If you pay for a portion of your employees' disability coverage, that portion of the benefits then becomes taxable. You may also get a policy with a so-called "residual benefits" feature, which pays a partial benefit to a person with a disability that prevents him or her from working full time. Lastly, consider getting a cost-of-living adjustment rider, which increases a benefit payment by a set percentage or in accordance with changes in inflation and helps retain the purchasing power of a policy's benefits.

✔ **Get benefits through age 65.** A good disability policy should pay benefits through an age at which the employee becomes financially independent, which for most people occurs around age 65 (the approximate age at which Social Security retirement benefits begin).

If you'd like to offer your employees coverage but find that policies until age 65 are too costly, you can get five-year benefit policies instead.

✔ **Use an adequate definition of disability.** An *adequate definition of disability* in a policy is that the policy pays benefits if you can't perform work for which you are "reasonably trained." *Own-occupation policies,* which pay benefits if you can't perform the duties of your current occupation, are the most expensive because there's a greater chance the insurer will have to pay out benefits.

✔ **Buy policies that are noncancelable and guaranteed renewable.** These features ensure that the disability policy can't be canceled because an employee develops health problems.

✔ **Accept a lengthier waiting period.** The *waiting period,* which can also be thought of as the deductible on the policy, is the time between the onset of your disability and the time you begin collecting benefits. Accepting a longer waiting period — at least three months, and preferably six months — greatly reduces the cost of the disability insurance.

✔ **Shop around.** In addition to soliciting proposals from insurance agents who specialize in disability coverage, check through professional associations to which you already belong or can join.

Life insurance

We recommend that you not waste your precious compensation and benefits dollars on life insurance. Why?

✔ **Few small business employers offer life-insurance coverage.** Why waste your precious benefit dollars on something that your competitors are unlikely to provide?

✔ **Many of your employees won't need it.** This means it isn't a wise benefit to offer. Those who don't have financial dependents don't need life insurance. The vast majority of your single employees, childless employees, and employees with grown children won't have the need for life insurance, either.

Should you decide that you really want to offer the Cadillac of benefits packages, buy term life insurance, not cash-value life insurance. With *term life insurance,* you pay an annual premium for a set amount of life-insurance coverage. During the term of the policy, if you stay alive, your beneficiaries collect no death benefit and you're out the premium, but of course you're

Employee Assistance Programs

Employee Assistance Programs (EAPs) provide support for employees' mental and physical health beyond what a traditional health-insurance plan provides. Specifically, EAPs help employees struggling with

✔ Substance abuse (alcohol and drugs)

✔ Marriage and family problems

✔ Stress

✔ Workplace concerns (including layoffs, reorganizations, and workplace violence concerns)

Although far more common to large employers, EAPs are increasingly found in smaller businesses. A basic EAP involves simply providing printed material, usually in the form of pamphlets, to interested employees. More sophisticated

EAPs provide confidential telephone hot-line services to employees in need and counseling referrals to psychological professionals. Larger businesses sometimes include counselors on staff.

Just about everyone is touched by the problems addressed by EAPs, so such plans do get utilized and are appreciated by employees — so long as confidentiality is ensured and the quality of services is reliable. To find out more about EAPs, consider subscribing to the quarterly magazine *EAP Digest* by calling 800-453-7733 or going online to `www.prponline.net/Work/EAP/eap.htm`. For referrals to EAP professionals, contact the Employee Assistance Professionals Association at 703-387-1000 or visit `www.eapassn.org`. Health-insurance providers can also submit suggestions for EAPs.

eternally grateful you're not deceased! With *cash-value life insurance* (also known as whole life, universal life, or variable life), you pay a much higher premium for a combination of life insurance coverage and a savings type account. For the same amount of coverage, cash-value policies cost a whopping eight times more than comparable term policies.

Dependent care plans

A *dependent care plan* enables you and your employees to put away money from your paychecks on a pretax basis, which you can then use to pay for child-care expenses or to care for an ill or aging parent. Doing so saves you federal, state, and even Social Security taxes. These plans allow you to put away up to $5,000 per year in a reimbursement account to be used to pay for eligible dependent-care expenses ($2,500 for those who are married and filing separately).

Dependent-care spending accounts are a "use it or lose it" benefit. If you or your employees aren't able to spend the money for child-care expenses in the current tax year, at the end of the year the IRS forces you to forfeit all the money you haven't used.

Vacation

We all need downtime, and weekends just don't cut it. A full week or two off can do wonders for you and your employees.

Two weeks of paid vacation is the norm for new hires in the world of small business. For key employees and employees who have been with you for several or more years, three weeks is the norm. Many small businesses offer a graduated vacation schedule that may, for instance, offer four weeks after 10 years and five weeks after 20.

Some employees may value vacation flexibility and more time off, so if your business allows, try to accommodate such wants to keep good employees happy. For example, if an employee would rather have an extra week's vacation each year rather than a 2-percent pay raise, financially you should be indifferent — unless, of course, that employee is difficult or impossible to replace during that extra vacation period.

Flexible hours

A wide variety of options are available when it comes to offering flexible hours. Families with children are especially starved for time, and most employed parents greatly value flexible work hours and the ability to take additional time off, even without pay. Sensitive employers who create a family-friendly work schedule and business environment reap enormous benefits, including happier, more loyal employees.

Here are a few options that are becoming more popular for some small-business owners:

- Four 10-hour days
- The option of allowing employees to vary their working hours depending upon personal requirements (for example, employees with health or child-care issues)
- Working from the home (telecommuting)

Finally, offering flexible hours in advance of, or during, holidays also makes a lot of sense, because, by and large, worker productivity falls off drastically during these times anyway. We know of one business, for instance, that, during the week between Christmas and New Year's, works only four-hour days (from 8:00 a.m. to noon).

Flexible benefit plans

Flexible benefit, or "cafeteria," plans allow employees to pick and choose the benefits on which to spend their benefit dollars. (These plans are also known as Section 125 plans, after the part of the IRS tax laws that sanctions such plans.) Under a flexible benefit plan, your employees can choose to receive a portion of their compensation as pay or to put those dollars toward purchasing benefits of their own choosing from a menu you offer.

The virtue of a flexible plan is that it allows employees to customize their benefits packages to suit their needs and wants. For example, a married employee with young children may prefer to spend his benefit dollars on dependent-care expenses or more vacation days, whereas a single employee may prefer simply to receive more cash compensation.

Another significant advantage of a flexible benefit plan is that the associated tax benefits produce greater value for employees from their compensation dollars. Rather than receiving some of their annual pay as taxable income, employees can elect to purchase benefits with pretax dollars, thus saving on income taxes.

Unless and until you offer a number of insurance benefits to your employees, offering a flexible plan won't be appropriate and worthwhile. However, if you're offering a generous number of benefits and would like to offer your employees maximum flexibility in using their benefits, a flex plan may make sense.

Among the types of benefits that you may want to consider offering to your employees in a flexible plan are the following:

- Health insurance and health-care spending accounts
- Group life insurance
- Disability insurance
- Vacation days
- Employee contributions to a 401(k)
- Dependent-care plans and spending accounts

Don't bother including the following benefits in your flexible benefit plan:

- Dental and vision insurance
- Group legal insurance plans

These insurance programs ultimately cover small-potato items. You should spend your insurance dollars on coverage options that protect you and your employees against potentially financially catastrophic losses, such as those that could be incurred from a long-term disability or major medical problem.

Because flexible benefit plans are time consuming and fairly costly for small businesses to establish and administer, your small business likely won't have one, especially if you have fewer than ten employees. You should hire competent tax and benefit advisors to help you design your flexible benefit plan and to help you comply with the myriad tax issues that you must deal with on an ongoing basis with such plans.

If you're going to go to the trouble and expense of putting a flexible benefit plan in place at your company, also invest the necessary time and cost to explain the specific benefits in the plan and how employees can choose among them. For many employers, small and large, too many employees don't understand the flexible plan, which hampers them from making good use of and appreciating the plan.

Chapter 17

Handling Regulatory and Legal Issues

*O*ne of the least-pleasant aspects of starting and running a small business is comprehending and adhering to the myriad government regulations that affect how and where you do business. Not to mention the plethora of legal issues that can blow up in your face and culminate in a lawsuit. So we can understand what's probably a strong desire on your part to skip this chapter. But please don't; doing so could ensnare you in government fines and legal fees that could prove disastrous, if not fatal, to your business.

And if the thought of these penalties isn't enough, we have what we hope is an incentive for you to familiarize yourself with the issues raised in this chapter: We can save you time and headaches. How? By showing you how to efficiently and correctly complete important legal and regulatory tasks. We rest our case.

Navigating Small-Business Laws

You may think that if you're starting or operating a truly small, small business, you don't need to know much on the legal and regulatory fronts. We wish that were true, but it's not. Consider the following types of issues that most small-business owners must grapple with, both in the early years of their businesses and on an ongoing basis:

✔ **Selecting a name for your business:** You can't choose any name and start using it for your business, because you may select a name that another business is already using and that owner could take legal action against you. Besides, you'll probably be spending a lot of marketing money over the years to distinguish *your* business, and you don't want it being confused with someone else's.

✔ **Complying with government licensing and permit requirements:** Federal, state, and sometimes even local governments regulate and license certain types of businesses, such as restaurants, taxicabs, or beauty shops.

If you're operating a business that requires registration with particular government entities, the passing of certain exams, or the satisfaction of specific licensing requirements (see the later sections of this chapter), you'll be breaking the law and may be put out of business if you don't comply. The possible penalties for running afoul of business laws can be steep, including monetary fines and outright prohibition against practicing your line of work for months or even years. And if that isn't bad enough, your transgressions may become public knowledge, which can hamper your ability to get your business up and running again when you're legally able to do so.

✔ **Protecting your ideas and work:** If you prepare a business plan and distribute it for comment or to raise money (see Chapters 4 and 5), you don't want your ideas stolen, do you? If you invent or brainstorm something new and unique, you don't want someone to copy your creation and profit from it, do you? Well, if you don't properly protect your ideas, work, and other creative developments through trademarks, copyrights, and patents, someone could rip you off and you'll have little, if any, legal recourse. (See the later section "Protecting ideas and plans: Trademarks, patents, nondisclosures, and copyrights.")

✔ **Establishing a retirement plan:** Perhaps you've heard of retirement plans such as profit sharing, money purchase pension plans, SEP-IRAs, and so on. Over the years, these plans can slash tens, and maybe even hundreds, of thousands of dollars off your tax bill. However, if you have employees, they're entitled to certain benefits in retirement plans subject to federal regulations. Your reward for violating retirement-plan rules can be the disallowance of your contributions into the plan, thereby causing you to owe the IRS taxes and penalties — ouch! (We cover retirement plans in Chapter 16.)

✔ **Filing your taxes:** As a business owner and self-employed person, you're responsible for the proper filing of all federal, state, and local taxes for yourself and your business. And when you employ others, you must withhold appropriate taxes from their wages and submit the withheld taxes in a timely fashion to the various tax regulatory authorities. More than a few small businesses have failed because the owners fell behind on taxes and subsequently were buried by past-due payments. (Chapter 18 helps you stay in the good graces of the IRS.)

✔ **Hiring and managing employees:** Employment law is a vast and growing area of the legal profession. When you hire and employ workers, you must be careful about what you say to them and how you manage and behave around them. If you're not careful, you can face big legal bills and possible lawsuit damages, while your and your hard-earned business's reputations are dragged through the mud during legal proceedings. (Refer to Chapter 15 for more on finding and hiring employees.)

✔ **Preparing contracts:** In many ways, contracts make the business world go 'round. When properly prepared, contracts function as legally binding and enforceable agreements that your business makes with suppliers, employees, and others relating to the operation of your business. If you offer a contract to another person or business or seek to change the terms and conditions of an existing contract, you must understand, up front, the legal ramifications. If you don't understand these ramifications, at a minimum you'll have to deal with upset parties on the other end of the contract; in the worst cases, you could end up in court with soaring legal bills and potential lawsuits (see the later section "A business prenup: Contracts with customers and suppliers" for more).

Suffering through Start-Up Regulations

Before you begin working with your first customer, you should invest time and money into getting your legal and regulatory ducks in a row. In the start-up phase of a small business, however, few business owners have the luxury of spending hard-to-spare time or money on these issues. Thus, in this section, we attempt to assist you in saving some of both while helping you protect your business.

Complying through licensing, registrations, and permits

Years ago, when Eric started his financial counseling practice, the first thing he did was investigate what government regulatory organizations he needed to register with. To his surprise, he had to register both with the federal Securities and Exchange Commission (SEC) and his state's Department of Corporations. He was surprised because he figured that a profession as full of deception, conflicts of interest, and outright cases of corruption as the financial planning profession would've had little government oversight. (Then again, government "oversight" of a profession can literally result in oversights!)

To discover the various ways in which different government bodies regulate your line of business, we suggest you check with the following; and after the list, we dig deeper into the realities of compliance and the local, state, and federal regulations you must follow:

✔ **Trade associations for your business or profession:** Zillions of trade associations exist, and the better ones can provide a wealth of information on government regulations and other such subjects. The *Small Business Sourcebook* (Gale; see Chapter 7) can help you locate the associations in your industry or conduct a search via the Internet.

✔ **Peers in your profession:** The simplest way to network with others in your line of work is to attend conferences or conventions for your industry or profession. Again, trade associations should be able to help you locate such events, or you can network in your local area.

A downside of the local-area strategy is that people in the same line of work in your town may view you as competition and be less than forthcoming with assistance.

✔ **The state agency that oversees corporations and/or small businesses:** Check the state government section in your local white pages phone directory for the phone number. Be persistent, because if the person who answers the phone is poorly trained or having a bureaucratic bad day, you may not get the information you need or you may be transferred to the wrong department. Look for any or all of the following state government agencies: economic development department, department of commerce, or the office of small business

✔ **Trade publications:** You may be surprised at how many specialized occupational publications exist. (See Chapter 7 for tips on how to identify and locate them.) You can research past articles on industry regulations in such publications. (You may need to contact the publication for a listing of topics covered in prior issues.)

✔ **The local Chamber of Commerce:** Most communities have a local Chamber of Commerce; an employee there may be able to suggest the applicable government organizations for you to check in with and other people to speak to.

✔ **Small Business Development Centers (SBDCs):** Every state has an SBDC, and most SBDCs have extensive small-business libraries, as well as a wide variety of pamphlets and brochures, compliments of the applicable government organizations.

The realities of compliance

Various government agencies — at the local, regional, state, and federal levels — impose all sorts of licensing, registration, and permit requirements on small-business owners. If you've ever arrived in a new city without a map and tried to get around by yourself in a car, you should understand what it may be like as you try to discover all the agencies and paperwork required for the type of business you want to operate.

If you overlook applying for one important permit or license, the government can slap you with hefty fines, and disgruntled customers can sue you, using your lack of compliance with government regulations as an indicator of slipshod business practices. And, even if you're a good enough detective to ferret out and understand every government regulation with which you must comply, you may tear your hair out when you realize that the order in which you obtain your permits and licenses is critical — and the only correct order is one that isn't readily apparent to most new business owners.

Okay, so life could be a lot worse — you could live in a Communist country where such permits are available only to the highest bidders! Just remember to keep your eyes and ears open. Talk to as many people as you can (see the previous list) and remember that the burden for compliance falls on your shoulders. Don't toss your hands in the air, say that compliance with government regulations is too hard to figure out, and just wing it.

The success or failure of a business often lies in the details — or, more specifically, in the owner's willingness to pay attention to them. Applying with all applicable regulations is an early test!

Local regulations: Taxes, zoning, and health

The town, city, and county in which you operate your business more than likely will impose some requirements on businesses like yours. Even if you operate a home-based business (see Chapter 20), you can't assume that you can do what you want when and where you want to do it because home-based businesses often are more restricted than their office-park counterparts.

Some common local regulations that affect small-business owners include:

- **Taxes:** In most areas, if you're selling products through a retail store, you'll probably have to collect sales tax. Even if you don't operate a retail store, you may have to collect sales tax on products you sell. And some cities tax all revenue from small businesses. Plus you may be surprised to discover that some communities levy an annual property tax on certain business assets such as inventory, equipment, and furniture.

- **Fictitious name:** If the name of your business is different from your own, you need to file what's known as a *fictitious name* or *doing-business-as* (DBA) form. Filing usually is done through the county, and you may have to publish your DBA filing in a local newspaper.

- **Real estate:** All real estate is affected by *zoning*, which restricts the usage of a given property. If you don't like the idea of local government telling you what you can and can't do on your property, consider how you'd feel if your next-door neighbor opened a chicken and pig farm on his property! Whether you're leasing or buying a property, your business will be affected by zoning ordinances.

You need to investigate whether you can operate your business at a given location, as well as plan on dealing with the good folks in City Hall if you want to do any renovations to your place of business. And if those renovations raise any environmental concerns — such as disturbing or removing potentially hazardous substances like asbestos — your local health department may get involved as well (see the following bullet). Zoning and renovation issues often come into play when a home-office business steadily grows and the owner finally decides he needs to add on to his house or garage in order to hire another employee or carry more products in inventory, or when the business generates a level of activity that affects noise levels, traffic, and parking demands.

✓ **Health and safety:** Small-business owners whose enterprises involve food are subject to all sorts of regulations from the local health department. You may need to have your water occasionally tested if you're lucky enough to live in a less-densely populated area that uses well water. And, don't overlook the myriad safety regulations such as local fire codes and elevator inspections.

So, you may be wondering how the heck you find out what local regulations affect your type of business. Here's a short list of the best ways that we know of to help you find out more:

✓ **Call relevant local government agencies.** Let your fingers do the walking through the government pages section of your local phone directory. For tax issues, look under "Tax Collector." For real-estate issues, look under terms like "Planning Department" or "Building Inspection Department." For health-related issues, the heading in the phone book is almost always "Health Department." If you get stuck and can't reach the correct department, most cities and towns have a city clerk or town clerk who can transfer you to the right department.

✓ **Cruise your state's Web site for applicable small-business agencies.** You never know what you'll find here. Many states have an Office of Small Business, which may serve as a one-stop resource for all your needs. If your state doesn't have an Office of Small Business, try the state's Commerce Department or the Economic Development Department.

✓ **Contact your local Chamber of Commerce or Small Business Development Center (SBDC).** Most communities have a Chamber of Commerce; the better ones have helpful information for prospective and current small-business owners. SBDCs, which specialize in instructing start-up businesses, often have the needed regulatory information at their fingertips.

✓ **Speak with other small-business owners in your field.** Those who have been there and done that can tell you about their experiences and what they've discovered. Although you can find out a tremendous amount by speaking with fellow small-business owners, keep in mind that others may or may not have done a thorough job of researching regulatory requirements and may have chosen not to comply with certain regulations.

If you're fortunate enough to live in a community that has a business incubator (see Chapter 14), stop in and inquire about one or more of its lessees. They are, by definition, people who recently went through the same thing you're going through now.

✔ **Tap the collective experience of trade associations.** Most lines of business have active trade associations (see Chapter 14 for information on how to locate a trade association) whose management and members can share war stories and information about regulations. Obviously, association members in your local area will have far more relevant experiences to share.

✔ **Chat with real estate agents and building contractors.** If your business will operate in a commercial or retail space, you can acquire much knowledge by conversing with agents who sell or lease space and/or contractors who develop and renovate space similar to what your business will occupy.

✔ **Work with experienced small-business advisors.** Tax and legal advisors, as well as consultants experienced with businesses like yours, can help point you in the right directions. Although such advisors generally charge a hefty hourly fee, the advice can be well worth the price if you select a good advisor. An advisor may even be willing to offer gratis tips on general regulatory issues in order to cultivate your future business.

State regulations: More taxes, along with licensing, insurance, and the environment

In addition to regulations at the local level, states impose requirements on businesses, and you need to be aware of and comply with these requirements. Fortunately, most states have established agencies to assist business owners with doing business in the state (see the previous section). States do have some vested interest in trying to attract and retain businesses because business tax revenues fill their coffers.

Here are the primary issues that may affect your small business due to state regulations:

✔ **Licenses:** State licensing is primarily intended to reduce the consumer's likelihood of being fleeced or victimized. Although some occupations (such as doctors and lawyers) are universally required to be licensed, each state has a unique list of occupations it regulates. The only way you can know for sure if your occupation requires a license in your state is to ask.

State licensing requirements vary by occupation and by state. In some states, you can get certain licenses after you complete a few forms and pay the state a fee. In most cases, however, you have to take a test or complete some form of certification in order to get a license.

✔ **Taxes:** As we discuss in the local regulations section, some businesses, such as retailers, need to collect sales tax on products sold. And in most states, all businesses must pay income taxes at the state level (see Chapter 18 for more on taxes).

✔ **Insurance:** To you, the small-business owner, having to pay for employee-related insurance will feel like another tax. Common state-required coverages include workers' compensation, which compensates workers for lost wages due to job-related injuries, and unemployment insurance, which pays laid-off employees for a certain period of time or until they secure another job.

✔ **Environment:** If you're a manufacturer and your plant emits unsavory smoke, particles, or odors into the air or water, you can be certain that your state (and possibly other government agencies) will regulate your activities — and for good reason. Left to their own devices, some business owners would happily pollute a state's natural resources because installing control devices would add to the cost of doing business, effectively reducing profits.

Federal regulations: Still more taxes, licenses, and requirements

In addition to local and state regulations, small-business owners must comply with U.S. federal government regulations, which cover taxes and licenses as well as the health, safety, and welfare of your employees.

Not all federal labor laws affect all small businesses, because some issues apply only to employers with a specific number of employees. So, the good news may be that your small business is small enough that you don't have to concern yourself with the following topics. (How to find out? Consult the list at the very beginning of this section.)

Here are the key federal regulations most small business owners need to think about:

✔ **Licenses:** Most businesses that require a license or permit to operate generally obtain the documentation at the state level. Some businesses, however, are permitted and licensed at the federal level. They include alcohol and tobacco manufacturers, drug companies, firearm manufacturers and dealers, investment advisors, meat packing and preparation companies, radio and television stations, and trucking and other transportation companies.

✔ **Taxes:** All incorporated businesses, or their owners if the business isn't incorporated, must file a federal income tax return. Additionally, most small-business owners — especially those who hire employees — will apply for and utilize a federal Employer Identification Number (EIN). See Chapter 18 for the lowdown on small-business tax issues.

✔ **Americans with Disabilities Act (ADA):** In 1991, Congress passed the ADA, which was sweeping legislation to prohibit employers with 15 or more employees from discriminating against prospective and current employees or customers with disabilities. Such discrimination is barred in the hiring, management, and dismissal of any employee.

For example, during the process of interviewing job applicants, you can get yourself into a heap of legal hot water if you exclude from consideration qualified candidates who are in some way disabled.

✔ **Family and Medical Leave Act:** Employers with 50 or more employees (within 75 miles) are required by this 1993 legislation to provide up to 12 weeks of unpaid leave to employees who desire or need the leave for personal health issues due to a serious medical condition that affects the employee's ability to perform the regular duties of his or her job; to spend time with a newborn or adopted child; or to care for a family member who has a serious medical condition.

During the term of an employee's leave, the employer must continue to cover the employee under the company's group health-insurance plan under the same conditions as when the employee was working.

Eligible employees (who have been with the employer for at least one year and who have worked at least 125 hours over the previous year) who take a leave under the Family and Medical Leave Act generally can do so with the understanding that they can return to their same positions with the same pay and benefits. So-called highly paid "key" employees aren't guaranteed the same positions and compensation packages if their returns would lead to significant economic harm to the employers. (A *key employee* is defined by the Department of Labor as a salaried employee ". . . who is among the highest paid 10 percent of employees within 75 miles of the work site.")

Selection of a business entity

In the start-up phase of your business, be sure to consult your attorney or tax advisor about what type of organization or business entity — for example, sole proprietorship, partnership, corporation, or limited liability company (LLC) — makes sense for your enterprise. Although the different corporate entities that you may form for your business can provide some legal protection for you and your personal assets, establishing such entities involves significant time and expense and doesn't completely insulate you and your company from lawsuits.

Given the excitement and stresses inherent in the early days of running a small business, we can understand why you may not care to spend your precious time and money on researching and consulting with legal and tax experts about what type of organization you should establish. As we discuss in Chapter 5, however, because of tax and other issues, you should choose sooner rather than later which entity will best serve your needs.

Focusing on where you can affect change

Small-business problems fall into two general categories:

- Category #1: Problems you (as a small-business owner) can do something about — such as employees, marketing, sales, systems, and controls

- Category #2: Problems someone else can do something about — such as effecting new laws, rules, and regulations or changing old ones

Given those two general categories, your time and energy is best spent on Category #1 problems, leaving those in Category #2 to outside parties who are trained to solve them. Such outside parties may include your local Chamber of Commerce, local or national trade associations, national or state business associations, and so on. In most cases, your best results with these Category #2 problems will come through your support of those organizations that you feel have the best leverage to resolve the problem du jour.

What specifically are Category #2 problems? A poll of small-business owners itemizes the top ten in order of importance:

- Health-care reform

- Tax parity (businesses tend to pay higher tax rates than individuals)

- Availability of capital

- Death (estate) tax elimination

- The Fair Tax (fundamental tax reform)

- Pension reform and simplification

- Support of the SBA Office of Advocacy

- Bankruptcy reform

- Regulatory reform

- Capital for small-business technological development

Protecting ideas and plans: Trademarks, patents, nondisclosures, and copyrights

Your business idea and business plans probably aren't unique. After all, the United States alone is home to over 25 million businesses. Some business owners, however, have taken a different twist on something or have created a truly unique product or service to offer. But even if you don't have a unique or different product or service to offer, you don't want to have your plans and ideas stolen by others. By circulating copies of your business plan (see Chapter 4), you may be giving away much of your hard work and ideas to an individual or another business that can end up being a competitor.

In addition to hiring an attorney to handle the more-complex issues (which we discuss in Chapter 10), you can check out books and other resources explaining small-business law. We strongly encourage you to understand as much as you can *before* sitting down with a lawyer.

General tips for protecting your ideas

Here are some tips for how to protect your business plan and ideas:

- ✔ **Be careful about who sees the plan.** A friend or advisor who happens to know a lot about your type of small business, or small businesses in general, is unlikely to have unfriendly motives in looking at your plan. On the other hand, an industry insider or a potential competitor who peruses your plans may not have your best interests at heart.

- ✔ **Keep proprietary information out of your plan.** Product designs, manufacturing specifications, unique resources, and other information unique to your company shouldn't be included in copies of your business plan that you distribute to others. Share such information with serious investors only if needed to gain their investments, and with a nondisclosure agreement attached.

- ✔ **Place a nondisclosure statement in the front of your business plan.** If your plan does fall into the hands of someone who may be inclined to steal your ideas, a nondisclosure statement (discussed in the next section) should scare them off.

- ✔ **Get legal assistance where necessary.** If your work and ideas are proprietary and protectable, speak with an attorney who specializes in intellectual property, including copyrights, trademarks, and patents. We explain these important legal protections in the upcoming section "Patents, trademarks, and copyrights."

Nondisclosure agreements (NDAs)

A *nondisclosure agreement* (NDA) should always be attached to the beginning of a business plan before you circulate it for review. Its purpose is to warn the reader that the enclosed contents are private property and are not to be spread around without your consent. (***Note:*** You don't need an attorney to craft this agreement.)

It isn't enough, however, to simply include the NDA with the plan; never hand out your plan without first having the recipient sign the NDA.

Following is a sample nondisclosure agreement:

> This confidential Business Plan has been prepared in order to raise financing for Wowza Widgets, Inc. This material is being delivered to a select number of potential investors, each of whom agrees to the following terms and conditions:

> Each recipient of this Business Plan agrees that, by accepting this material, he or she will not copy, reproduce, distribute, or discuss with others any part of this plan without prior written consent of Wowza Widgets, Inc.

> The recipient agrees to keep confidential all information contained herein and not use it for any purpose whatsoever other than to evaluate and determine interest in providing financing described herein.

This material contains proprietary and confidential information regarding Wowza Widgets, Inc., and is based upon information provided to Wowza Widgets, Inc., by sources deemed to be reliable. Although the information contained herein is believed to be accurate, Wowza Widgets, Inc., expressly disclaims all liability for any information, projections, or representations (expressed or implied) contained herein from omissions from this material or for any written or oral communication transmitted to any part in the course of its evaluation for this financing. The recipient acknowledges that this material shall remain the property of Wowza Widgets, Inc., and Wowza Widgets, Inc., reserves the right to request the return of the material at any time and in any respect, to amend or terminate solicitation procedures, to terminate discussions with any and all prospective financing sources, to reject any and all proposals, or to negotiate with any party with respect to the financing of Wowza Widgets, Inc.

The projections contained in the pro-forma Financial Section are based upon numerous assumptions. Although Wowza Widgets, Inc., believes that these assumptions are reasonable, no assurance can be given as to the accuracy of these projections because they are dependent in large part upon unforeseeable factors and events. As a result, the actual results achieved may vary from the projections, and such variation can be material and adverse.

Signature (print): _____

Signature: _____

Patents, trademarks, and copyrights

You may have created a product, service, or technology unique enough that you want to prevent others from copying it. Or maybe you simply want to restrain others from using and profiting from the name of your business or literary, musical, or artistic creations.

Welcome to the wonderful and often confusing world of patent, copyright, and trademark law. You'll be relieved to hear that this isn't a legal book, in part because your two humble authors are, happily (for us at least), not lawyers. And most small-business owners don't need to spend much time or legal expense on these issues.

Here, then, are some brief definitions of some very important terms:

- **Patent:** If you've invented something (such as a new type of toy or computer disk), you may want to explore patenting your invention. The reason: By filing a *patent* with the federal government, you have exclusive rights to manufacture, sell, and use the patented invention. You can, if you so choose, license usage of the patent to others.

- **Trademark:** Companies invest significant time, effort, and money into creating brand names (for example, Coca-Cola and *For Dummies*), marketing strategies, advertising slogans (A Reference for the Rest of Us!), logos (the Dummies Man on this book's cover or the Nike swoosh, for instance), and so on. The point of the *trademark* is to protect your brands and prevent other enterprises from using and profiting from the recognition and reputation you've developed through your business's brand names, marketing/advertising images, and the words associated with your product.

Trademarked items can also include things such as the packaging, shape, character names, color, and smell associated with a product. If you think your business has identifying characteristics you don't want copied by competitors, think about applying for trademark protection. (***Note:*** Patents and trademarks are handled by the U.S. Patent and Trademark Office; copyrights are the domain of the U.S. Copyright Office.)

Most small-business owners don't have to be as concerned with protecting their own trademarks as with infringing on someone else's. For example, when starting your business, make sure that the business name you have in mind isn't currently in use by another small business.

✔ **Copyright:** *Copyright* laws cover such works as musical and sound recordings, literary works, software, graphics, and audiovisuals. The owner of the copyright of a work is solely allowed to sell the work, make copies of it, create derivations from it, and perform and display the work. The creator of the work isn't always the person or part of the organization that holds the copyright, though. For example, writers sometimes do freelance writing for publications that hold the copyright to the work that their writers create for them.

In the less-complex cases, you can copyright your idea, product, or authorship yourself to save money. A two-page form is available from the U.S. Copyright Office (202-707-3000, or www.loc.gov/copyright). Follow the directions and you can register your copyright yourself. You must pay a $45 filing fee for each request, but you can put similar works on one form.

You must realize that there are no copyright cops out there searching for people violating your copyrights. The burden is on you to perform the detective work yourself.

A business prenup: Contracts with customers and suppliers

All small businesses have customers as well as suppliers. In both of these relationships, the small-business owner will find himself or herself engaging in contracts, whether formally written or verbal. Certain expectations are created as well in these relationships due in part to advertising. Here are our tips for dealing with contracts with your customers and suppliers:

✔ **Get it in writing.** Otherwise, you have little or no recourse if someone (such as a supplier) doesn't deliver as promised.

✔ **Don't make promises verbally that you aren't willing to put into writing.** Yes, this may sound like it contradicts our first tip, but especially when it comes to your customers and advertising, what you say can get you into trouble.

✔ **Get a legal perspective.** As we discuss in Chapter 10, there will be various times when you should seek legal assistance for small-business operation issues. When you're drafting contracts is one of those times.

Laboring over Employee Costs and Laws

When your business begins to hire employees, the good news is that your business has probably gotten off the ground sufficiently well enough to afford the cost of hiring employees. The bad news is that, besides the salary you pay your employees, significant "hidden" costs to hiring and retaining employees will arise, such as the following (Chapter 15 covers any remaining employee hiring concerns you may have):

✔ **Taxes:** On top of your employees' salaries, you'll also be responsible for paying Social Security taxes on their earnings, as well as other taxes, such as for unemployment insurance. When hiring, you also must be careful about whether you hire people as employees or independent contractors. Many small-business employers prefer to hire people as independent contractors because it lowers their tax bills, but the IRS has strict rules for who qualifies as an independent contractor. If you classify someone as a contractor who should be considered an employee, you could end up with stiff penalties. (We cover small-business tax issues in detail in Chapter 18.)

✔ **Employee benefits:** Various insurance programs, paid vacation, and retirement plans are provided to attract and retain employees. Most truly small, small businesses can't afford to offer many employee benefits, but you should know your options and what your competition is offering. (We cover employee benefit programs in Chapter 16.)

✔ **Complying with government regulations:** Are you surprised that a host of local, state, and federal government regulations dictate, mandate, and cajole your hiring, management, and dismissal of employees? You shouldn't be if you've read this chapter all the way through!

✔ **Employee lawsuits:** Don't think that just because you're not running a billion-dollar enterprise you can't and won't be sued. Although some employee suits are frivolous, others are caused by employers not exercising proper care when dealing with employees. Check out Chapter 10 for info on working with a small-business-experienced attorney.

Chapter 18

Mastering Small-Business Taxes

· ·

In This Chapter

▶ Managing your business taxes

▶ Maintaining sound financial records

▶ Working within your income bracket

▶ Understanding employee tax issues

▶ Using sensible tax write-offs

▶ Choosing a tax-friendly corporate entity

· ·

*O*ne of the more painful aspects of owning your own business is the far-too-many hours you'll spend on bookkeeping chores related to tax reporting and on completing and filing numerous tax forms. In addition to federal income tax requirements, most states assess income taxes and, as we discuss in Chapter 17, some local governments levy taxes on small businesses, too. This chapter is all about helping you understand small-business taxes.

When you were an employee, you probably took for granted how much simpler your tax life was. As a wage-slave, you had the appropriate taxes withheld by your employer from each of your paychecks, and your employer submitted the money to the required government entities. When it was time to file your annual tax return, your employer provided you with Form W-2, which neatly summarized on a postcard-size document your total pay for the year just passed, as well as the dollar amount of taxes paid at the federal, state, and local levels. Being a wage-slave, from a paperwork standpoint anyway, has benefits!

By contrast, as a small-business owner, you're now the employer, and you have many new tax responsibilities. Throughout the year, you're personally responsible for paying estimated taxes as you earn money, and you must withhold and submit payroll taxes for all your employees. And, then, when the time comes to file your annual tax return, the real fun begins. For all these reasons, many small-business owners seek help from tax professionals to complete their annual income tax returns and to file their payroll tax payments throughout the year. As we discuss in Chapter 10, after your company starts growing, you may choose to hire an in-house bookkeeper. Even then, however, you probably won't be able to go it alone on your income and pay-roll taxes and still be assured of avoiding errors and taking advantage of legal ways to minimize your tax bills.

That last point is important, because whether you hire professional tax help or not, we don't want you to pay more taxes than you're legally required to pay. Although you may have heard tales of small-business owners who cheated on their taxes, surprisingly, we know some small-business owners who pay *more* taxes than they should. Either they haven't taken the time to understand the tax laws or they (or their tax preparers) are being too conservative in prepar-ing their tax returns. Also, some small-business owners (and sometimes their tax preparers) believe that it's better not to claim legal deductions if doing so will trigger an audit. Frankly, we find that approach foolish. As long as you stay within the boundaries of the tax laws, you have no reason to fear an audit, except for the hassle of time and possible out-of-pocket expense for representa-tion if you so choose. So, throughout this chapter, we highlight strategies for reducing your small-business taxes.

One final point before we get into discussing specific tax solutions. There may come a time in your business's growth when cash becomes tight. When this happens, you have a number of options for generating, or saving, cash:

- ✔ Collect your receivables faster.
- ✔ Convert your inventory into cash faster.
- ✔ Pay your vendors slower.
- ✔ Pay your taxes late.

Whoa, not so fast! We were just kidding about the last of the four! Paying your taxes late is *not* an option — not a viable one anyway. Although just about anything else goes when the cash-flow blues arrive, the tardy payment of taxes is a no-no. The government has too many options to collect their due and they nail you with stiff costs for late and missed payments, so be sure to pay the government's share of your taxes on time. Of course, there's nothing wrong with making your tax payments just before the due date, but make sure you've earmarked the cash for those payments.

Getting Smarter about Taxes

Whether you decide to hire tax advisors or deal with taxes completely on your own, your best strategy for reducing your small-business taxes and com-plying with tax laws is to educate yourself. For those who can afford to and who prefer doing so, you can hire outside bookkeeping and tax preparers or advisors. However, we believe it's a mistake to seek such assistance without first investing a small amount of time to better understand the tax laws and how they fit into your small-business and personal financial situations.

In this section, we cover resources that can help you deal with taxes on your own, as well as how to go about hiring tax preparers and advisors.

Reading income tax guides

Free for your asking (call 800-TAX-FORM or visit the Web site www.irs.gov) — actually, you've already paid for them through your tax dollars — are the following helpful booklets from the Internal Revenue Service (IRS):

- ✔ Publication 17, Your Federal Income Tax, is designed for individual tax-return preparation.

- ✔ Publication 334, Tax Guide for Small Business, is for small-business owners to use in their tax-return preparation of Schedule C or C-EZ.

In its publications, the IRS (as you can guess) doesn't go out of its way to suggest ways for you to cut your income tax bill. Not surprisingly, the IRS doesn't exactly have a knack for clearly and concisely stating things in plain English. If it did, we wouldn't all get frustrated and annoyed when it comes time to complete our tax forms.

Fortunately, you don't have to rely solely on IRS booklets to understand taxes and file your tax returns. You can obtain many tax-preparation, -planning, and -advice books that highlight wise and legal tax-reduction moves. We're partial to *Taxes For Dummies* (Wiley), which Eric co-authored. Another good book to check out is J. K. Lasser's *Your Income Tax* (Wiley).

Don't be put off by the girth of these books — the portions relevant to small-business owners aren't lengthy and are well worth your time to read. If you understand the tax system, you can legally reduce your tax bills by tens of thousands of dollars during your working years. Compound these savings over the life of your business and you'll see why we're so adamant on the subject of figuring out how to play the tax-saving game.

Using tax-preparation software

Good tax-preparation software has many benefits, including the following:

- ✔ Explains how to complete your tax return
- ✔ Highlights what could trigger an audit
- ✔ Suggests some tax-reduction strategies
- ✔ Enables you to quickly recalculate all your tax numbers if something changes

Among the major programs, our favorites are TaxCut (www.taxcut.com) and TurboTax (turbotax.intuit.com). If you use bookkeeping software, check to see if the income tax package you're interested in allows you to transfer data easily from your financial program into the tax-preparation program.

Hiring help

Hiring a tax preparer or advisor — particularly when confronted for the first time with completing a tax return as the owner of your own business — can save you time *and* reduce your tax bill. If and when you end up seeking the services of a tax practitioner (as most small-business owners will), do your homework to find a good one. Like any other professional, the quality and competence of tax preparers and advisors vary widely. Hire them with the same care, concern, and due diligence as you would a key employee (see Chapter 15).

What's in a title?

In the income tax field, you'll find practitioners who go by all sorts of names and titles. Here are the common ones you'll encounter along with our take on when each may be appropriate for you to hire:

✔ **Tax preparers:** Tax preparers (such as those who work for large chains such as H&R Block and Jackson Hewitt), as well as scads of sole practitioners and small partnerships, tend to focus on tax preparation and sometimes don't work in the tax field year-round. Although they're among the least costly of tax people, most preparers don't have adequate expertise to handle the typical small-business owner's tax returns and other tax questions.

As is the case with so-called financial planners, no regulations or licensing applies to preparers. A good preparer who has completed an adequate training program makes sense for small-business owners with simple situations and businesses.

✔ **Enrolled agents (EAs):** Enrolled agents tend to focus their practices on income tax return preparation. EAs, whose prices tend to be higher than those of preparers, complete significant training as well as continuing education. Unlike a preparer, if you ever get audited, an EA can represent you before the IRS or state tax authorities.

✔ **Certified public accountants (CPAs):** Similar to enrolled agents, CPAs go through significant training and examination to receive their credentials and then must complete continuing education. CPA fees tend to be a bit higher than EA fees.

✔ **Tax attorneys:** Most tax attorneys don't prepare tax returns; instead, they typically get involved in court cases dealing with tax problems. Attorneys with sufficient small-business experience also can help with your buying or selling of a business.

Note: A tax person with a credential isn't necessarily competent, ethical, or cost-effective. Whatever credential a given tax advisor has should have little impact on your decision about whether to retain his or her services.

When searching for tax help, as with seeking out any other competent professional, take the time to get the names of several leads and interview your prospects. Then check their references carefully. Word-of-mouth referrals are useful places to start. For instance, networking with other small-business owners is the best way to find an experienced and capable professional (lawyers and bankers are other traditional sources for referrals).

What should you be looking for and asking about? We're glad you asked! Here are our suggestions:

- **Small-business focus:** As a small-business owner, you have unique income tax requirements, quite different from those of a retired person or employee who draws an employer's paycheck. As a result, one of the first questions you need to ask a tax person you're interviewing is to describe the makeup of his or her practice in terms of income, assets, and client occupation.

  Don't say that you're a small-business owner because that may bias his or her answers. Another way to verify the tax advisor's experience with businesses like yours is to ask for such references.

- **Tax focus:** The United States income tax system can get complicated. Good tax advisors will tell you that keeping up with it is a full-time job. Thus, you should seek the services of a tax person who focuses full time on tax preparation and advice.

  Be careful — some tax preparers struggling to build their businesses or seeking fat commissions try to sell financial products under the guise of performing financial planning for their clients. You don't want or need a sales pitch for investments and insurance products. Hire professional tax advisors who are selling their time and tax expertise — and nothing else.

- **Solid training and experience:** As we discuss in the sidebar "What's in a title?" tax advisors come with varied credentials. Far more important than a credential is the relevant training and experience the tax advisor brings to the table.

- **Tax advice, not number crunching:** Some tax practitioners only complete tax returns and don't offer advice or much other assistance throughout the year. We suggest that you seek out the services of a tax advisor — someone who has a broader view of the job than simply plugging numbers into your annual tax return and then forgetting about you until the next spring.

  A good tax advisor should help you plan ahead to reduce your taxes and help you file other important tax documents throughout the year. He or she should also make sure that you don't overlook deductions or make costly mistakes that may lead to an audit, penalties, and interest.

If your current tax advisor isn't asking to meet with you every November or December for planning purposes, you're probably using the wrong person. Tax planning for the upcoming year and last-minute tax planning for the current year are as much a part of the tax process as crunching the numbers. The small incremental cost of a tax-planning session can be well worth the investment. If you aren't currently planning, get busy right now.

✔ **Reasonable prices:** As you interview them, ask prospective tax advisors what their hourly billing rates are and what total fees they expect to charge you for specific services (such as completing your annual income tax returns, helping with employee payroll tax issues, preparing financial reports, and so on). You should hold them to their quotes unless you dump more work on them than you originally planned. And make sure their invoices break down their billings into hourly charges.

More-experienced advisors charge a higher hourly rate, but they should be able to complete your work more efficiently than someone less experienced. Ask exactly who will be preparing your return and what the fees are; if it is someone other than the person you're interviewing, ask also who will be reviewing the preparer.

✔ **Insurance:** When interviewing prospective tax advisors, ask if they carry liability, or what's sometimes known as errors and omissions (E & O), insurance. If your tax advisor makes a gaffe, especially a major one, the insurance increases your chances of being compensated for your damages.

✔ **Glowing references:** Ask a tax advisor candidate to provide you with three clients in similar work to yours who have used the advisor's services the past couple of years. As you check references with these clients, ask them such questions as what they like or don't like about working with that tax advisor and how aggressive and proactive the advisor is with regard to tax-reducing tactics.

✔ **An ability to speak your language:** Advisors who use a lot of confusing jargon and don't give straight answers are a waste of your time and money. Sure, taxes can get complicated. But a good advisor should be able to explain your situation in plain English. If he or she can't, you'll be going on blind faith that the advisor is taking the best path for you.

You can be your own best tax advisor. Understanding how the income tax system works and how to make it work best for you can save you tens of thousands of tax dollars, as well as tax advisor fees. Use advisors to increase your knowledge and save you money, not as replacements for your own responsibility. And if you have a static tax situation year after year, or if you take sufficient interest in understanding the income tax system, we don't believe you need to hire a tax person, unless you feel you have something better to do with your time.

Keeping Good Financial Records

As small-business owners who've survived more than a few years running our own shops, we know from experience the value of tracking and documenting business financials. Along with our word, consider the following tax benefits that come from keeping good records and staying on top of your business bookkeeping:

- ✔ **Reduced taxes:** The better the financial records you keep for your business, the better able you'll be to come up with lawful, tax-reducing deductions when the time comes to fill out that dreaded annual tax return. Also, good records enable you to stay on top of your income tax payments for yourself and your business and payroll tax payments for your employees throughout the year — saving you late interest and penalty charges.

- ✔ **Easier and less-costly income tax return preparation:** If you don't keep a proper accounting of your income and expenses during the tax year, you won't be able to complete the necessary tax forms accurately when the time comes to file them for your business. A tax preparer may actually be happy with your slipshod practices, however — the more time he or she needs to spend assembling and organizing your documentation, the fatter the tax-preparation fee you'll need to pay.

- ✔ **Documentation for audits:** Because the IRS uncovers more mistakes and fraud on small-business returns than on ordinary employee returns, small-business owners get audited at a much higher rate than employees who draw a paycheck. The better records you keep, the better able you'll be to effectively substantiate your tax return in the event you do get audited.

- ✔ **Planning for subsequent years:** The better your records from last year, the better the decisions you'll make when planning for the coming year.

In Chapter 10, we discuss how to establish a bookkeeping system for your small business.

Knowing (And Managing) Your Tax Bracket

Over the years that you own and operate your small business, your income will, hopefully, increase; most likely, your income will also fluctuate. Because of the way the IRS and most states tax that income, your changing income from year to year probably will place you in different income tax brackets from year to year.

So, you may be thinking, who cares? Well, you should care! And here's why it matters.

You may be able to legally shift some of your business's income and expenses from one tax year to another, saving yourself some tax dollars in the process — perhaps even thousands of dollars. If you operate your business on a *cash basis* — meaning that you recognize or report income in the tax year in which that income was received and expenses in the tax year that you paid them — you can exert some control over the amount of profit that your business reports in a given tax year.

Sole proprietorships, partnerships, S Corporations, limited liability corporations (LLCs), and personal service corporations, for instance, typically can shift revenue and expenses. On the other hand, C Corporations (and partnerships that have C Corporations as partners) may not use the cash accounting method.

Suppose that, like most business owners, you expect your next year's income to be higher than this year's, and you expect to be in a higher tax bracket next year (see Table 18-1 to approximate your federal income tax bracket). In this case, you can likely reduce your total tax bill for both this year and next by paying more of your expenses in the following year, thus reducing your next year's taxable income, which you expect to be taxed at a higher rate. Although you can't expect your employees to wait until January for their November paychecks, maybe you can delay buying a new photocopying or fax machine or delay paying a December invoice for expenses (as long as no penalties are involved) until the beginning of the next tax year.

Table 18-1	Estimating Your Federal Income Tax Bracket*	
Singles Taxable Income	*Married-Filing-Jointly Taxable Income*	*Federal Tax Rate (Bracket)*
Up to $8,025	Up to $16,050	10%
$8,026 to $32,550	$16,051 to $65,150	15%
$32,551 to $78,850	$65,151 to $131,450	25%
$78,851 to $164,550	$131,451 to $200,300	28%
$164,551 to $357,700	$200,301 to $357,700	33%
Over $357,700	Over $357,700	35%

* For 2008 tax year

Your *marginal tax rate* is the rate of tax that you pay on your last or so-called highest dollars of income. In the example of a single person with taxable income of $40,000, that person's federal marginal tax rate is 25 percent. In other words, she effectively pays 25 percent federal tax on her last dollars of income — those dollars in excess of $32,550.

Staying on Top of Employment Taxes

As we discuss in Chapter 15, hiring and keeping good employees is no small challenge. One of the administrative unpleasantries that comes with hiring employees is needing to withhold proper taxes for various government entities. This section contains our advice for dealing with the sometimes sticky issues of employee taxes.

Be aware of your benefits options

As a small-business owner, you can deduct the cost of various benefits — including retirement savings plans and insurance — which are there for you as well as the employees in your company. As a self-employed person, you may find thinking of yourself as an employee funny, but you are an employee in addition to being the owner. You have to look after your own, as well as your employees', benefit needs.

Please be sure to read Chapter 16, which covers the ins and outs of benefits, including which benefits are tax deductible as an expense related to your business.

Stay current on taxes

When you're self-employed, you're responsible for the accurate and timely filing of all taxes owed on your income. Without an employer and a payroll department to handle the paperwork for withholding taxes on a regular schedule, you need to make estimated tax payments on a quarterly basis.

If you have employees, you also need to withhold payroll taxes on their income from each and every paycheck you cut them. You then must make timely payments to the IRS and to the appropriate state authorities. To discover all the amazing rules and regulations of withholding and submitting taxes from employees' paychecks, ask the IRS and your state agencies for informational brochures (and refer to Chapter 17).

In addition to withholding federal and state income tax, you need to withhold and send in Social Security and any other state- or locally mandated payroll taxes from your employees' paychecks.

If you doubt your ability to keep current on taxes for yourself and your employees, you should hire a tax advisor and/or payroll service (good tax advisors can recommend a payroll service) who will force you to jump through the necessary tax hoops. (Oftentimes such firms offer a bevy of other human-resource related services.) Falling behind in taxes has sunk too many small businesses. The earlier section "Hiring help" shows you the way.

As we note in Chapter 17, all businesses except certain sole proprietors are required to obtain an Employer Identification Number (EIN) from the Internal Revenue Service. The application form, known as an SS-4, is available at your local IRS or Social Security office, by calling 800-TAX-FORM, or by visiting the IRS Web site at www.irs.gov.

Be careful with "independent contractors"

Many small businesses start off hiring people as part-time independent contractors rather than full-time employees. Why? For the simple reason that hiring a contractor is less of a financial commitment:

✔ If you hire an employee, your business must withhold federal (including your share of the employee's Social Security taxes) and state taxes, as well as any other mandated taxes, and then send those tax payments to the appropriate tax authorities.

✔ You don't have to offer an independent contractor benefits, such as health insurance or retirement plan coverage.

Although you as the small-business owner may be attracted to hiring people as contractors rather than employees, the people you hire also may prefer to be classified as independent contractors. Why?

✔ Contractors have a greater ability to write off business expenses on their personal income tax returns.

✔ Being themselves self-employed, contractors can establish and fund retirement savings plans, such as SEP-IRAs or Keoghs (see Chapter 16), which allow for tax sheltering as much as 20 percent of employment income.

 The IRS dislikes independent-contractor arrangements because it believes such workers tend to underreport their income and inflate their business expenses. Not surprisingly, the IRS has rules for determining whether someone you hire should be classified as a contractor or as an employee. The general rule is that unless the person doing the work is clearly another business, you have an employee. Neither the length of employment nor how much you pay matters. Even if you and the other person both agree that you're using an independent contractor, the only thing that matters is whether the business (person) meets both state and federal guidelines.

Here are some of the many guidelines for making the determination:

✔ **Amount of employer's direction:** Employers direct employees in their work. Independent contractors largely figure out for themselves — without much instruction from the employer — how to accomplish the work that they're hired to do. Employees also usually have established hours of work, whereas independent contractors have more freedom in setting the hours that they'll work for a given employer.

✔ **Number of employers:** Independent contractors tend to perform work for many employers at the same time; they may even have their own employees. Employees typically work for just one employer.

✔ **Where the work is performed:** Employees typically do their work at the employer's place of business; independent contractors usually do their work elsewhere.

IRS Publication 15, *Circular E, Employer's Tax Guide,* spells out all the parameters to consider in classifying someone who works with your firm as an employee or independent contractor. If that still confuses you — and you're not alone if it does — seek out the help of a tax advisor experienced in working with small-business owners (see the earlier section "Hiring help"). You can also allow the IRS to make the determination by completing Form SS-8, Determination of Worker Status for Purposes of Federal Employment Taxes and Income Tax Withholding, and mailing it to the IRS.

If your business legitimately hires independent contractors to perform work, the contractors are responsible for paying their own taxes. However, this doesn't absolve you, as the small-business owner, from reporting on independent contractors that your firm works with. In fact, you're required to file Form 1099 with the IRS (and some state tax agencies), which details the amount of money paid to companies (that are not corporations) that receive $600 or more from your business for services (not the product provided).

Hire your kids!

If your kids can perform a useful job in your business, consider hiring them. Here's why:

✔ You'll be showing them firsthand the value of their efforts.

✔ This could be an important bonding opportunity for you and your kids. (Just be sure they wash their greasy popcorn hands before coming to work!)

✔ If you're a sole proprietor, you could save your family taxes. Your kids surely are in a lower income tax bracket than you (wouldn't it be nice if they weren't!), so by paying them some of your income, you're effectively lowering your income tax bill. Also, if your kids are under the age of 18, they won't have to pay the same Social Security on their earnings as you must.

To make the most of hiring your kids, follow these guidelines to keep the IRS off your back and you and your kids happy:

- ✔ Make it real work.
- ✔ Pay fair market wages.
- ✔ Highlight the value of working for work's sake and for the accomplishment of broader goals, such as saving for college, a home, or for major purchases.

Don't make the work part of their household chores, and don't treat your child differently than you treat your other employees. Keep your business relationship businesslike.

Spending Your Money Tax-Wisely

As a small-business owner, you'll have many opportunities for how and where to spend your start-up funding and the cash you generate from your business's operations. In this section, we explain how part of your spending decisions should hinge on tax factors.

Take equipment write-offs sensibly

When you buy equipment — such as computers, office furniture, bookshelves, and so on — each item can be *depreciated,* meaning that each year you can claim a tax deduction for a portion of the equipment's original purchase price. Alternatively, through a so-called Section 179 deduction, you can deduct the entire amount you spent on the equipment as long as the deduction doesn't contribute to showing a tax loss. You must also be within IRS limits for the amount of equipment purchases expensed for your business — for tax year 2008, the limit is $128,000.

Although you may want to expense the full amount of an equipment purchase in the tax year that you made the purchase, doing so isn't always the best option. Looking ahead, if you expect your business profits to increase and push you into a higher tax bracket, you may be able to reduce your taxes by depreciating (over a period of time) rather than deducting (immediately) — pushing more tax write-offs into future years when you expect to be in a higher tax bracket. (See the section "Knowing [And Managing] Your Tax Bracket" earlier in this chapter for more.)

Don't waste extra money on a business car

If you use your car for business, you can claim a deduction. Some small-business owners mistakenly buy a costly car for business use. The reasoning is that a splashy car will impress clients and customers and, because auto expenses for businesses are tax deductible, the IRS is helping to foot the bill.

We think you should buy a car within your means — just as you should buy any other piece of business equipment within your means. Money not spent on an expensive business car can be much better spent on marketing, customer service, a new computer system, and so on.

You should also know that the IRS limits the depreciation write-off you can take for a car, thus negating some of the potential tax write-offs on more expensive cars. Without boring you with the details, suffice it to say that, for tax purposes, you shouldn't spend more than about $25,000 on a car for business use.

Minimize fun and travel expenditures

With meal and entertainment expenditures, only 50 percent of your business expenses are deductible. The IRS doesn't allow deductions for club dues such as health, business, airport, social clubs, or entertainment facilities (like executive boxes at sports stadiums, apartments, and so on).

The IRS has clamped down on writing off travel, meal, and entertainment expenses because of abuse by business owners and employees who try to write off nonbusiness expenses.

Grasping the Tax Implications of Your Entity Selection

Corporations, as we note in Chapter 5, are taxed as entities separate from their individual owners. This situation can be both good and bad. Suppose that your business is doing really well and making loads of money. If your business isn't incorporated as a C Corporation, all the profits from your business are taxed on your personal tax return in the year that you earned those profits.

If you intend to use these profits to reinvest in your business and expand, incorporating can potentially save you some tax dollars. If your business is incorporated (as a regular or so-called C Corporation), the first $75,000 of profits in the business should be taxed at a lower rate in the corporation than on your personal tax return (see Table 18-2 for an illustration). One exception to this rule is personal-service corporations, such as accounting, legal, and medical firms (which pay a flat tax rate of 35 percent on their taxable income).

Table 18-2	Corporate Tax Rates for C Corporations
Income	*Tax Rate*
$0–$50,000	15%
$50,001–$75,000	25%
$75,001–$100,000	34%
$100,001–$335,000	39%
$335,001–$10,000,000	34%

Another possible tax advantage for a corporation is that corporations can pay — on a tax-deductible basis — for employee benefits such as health insurance, disability, and up to $50,000 of term life insurance (see Chapter 16 for the details). Sole proprietorships and other unincorporated businesses can only take tax deductions for these benefit-related expenses for employees. Benefit expenses for owners who work in the business aren't deductible.

However, you should resist the temptation to incorporate just so you can have your money left in the corporation, which may be taxed at a lower rate than you would pay on your personal income (refer to Table 18-1 for the personal income tax rates). Don't be motivated by this seemingly short-term gain. If you want to pay yourself the profits in the future, you could end up paying *more* taxes. Why? Because you pay taxes first at the corporate tax rate in the year your company earns the money. Then you pay taxes again on the profits (this time on your personal income tax return) when you pay yourself from the corporate till in the form of a dividend.

Another tax reason not to incorporate — especially in the early days of a business — is that you can't immediately claim the losses for an incorporated business on your personal tax return. You have to wait until you can offset your losses against profits. Because most businesses produce little revenue in their early years and have all sorts of start-up expenditures, losses are common.

With all entities except C Corporations, the business profit or loss passes through to the owner's personal tax returns. So if the business shows a loss in some years, the owner may claim those losses in the current year of the loss on the tax returns. If you plan to take all the profits out of the company, an S Corporation may make sense for you.

The only significant advantage for most businesses to incorporate is that the corporate "shield" protects owners from some liabilities, such as suits against the company — if the corporation is properly organized. Because incorporation has legal and tax consequences, we recommend that you consult a tax preparer and an attorney before making a decision. See Chapter 5 for a full discussion of the pros and cons of incorporation.

Chapter 19

Cultivating a Growing Business

In This Chapter

▶ Understanding the evolution of a growing business

▶ Addressing human resources issues

▶ Managing time in a growing business

▶ Pairing a management system with your growing business

▶ Finding solutions for business problems

▶ Making the transition from entrepreneur to manager (or moving on)

*G*iven the choice, most small-business owners would prefer that their companies grow rather than not grow, stagnate, or even fail. After all, growth *is* the American way — not to mention that it's also one of the typical entrepreneur's primary motivators.

This chapter is for you if your business is presently on a growth track or (hopefully) soon will be. We provide you with insights into what awaits you on your journey, along with tips on how to survive the trip and prosper as you go. We warn you, however, that growth — especially that of the consistent and relentless variety — can feel like a climb up an uncharted mountain. And the climb becomes even steeper if you set out on the journey unprepared to make the change that has eluded so many small-business owners before you: the transition from entrepreneur to manager.

The changes to your growth-fueled business will be apparent everywhere. Five years from now, your customers will be different, their demands and needs will be different, and many of the products and services you offer them will be different, too. You'll also have a number of brand-spanking-new, superstar employees, and employee-related matters will take up more and more of your time. (Sadly, some of your earlier hires will have departed or won't have the necessary skills to keep up with your growth.)

Finally, you — Mr. or Ms. Grand Poobah yourself — will be constantly in the midst of change, engrossed in the not-always-enjoyable-but-always-necessary process of making the transition from entrepreneur to manager. Along the way, you'll adopt skills such as delegation, focus, and holding people accountable — skills that every successful manager must eventually acquire in order to effectively lead a growing team of employees. Your financial, communication, and leadership skills also will be tested and, we hope, improved. In other words, you won't be the same Grand Poobah as you are today!

The only characteristics of your business that won't change (hopefully) as your company grows are its mission, ethics, and principles. However, if your top management (which is probably just you at this point) changes during the business's growth years, as happens in so many growing entrepreneurial companies, even your company's mission, ethics, and principles may be subject to change. Growth holds nothing sacred!

Recognizing Growth Stages

Small business success doesn't just happen. Some fairly predictable but not-very-orderly stages characterize its evolution. Most entrepreneurs caught up in the day-to-day goings on in a business don't recognize these stages until they've passed, though. Time to open your eyes. The following sections describe the three stages of business evolution.

The start-up years

The *start-up years* are the years when survival motivates your thoughts and actions. Everything that happens within the business is dominated by you; words such as *delegation, team,* and *consensus* generally are not yet part of the business's vocabulary. These are the hands-on years. For some owners, they're the most enjoyable years of the business; for all owners, they're an integral part of the learning process.

The work during this time is hard — often the physically and emotionally draining kind of hard. The hours are long and sometimes tedious, but by the end of the day, you can see, touch, and feel the progress you've made. The gratification is instantaneous.

The duration of this first stage can vary greatly. Some businesses may fly through the start-up stage in less than a year, but most spend anywhere from one to three years growing out of the stage. Others — oftentimes those in the more competitive niches — spend as many as five or more years in the start-up stage.

You'll know you've graduated from the start-up stage when profitability and orderliness become a dependable part of your business. The hectic days of worrying about survival are replaced by the logical, orderly days of planning for success.

The growth years

The *growth years* are the years when your business achieves some sense of order, stability, and profitability. Your evolving business has survived the mistakes, confusion, and chaos of the start-up years, and now optimism, camaraderie, and cooperation should play an important role in the organization. Key employees surface, efficient administrative systems and controls become part of the business's daily operating procedures, and the need to depend on you for everything disappears.

The business of doing business remains fun for most small-business owners in this stage, because increasing sales translate into increasing profits — every small-business owner's dream. The balance sheet puts some flesh on its scraggly bones as you generate cash as a result of profitability. You learn to delegate many of those unpleasant tasks that you performed in the past. And survival is no longer your primary motivator. At last, the daily choices that you make can be dictated by lifestyle goals instead of by survival.

We have further good news: This stage can last a long time if the growth is gradual and remains under control, and if you manage the business and its expanding population of employees properly. (For information on out-of-control growth, see the upcoming sidebar.) More than likely, however, this stage will last anywhere from a few years to six or seven years or so before the next stage raises its ugly head.

The transition period

The third stage, the *transition period,* can also be called the *restructuring stage* or the *diversification stage.* This is the stage when something basic to the success of the growth years has changed or gone wrong. As a result, in order for the business to survive, a strategic change in direction, or transition, is required. (See the final section of this chapter for more on this topic.)

Many factors can bring about the transition period, including the following:

- ✔ **Relentless growth:** This is because relentless sales growth requires relentless improvement in the business's employees, systems, procedures, and infrastructure — and many businesses simply can't keep up with such pressures.

- ✔ **Shrinkage of sales and the disappearance of profits, or even prolonged periods of stagnation:** This is the opposite of growth. The causes for this shrinkage or stagnation can come from anywhere and everywhere, and they often include such uncontrollable factors as new competitors, a changing economy, new technology, and changes in consumer demand.

The solution to transition-period problems involves the business and you making a strategic change — a transition — in the fundamentals of the company. This transition often involves a change in top management. It isn't unusual for a rapidly growing company to outgrow its founding entrepreneur (that's you!). Additionally, the transition may involve the introduction of new products or services, the establishment of new distribution systems, the adoption of new technology, or the paring of underperforming parts of the business.

The good news to a displaced founding entrepreneur? If yours was a profitable company and you can sell it on the way out, you can then afford to go back to what you do well and what you enjoy. You can go back to entrepreneuring and start all over again. Or, if you're financially able, you can move on to other pursuits.

Handling Human Resources Issues

As we discuss in Chapter 15, the day that you hire your first employee is the same day that the bottomless pit of human resources (HR) issues appears on your path. After all, that newly hired employee has needs, privileges, and rights — the last of which, lest you forget, is protected by a host of government agencies. In the following sections, we raise some important HR concerns and suggest how to handle them.

Cutting the red tape of human resources concerns

Consider, if you will, a partial list of human resources issues, the mere mention of which make a government inspector's mouth water:

- Sexual harassment
- Discrimination
- Wrongful discharge
- Hiring violations
- Workplace safety violations
- Working conditions violations
- Wage and hour violations

Unfortunately, much of the concern for the employee's welfare is well founded and necessary, because some greedy and uncaring business owners over the years have created the need for such government scrutiny. This means that

---

Is your business growth healthy growth?

Growth is good, as long as it's healthy growth. Here are two ways to figure whether your business's growth is trending toward healthy or unhealthy:

✔ Using your profit and loss statement (see Chapter 13), compute the percentage growth of your sales. Then compute the percentage growth of your earnings. If your sales are growing faster than your earnings, this is an early sign of unhealthy growth. (The bigger the spread, the more unhealthy the trend.)

✔ Using your balance sheet (see Chapter 13), compute the combined percentage growth of your key noncash asset categories: accounts receivable, inventory, and equipment. If the combined percentage growth of these three categories exceeds the percentage growth of your sales (see the preceding paragraph), this is another early sign of unhealthy growth. (Again, the bigger the spread, the more unhealthy the trend.)

For your business's long-term growth to be trending in a healthy direction, two things should be taking place:

✔ Your percentage growth in earnings should keep up with, or exceed, your percentage growth in sales.

✔ The combined percentage increase in the key asset categories (accounts receivable, inventory, and equipment) should be less than your percentage increase in sales.

The financially astute small-business owner is no different than the financially astute homeowner. The homeowner must figure out how to keep his expenditures in line with his income. The small-business owner has similar goals: She must figure out how to keep her income in line with her sales (which amounts, in large part, to controlling her expenses), all while controlling the purchase of those key assets (inventory, receivables, and equipment) — the increase in which must be paid for by cash generated through future earnings.

Managing a small business is like creating a vaudeville juggling act — the successful small-business owner must figure out how to keep a number of balls in the air at the same time. This exercise is simply one way of measuring your juggling talent.

---

law-abiding and people-caring small-business owners like you must pay the price in the form of red tape and regulations. And the more your company grows, the larger that price becomes. (We deal with legal and regulatory issues in Chapter 17.)

Thriving in the three stages of human resources development

How do you deal with such a wide spectrum of human resources issues? The answer depends on which of the three stages of human resources development your company happens to be in.

Stage 1: Dealing with human resources issues yourself

Stage 1 is the start-up stage when your business has, for example, fewer than ten employees, and you have no one on the payroll to whom you can delegate the wide variety of human resources issues. In this stage, you must interrupt the activities that you probably prefer performing (sales, product development, and customer service) and deal with those that you don't (working conditions, drug and alcohol policies, and employee conduct).

Stage 1 is the hands-on stage when you're up to your neck in the day-to-day details of running a business (see the earlier section "The start-up years"). The good news is that the human resources lessons you learn at this stage of your business will remain with you forever. The bad news is that dealing with some human resources issues may consume a large part of your time.

If you're struggling through Stage 1 right now, turn to Chapter 15 for helpful advice. Also, when dealing with those sticky issues that have the potential to become even stickier — harassment, wrongful termination, employee theft, and the like — consult a professional (a human resources consultant or lawyer) before you act (see Chapter 10).

Stage 2: Delegating human resources responsibilities to others

As the number of employees in your company grows, you should look for the opportunity to offload some human resources details onto someone else in the business — most likely a full-time bookkeeper or the person who manages your office — or a professional employer organization. Whatever option you choose, the basic human resources functions will remain as a part of your day-to-day business procedures until your business enters Stage 3.

Stage 3: Hiring a human resources director

You may think you're in heaven when your business grows to the point where you finally can afford the small-business owner's greatest luxury: your very own human resources director. (Our experience is that this will happen when you have somewhere in the neighborhood of 50 to 100 employees.) We know that it's hard to believe that people actually make a 9-to-5 living dealing with and actually enjoying the seemingly endless details involved in HR. Imagine, someday you could have one on your payroll!

Strangely, people capable of becoming human resources directors are like consultants: There seems to be one on every street corner. Run an ad for a "Human Resources Director" in the newspaper or on one of the many online resources (national organizations such as Monster or Craigslist or regional/local sites) and measure your responses in the dozens. You can expect a number of quality applicants. (See Chapter 15 for tips on how to hire the best one.)

Addressing Time-Management Issues

The faster a company grows and the bigger it becomes, the more important time-management issues become. The increased size of an organization requires increased communications between its members — which in turn increases the demands on your time and that of your employees.

Time, and the efficient use of it, is one of those cultural issues that starts at the small-business owner's desk. You, by way of your actions, determine how your business uses its time. If you ensure that meetings start on time, that the workday begins at 8 o'clock sharp, and that prolonged gatherings around the copy machine are not acceptable behavior, your company will have a culture of efficient time management. On the other hand, if you don't pay attention to such issues, human nature will take its natural course, which doesn't bode well for your business's efficient management of time.

Here are a number of ways that a small business team member's time can be wasted:

- ✔ By missed deadlines and appointments

- ✔ By meetings that should last only ten minutes lasting an hour

- ✔ By people who arrive late to meetings

- ✔ By meetings that shouldn't be held in the first place

- ✔ By the telephone, in so many ways: long voicemail messages, phone calls not returned, ringing phones not picked up, and unnecessary calls

- ✔ By unnecessary or long-winded e-mails

- ✔ By employees conducting personal matters on the job (making calls to friends, surfing the Internet looking for their next vacation, and so on)

- ✔ By people taking 15 minutes to say what could be said in 5

- ✔ By waiting — in waiting rooms, outside offices, or for someone to get off the phone or fax machine or away from the copier

- ✔ By equipment that malfunctions, by systems that don't work, and by supplies that run out of whatever is necessary at that instant

Imagine what your company would be like if effective time management were practiced by everyone. How much additional work would each employee get done? How much time would he or she save? Five hours a week? Ten? What could every employee do with another five hours a week — 250 hours a year from any given employee? And what could your company do with those 250 hours a year, multiplied by your number of employees?

You, and you alone, can insist on employee attitudes that value rather than abuse time, and respect the fact that, because they're paid to do the work of your business, they should focus on that end while at work.

For example, you can insist on a culture within your business that

- ✔ Requires people to be on time for the start of the day, for meetings, for conferences, for whatever.
- ✔ Never holds a meeting when it isn't necessary.
- ✔ Requires every employee to use some kind of time-management system, whether it be a simple to-do list, an intricate store-bought system, or the latest handheld device.
- ✔ Has definitive rules governing such issues as surfing the Internet for personal purposes and playing computer games on company time.
- ✔ Deals with its in-house nonstop talkers and time abusers (every office has them).
- ✔ Requires that telephones be picked up after the first or second ring, voice-mail messages be shortened, and telephone calls be returned promptly.
- ✔ Respects visitors' time. (How do you like it when you visit another business and you're made to wait in the lobby for half an hour?)
- ✔ Encourages delegation. (Don't waste your time doing a task that someone else can do faster — or better.)
- ✔ Understands that shorter and quicker is better when it comes to meetings, memos, letters, manuals, and rules.
- ✔ Insists on employee accountability. (Count on employees to perform such tasks as keeping the supply inventory at adequate levels, maintaining equipment to minimize downtime, and designing and implementing workable internal systems and controls.)
- ✔ Uses time-proven technology.

Time management itself is impossible to measure. What you *can* measure are results — results when compared to plans, budgets, and goals. You can usually figure that whenever you see improving results in the areas you *can* measure, your management of time is improving, too.

You alone can make effective time management a part of your company's culture. After hiring the best people that you can (see Chapter 15), set the right example. Your employees will take it from there.

Choosing Your Management Tools

Little is new in the world of small business. Other organizations have needed restructuring, other employees have needed motivating, and other cultures have needed change.

So what are you, the small-business owner who's looking for ways to continue growing your company, supposed to do when you think it's time for a dose of something new? What management tools should you use to assure continued growth? Whose advice should you take? And how can you possibly know which of the latest fads to glom onto?

You can't. The truth of the matter is, there isn't just one management tool that will turn your company around. And there isn't just one tool that will change your culture, correct your infrastructure, or unite your employees, just as there isn't one strategy that wins football games or produces profitable customers.

We suggest that when you're considering adopting the latest management tool, wait instead and let someone else be the pioneer. (Like someone once said, "You can always tell the pioneers — they're the ones with the arrows in their backs.") Be aware of the fads making the rounds of the small-business arena, but don't bet the farm on the latest one. Cherry-pick a fad's key components that make the most sense to you.

The following tips will help you determine whether the tools inherent in a management system will work for you:

- ✓ **Don't be the first kid on the block.** See if you can determine which similarly sized businesses have already pioneered the system and/or utilized any of its most appropriate tools, and then solicit their suggestions and advice.

  This is particularly true of new, costly software-driven applications. Make sure the program you're considering has been time-tested and has many satisfied users.

- ✓ **Ensure that your key employees agree with the need and the basics of the new tools before you introduce them.** Include them in the purchasing, planning, and implementation processes.

- ✓ **Consider the downsides of utilizing the new tools as well as the upsides.** Make sure you know what it will cost you to pull the plug midstream if the tools aren't working.

- ✓ **Understand the time frame needed to implement the tools and measure their success.** Be sure you can live within the time frame. (Whatever figure you come up with, you generally can multiply that number by two.)

> ✓ **Be certain that you, the owner and chief culture-setter of your business, have the time and energy to devote to the proper implementation of the new management tools.** The implementation of new tools always requires total commitment from the Grand Poobah; if you aren't willing — or able — to make that commitment, don't even think about introducing them.

If your business is working well (as measured primarily by profitability), don't break it. (It's okay, however, to bend it.) If it isn't working, consider a change. Your job is to be the systems and tools matchmaker. Keep current of the latest and greatest management systems and the tools within them, and then match your need for change with the applicable system.

Consider the management fads in the following sections. Each of the fads has at least one key management tool that makes sense — ranging from setting goals to redefining processes, from paring expenses to sharing financial information. Every fad offers a degree of management wisdom and an accompanying management tool, but that doesn't mean that you need to adopt the entire system. Cherry pick as you see fit.

Management by objective

An old-timer for sure, the basic components of *management by objective* (MBO) — setting and reaching goals — have endured and are still used, to one degree or another, by many successful businesses. We discuss the process of goal setting at length in Chapter 15; most businesses — small and large — use the management tool of goal setting in one form or another. So should yours.

Participatory management

Great in theory, *participatory management* (the primary tool of which is that all employees take part in determining the direction and policies of the company) can work wonders when organized carefully and phased in over long periods of time.

The participatory tools inherent in this system work for two reasons:

> ✓ Given a voice in the decision-making process, employees are much more likely to make a personal commitment to the decisions reached.

> ✓ Given the fact that employees see the business through eyes that the owners don't, their input enhances the quality of the decisions made.

But don't give away the keys to the car too soon. Figuring out how to drive a small business takes years of training and preparation. Besides, not all employees *want* the responsibility that goes with being behind the wheel.

Employee ownership

Although we're certainly proponents of the motivation tool inherent in offering employees the opportunity to own a piece of the company, sharing the pie isn't always as easy as it sounds. Sometimes you don't have enough pie to go around; sometimes the pie isn't divided the way everyone would like it to be; and sometimes your employees would rather bet their futures on T-bills than on small-business pie. Besides, minority shareholders can be a pain in the rear.

But, for many people, there's no better motivator than ownership. That's why, despite the problems that come with sharing the pie, we see more and more pie-sharing going on today than ever before. Even the federal government recognizes this fact, which is why it offers a number of incentives to companies to establish such employee-empowering tools as Employee Stock Ownership Plans (ESOPs). For much more on offering employees equity in your company, see Chapter 16.

Quality circles

Quality circles are ad hoc groups or temporary teams (also known as *ad hoc committees*) of employees assembled to solve specific problems. Forms of this team approach to problem solving are used every day in most successful businesses. In many cases, specially formed teams are assembled to solve a problem and then quickly disbanded after the issue has been resolved.

The appeal of the problem-solving tool inherent in quality circles is the age-old theory that two heads are better than one. This is especially true when those two (or more) heads are focused on solving a specific problem, and especially when those heads bring differing perspectives to the problem-solving table.

Total Quality Management

Total Quality Management (TQM) is an all-encompassing phrase that means "the involving and empowering of employees to increase profits by increasing quality, increasing focus on the customer, and decreasing costs." Whew. Sounds like a synonym for "sound business practices" to us.

After all, the tool involved in managing quality, focusing on customers, and controlling expenses is nothing more than plain-old common sense, which, come to think of it, is what TQM is all about. What makes it a fad is beyond us.

Reengineering

Called *process analysis* by some and *Business Process Reengineering* (BPR) by others, *reengineering* refers to putting each of a business's functions under the microscope and refining them. Given the choice, we'd call reengineering either "expense management par excellence" or "fat cutting extraordinaire." The primary tool is, of course, the management of expenses.

Similar to TQM, reengineering is just another fancy word for "managing your business efficiently and logically," which makes the fad itself another excuse for consultants to write books on the subject.

Open-book management

Open-book management teaches that informed employees are capable of making key decisions usually reserved for management — within, that is, their areas of expertise. An *informed employee* is one who's privy to nearly everything that goes on within the company, including a variety of tools usually reserved for management, such as financial statements.

Similar to any other management system, there are upsides and downsides to the open-book management system:

- ✔ The downside is that your employees may find out things that you'd prefer they don't know, like how much you spend on travel and entertainment in a year and how much your new Lexus costs the company.

- ✔ The upside is that informed employees tend to make better day-to-day decisions than uninformed ones. Informed employees are also more likely to be committed to the cause — in this case, to increasing the profitability of the company.

Troubleshooting Your Business

From time to time, businesses call in small-business consultants to troubleshoot. Although troubleshooting can be an effective tool any time, sadly it's usually done only when a growing business suddenly slows down. Consultants can help a struggling business by evaluating important areas of the business — such as finances, employee morale, and business appearance — and then making suggestions for improvement. Find out how in the following sections.

TRUE STORY

The faster the growth, the harder it is to keep up

Joan, a friend of co-author Jim, owned what had been (for its first five years) a very successful sign company. Her sales had grown at an annual rate in excess of 25 percent and had reached $15 million per year in less than eight years. As a result of Joan's previous job in sales, she'd developed an effective sales staff within her company, a group that kept the orders coming — and coming.

Unfortunately, her business's systems and controls had not kept up with the 25 percent annual increase in sales. Neither had the skills of her managerial, administrative, and production employees. As a result, despite the consistent increase in sales, Joan's inefficient business lost money in its sixth, seventh, and eighth years, eventually forcing her to file for bankruptcy.

"The more rapid the sales growth," Joan told us later, "the more difficult it is to keep up. A 5-percent sales-growth rate provides ample time for the employees to learn and react. A 25-percent sales-growth rate and the accompanying crush of new problems do not."

Here are some lessons to take from businesses like Joan's that get consumed by sales growth:

✔ **Unless your business has large fixed costs that you can lower, you can't grow yourself out of profitability difficulties.** Consequently, never try to throw more sales at profitability problems. More sales generally magnifies existing deficiencies. Forget focusing on sales growth. Focus instead on improving profitability (see Chapter 13).

✔ **A strategic change (that is, a transition) is needed at this stage in your business.** Missions, goals, and strategies must be evaluated and changed. Systems and controls must be repaired or, more often, replaced. The organizational structure must be reviewed and upgraded. Most important, key employees must be trained and, where necessary, replaced — including, when the shoe fits, you, the founder. (See the advice in the sections "The transition period" and "Redefining Your Role in an Evolving Business" for more.)

✔ **Don't give yourself, your managers, and your key employees cheerleading speeches when they require training.** A fight for life is going on here, and the fight will be won or lost by you and your employees.

✔ **Be willing to go outside of the organization for management help.** A promote-from-within strategy in the face of exploding sales may mean a team of more secure employees, but the strategy can also mean that their secure days will be numbered if your staff doesn't have the objectivity to honestly evaluate the business's weaknesses. Most employees of rapidly growing but struggling companies welcome the infusion of new blood.

Filling out a troubleshooting checklist

Most consultants use checklists to help them determine the seriousness of the problems. Here's a checklist that one troubleshooting consultant we know uses.

Rank each category from 1 to 10; 1 = poor, 10 = excellent:

___ **Quality of cash-management procedures (cash-flow reporting and forecasting)**

___ **Quality of financial reporting (profit and loss statement and balance sheet)**

___ **Quality of financial forecasting (budgets)**

___ **Dependence upon borrowed funds (1 = heavy, 10 = none)**

___ **Late with payroll tax deposits (1 = often, 10 = never)**

___ **Lag between sales growth and profit growth (1 = substantial, 10 = none)**

___ **Employee turnover (1 = heavy, 10 = nonexistent)**

___ **Quality and frequency of strategic planning**

___ **Owner has more work to do than time to do it (1 = too much work, 10 = balances time efficiently)**

___ **Owner's feelings about the business (1 = hates it, 10 = loves it)**

If you were your own troubleshooting consultant, how would you rate your business overall? What areas would you target for improvement? Using this checklist, how does your business check out? On how many items would you give yourself close to a 10? How many receive only something near a 1?

Although there's no overall key to grading the answers, we suggest that where you answered any of these questions with a 5 or below, you should give immediate attention to upgrading the number. For the 6s or 7s, put the issue on your long-range to-do list. For the 8s and above, pat yourself on the back and make sure that the employees responsible for the rating are publicly recognized and, where possible, rewarded.

Taking the five-minute appearance test

Your business's appearance is important. With this in mind, we devised a simple "appearance test." Five minutes is all it takes. (For more on the importance of appearance, see the later sidebar "You *can* judge a business by its looks.")

Start with a business other than your own. For instance, you can offer to give a friend's business the following five-minute appearance test. Simply drive into the parking lot, walk into the general office area, peek into a few offices here and there, step into the restroom for a quick look around, and then check out the areas around the coffeemaker and fax and copying machines on your way out the door.

Note the following as you go, ranking your observations from 1 (poor) to 5 (excellent):

THE EXTERIOR

___ **Parking lot:** Indicates care and upkeep

___ **Grounds and exterior:** Well maintained, trimmed, and inviting

___ **Windows:** Clean, unsmeared, and uncluttered when viewed from the outside

___ **Signage:** Well maintained, readable, and understandable

THE INTERIOR

___ **General neatness:** Desks and working areas neat and uncluttered

___ **Restrooms:** Neat and clean

___ **Expense awareness:** Unnecessary lights and unused equipment turned off, no original Van Goghs in the lobby

___ **Time management:** Employees appear focused and busy, no gossipy gatherings around the coffeemaker or copy machines

___ **Employee attitudes:** Polite, alert, attentive, and focused

___ **Employee appearance:** Neat, clean, and dressed appropriately

___ **Sense of urgency:** Employees going about their business at a pace that indicates they don't have time to waste

THE BEST AND THE WORST

The one thing I saw that impressed me the most:

_____

The one thing I saw that bothered me the most:

_____

Then give the questionnaire to the owner. Ask your friend to repay you the favor. Your business could use the five-minute appearance test, too.

Redefining Your Role in an Evolving Business

Owning a business is like raising a teenager: As it grows, the business is sure to get into trouble, yet you can never be sure what the trouble will be, how severe it will be, and how the company will weather the experience. Whether the business (and the teenager) will survive and subsequently thrive or fail depends on the quality of leadership provided.

That leadership, in the case of your business anyway, must come from you.

So why is growth, especially that of the rapid variety, so hard on the typical small-business owner? The reasons are twofold:

- ✔ **Most small-business owners aren't prepared for the managerial demands of a growing business.** In most cases, the owner's expertise is in a specialized area, such as sales or accounting, or is related to his craft or to the product or service that the company offers. As a result, he's untrained and unskilled in the management aspects of running a business. To make matters worse, many of the management skills required to run a growing business usually run counter to the way the owner is accustomed to doing things.

- ✔ **The bigger your company becomes, the farther you fade from the center of the action.** Visions get blurred as a result of that distance, missions fade, and communications falter. Also, the more the business grows, the more layers there are to separate you from your customers, vendors, and employees. It's an entrepreneurial axiom that with distance comes misdirection — unless the management skills of the owner can keep pace with the growth.

A number of traits are required of a proficient manager. Most of these traits aren't required for a successful start-up, but only come into play as a company grows. The ability, or inability, of the entrepreneur to adopt these skills determines the ultimate success of the business.

Making the transition to manager

Here's a popular entrepreneurial axiom: "The day you hire your first employee is the same day you begin making the transition to manager." This isn't an easy transition to make because many of the typical small-business owner's personal traits run counter to those of a successful manager. Consider the following required traits and job descriptions of the successful manager — traits that aren't always near the top of the typical entrepreneur's list of skills:

- ✔ **Focus:** The successful manager focuses on the project at hand, no matter what else is going on around him. The typical entrepreneur stops in the middle of the task to respond to the latest crisis.

- ✔ **Attention to detail:** The successful manager devoutly dots her *i's* and crosses her *t's*. The typical entrepreneur is often too busy or simply not the type that enjoys dealing with details.

- ✔ **Follow-up:** The successful manager knows that employees need to know that their work will be evaluated. The typical entrepreneur thinks that employees' work shouldn't have to be followed up; he believes that the employees should do it right the first time.

You *can* judge a business by its looks

Most people who work with small-business owners have discovered that the health of a business can often (but not always) be pre-judged accurately by its physical appearance. Here's a telltale example of how a few simple details can provide a surefire indication of what a growing business's culture is really like and how it can be translated into the health of that business.

Co-author Jim was asked to visit an automobile recycling business (also known as a "junkyard") to help the owner devise a commission plan for his sales employees. Driving into the parking lot, Jim noticed the well-kept wooden fence, the neat landscaping lining the front office, and the freshly asphalted and well-marked parking facilities. Upon entering the office, he was immediately struck by the neatness and cleanliness of the facilities, the professional counter and wall displays of the company's "recycled" products, and the staff of employees with matching, embroidered shirts. The

busy atmosphere and the prevailing sense of urgency reminded Jim of a well-managed McDonald's restaurant at lunchtime.

Well, Jim could tell you one thing about this man's business within 30 seconds of walking into the place, without so much as talking to its owner or glancing at its financial statements. The business looked, felt, and, yes, even smelled like a profitable business.

And so it was. The financial statements revealed rapidly growing sales and robust profitability in excess of a 10-percent return on those sales. Additionally, the company boasted a low employee turnover, excellent employee benefits, and an inventory system that was second to none that Jim had seen in any small business.

In short, this business's financial performance lived up to its appearance, a relationship that almost always goes hand in hand.

> ✔ **Conflict resolution:** The successful manager views resolving conflict as an important part of her job description. The typical entrepreneur sees it as an intrusion on her time.

> ✔ **Training:** The successful manager views training as an investment. The typical entrepreneur sees it as an expense.

Of course, not all small-business owners fit this entrepreneur's profile. You can make changes in some, if not all, of those managerial traits that you lack. However, the transition to manager isn't an easy one and involves some basic — and often wrenching — changes in the entrepreneur who originally founded the business.

Implementing strategic changes

The *Peter Principle* (which says that, sooner or later, everyone peaks and ends up in a job beyond his or her capabilities) constantly creeps up on all small-business owners as their companies grow. For one entrepreneur, it may arrive when his company has only one employee; for others, it may creep up when their companies reach 1,000 employees. But everyone has limitations — managerial and otherwise. Having limitations doesn't make you a bad person; it only means that, where the management of your business is concerned, there may come a time when you should either move over or move on.

When you notice that the Peter Principle is hanging over your management skills and you're having a difficult time making the transition from entrepreneur to manager (you'll know its happening when your business isn't fun anymore), it may be time to consider the four alternatives in the following sections.

Downsizing your business

Downsizing involves shrinking your business back to the point where you're able to spend your time doing those things you enjoy and are best at. For example, you may decide to limit your customer base to only those within your market area, thereby cutting your sales and allowing you to shrink the number of employees you must manage.

Before making this choice, ask yourself the following questions:

✔ What are the downsides of shrinking the business (loss of income, reduction in the market value of the business, letting go of customers, and possibly laying off employees)?

✔ Will you be able to emotionally and financially cope with these losses?

If the answer to either of these questions is no, consider the alternative in the following section.

Taking a personal inventory

Taking a personal inventory includes assembling your own *managerial defect list* — a list of personal traits that make managing your business difficult, such as inattention to detail or fear of conflict. Consider which entries on the list you could, and would, change in order to make the managerial transition.

Ask your spouse, friends, and key employees to help you make the list.

Questions that you should ask yourself include the following:

✔ How many of the traits on your managerial defect list can you hire around?

✔ How many of the traits can you train around?

✔ How many of the traits can you delegate around?

✔ Of those traits that you can't hire, train, or delegate around, which can you reasonably expect to change?

This exercise will tell you what you need to do to improve your managerial skills and how to go about it. Assuming, as a result of the answers given, you decide you can make the transition, get busy! Start hiring, training, delegating, and, where applicable, making changes in your organizational structure (see the earlier section "Choosing Your Management Tools").

Assuming you decide you can't — or won't — make that transition, it's time to consider the following alternative.

Hiring a replacement

Hiring a replacement includes hiring a president or Chief Operating Officer (COO) to run your company while you become Chief Executive Officer (CEO). The president or COO takes control of the day-to-day management of the business, while you concentrate on long-range, strategic matters.

Before hiring a replacement, ask yourself the following:

- Is your company big enough and profitable enough to afford a president or COO?
- Are you capable of letting go and keeping your nose out of the day-to-day operating functions of your business?

If the answer to either of these questions is no, you have to either go back to the preceding alternatives (downsizing your business or making personal changes) and decide how you can adapt one (or both) to your situation, or consider the fourth alternative.

Selling the business

Before you decide to take such a big step as selling your business, ask yourself the following:

- Will you emotionally be able to sell and walk away from the company you've built?
- Is your company salable at a price that works for you?

Ultimately, you may decide to sell your business and move on to something you're better suited for or more ready to do.

Part V
The Part of Tens

The 5th Wave   By Rich Tennant

"I like getting complaint letters by e-mail.
It's easier to delete than to shred."

In this part . . .

This part provides lists of things you need to know in order to build your business and keep it growing. We provide wisdom on such topics as operating a home-based business, effectively using technology, and improving your personal management skills.

Chapter 20

Ten Tips for Home-Based Businesses

. . . .

In This Chapter

▶ Preparing yourself for the challenge and avoiding common mistakes

▶ Balancing your personal and professional lives

▶ Putting technology to work for you

. . . .

Make no mistake about it: Opening a home-based business is in vogue these days. A study by *Inc.* magazine indicates that home-based businesses account for nearly half of all businesses in the United States today. We're not talking hobbies here, either. As evidence, consider the fact that in one study several years ago, a whopping 48 percent of *Inc.* 500 businesses (the nation's fastest-growing, privately held businesses) reported starting their companies in their homes.

Your humble authors account for two home-based businesses, and we can tell you from experience that starting a home-based business definitely has its advantages. The four most typically cited advantages include lower start-up costs, less overhead, tax benefits, and lifestyle advantages gained by being "close to home."

For us anyway, having our own home-based businesses sure beats the heck out of being someone else's employee — punching a time clock, packing a cold lunch, or sharing a cubicle with someone who often makes loud, personal phone calls. Furthermore, when compared to owning our own office-based retail, manufacturing, or service business (again, for us anyway), running our home-based businesses sure beats the heck out of managing a warehouse filled with inventory, motivating a team of march-to-their-own-drummer employees, or attempting to comply with ever-more-complicated government regulations (see Chapter 17).

Not everyone, however, is home-based business material. You need more than a desk, phone, and computer to create a successful home-based business. You also need large doses of dedication, discipline, and self-accountability.

In this chapter, we share a collection of tips we've learned from our home-based business experience and borrowed from other home-based business owners we've known.

Decide if Home-Based Is Right for You

Some small-business owners believe that they're getting something for nothing by working from home rather than from a business office. The truth is, the space your business occupies in your home and the costs of that space are real, not imaginary.

Sure, assuming that you qualify, you get tax deductions for the costs of operating your business out of your home (see Chapter 18 for more tax information). But that's no different than if you operated a business outside your home and paid for office space, the expense for which would be tax-deductible, too.

If you have the choice of running your business from your home versus securing outside office space, base the decision as much as possible on what makes the best overall business sense for your enterprise. Consider your business's and customers' needs:

- ✔ If you don't need fancy office space to present an image of success or in which to meet with clients, working at home may be fine. Likewise, if you're in a creative enterprise, such as copywriting or graphic design, you can work your magic at any time of the day or night, so working at home can be ideal.

- ✔ If you operate a retail business that requires a constant flow of customers, obtaining outside office space is probably the best (and legally correct) choice. Likewise, if you're in warehousing or manufacturing, you may have problems in a home environment.

- ✔ Professionals such as doctors, lawyers, or accountants and tax consultants may have more versatility in their choice of work setting, depending on their specialties and the customers they want to attract.

Be sure to check with the governing authorities of your town or city to find out what regulations exist for home-based businesses. You may find that government regulations prohibit you from conducting certain kinds of business from your home.

Also ask yourself what it will cost you personally to work from home. At home, you must have the discipline to get your work done in spite of a wide variety of interruptions. Will you be tempted to make half a dozen snack trips to the kitchen and turn on the television for late-breaking news? Will you get caught up in the details of running your house rather than running your business?

The hardest time to discipline yourself usually is in the early days of your business when you don't have enough work to fully occupy your time. The sometimes-amorphous challenge of figuring out how to grow the business may cause you to focus your energies elsewhere.

Above all, ask what conducting business within your house will cost in terms of your home life. If you're single and living alone, home life may be less of an issue because you need to consider only your own needs and schedule. Working at home may be an advantage if you're a parent because you can be more involved with your kids. If nothing else, the one to two hours per day that you may spend commuting are hours that you can spend with your kids! Just be sure to set specific work hours and expectations with family members.

Before you make your decision to set up at home, talk to other family members to find out how they feel about having you around during the day. Get specific about what you plan to do, as well as where, when, and how you intend to do it. Will you have clients come to your home? What time of day and where in the home will you meet with them? How will you assure that your home-based business won't override the needs of your family and vice versa?

Run Your Business like a Business

After you've made the decision to set up shop in the den or the extra bedroom of your home, remember that this is a business you're running, not a hobby. Businesses are intended primarily to be profitable and financially sustainable; hobbies are intended primarily to be fun. (The key word here is *primarily.* Businesses can obviously be fun, and hobbies can also be profitable.)

If your business *is* a hobby, feel free to let the daily events of the home come first. Do the dishes between phone calls, let the kids doodle on your business stationery, or chat with a neighbor in your office over a cup of coffee. Be cool. Stay relaxed. Have fun.

If, however, you've started what you intend to be an honest-to-goodness business, treat the door to your office as an imaginary line in the sand; cross it and you enter into the world of debits and credits and business deals. Set rules for whoever is on the other side of that line, and then make sure that you enforce those rules.

We're not saying that you can't take time out to answer the doorbell or have lunch with the family. But we *are* saying that, during the course of your stated business hours — whatever those hours may be — business should come first, just as business would come first if you had an office on the corner of Elm and Main streets.

Keep Things Legal (And Safe)

Perhaps in part because working out of the home isn't like working in a downtown, high-rise office building, some home-based business owners feel that they can cut corners legally. Of course, some people who run their businesses out of glitzy high-rises break the law, too.

Just because you work out of your home, don't assume that you won't get caught or you won't draw attention to yourself if you do break the rules. If you cheat on your taxes or don't obtain the proper licenses and permits to run your business, you should expect to get caught and to pay a dear price.

Do your upfront due diligence the same way you would if you were to operate remotely. Contact an attorney and make sure you've selected the right entity (see Chapter 5). Do everything the right way, the first time around.

We also suggest you protect yourself in the insurance department. You're in the consulting business? You'll probably need some business liability protection. Customers or vendors visiting your home office regularly? You may need an add-on to your homeowner's insurance to cover personal liability. Your business is up, running, and successful? You may want to consider business interruption insurance. (For more about insurance, see Chapter 10.)

Chapter 17 explains how to comply with the myriad legal and regulatory issues that small-business owners face, and Chapter 18 details how to stay on the right side of the various tax authorities.

Put On a Professional Face

Someone once said, "You don't get a second chance to make a first impression" — a statement that's especially true where a home-based business is concerned.

Part of making a good first impression is making a professional one. Today's customers, at least the ones who will be willing (and able) to pay top dollar for better products or services, are looking for professionalism from their vendors, and equate professionalism with quality.

Use these tips to help you make that first impression a professional one:

- **Office:** Physically separate your office from the rest of the house. If that's not possible, find a way to close the doors and shut out the sounds (and smells) of the house. Try to keep background noise (the television playing, children crying, carpenter hammering, washing machine churning) to a minimum.

✔ **Telephone:** The telephone is the front door of your business and is often-times (with the possible exception of your Web site) the gateway to the first impression a potential customer has of you. If your customer must dial your number six times before getting through; if your answering machine sounds scratchy and unprofessional; or if you don't return your customer's call within a reasonable amount of time, your relationship is off to a rocky start.

Voicemail provides you the benefit of having your calls answered while you're on the phone. Another option is to get two telephone lines — one for incoming calls and/or one for outgoing calls and (where necessary) a dial-up modem and fax. Obviously, the more phone lines, the greater the expense.

✔ **Answering service and/or voicemail:** Unless you can afford a full-time secretary, this is your best alternative. (It's our experience that most people would rather leave their message on voicemail than with a secretary — voicemail doesn't lose words or garble messages in the translation.)

✔ **A toll-free number:** Toll-free numbers are relatively inexpensive yet present a professional image to your potential customers. At the same time, they send a message that yours is a sales-minded, customer-responsive business.

✔ **Fax:** Over an extended period of time, you can pay for a fax machine with the money you save by not using the mail or the various overnight services. Besides, with faxing, you don't waste telephone time by chatting or being put on everlasting hold or having to convince a secretary to let your call through. (Be sure to develop a professional-appearing cover sheet; it can serve as an advertising piece as well as an introduction to your communication.)

✔ **E-mail:** E-mail is usually the quickest and least-expensive method of communication. Type away to your heart's content, regardless of where the message is headed. (Sending a message to Rome costs the same as sending a message to Chicago.)

✔ **Letter writing:** Despite all the new technology, sooner or later you'll have to write letters, and your business will be judged by the professionalism of those letters. You should use the software program on your computer, because most word-processing programs come with spell-check and grammar-check features, assisting you in giving your written communications a professional appearance. If you're unable for some reason to word-process your letters, be sure to have a secretarial service lined up to handle your important written communications.

✔ **Business cards:** Don't scrimp on business cards; they'll probably turn out to be one of your primary marketing vehicles. (Don't believe it? The next time someone slips you his or her business card, make a mental note of how you judge that person's business by the appearance of the card.)

✔ **Web site:** If you know how to construct it and market it (drive people to it, in other words), your Web site can be your brochure, your business card, your e-mail, and even your telephone, all wrapped into one. (But don't just settle for any old Web site — do it right or don't do it at all. Remember, a schlocky Web site is worse than no Web site at all.)

So why all this fuss about your business's appearance? After all, are you in the image business or are you selling widgets? The answer is: You're in both the image business *and* the selling business. The selling of your widgets is made easier by the professional display of your image. Like it or not, people (potential customers) *do* judge businesses by their appearance and image. If yours doesn't stack up on first impression, chances are those people won't even try to do business with you.

Choose the Right Technology

We can't imagine a home-based business today that wouldn't benefit from a computer and some of its related technologies. No matter what service you provide or what product you sell, you must perform one or more of the following duties in the conduct of your home-based business:

✔ **Write anything from a business plan (see Chapter 4) to business letters.** A good word-processing program on your computer is worth its weight in gold.

✔ **Communicate efficiently with other businesses in the same town or halfway across the world.** Nothing compares in price or quickness to a fax or e-mail. Of course, where a personal touch is needed, don't use such impersonal communication methods.

✔ **Market to your customer base.** E-mail is the least expensive, quickest, and most effective marketing medium in the world. It's the fastest growing, too.

✔ **Invoice a customer, pay your bills, and track your business financials.** Scores of financial software packages are available, and even the most inexpensive can be cost-effective compared to a manual system.

✔ **Maintain a customer database.** You can store customers' names, addresses, and whatever else you need to know — ranging from the name of the purchasing agent's spouse, to the date of his or her birthday, to a history of client requests and purchases, service preferences, contact summaries, and other information to help you form and maintain client relationships. A computerized database package has far-reaching advantages over a manually maintained system.

✔ **Maintain a to-do list and an appointment calendar.** Manual versus computerized to-do list? The jury's out on which one works the best. (One man's meat is another man's potatoes.)

Here's a quick overview of the technology that you should consider when starting your own home-based business:

✔ **Hardware:** Hardware is the computer itself. The choices you'll have to make include

- PC or MAC
- Laptop or desktop
- New or used
- A wide range of horsepower options

Your choices should be dictated by the kind of business you're in, your budget, and your personal preferences.

✔ **Software:** Software is what you need to tell your computer what to do and how to do it. Your software needs depend on what applications you intend to use: word processing for letter-writing and reports; spreadsheets for accounting and other number-crunching functions; a graphic design program for artwork, charts, and graphs; scheduling and e-mail programs; presentation graphics for slides; or database packages for customer information.

If your budget allows, you may want to consider purchasing one of the many office-manager suites available. (Microsoft Office is the best-selling package.) The applications in a typical suite include all the ones we list here, and because they're from the same manufacturer, they're designed to work more easily together.

✔ **Printer:** Your first decision is whether you need a color printer or just a black-and-white printer. If you plan on preparing your own marketing materials, you need a color printer. Also, if you plan on downloading and printing from the Internet, color is preferable. Your next decision is whether to buy an inkjet or a laser printer. Both are available for color printing, although most color laser printers come with a higher price tag than their inkjet cousins. The price difference can be offset, however, by the cost of the laser printer's long-lasting toner drum compared to that of the short-lived cartridges you'll need to buy on an ongoing basis for an ink printer. Add to that the fact that laser printers are better suited for high-volume work, and you'll see why they win out in most businesses.

✔ **Modem:** The *modem* is the mechanism that enables a computer to transmit data over telephone or cable lines, thereby allowing you to connect with the Internet and to get and send e-mail. Modems come in both internal (as part of the computer) and external models and can vary in price, depending on the speed of the modem. The faster the modem, the less time you wait to receive and send information (and the more you pay). Most communities are now serviced by high-speed or broadband Internet service, accessed via cable modems, DSL (Digital Subscriber Lines), or other technologies that provide much faster Internet connections than the original dial-up modems.

✔ **Fax machine:** The fax machine (short for *facsimile*) is behind only the telephone, computer, and printer in importance to the typical home-based business. Fax machines send images via telephone lines and allow you to transmit documents in a matter of seconds.

You can also use fax-machine services at most copy centers, so you don't have to purchase the machine yourself to send or receive faxes. (You can use the copy center's fax number and have incoming faxes held there for you.)

Sending your documents via a fax machine is, in most cases, less expensive than alternative methods, including the U.S. mail and the various overnight services.

✔ **Answering machine:** Answering machines record incoming messages on a tape recorder and come in two different models: digital and tape. Although both are effective, digital models are faster because you don't have to wait for the tape to rewind before you can hear your messages. Some people prefer voicemail because it sounds more professional and can answer a number of calls at once.

You can buy both fax machines and answering machines as add-on features to your printer and computer. Our experience is that, although stand-alone faxes and answering machines may be a bit more expensive than the add-on units, the additional expense is worth it. Stand-alones generally perform better and aren't subject to the unpredictable moods of your hard drive.

Develop a Marketing Strategy

If you're like most people who operate home-based businesses, your number-one critical issue from day one will be your need to sell and market your services or products. This task is almost always the most difficult one — and not surprisingly either, because it's also one of the issues at or near the top of the office-based business's list as well.

The most frequently used marketing tool for the home-based business is word-of-mouth referrals from satisfied customers, leading to more satisfied customers and more referrals. This is the major reason that the typical home-based business takes so long to become successful — a solid base of satisfied customers takes time to build.

The best home-based marketers are those who can take that base of satisfied customers and do something with them. Although they may be satisfied, these customers may also need to be encouraged to broadcast their satisfaction, which is where the assertive home-based business owner comes in. The meek may well inherit the earth, but they shouldn't own home-based businesses.

Word-of-mouth referral techniques vary. Use the following techniques and others that you may come up with to "advertise" your business:

- ✔ Call your satisfied customers and ask them to call one potential customer for you.

- ✔ Ask for the names of potential customers and the right to use the satisfied customer's name in a conversation with, or in written materials sent to, a potential customer.

- ✔ Use your satisfied customer's name and a quote of praise in such advertising materials as flyers, brochures, and media ads.

- ✔ Market to your existing customers. Ask for their permission to send them focused e-mails.

Second only to word-of-mouth advertising is networking. Networking comes in many forms, from joining the Chamber of Commerce, to volunteering to flip burgers at the Rotary picnic, to introducing yourself to the person sitting next to you on the airplane.

The best way to find out about the marketing techniques that work (or don't work) in your industry is to join your industry trade association, become a member of one of the home-based business associations, or subscribe to a home-based business magazine. Any of these resources worth its salt will include a number of self-training vehicles and suggestions on how to market your products or services.

No matter how good you are at performing your service or how wonderful your product is, your home-based business will sink or swim based on your ability to promote and sell your product or service, get paid for it, and account for the proceeds. In other words, the key to your success will be your ability to manage your business (see Chapter 10), which is, when you get right down to it, no different than those businesses with ten, a hundred, or a thousand employees.

Manage Your Time Effectively

Effective time management is especially difficult for the typical home-based business owner, primarily due to the fact that within most home-based businesses, there's typically no one to delegate all those mundane details to, so you must do them all yourself.

Out of stamps? *You* buy them. UPS driver knocking at the door? *You* answer it. Dog needs to find a fire hydrant? *You* open the door and let him out. You must also clean up the office at the end of the day, answer the telephone, and monitor your accounts receivable — all this while solving your customers' problems. Everything that happens in your home-based business either goes *through* or goes *to* you.

Similar to the office-based small-business owner, you, too, must use a time-management system of one sort or another. Whether it's a simple to-do list (we suggest two to-do lists — one for short-term issues and one for long-term projects) or one of the many commercially developed systems (manual or computerized) that manage your time down to the nanosecond, you must make the commitment to initiate and stick to a time-management plan.

Always end your workday by preparing the next day's to-do list. This allows you to get off to a good start in the morning, cuts down on the likelihood of your omitting an important item from the list, and reduces the stress of feeling that you have a zillion things hanging over your head without a plan for how to tackle them.

Keep your to-do list alongside your appointment calendar. (If you use one of the commercially prepared or computerized time-management systems, the appointment calendar likely is a part of the system itself.) Get in the habit of consulting both the to-do list and your appointment calendar first thing when you enter your office in the morning. Doing this will cut down on missed appointments — something that's often a problem for most home-based business owners.

Also, get in the habit of using e-mail rather than the telephone — especially when your phone call is a reminder call or a call that doesn't require a give-and-take conversation. You won't get dragged into a one-hour conversation on e-mail, you won't be hung up on, and you won't get involved in playing telephone tag. E-mail can't put you on hold, either. And e-mail gives you a record of your action, complete with time and date.

Finally, don't try to do every menial chore yourself, in the interest of saving a few bucks. Allocate your time, making sure to spend it where the leverage is. Plenty of outsourcing companies are available to perform many of the menial tasks of business. For instance, if you have a direct-mail piece to get out and it's going to take four hours to do the addressing and stamping, outsourcing the project to a mailing house may be a better choice. This allows you to spend those four hours on a project that's more worthy of your time.

Review the section on time management in Chapter 19. Most of the parameters that apply to office-based businesses also apply to home-based businesses.

Get Motivated!

Goal-setting exercises are important when it comes to motivating you in your personal life, as well as in your home-based business. See Chapter 15 for tips on setting goals for your business and, where applicable, your employees.

Setting the goals isn't what will make you achieve them. Writing goals down and then publishing them will help motivate you to achieve them.

By publishing your goals, we don't mean sending them to *The Wall Street Journal* and hoping that they get included in the next press run. We mean showing them to your spouse, mounting them on the refrigerator, and including them in your business plan right below your mission statement (see Chapter 4).

Include Your Family

If your office is in your home, that makes your spouse and other family members — whether they're around the house during the day or at work or school — at least silent partners in your venture. After all, your spouse, in addition to being your dinner date, is your landlord, investment partner, and eternal soulmate, and as such has a vested interest in the stresses and successes of your business.

Use these tips to help you work with your family in regard to your home-based business:

- ✓ **Before opening the door of your business, you should all agree to ground rules for the input each of you will have when it comes to the direction of the business.** Minimize down-the-road surprises by defining each partner's input and the parameters from the beginning. The silent partner will be able to contribute some things, but not all.

- ✓ **If your spouse is involved in your business, be sure that he or she knows what's going on.** This is especially important when, from time to time, your spouse is involved in talking to your customers, greeting the UPS driver, picking up your fax paper when you run out, and so on. Keep your spouse in the loop.

- ✓ **In the event that you and your spouse are considering working together in the business, recognize that if you haven't been able to solve your personal problems amicably in the past, being in business together will probably make things worse.** Don't burden your marriage with the heightened difficulties of being in business together if the marriage isn't strong. Address your relationship issues before going into business together.

The best partnerships we know are those in which the partners bring different skills to the table. If you and your spouse don't have complementary skills, don't consider going into business together.

- ✓ **Always make sure that your marriage and family come first.**

- ✓ **Remember to expend your energy competing with your competitors and not with each other.**

Stay in the Loop

One of the common misconceptions about the home-based business is that it's a safe place for people who are hermits or loners (Howard Hughes types). Old stereotypes abound: Many home-based business owners are perceived as people who don't need or like other people.

Although some small-business owners have had less-than-desirable experiences with their fellow *homo sapiens* — either as part of a team of employees or as the leader of a team — this doesn't mean that they chose to start home-based businesses because they wanted to lose contact with the world. In the end, your success in business will be because you've discovered a way to interest people (customers) in your product or service. You've discovered a way to provide a service or deliver a product that people are willing to pay for, solving their particular problem in the process. In truth, all small-business owners depend, in some way, on other people.

What this dependence on people means is that when you're working out of your home office, you must find a way to stay in the local business and social loops, or you risk losing touch with the very people whose needs can influence your product or service.

Here are several of our suggestions for staying in the loop:

- ✔ **Join at least one local business organization.** Examples include the Chamber of Commerce, the Rotary, or one of the community's business networking organizations.

- ✔ **Join at least one national organization, such as a home-based business association or an industry trade association.** Not only will membership in a national organization help you remain in the loop, but also many associations offer their members a number of other advantages, such as health plans, travel discounts, and educational programs. (See Chapter 14 for more on associations.)

- ✔ **Make an educational goal for yourself each year, and then stick to it.** Goals should include such activities as schooling, reading books, and attending educational seminars (especially those put on by your trade association), conferences, and industry trade shows.

- ✔ **Familiarize yourself with the Internet (without getting addicted to it).** Find out which Web sites have helpful information related to your industry. (See Chapter 21 for how to best use the Internet in your small business.)

Every business, home-based and otherwise, is a living, breathing organism, and, thus, is always in one stage or another of growing or dying. In order to keep your business growing, you need to have a constant grip on how the world is changing. The best way to keep your finger on the world's pulse is by staying in touch.

Chapter 21

Ten Smart Ways to Harness Technology

In This Chapter

▶ Bringing time management and research into the 21st century

▶ Supplementing your administration and customer service with technology

▶ Reaching customers and network contacts over the Web

*M*ost of the time, technology enables small-business owners to run their businesses more efficiently and profitably. We encourage you to keep a finger on the pulse of technology and its role in your type of business. In fact, if you fail to track and take advantage of useful technology, your business could end up getting thumped by your competition (for more on the needs of a growing business, head to Chapter 19). However, like any tool, technology can be misused or overused and become more costly than necessary.

We need to warn you against embracing new technology blindly. As a group, small-business owners are particularly susceptible to buying software programs that they don't need. At the entrance to every software program or Web site, we'd like to post a sign that says: "Small-business owners, proceed at your own risk." Why? Because adopting new technology takes time, and whether you're a current small-business owner or a wannabe entrepreneur, time is probably your most precious commodity.

Effective technology can do many things to aid your business:

✔ Save you time

✔ Stimulate ideas that can help make your business grow larger and more profitable

✔ Manage your and your business's finances (online banking and accounting software)

✔ Deliver advertising and marketing to targeted sectors

Never buy expensive new business hardware and software until you've talked with several other small-business owners who've used the product for at least a year. Be sure to exercise self-discipline when you're surfing the Web for small-business services or to identify software you may want to purchase. Computers and handheld time-management hardware, for instance, are incessantly sold as time and money savers, but anyone who has dealt with those products knows that they can also make things more difficult and stressful and can end up costing more than they save if used inefficiently.

Few Web sites offer useful information for the sake of offering information; more often, Web sites offer "free" small-business services and business news, business plan advice, and so on in order to keep you clicking through the site. The goal, of course, is to sell you something, not to educate you. Don't get sucked into these time-wasting and money-burning sites.

Now that we have the warnings over with, we can proceed with the good stuff — the ways in which you can use technology to better conduct your business and separate your company from the pack. This chapter contains our suggestions for the best ways to utilize technology in your small business, including our recommendations for software programs and Web sites.

To Manage Your Time

In the early stages of your business, only one person will make or break your business. That one person is you, which means that every minute of your time is valuable. Because time is finite, if you waste an hour, that hour, along with whatever you could've accomplished during the course of it, is gone forever. Thus, the management of time — especially that time that belongs solely to you — is potentially the most valuable service that technology can provide.

Every small-business owner manages his or her time differently. Some still use the ubiquitous manual methods — to-do lists, calendars, and various forms of the good old-fashioned DayTimer. Today, however, more and more successful small-business owners are turning to technology to manage their time, whether via computer-based calendars, e-mail, or the scheduling programs on cell phones and handheld devices. The cell phone, of course, ranks at the top of the list of time-management devices. With the cell phone, you can always be on the job, no matter where you are or what you're doing (often to the distraction of others, of course, but we'll save that discussion for another day).

Also, such handheld devices as Blackberrys, Treos, and iPhones, which double as cell phones and Internet-access and e-mail devices, are increasingly considered a must-have time-management device for today's fast-paced entrepreneurs. Despite the addictive nature of such devices, the opportunity to manage schedules, multitask, and get the most out of your day is enhanced by their use. Every small-business owner should at least experiment with the use of handheld devices, because when used appropriately, they can make the user undeniably more efficient.

Another great time-management tool is computer networking. You can network your computer at home to one at the office to manage your calendar, and be on the job from either location. Just be careful not to become a workaholic!

Finally, e-mail is the second-most efficient communication device of them all (behind only cell phones). No waiting for someone to pick up the phone, no wasting time with idle conversation, no telephone bills at the end of the month. Just type your message, click send, and wait for the response. Communication doesn't get much more efficient than that.

To Brainstorm and Research Business Ideas

The Internet can be a useful place to jog your imagination and brainstorm your business ideas. And, no, we're not referring to the business pitches that junk up your e-mail inbox every day. For instance, even if you're more interested in starting a business than buying one, you can check out a few Web sites that list businesses for sale, such as BizBuySell (www.bizbuysell.com). Such an exercise will often expand your horizons and can perhaps steer you into your true life's calling — running a surf shop in Hawaii, for example.

The Small Business Administration (SBA) offers the most extensive array of information and services to aspiring and current small-business owners at www.sba.gov. If you're trying to develop and research a list of opportunities, be sure to peruse the Business Opportunities section of the site. The SBA is also responsible for the creation of another useful site, the U.S. Business Advisor (www.business.gov), which is a compilation of useful business information and regulations from the dozens of various federal agencies that assist or regulate business (for more on business regulations, see Chapter 17). And if you're a data hound, you can access the more than 100 federal agencies' data through www.fedstats.gov, which can assist you with evaluating market opportunities and conducting other research.

Trade association sites can be a great resource for getting information on a specific line of work. The popular search engine, Yahoo! (www.yahoo.com), has a good list of these types of sites under Trade Associations. Also, you can try adding .org to a type of business that you're interested in and plugging that into the address bar in your Web browser; you'll be amazed how often this works. If you're skeptical that a site is available for a particular kind of business, remind yourself that www.coinlaundry.org exists! (For more advice on trade associations and the like, refer to Chapter 14.)

If you don't yet have a computer or Internet access, try the public libraries in your area, many of which can perform computer searches (sometimes for free and sometimes for a nominal fee) for small-business owners and help you get on the Internet. Most also have banks of Internet-connected computers available for public use.

To Provide Supplemental Web Site Services

In addition to using your Web site for marketing purposes (see Chapter 11), you can use your Web site for various operational and customer-service functions that would otherwise require the time and energy of you or one of your employees. For instance, your Web site, when properly configured, can

- **Provide order-entry service for your customers.** A few clicks of the mouse by your customer and his or her order can be entered, printed, subtracted from inventory, and invoiced, all without the involvement of a human being. Yes, someone still has to pack it and ship the order, but stay tuned; someday maybe even that function can be automated. For those small businesses in the hospitality industry (restaurants, bed and breakfasts), a Web site can also be used to take reservations and send confirmations.

- **Accept payment for products and services.** Talk about simplicity; either your credit-card company accepts the number or it doesn't. No bounced checks, no endless phone calls, no unheeded promises, no collection agencies.

- **Solicit customer feedback.** Interested in what your customers think about your company but don't want to go to the expense required in mailing a printed questionnaire? You'll get a better return rate, the returns will come faster, and the costs will be less when you e-mail your questionnaire to the proper people.

To Aid in Administration

Computers, when properly configured and used, can provide a number of administrative services. Consider the following:

- **Letters and memos:** Write the letter or memo, print it, sign it, and mail it instead of dictating it, having someone else type it and send it back to you to edit and sign, and *then* mailing it. Computers make this task quicker, less expensive, and more private (no administrative assistants nosing around in your hallowed company secrets).

TIP

✔ **Communications:** E-mail is the quickest, easiest, and least-expensive way to communicate.

✔ **Filing:** Electronic filing of letters, worksheets, financial statements, and so on is quicker, neater, less expensive, and less space consuming than manual filing.

Just make sure that you back up your files in case your computer crashes — which it inevitably will!

✔ **Worksheets:** When you know how to work with the software, you can develop and fill out electronic spreadsheets in half the time (or less) of manual spreadsheets. Also, they're more professional looking, easier to file, and easier to update and change.

✔ **Office supplies:** Why waste your time and aggravate yourself driving to an office-supply store when you can more quickly and cheaply buy most office supplies for your business online? Our favorite sites are those such as `www.pcconnection.com`, `www.staples.com`, and `www.office max.com`, which offer competitive prices and good service (including by phone if you need it).

✔ **Mailing:** Computer-generated mailing labels are much faster than creating hand-addressed postcards or envelopes. Remember, direct mail is only considered to be "junk mail" when it doesn't seem relevant and personal! For all its bad press, mass mailing, when done right, can result in increased sales.

Of course, computers and the accompanying technology can also waste your time if you happen to get hooked on surfing the Internet, fiddling with the latest presentation software, or reading endless computer manuals. Be aware that, as with any other item that's part-tool/part-toy, using a computer can become an obsession.

To Buy a Business or Franchise

The Internet still has a ways to go before it becomes a major meeting place for business buyers and sellers, but you may find promising leads with the sites in this section (for more on selling your business, see Chapter 19).

BizBuySell (`www.bizbuysell.com`) has all the ingredients for a good business-for-sale online database: a pleasing design, a smooth search engine, and a decent description of each listed business that includes the asking price, gross income, cash flow, year established, number of employees, facilities description, details on the competition, and growth possibilities. We've seen such entries as a smoothie franchise in Texas and a pet store in California. This site helps jog your entrepreneurial imagination!

If you're interested in owning a franchise business, check out Franchise Advantage (www.franchiseadvantage.com), a site that matches up its client franchise companies with your selection criteria and profile as a potential franchise owner. The site gives good specs on each franchise, including the company history, number of stores, description of company support, franchise fee, and necessary capital to get started.

To Scan Inventory

Inventory scanning is especially useful for retail- and manufacturing-based small businesses that include extensive, and expensive, quantities of inventory.

 For those business owners who must depend on managing their inventory, handheld, wireless scanners make the counting of inventory a relatively easy task — especially when compared to the tried-and-true, yet slow and less-accurate, manual method. The best small businesses we know take frequent inventories, quarterly or even monthly. Without the requisite scanning technology, the process of tabulating inventory can be time consuming and inaccurate. And the more SKUs (Stock Keeping Units) you have in your inventory, the more important inventory scanning becomes.

Scanning devices are proliferating within the inventory-carrying small-business sector. For instance, one scanning device is designed to measure the amount of beer that has been consumed from a keg, certainly a valuable tool for the bar and restaurant industry. Check with your industry trade association; it can make you aware of the latest technologies available in scanning.

Inventory scanning technology for small-business owners in the retail industry can either be a stand-alone function or bundled into a complete management software system (see Chapter 19). For instance, one national vendor we know offers a system that includes a bar-code scanner, a credit-card reader, a receipt printer, and a cash drawer. Such a configuration of products allows the retailer to track inventory, create purchase orders, determine sales taxes, and avoid much of the time-consuming minutiae that often plagues the typical retailer.

To Network Online

Ask any small-business owner the question "Who's advice do you trust the most?" and the answer will seldom be a consultant, an accountant, or an attorney. Rather, the most consistent response to this question is that the typical business owner receives his or her most valuable and trusted advice from another small-business owner — preferably one who's experienced in this career field and has a successful business to his or her credit. The concept of online business networking among small-business owners makes sense. You're receiving advice from your peers.

Online business networking involves the virtual (online) assembling of small-business owners with the intent of identifying other owners, meeting, and sharing information. Oftentimes, such networking groups include small-business owners operating within the same industry sector — retail, technology, manufacturing, and so on. The most effective business networking, of course, results when you can hook up with other small-business owners within the same specific niche — outdoor retailers, computer printing service providers, or widget manufacturers, for instance.

 Just as Web sites such as Friendster and MySpace have been successful in bringing singles and homogeneous groups together, business-networking providers now offer a similar experience. You can access a number of popular online business-networking providers, including LinkedIn (`www.linked in.com`), Ryze (`www.ryze.com`), and Tribe.net. To find other business-networking providers, simply type the term "Online Business Networking" into your favorite search engine and take your pick.

You don't have to be a techie to participate in a networking group. You can do it by phone, by e-mail, or by subscribing to an online service. Or, for those tech geeks among you, there are more-advanced online collaboration tools, such as Skype, forums, blogs, and even wikis — tools that can take business networking to the next step.

Oh yes, and there's one other advantage to online networking with other business owners: Not only do you receive trusted advice on how to run your business, the advice you receive is free (other than the cost of belonging to the Web site).

Imagine: Trusted advice at no cost. A match made in heaven for the cost-conscious small-business owner.

To Manage Finances

A recent survey reveals that only 37 percent of small businesses take advantage of online banking, but that number is steadily increasing every year. Eventually, the lure of not having to lick envelopes (which takes time) and buy stamps (which costs money) will drive even the most technologically challenged small-business operators to opt for online banking.

There are a number of benefits to banking online, in addition to the time and money you'll save:

- ✔ You can check your account balances 24 hours a day.
- ✔ You can view your account activity and history whether you're at home or on the road.
- ✔ You can transfer money immediately.
- ✔ You can reorder checks instantly.
- ✔ You can perform myriad generic banking functions without having to leave the comfort of your home or office.
- ✔ You can cut down on late fees because you can pay your bills instantly.
- ✔ You can utilize most online banking services free of charge — and "free," in the world of the profit-conscious small-business owner, is usually good.

Certainly, there are still valid reasons why some small-business owners are reluctant to make the step to online banking. The ever-present Web scammers continue to find creative ways to trick the unwary Web user, including fake e-mails and phony Web sites. But the careful online-banking customer has learned how to recognize today's scams and has thus made the decision to go with the efficiency, timeliness, and transparency of online banking.

The banks, of course, want their customers to opt for online banking, too. Electronic banking is less expensive than paper transactions, online customers require less customer service, and, experience has proven, a bank's online customers are less likely to switch banks.

The same logic, incidentally, can be applied to the small-business owner who should be looking for ways to entice his customers to conduct their e-business on his Web site. A small business's customers are less likely to switch, too, after they get used to the convenience of doing business over the Web.

Finally, note that online banking is just as beneficial to the individual business owner as it is to the business itself. Tens of millions of Americans utilize online banking. All of which means, after you've learned how to master the skills of online banking at the office, there's no reason why you shouldn't be doing the same thing at home.

To Market over E-mail

E-mail marketing has proven to be more efficient and less expensive than any other form of marketing (see Chapter 11). Of course, for such a virtual tool to be successful, the marketer must first garner some sort of "permission" from the target audience to accept his or her e-mail advances. This "permission," then, is what separates e-mail marketing from spam.

Think about it. If you receive an e-mail from someone you know or are familiar with, you're liable to open the e-mail. On the other hand, e-mail from a stranger is less likely to be opened. Thus, the e-mail marketer's goal is to turn those otherwise strangers into acquaintances and then those acquaintances into friends.

The trick, of course, is to first get permission from the person you're marketing to. Most often, the best source for e-mail marketing is your existing customer base. Using that base, you have a number of ways to expand it. Such tools for expansion include events, opt-in gifts, and, most of all, an effective Web site that encourages visitors to sign up for, say, your newsletter, marketing program, or latest product release.

Effective e-mail marketing is based on the concept of one-to-one marketing — marketing to an individual who's already known to the marketer, as opposed to the more typical marketing shotgun-based methods. These include direct mail, which reaches a long list of prospects who match a predetermined target customer profile, or the various forms of mass-media advertising that reach one and all in a radio, television, newspaper, or magazine audience. After you establish this one-to-one relationship, the success of your marketing program rests on making sure that the products or services offered are relevant to the recipient's need. Remember, no marketing medium, no matter how inexpensive and efficient, can overcome poor offerings of products or services.

To Educate with E-Newsletters

The ultimate purpose of an e-newsletter is to enhance the relationship between your business and whomever it is that you're sending it to, with the intended result of increasing awareness and regard for your business and ultimately causing increased sales.

Because the initial glimpse of your e-newsletter is when the recipient will make his or her decision whether or not to hit the delete button, the first rule of success is that it must be pleasing to the eye and professional in appearance. There are myriad e-newsletter templates available to help you achieve these goals, including those available from MyNewsletterBuilder, Topica, and eNewsletter Pro.

After you've captured your readers' attention with an e-newsletter, the next step is to provide enticing content. A recent survey shows that e-newsletter readers are more likely to become avid readers when you provide:

- ✔ Specific information on whatever subject you happen to be writing about
- ✔ Timely, up-to-date facts and figures on the topic

Failure to fulfill these two objectives on an ongoing basis will result in your e-newsletter being regarded as just another piece of unwanted spam.

Sure, an e-newsletter is really just another form of an e-mail marketing tool, but if the recipient doesn't perceive it as an educational opportunity, your e-newsletter won't be around very long. So your electronic newsletter must include informative news and relevant commentary on subjects that will be of interest to the person or persons receiving it. In other words, there must be educational benefits involved.

In addition to providing enticing content, you also want to make sure that your mailings aren't too frequent (once every two months would be our recommendation). Also, readers won't want to receive other material from you for which they haven't signed up, and they won't look kindly on e-newsletters that include pop-up ads. Finally, make sure, when purchasing an e-newsletter template, that the software tracks a variety of relevant statistics, including number of views, opens, and clicks on each link.

You can measure the degree of enhancement created by your newsletter by such activities as gathering data on the number of visits to your Web site, tracking the number of sales made to the e-newsletter recipients, or tracing the number of phone calls by recipients to your sales department. Whatever measure of success you deem to be most relevant, be sure to track it diligently.

Chapter 22

Ten Tips for Managing Your Growing Business

*L*ike it or not, the larger your company grows, the more you must practice taking off your entrepreneur's hat and putting on your manager's hat. This transition isn't an easy one for most small-business owners to make, and it involves adopting a number of new management skills that don't come naturally to many people. This chapter provides a collection of time-tested tips that will help you work through this transition and better manage your growing company.

Focus On What You Do Best

How many small businesses do you know that try to offer too many services or products — more than they can successfully provide? How many do you know that try to provide the best quality along with the fastest delivery as well as the lowest prices — all at the same time?

The successful small business is one that's operated with the recognition that its resources are finite — that the business can only do so much and still do it well. Hence, the business is focused on what it does best; then, it goes ahead and does it *better* than anyone else.

You, as the owner of a growing business, must recognize your need to focus, too. Your personal resources are finite, and you can only do so much before you start doing *too* much and losing your focus. Keep your focus on what you can reasonably accomplish, leaving that which you can't do well to someone else — an employee, an outside vendor (lawyers or accountants, for example; see Chapter 10), or perhaps a consultant or mentor (see Chapter 14).

Use these tips to help you focus appropriately and, therefore, better manage your time and talents:

- ✔ An overflowing plate is the enemy of focus. You don't have to be all things to all people. Determine what you can delegate, to whom you can delegate it, and how soon it needs to be done.

- ✔ When one project must give way to another, make sure that the first project is temporarily concluded at a convenient spot. Then adopt a steadfast plan for its resumption.

- ✔ Interest and focus are directly related. Don't expect to focus for long periods of time on subjects that don't interest you. Delegate them to someone else who *is* interested in such projects.

- ✔ Focus, and the lack thereof, is an issue related to company culture. If you, the owner/boss, don't finish the projects you begin or don't follow up on your initiatives, your employees will most likely adopt the same behavior over time. Your lack of focus can lead to their lack of focus; little will get done well or on time, and you'll be left with plenty of time to focus on the failure of your business.

The best small-business managers know that the ability to focus pays dividends. They've discovered that solving one problem is far better than having three problems in various stages of irresolution.

Bend the Rules when Necessary

A small business is a place where Katharine Hepburn undoubtedly would've enjoyed herself. You may recall that Hepburn was once quoted as saying: "If you obey all the rules, you miss all the fun." And, with one slight change, Katharine's quote works for today's successful small businesses: "If you obey all the rules, you miss many of the opportunities."

We certainly aren't suggesting that rule-bending be considered lightly. Those for whom the rules are bent need to understand why the rules are being bent, and that the bending is an exception. The same holds true for when the rules need to be bent because of circumstances rather than individuals.

When people and institutions become perfect and problems become predictable, rigid and inflexible rules may work. Until then, however, flexibility is the key to making the best of any imperfections.

Hold Your Employees Accountable

Remember the best teacher you ever had? Chances are, that teacher made you accountable — accountable to do your homework, to participate in class, and to pay attention to whatever it was he or she happened to be teaching. When the teacher told you to do something, by golly, you did it.

In the process of making you accountable, this teacher no doubt communicated to you in advance what would happen if you didn't do what was asked of you. Conversely, he or she also told what would happen if you accomplished what was requested. So, you knew exactly what to do and exactly what to expect in terms of reward or punishment. Most importantly, you knew that the teacher would follow up his or her words with actions. You could control the outcome by your choice to follow or not follow instructions. Somewhere along the line, your best teacher had discovered the necessary role of accountability in attaining desired results.

Two elements make up this process of establishing accountability:

✔ Communication of expectations

✔ Follow-up

Without the two working in unison, you can forget about accountability. And the lack of accountability will result in spotty performance at best, and at worst no performance at all. Most small businesses can't afford continued poor performance.

Right or wrong, people need a rationale — a sense of the purpose and consequences of the task — before they can do whatever it is you want them to do. Providing this rationale is the role of accountability — yours for setting expectations and follow-up, the employees' in accomplishing the expected result — in managing your employees.

The same tools that worked for your best teacher can also work for you. If your employees aren't held accountable for their actions, they usually won't succeed. And, in the long term, if your employees don't succeed, your company won't, either. The time-tested "win-win" formula won't kick in unless both sides are involved.

Consider the 80-20 Rule

The 80-20 rule is alive and well in the small-business world. Consider the following examples of the 80-20 rule:

- **The 80-20 rule for your customers:** "Eighty percent of your profits come from 20 percent of your customers."

  What this means to you: Focus your time and energy on those customers who have the potential to be profitable. Stop wasting your time on those who don't. (For more on identifying the best customers, see Chapter 12.)

- **The 80-20 rule for your employees' output:** "Eighty percent of your company's output will come from 20 percent of your employees."

  What this means to you: Work harder to improve, or cull, the 80 percent that isn't contributing (see Chapter 15) and take good care of the 20 percent doing so much of the work (see Chapter 16).

- **The 80-20 rule for your employee problems:** "Eighty percent of your employee problems come from 20 percent of your employees."

  What this means to you: Do something about that 20 percent. Either solve *their* problems (by training or motivating them) or solve *your* problem (by replacing them).

- **The 80-20 rule for your expenses:** "Eighty percent of your waste comes from 20 percent of your expense categories."

  What this means to you: Focus on the 20 percent — that's where your leverage lies for increased profitability.

- **The 80-20 rule for your accounts receivable:** "Eighty percent of your slow pay dollars come from 20 percent of your customers."

  What this means to you: Determine the source of that 20 percent; you usually find a common denominator. One salesperson, maybe? One product? One market?

- **The 80-20 rule for your success:** "Eighty percent of your successes will come from 20 percent of your efforts."

  What this means to you: Find out how to leverage your talents as well as your time. Find a way to spend more time on the things you do well (and that benefit your business) while delegating those things that you don't.

Think Ahead

Have you ever noticed that the hottest month of the year is July, even though the sun is at its peak in June? Ditto with any given day: The hottest time of the day is midafternoon, even though the sun is at its highest around noon.

Our point? Lags in time are a reality of life, and you have to figure out how to live with them. Such lags in time have a place in the small-business world as well. Use the following examples to help you deal with your business's hot spots:

✔ When your sales hit the skids in June, it isn't because your salespeople have suddenly become ineffective. They may have become ineffective months earlier. The results have just caught up.

✔ When your inventory soars out of sight, it isn't because of what you ordered last week. Your prior month's purchases have killed you.

And so it is with most small-business problems. What happens today is yesterday's fault.

So how do you compensate for this lag in small-business time? Using the previous examples, you do the following:

✔ **Use an early-warning system, such as a Salesperson's Call Report.** This report will tell you how many calls your salespeople are making, which gives you an indication of how successfully they're working in those months before the actual sales will increase.

✔ **Put a purchasing system in place that sounds bells and whistles when purchases exceed a certain level.** Today's bells and whistles will negate any chance of tomorrow's soaring inventory.

The business of doing small business is a 12-month proposition, but people and business cycles have their ups and downs, as does performance. Your job is to manage your small business around those ups and downs, making sure that this lag in time doesn't cause a lag in results.

Sleep On Important Decisions

Following are the guidelines the president of the United States is supposed to observe when there's an important decision to make. These guidelines also apply to the president of General Motors and the president of Acme Plumbing. You should apply them to your business decisions as well:

✔ **Be steady.** That's what Americans most want from their president and what adversaries most respect.

✔ **Don't get captured by the event.** History is full of presidents who have been obsessed with a crisis or an impending decision and, as a result, made a bad choice.

✔ **Don't act until you must.** Rash decisions based on emotion and insufficient information are the biggest dangers in a crisis.

✔ **Talk, think, negotiate.** Take your time, consider all the options, and don't rush into something that you'll later regret.

The underlying strategy here for all presidents of organizations large and small is to keep cool, stay in control, and allow plenty of time to reach a decision. Wait until your emotions are subdued before making important decisions.

Whether you like it or not, the biggest decisions in life and in business usually come around only once. Rarely will you be allowed a second chance. "I'll get back to you tomorrow" are the words for those make-it-or-break-it times. Then go home. Take a drink of something tall and cool. Go for a bike ride with the kids.

And sleep on it.

Resolve Conflicts

The meek may inherit the earth, but their employees may revolt at the same time. Employees and conflict are directly related. The more employees you have, the more conflict you'll have to deal with. Also, the stakes involved in that conflict become more significant and the antagonists become more skilled at that conflict as your company grows.

Effective managers must also be professional conflict resolvers. Conflict and the quick and easy resolution of it doesn't come naturally to most people. Resolving conflict almost always calls for compromise and understanding in the heat of emotion, something many people are unable or unwilling to do.

The best way to resolve conflict? Face it. Immediately. Festering conflict is always worse than new conflict. Don't let yours get cold or old.

Accept that Perception Is Reality

As a small-business owner, the message you send is vital. Imagine the following scenario:

Annual performance review time has come (see Chapter 15). One of your employees fidgets nervously on the far side of your desk. You begin the review with a complimentary remark and then dive into the guts of the presentation. Your intent? To improve that employee's performance. Ten minutes later, your employee storms out of your office, slamming the door behind him. He perceived that you were attacking him personally.

And that's how perception works. Facts and intent don't mean diddly-squat. It's only perception that counts — and that perception is reality until the perception is changed. So what, you ask?

- When leading people (as small-business owners are supposed to do), what *you* think or believe doesn't matter. What matters is what your employees *perceive* that you think or believe. If they perceive that you don't give a hoot about their problems, they won't give a hoot about your problems. If they perceive that quality isn't important to you, quality won't be important to them. If they perceive that you think the customer is a pain in the posterior, so the customer shall be to them.

- Presentation is crucial. Employee review? Shareholder meeting? Customer presentation? Association talk? What you intend to communicate isn't the issue here; the way your presentation is perceived is what counts.

Try this: Ask a collection of your employees (allow anonymity, of course) how you and your company are perceived. Ask them for a 1-to-10 rating on whatever you deem important to the success of your business. Ask about cultural issues, management issues, leadership traits, ethics, respect for the individual, customer responsiveness, trust, follow-up, accountability, focus — whatever perception you want to measure. Then compare your employees' ratings to yours. Do their perceptions agree with yours?

Our guess? On some issues, it isn't even close. Like it or not, when it comes to dealing with people or being dealt with by people, facts hardly matter at all. Perception is what counts.

Remember that Cash Is King

Profits are what you pay taxes on; cash is what you take home. When co-author Jim ran into a business friend of his he hadn't seen in a year, he asked "How was your business last year?"

"Great," she replied. "Sales were up and profits were up. Best year we ever had."

"Paying all your bills on time?" Jim asked

"Well, not exactly," she said, frowning. "As a matter of fact we're having a harder time paying our bills than a year ago."

It turns out Jim's friend had too much cash tied up in inventory and had purchased more new furniture and equipment than she had the cash to pay for. (These are items that don't affect your business's profitability but do eat up the cash.)

Chalk up another lesson learned the hard way: Cash flow is king in the world of small business (and big business, too!). The answer to generating cash in your business? Find out how to track it, then to forecast it, and finally to savor it (see Chapter 13 for our advice).

Follow the Rule of Many Reasons

If your business is successful, myriad reasons are behind that success. You've hired right and fired right, focused, made a great product or provided a great service, put the right distribution system in place, planned and strategized, managed your cash . . . the list of the things you've done right goes on forever.

And if your business is in trouble, you'll find a number of reasons why, too. You've hired poorly, you haven't fired when you should, your product quality is poor, your sales force needs training, your culture lacks accountability, you have a warehouse full of inventory that won't sell . . . you get the idea.

That's how the *Rule of Many Reasons* works, and it applies to everything you do — whether it's running your company, raising your kids, or shuffling along the back roads of life. So what does this Rule of Many Reasons mean when your company hits one of the many speed bumps that lurk along the road to success?

It means that no easy fixes are available. Sure, you have priorities, but your company won't do an about-face tomorrow simply because you've put a quality program in place, started a program to improve your hiring techniques, decided to install accountability in your culture, or whatever it is you've started to do that you weren't doing before.

And it means that the winner in the small-business game is the owner who has discovered that it's everything that makes the difference — the big things and the little things and all the in-between things. Success is the result of everything that you do.

Index

BUSINESS, CAREERS & PERSONAL FINANCE

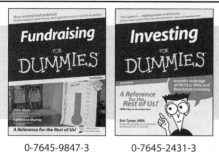

0-7645-9847-3   0-7645-2431-3

Also available:
- Business Plans Kit For Dummies
  0-7645-9794-9
- Economics For Dummies
  0-7645-5726-2
- Grant Writing For Dummies
  0-7645-8416-2
- Home Buying For Dummies
  0-7645-5331-3
- Managing For Dummies
  0-7645-1771-6
- Marketing For Dummies
  0-7645-5600-2

- Personal Finance For Dummies
  0-7645-2590-5*
- Resumes For Dummies
  0-7645-5471-9
- Selling For Dummies
  0-7645-5363-1
- Six Sigma For Dummies
  0-7645-6798-5
- Small Business Kit For Dummies
  0-7645-5984-2
- Starting an eBay Business For Dummies
  0-7645-6924-4
- Your Dream Career For Dummies
  0-7645-9795-7

HOME & BUSINESS COMPUTER BASICS

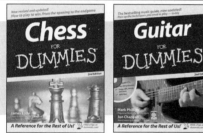

0-470-05432-8   0-471-75421-8

Also available:
- Cleaning Windows Vista For Dummies
  0-471-78293-9
- Excel 2007 For Dummies
  0-470-03737-7
- Mac OS X Tiger For Dummies
  0-7645-7675-5
- MacBook For Dummies
  0-470-04859-X
- Macs For Dummies
  0-470-04849-2
- Office 2007 For Dummies
  0-470-00923-3

- Outlook 2007 For Dummies
  0-470-03830-6
- PCs For Dummies
  0-7645-8958-X
- Salesforce.com For Dummies
  0-470-04893-X
- Upgrading & Fixing Laptops For Dummies
  0-7645-8959-8
- Word 2007 For Dummies
  0-470-03658-3
- Quicken 2007 For Dummies
  0-470-04600-7

FOOD, HOME, GARDEN, HOBBIES, MUSIC & PETS

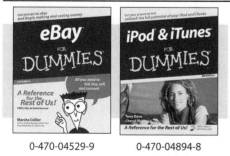

0-7645-8404-9   0-7645-9904-6

Also available:
- Candy Making For Dummies
  0-7645-9734-5
- Card Games For Dummies
  0-7645-9910-0
- Crocheting For Dummies
  0-7645-4151-X
- Dog Training For Dummies
  0-7645-8418-9
- Healthy Carb Cookbook For Dummies
  0-7645-8476-6
- Home Maintenance For Dummies
  0-7645-5215-5

- Horses For Dummies
  0-7645-9797-3
- Jewelry Making & Beading For Dummies
  0-7645-2571-9
- Orchids For Dummies
  0-7645-6759-4
- Puppies For Dummies
  0-7645-5255-4
- Rock Guitar For Dummies
  0-7645-5356-9
- Sewing For Dummies
  0-7645-6847-7
- Singing For Dummies
  0-7645-2475-5

INTERNET & DIGITAL MEDIA

0-470-04529-9   0-470-04894-8

Also available:
- Blogging For Dummies
  0-471-77084-1
- Digital Photography For Dummies
  0-7645-9802-3
- Digital Photography All-in-One Desk Reference For Dummies
  0-470-03743-1
- Digital SLR Cameras and Photography For Dummies
  0-7645-9803-1
- eBay Business All-in-One Desk Reference For Dummies
  0-7645-8438-3
- HDTV For Dummies
  0-470-09673-X

- Home Entertainment PCs For Dummies
  0-470-05523-5
- MySpace For Dummies
  0-470-09529-6
- Search Engine Optimization For Dummies
  0-471-97998-8
- Skype For Dummies
  0-470-04891-3
- The Internet For Dummies
  0-7645-8996-2
- Wiring Your Digital Home For Dummies
  0-471-91830-X

* Separate Canadian edition also available
† Separate U.K. edition also available

Available wherever books are sold. For more information or to order direct: U.S. customers visit www.dummies.com or call 1-877-762-2974.
U.K. customers visit www.wileyeurope.com or call 0800 243407. Canadian customers visit www.wiley.ca or call 1-800-567-4797.

 WILEY

SPORTS, FITNESS, PARENTING, RELIGION & SPIRITUALITY

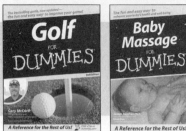

0-471-76871-5

0-7645-7841-3

Also available:
- Catholicism For Dummies
  0-7645-5391-7
- Exercise Balls For Dummies
  0-7645-5623-1
- Fitness For Dummies
  0-7645-7851-0
- Football For Dummies
  0-7645-3936-1
- Judaism For Dummies
  0-7645-5299-6
- Potty Training For Dummies
  0-7645-5417-4
- Buddhism For Dummies
  0-7645-5359-3

- Pregnancy For Dummies
  0-7645-4483-7 †
- Ten Minute Tone-Ups For Dummies
  0-7645-7207-5
- NASCAR For Dummies
  0-7645-7681-X
- Religion For Dummies
  0-7645-5264-3
- Soccer For Dummies
  0-7645-5229-5
- Women in the Bible For Dummies
  0-7645-8475-8

TRAVEL

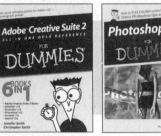

0-7645-7749-2

0-7645-6945-7

Also available:
- Alaska For Dummies
  0-7645-7746-8
- Cruise Vacations For Dummies
  0-7645-6941-4
- England For Dummies
  0-7645-4276-1
- Europe For Dummies
  0-7645-7529-5
- Germany For Dummies
  0-7645-7823-5
- Hawaii For Dummies
  0-7645-7402-7

- Italy For Dummies
  0-7645-7386-1
- Las Vegas For Dummies
  0-7645-7382-9
- London For Dummies
  0-7645-4277-X
- Paris For Dummies
  0-7645-7630-5
- RV Vacations For Dummies
  0-7645-4442-X
- Walt Disney World & Orlando
  For Dummies
  0-7645-9660-8

GRAPHICS, DESIGN & WEB DEVELOPMENT

0-7645-8815-X

0-7645-9571-7

Also available:
- 3D Game Animation For Dummies
  0-7645-8789-7
- AutoCAD 2006 For Dummies
  0-7645-8925-3
- Building a Web Site For Dummies
  0-7645-7144-3
- Creating Web Pages For Dummies
  0-470-08030-2
- Creating Web Pages All-in-One Desk
  Reference For Dummies
  0-7645-4345-8
- Dreamweaver 8 For Dummies
  0-7645-9649-7

- InDesign CS2 For Dummies
  0-7645-9572-5
- Macromedia Flash 8 For Dummies
  0-7645-9691-8
- Photoshop CS2 and Digital
  Photography For Dummies
  0-7645-9580-6
- Photoshop Elements 4 For Dummies
  0-471-77483-9
- Syndicating Web Sites with RSS Feeds
  For Dummies
  0-7645-8848-6
- Yahoo! SiteBuilder For Dummies
  0-7645-9800-7

NETWORKING, SECURITY, PROGRAMMING & DATABASES

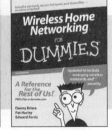

0-7645-7728-X

0-471-74940-0

Also available:
- Access 2007 For Dummies
  0-470-04612-0
- ASP.NET 2 For Dummies
  0-7645-7907-X
- C# 2005 For Dummies
  0-7645-9704-3
- Hacking For Dummies
  0-470-05235-X
- Hacking Wireless Networks
  For Dummies
  0-7645-9730-2
- Java For Dummies
  0-470-08716-1

- Microsoft SQL Server 2005 For Dummies
  0-7645-7755-7
- Networking All-in-One Desk Reference
  For Dummies
  0-7645-9939-9
- Preventing Identity Theft For Dummies
  0-7645-7336-5
- Telecom For Dummies
  0-471-77085-X
- Visual Studio 2005 All-in-One Desk
  Reference For Dummies
  0-7645-9775-2
- XML For Dummies
  0-7645-8845-1